T0297659

Computational Intelligence and Blockchain in Complex Systems

Advanced Studies in Complex Systems

Computational Intelligence and Blockchain in Complex Systems

System Security and Interdisciplinary Applications

Edited by

Fadi Al-Turjman

Artificial Intelligence, Software, and Information Systems Engineering Departments., Research Center for AI and IoT, AI and Robotics Institute, Near East University, Nicosia, Mersin10, Turkey

Series Editors

Valentina Emilia Balas

Dumitru Baleanu

Hemen Dutta

Morgan Kaufmann is an imprint of Elsevier
50 Hampshire Street, 5th Floor, Cambridge, MA 02139, United States

Copyright © 2024 Elsevier Inc. All rights are reserved, including those for text and data mining, AI training, and similar technologies.

Publisher's note: Elsevier takes a neutral position with respect to territorial disputes or jurisdictional claims in its published content, including in maps and institutional affiliations.

No part of this publication may be reproduced or transmitted in any form or by any means, electronic or mechanical, including photocopying, recording, or any information storage and retrieval system, without permission in writing from the publisher. Details on how to seek permission, further information about the Publisher's permissions policies and our arrangements with organizations such as the Copyright Clearance Center and the Copyright Licensing Agency, can be found at our website: www.elsevier.com/permissions.

This book and the individual contributions contained in it are protected under copyright by the Publisher (other than as may be noted herein).

MATLAB® is a trademark of The MathWorks, Inc. and is used with permission. The MathWorks does not warrant the accuracy of the text or exercises in this book. This book's use or discussion of MATLAB® software or related products does not constitute endorsement or sponsorship by The MathWorks of a particular pedagogical approach or particular use of the MATLAB® software.

Notices
Knowledge and best practice in this field are constantly changing. As new research and experience broaden our understanding, changes in research methods, professional practices, or medical treatment may become necessary.

Practitioners and researchers must always rely on their own experience and knowledge in evaluating and using any information, methods, compounds, or experiments described herein. In using such information or methods they should be mindful of their own safety and the safety of others, including parties for whom they have a professional responsibility.

To the fullest extent of the law, neither the Publisher nor the authors, contributors, or editors, assume any liability for any injury and/or damage to persons or property as a matter of products liability, negligence or otherwise, or from any use or operation of any methods, products, instructions, or ideas contained in the material herein.

ISBN: 978-0-443-13268-1

For Information on all Morgan Kaufmann publications
visit our website at https://www.elsevier.com/books-and-journals

Publisher: Mara Conner
Acquisitions Editor: Chris Katsaropoulos
Editorial Project Manager: Palak Gupta
Production Project Manager: Neena S. Maheen
Cover Designer: Matthew Limbert

Typeset by MPS Limited, Chennai, India

Dedication

Live on the island like a continental.

—Dr. Suat I. Gunsel

To my wonderful family at home and at the school. To whom it may concern. I dedicate this book and hopefully the best of it.

And remember, when you start flying, a few stones will be thrown at you. So, don't look down. Just fly higher so the stones won't reach you.

—Prof. Fadi Al-Turjman

Contents

List of contributors   xvii

1. An overview of future cyber security applications using AI
   and blockchain technology   1
   RAMIZ SALAMA, CHADI ALTRJMAN AND FADI AL-TURJMAN

   1.1 Introduction   1
   1.2 Previous work extent   2
   1.3 Using blockchain technologies in cyber security   3
   1.4 Blockchain applications in cybersecurity   4
   1.5 The application of artificial intelligence technologies in cyber
       security   6
   1.6 The benefits of artificial intelligence in cybersecurity   8
   1.7 Here are a few advantages and applications of artificial
       intelligence in cybersecurity   8
   1.8 Conclusion   9
   References   9

2. A survey of issues, possibilities, and solutions for a
   blockchain and AI-powered Internet of things   13
   RAMIZ SALAMA, SINEM ALTURJMAN AND FADI AL-TURJMAN

   2.1 Introduction   13
   2.2 The volume of prior work   17
   2.3 Internet of things driven by 6G   18
   2.4 What is blockchain, anyway?   19
   2.5 Blockchain with artificial intelligence: challenges, opportunities,
       and solutions for the 6G internet of things   20

2.6 Discussion   21

2.7 Conclusion   22

References   23

3.   A simple online payment system using blockchain
     technology   25

HASAN KUREN AND FADI AL-TURJMAN

3.1 Introduction   25

3.2 Research and design   26

3.3 Conclusions   36

References   37

4.   Efficient spam email classification logistic regression model
     trained by modified social network search algorithm   39

BRANISLAV RADOMIROVIC, ALEKSANDAR PETROVIC, MIODRAG ZIVKOVIC,
ANGELINA NJEGUS, NEBOJSA BUDIMIROVIC AND NEBOJSA BACANIN

4.1 Introduction   39

4.2 Background and literature review   40

4.3 Proposed hybrid metaheuristics   42

4.4 Experiments and comparative analysis   48

4.5 Conclusion   53

References   53

5.   Reviewing artificial intelligence and blockchain innovations:
     transformative applications in the energy sector   57

OLUKAYODE AKANNI, M. VUBANGSI, SARUMI USMAN ABIDEMI,
ODUNLAMI ERIOLUWA AND FADI AL-TURJMAN

5.1 Introduction   57

5.2 Literature review   58

5.3 Applications of artificial intelligence and blockchain in the
     energy industry   60

5.4 Use cases   70

5.5 Discussions 70

5.6 Conclusion 71

References 72

6. Using artificial intelligence in education applications 77

RAMIZ SALAMA AND FADI AL-TURJMAN

6.1 Introduction 77

6.2 Extent of past work 78

6.3 Materials and methods 78

6.4 Result and discussion 80

6.5 Conclusion 82

References 82

7. Performance measurements of 12 different machine learning algorithms that make personalized psoriasis treatment recommendations with a database of psoriasis patients responding to treatment 85

HAMIT ALTIPARMAK, SERKAN YAZICI, İZEL YILMAZ, EMEL BÜLBÜL BAŞKAN, HALUK BARBAROS ORAL, KENAN AYDOĞAN, ŞEHIME GULSUN TEMEL, MAHMUT ÇERKEZ ERGÖREN AND FADI AL-TURJMAN

7.1 Introduction and literature review 85

7.2 Materials and methods 90

7.3 Experimental results 92

7.4 Conclusion and future work 94

References 94

8. Healthcare cybersecurity challenges: a look at current and future trends 97

RAMIZ SALAMA, CHADI ALTRJMAN AND FADI AL TURJMAN

8.1 Introduction 97

8.2 The amount of prior works 99

8.3 Difficulties 101

8.4 A review of current and future trends in cybersecurity
    challenges in healthcare   103

8.5 Discussion   103

8.6 Cybersecurity tools, defenses, and mitigation techniques   106

8.7 Conclusion   108

References   110

9.   EU artificial intelligence regulation   113
    ESRA ERSOY

9.1 Introduction   113

9.2 Background of the regulation   113

9.3 Scope of the regulation   115

9.4 Conclusion   118

References   118

10. The issue of personality rights and artificial intelligence   121
    GÖKÇE MARAŞLI

10.1 Introduction   121

10.2 Person and personality   122

10.3 Artificial intelligence and personality   123

10.4 Conclusion   124

References   125

11. Will artificial intelligence sit on the judge's bench?   127
    EYLEM ÜMIT ATILGAN

11.1 Introduction   127

11.2 Can artificial intelligence realize law?   128

11.3 Can artificial intelligence interpret or create law?   130

11.4 Conclusion   131

References   131

12. The effectiveness of virtual reality-based technology on foreign language vocabulary teaching to children with attention deficiency hyperactivity disorder   133

GÜL KAHVECI, ÇAĞDA KIVANÇ ÇAĞANAĞA AND AHMET GÜNEYLI

12.1 Introduction   133
12.2 Method   137
12.3 Results   140
12.4 Conclusion   142
References   143

13. BERT-IDS: an intrusion detection system based on bidirectional encoder representations from transformers   147

M. VUBANGSI, TEYEI RUTH MANGAI, AKANNI OLUKAYODE, AUWALU SALEH MUBARAK AND FADI AL-TURJMAN

13.1 Introduction   147
13.2 Review of related works   148
13.3 Dataset   149
13.4 Method   149
13.5 Results and analysis   152
13.6 Conclusion   153
References   154

14. Internet of Things and the electrocardiogram using artificial intelligence—a survey   157

HAMDAN H. SHEHAB AND FADI AL-TURJMAN

14.1 Introduction   157
14.2 Literature study on electrocardiogram   158
14.3 Electrocardiogram signal   160
14.4 Review of technique used in electrocardiogram   161
14.5 Conclusion   165
References   165

15. Evaluation of artificial intelligence in education and its applications according to the opinions of school administrators   167

GOKMEN DAGLI, FAHRIYE ALTINAY AND ZEHRA ALTINAY

15.1 Introduction   167
15.2 Method   168
15.3 Findings and comments   170
15.4 Conclusion and recommendations   171
References   172

16. Evaluation of tourism developments with artificial intelligence according to the opinions of tourism hotel managers   175

NESRIN MENEMENCI, MEHMET ALTINAY, ZEHRA ALTINAY, FAHRIYE ALTINAY AND GOKMEN DAGLI

16.1 Introduction   175
16.2 Artificial intelligence in tourism   176
16.3 Use of artificial intelligence in hotels   176
16.4 Methodology   177
16.5 Findings   177
16.6 Conclusion and recommendations   179
References   180

17. The manager's perspective on the effect of using artificial intelligence of things in work life   181

FURKAN OCEL, TOLGAY KARANFILLER AND ESER GEMIKONAKLI

17.1 Introduction   181
17.2 Literature survey   182
17.3 Methodology   183
17.4 Findings   184
17.5 Conclusion   185
References   185

18. Machine learning algorithms for blockchain-based security
    mechanisms in UAVs: a review   187

    ESER GEMIKONAKLI AND YONEY KIRSAL EVER

    18.1 Introduction   187
    18.2 Related works   188
    18.3 Results and discussions   192
    18.4 Conclusions and future works   195
    References   196

19. Artificial intelligence and sustainable educational
    systems   199

    KIFAH AMARA, FAHRIYE ALTINAY, ZEHRA ALTINAY AND GOKMEN DAGLI

    19.1 Introduction   199
    19.2 Conclusion   203
    References   203

20. Distributed mobile cloud computing services and
    blockchain technology   205

    RAMIZ SALAMA AND FADI AL-TURJMAN

    20.1 Introduction   205
    20.2 Integration of blockchain technology into mobile cloud
          computing   206
    20.3 Smart contracts for mobile cloud computing   208
    20.4 Blockchain-based supply chain management   210
    20.5 Results and discussions   212
    20.6 Conclusion   213
    References   213

21. Mobile cloud computing security issues in smart cities   215

    RAMIZ SALAMA AND FADI AL-TURJMAN

    21.1 Introduction   215

21.2 Amount of previously published work   221

21.3 Security concerns with mobile cloud computing in smart
       cities   223

21.4 Results and discussion   224

21.5 Conclusion   226

References   230

22. IoT-based river monitoring and alerting system to mitigate flood damage   233

*ALI MOHAMUD ABDULLE, ADAM SAED ALI, ABDIRAHMAN SALAD ALI,
MOHAMED ABDULLAHI ALI, SHARAMKE ALI KAHIE AND
NASRA ABDULKADIR MOHAMED*

22.1 Introduction   233

22.2 Literature review   234

22.3 Proposed system   235

22.4 Analysis and design   236

22.5 System architecture   237

22.6 Results   238

22.7 Send mobile short message service message   241

22.8 Conclusion and recommendation   242

References   243

23. Developing plant environment monitoring application using IOT sensors   245

*LIBAN AHMED ABDULLAHI, ABDIKARIM OMAR MOHAMED, NURADIN HASHI
ADAN, MOHAMED ABDULLAHI MOHAMUD, MOHAMED ABDI MOHAMED AND
SHARMAKE ALI KAHIE*

23.1 Introduction   245

23.2 Literature review   246

23.3 Methodology   246

23.4 Implementation of proposed system   247

23.5 Results and analysis of proposed system   247

23.6 Conclusion   252

References   252

24. An overview of how AI, blockchain, and IoT are making
     smart healthcare possible   255

     RAMIZ SALAMA, AZZA ALTORGOMAN AND FADI AL-TURJMAN

     24.1 Introduction   255

     24.2 The scope of prior work   256

     24.3 Using artificial intelligence, blockchain, and Internet of
           Things to provide smart healthcare   258

     24.4 A blockchain-based data recorder that is immutable,
           transparent, and secure   260

     24.5 The patient dealings process   261

     24.6 Access to the Internet of Things in the local area   262

     24.7 Findings and evaluation   262

     24.8 Conclusion   265

     References   265

25. An overview of artificial intelligence and blockchain
     technology in smart cities   269

     RAMIZ SALAMA, FADI AL-TURJMAN, SINEM ALTURJMAN AND AZZA
     ALTORGOMAN

     25.1 Introduction   269

     25.2 Extent of past work   270

     25.3 Smart cities with artificial intelligence and blockchain   271

     25.4 Result and discussion   272

     25.5 Conclusion   273

     References   274

26. IoT-based smart vending machine   277

MOHAMED NOR HASHI, YASIR SALAD ABDULLE, YAHYA AHMAD KAYRE,
ALI DAHIR MOHAMUD, MOHAMED ABDULLAHI KHALAF AND
SHARAMKE ALI KAHIE

26.1 Introduction   277

26.2 Related work   278

26.3 Methods and materials   279

26.4 Implementation   281

26.5 Discussion   285

26.6 Conclusion   285

References   286

Index   287

List of contributors

Liban Ahmed Abdullahi   Department of Computer Application, Jamhuriya University of Science and Technology, Mogadishu, Somalia

Ali Mohamud Abdulle   Department of Computer Application, Jamhuriya University of Science and Technology, Mogadishu, Somalia

Yasir Salad Abdulle   Department of Computer Application, Jamhuriya University of Science and Technology, Mogadishu, Somalia

Sarumi Usman Abidemi   Artifiical Intelligence Engineering Department, Research center for AI and IoT, AI and Robotics Institute, Near East University, Nicosia, Mersin, Turkey

Nuradin Hashi Adan   Department of Computer Application, Jamhuriya University of Science and Technology, Mogadishu, Somalia

Olukayode Akanni   Artifiical Intelligence Engineering Department, Research center for AI and IoT, AI and Robotics Institute, Near East University, Nicosia, Mersin, Turkey

Abdirahman Salad Ali   Department of Computer Application, Jamhuriya University of Science and Technology, Mogadishu, Somalia

Adam Saed Ali   Department of Computer Application, Jamhuriya University of Science and Technology, Mogadishu, Somalia

Mohamed Abdullahi Ali   Department of Computer Application, Jamhuriya University of Science and Technology, Mogadishu, Somalia

Fahriye Altinay   Societal Research and Development Center, Faculty of Education, University of Kyrenia, Northern Part of Cyprus, Kyrenia, Mersin, Turkey

Zehra Altinay   Societal Research and Development Center, Faculty of Education, University of Kyrenia, Northern Part of Cyprus, Kyrenia, Mersin, Turkey

Azza Altorgoman   Faculty of Engineering, Research Center for AI and IoT, University of Kyrenia, Mersin, Turkey

Chadi Altrjman   Artificial Intelligence, Software, and Information Systems Engineering Departments, Research Center for AI and IoT, AI and Robotics Institute, Near East University, Nicosia, Mersin10, Turkey

Fadi Al-Turjman   Artificial Intelligence, Software, and Information Systems Engineering Departments, Research Center for AI and IoT, AI and Robotics Institute, Near East University, Nicosia, Mersin10, Turkey

Sinem Alturjman   Artificial Intelligence, Software, and Information Systems Engineering Departments, Research Center for AI and IoT, AI and Robotics Institute, Near East University, Nicosia, Mersin10, Turkey

Mehmet Altınay   Faculty of Tourism, University of Kyrenia, Kyrenia, Northern part of Cyprus, Mersin, Turkey

Hamit Altıparmak   Department of Computer Engineering, Near East University, Nicosia, Cyprus

Kenan Aydoğan   Department of Dermatology, Bursa Uludag University, Nilüfer, Bursa, Turkey

Nebojsa Bacanin   Singidunum University, Danijelova, Belgrade, Serbia

Emel Bülbül Başkan   Department of Dermatology, Bursa Uludag University, Nilüfer, Bursa, Turkey

Nebojsa Budimirovic   Singidunum University, Danijelova, Belgrade, Serbia

Çağda Kıvanç Çağanağa   Faculty of Education, European University of Lefke, Lefke-Northern Cyprus, Mersin, Türkiye

Gokmen Dagli   Societal Research and Development Center, Faculty of Education, University of Kyrenia, Northern Part of Cyprus, Kyrenia, Mersin, Turkey

Mahmut Çerkez Ergören   Department of Medical Genetics, Near East University, Nicosia, Cyprus; DESAM Research Institute, Near East University, Nicosia, Cyprus

Odunlami EriOluwa   Artifiical Intelligence Engineering Department, Research center for AI and IoT, AI and Robotics Institute, Near East University, Nicosia, Mersin, Turkey

Esra Ersoy   Faculty of Law, Department of International Law, Kyrenia University, Kyrenia, TRNC

Yoney Kirsal Ever   Engineering Faculty, Computer Engineering Department, Cyprus International University, Nicosia, North Cyprus

Eser Gemikonakli   Computer Engineering Department, University of Kyrenia, Şehit Yahya Bakır Sokak, Karakum, Kyrenia, North Cyprus; Department of Computer Engineering, Faculty of Engineering, University of Kyrenia, Kyrenia, Mersin, Turkey

Ahmet Güneyli   Faculty of Education, European University of Lefke, Lefke-Northern Cyprus, Mersin, Türkiye

Mohamed Nor Hashi   Department of Computer Application, Jamhuriya University of Science and Technology, Mogadishu, Somalia

Sharamke Ali Kahie   Department of Computer Application, Jamhuriya University of Science and Technology, Mogadishu, Somalia

Gül Kahveci   Faculty of Education, European University of Lefke, Lefke-Northern Cyprus, Mersin, Türkiye

Tolgay Karanfiller   Management Information System, School of Applied Sciences, Cyprus International University, Nicosia, North Cyprus

Yahya Ahmad Kayre   Department of Computer Application, Jamhuriya University of Science and Technology, Mogadishu, Somalia

Mohamed Abdullahi Khalaf   Department of Computer Application, Jamhuriya University of Science and Technology, Mogadishu, Somalia

Kifah Amara   UNRWA, Deputy chief field education program\West Bank, Mersin, Turkey

Hasan Kuren   Artificial Intelligence, Software, and Information Systems Engineering Departments, Research Center for AI and IoT, AI and Robotics Institute, Near East University, Nicosia, Mersin10, Turkey

Teyei Ruth Mangai   Artifiical Intelligence Engineering Department, Research Center for AI and IoT, AI and Robotics Institute, Near East University, Nicosia, Mersin, Turkey

Gökçe Maraşlı   Faculty of Law, University of Kyrenia, Kyrenia, Northern Cyprus

Nesrin Menemenci   Faculty of Tourism, Near East University, Northern part of Cyprus, Nicosia, Mersin, Turkey

Abdikarim Omar Mohamed   Department of Computer Application, Jamhuriya University of Science and Technology, Mogadishu, Somalia

Mohamed Abdi Mohamed   Department of Computer Application, Jamhuriya University of Science and Technology, Mogadishu, Somalia

Nasra Abdulkadir Mohamed   Department of Computer Application, Jamhuriya University of Science and Technology, Mogadishu, Somalia

Ali Dahir Mohamud   Department of Computer Application, Jamhuriya University of Science and Technology, Mogadishu, Somalia

Mohamed Abdullahi Mohamud   Department of Computer Application, Jamhuriya University of Science and Technology, Mogadishu, Somalia

Auwalu Saleh Mubarak   Artifiical Intelligence Engineering Department, Research Center for AI and IoT, AI and Robotics Institute, Near East University, Nicosia, Mersin, Turkey

Angelina Njegus   Singidunum University, Danijelova, Belgrade, Serbia

Furkan Ocel   Management Information System, School of Applied Sciences, Cyprus International University, Nicosia, North Cyprus

Akanni Olukayode   Artifiical Intelligence Engineering Department, Research Center for AI and IoT, AI and Robotics Institute, Near East University, Nicosia, Mersin, Turkey

Haluk Barbaros Oral   Department of Dermatology, Bursa Uludag University, Nilüfer, Bursa, Turkey

Aleksandar Petrovic   Singidunum University, Danijelova, Belgrade, Serbia

Branislav Radomirovic   Singidunum University, Danijelova, Belgrade, Serbia

Ramiz Salama   Artificial Intelligence, Software, and Information Systems Engineering Departments, Research Center for AI And IoT, AI And Robotics Institute, Near East University, Nicosia, Mersin10, Turkey

Hamdan H. Shehab   Department of Biomedical Engineering, Faculty of Engineering, Near East University, Nicosia/TRNC, Mersin, Turkey

Şehime Gulsun Temel   Department of Medical Genetics, Bursa Uludag University, Nilüfer, Bursa, Turkey

Eylem Ümit Atılgan   Faculty of Law, University of Kyrenia, Near East University, Kyrenia, Cypruss

M. Vubangsi   Artifiical Intelligence Engineering Department, Research Center for AI and IoT, AI and Robotics Institute, Near East University, Nicosia, Mersin, Turkey; Computational Materials Science Lab, HTTTC Bambili, University of Bamenda, Bambili, NWR, Cameroon

Serkan Yazıcı   Department of Dermatology, Bursa Uludag University, Nilüfer, Bursa, Turkey

İzel Yılmaz   Department of Dermatology, Bursa Uludag University, Nilüfer, Bursa, Turkey

Miodrag Zivkovic   Singidunum University, Danijelova, Belgrade, Serbia

1

An overview of future cyber security applications using AI and blockchain technology

Ramiz Salama, Chadi Altrjman, Fadi Al-Turjman

ARTIFICIAL INTELLIGENCE, SOFTWARE, AND INFORMATION SYSTEMS ENGINEERING DEPARTMENTS, RESEARCH CENTER FOR AI AND IOT, AI AND ROBOTICS INSTITUTE, NEAR EAST UNIVERSITY, NICOSIA, MERSIN10, TURKEY

1.1 Introduction

Because blockchain technology is a distributed ledger based on cryptography, it enables trustworthy transactions between untrustworthy network participants. Since the initial Bitcoin blockchain was introduced in 2008, a number of new blockchain systems, including Ethereum and Hyperledger Fabric, have emerged in addition to the current fiat currencies and electronic voucher systems. Because of its unique trust and security qualities, blockchain technology has recently been the focus of an increasing number of scientific studies, which has piqued the interest of researchers, developers, and business experts. There is no doubt that blockchain technology has acquired worldwide traction. It has had a long-lasting impact on the world, in addition to just becoming well-known. It has, for example, been commercialized, affecting global financial markets and promoting the creation of harmful dark web marketplaces. It has also had a big impact on the rise of financially motivated attacks on online stores and other businesses, such as ransomware and denial of service. Actually, the uses and applications of blockchain have far surpassed its original role as the world's first decentralized cryptocurrency. Other companies attempting to apply the underlying concepts to their current business processes have recognized the value of a trustless, decentralized ledger with historical immutability [1–3]. Because of its unique qualities, blockchain technology is an intriguing prospect for many sectors, including banking, logistics, the pharmaceutical industry, smart contracts, and, most crucially in the context of this study, cyber security. The use of the blockchain, which may enable a new generation of decentralized apps without middlemen and serve as the foundation for critical components of Internet security infrastructures, stands out among those moving beyond bitcoin payments. It is vital to identify current studies directly related to the application of blockchain technology to the issue of cyber security to analyze how expanding technologies may give solutions to prevent escalating risks. It is critical to methodically map out major publications and scholarly works to determine what study has already been done in reference to blockchain and cyber security. This paper focuses on the existing research on the usage of blockchain as an additional technology for cyber security [4].

Artificial intelligence (AI) is a technology that has the potential to be more powerful than humans and can do difficult jobs that require human intelligence. AI applications include corporate sectors such as data privacy, security, integrity, and accountability, as well as its usage in cybersecurity. AI is one of the key engines driving industrial growth because it promotes the integration of cutting-edge technologies in the fourth industrial revolution (IR 4.0), such as blockchains, cryptocurrencies, cloud computing, and the Internet of Things (IoT). In fact, the vast amount of data created by IoT devices, social media, and online apps, which are then used to train machine learning (ML) algorithms, has propelled the expansion of AI. However, there are some reservations about AI. Privacy has emerged as a major issue, particularly in light of recent data breaches and other instances of misuse. The Facebook scandal is one such example, in which the political consulting firm Cambridge Analytical unintentionally targeted millions of users. AI cannot be judged or trusted because it cannot connect with or engage with human users. As a result, explainability and the trustworthiness of technology are two additional challenges that are becoming increasingly important [5]. The acceleration of AI and blockchain integration will change the future digital generation inspired by IR 4.0. Blockchain can provide explainability, privacy, and trust to AI-powered applications, in contrast to how AI can boost scalability and security while addressing customization and governance challenges for blockchain-based solutions. Despite significant technological differences, blockchain and AI may complement one another by compensating for one another's flaws. In this way, AI and blockchain are the yin and yang of digital business, with the former supporting in understanding, identifying, and making decisions, while the latter assists in execution, verification, and recording, thereby preventing security breaches. The lack of security given by AI in major companies that utilize AI to analyze their purchase alternatives, such as Walmart and Amazon, can be remedied if blockchain is made a payment option on such sites. Secure information encryption is utilized across the system to create an effective barrier between hackers and user data. A new set of cybersecurity goals may be established through the usage of encrypted data, decentralized information storage, and publicly accessible ledgers. These organizations would be able to swiftly identify potential assaults and the source of the altered data [6–8].

1.2 Previous work extent

Google: Since its inception 18 years ago, Gmail has utilized ML to filter emails. Almost all of its services now use ML, particularly deep learning, which allows algorithms to self-regulate and make more autonomous changes. Having more data used to be associated with facing more obstacles. In deep learning, more data is usually better. Elie Bursztein, director of the

Google IBM/Watson antiabuse research team, states that for "knowledge consolidation" jobs and ML-based threat identification, the IBM team is increasingly depending on its Watson cognitive learning platform. What if ML could be used to automate some of the repetitive or routine tasks currently performed in a security operation center? Koos Lodewijkx is IBM Security's vice president and chief technical officer of security operations and response. According to Juniper Networks, the networking industry is in serious need of innovative solutions to current network economics. Juniper says that the solution to this challenge is a production-ready, cost-effective self-driving NetworkTM [9−11].

1.3 Using blockchain technologies in cyber security

The largest security concern is now blockchain, a decentralized, user-operated secure digital registration and authentication system. Users' "private keys have cutting-edge encryption mechanisms that guarantee that the data is not claimed," preventing identity theft. When Satoshi Nakamoto published the paper exposing the cryptocurrency to the public in 2008, the Bitcoin blockchain technology was not generally understood. Many creative minds have expanded on Nakamoto's original focus on the blockchain as a Bitcoin platform and given it new applications. Authentication can be raised, edge computing can be safeguarded, and data mapping can be improved. Blockchain could improve cybersecurity in many ways; cybercrimes such as identity theft, fraud, and data theft can all be avoided by utilizing block-chain technology [12−14].

Using distributed key public infrastructure, blockchain enables security apps installed in companies to authenticate devices and individuals. The resilient domain name system (DNS) entry mechanism used by blockchains can improve security by eliminating a single point of failure. It enables the resolution of single attack points against multiple targets at a single access point, such as a database, network, or data center. It allows you to stop single-point attacks as well as multiple target attacks, such as a server-side attack, all at the same time. Here are a few ways that blockchain could improve cybersecurity: Cybercrimes such as identity theft, fraud, and data theft can all be avoided by utilizing blockchain technology [12−14].

In a series, distributed ledger technology, a decentralized ledger technology, tries to instill trust in an untrustworthy ecosystem. Every blockchain participant has transparent access to all data, and participant nodes can see, store, transmit, and record any encrypted transaction data on the blockchain. Companies all across the world can use blockchain technology to interact in their cloud settings without revealing sensitive information owing to security, privacy, and regulatory concerns. A few sectors have shifted to cryptographic technology based on the blockchain concept. Identity management, smart contracts, encrypted communications, and data encryption are some of the applications of ledger technology [15]. Parties can maintain complete privacy while collaborating to run computations or store data using this technique. It can include the entire network, including the cloud, cloud storage, and cloud computing, as well as endpoints. Blockchain technology is increasingly being used in cybersecurity to improve IT security. In the event of a breach, the blockchain can be kept in a single location rather than having to generate an exact clone. It is critical to distinguish between the use of blockchains in cybersecurity and the main flaws discovered by hackers who were able to steal from Bitcoin exchanges. Because data must be encrypted before processing, cryptocurrency exchanges believe that blockchain security is insufficient to protect transactions. This issue can be solved by integrating the blockchain with a decentralized system that is resistant to such attacks. Despite the fact that the blockchain is still in its infancy, fraudsters are already exploring ways to exploit it, according to a recent assessment by the US Department of Homeland Security. Online security may improve with the use of blockchain technology. When a user publishes his public key on the blockchain, the data in the register about previous blocks is linked and distributed to hundreds of millions of nodes. In the event of a network assault, this could risk not only the user's private key but also the network's overall security. Blockchain technology is here to stay and will help businesses, individuals, and governments protect their data, assets, and selves. Innovative blockchain utilization has already had an impact on other industries, such as cryptocurrencies, albeit it mostly benefits cybersecurity [16,17].

1.4 Blockchain applications in cybersecurity

Despite the fact that it is not completely impenetrable, blockchain has evolved into one of the most secure means of conducting transactions in the world of digital networks. The system has been recognized for upholding information integrity in accordance with how it was intended and built. It has the potential to benefit a wide range of industries if used correctly. Blockchain technology is versatile and has the potential to be useful in a variety of applications. One of the better applications would be to employ its integrity assurance to provide cybersecurity solutions for a wide range of other technologies [12,18−22]. Here are a few examples of how blockchain could be utilized to improve cybersecurity in the future:

1. **Protecting Private Messaging**: As the internet shrinks the world into a smaller, more connected village, more people are using social media. There are more social media outlets than ever before. As conversational commerce grows in popularity, more social applications are being released on a regular basis. These exchanges result in the collection of a large amount of metadata. The majority of social networking site users utilize weak, untrustworthy passwords to safeguard the platforms and their data. When compared to the end-to-end encryption used by messaging companies to protect user data, blockchain is becoming a more appealing solution. A universal security protocol can be created using blockchains. Blockchain technology could be used to create a uniform API architecture for facilitating cross-messenger communication. In recent months, there have been numerous attacks on social media platforms such as Twitter and Facebook. As a result of these attacks, millions of accounts and user information were compromised. If properly integrated into these communication systems, blockchain technology may be able to thwart future attacks of a similar type.

2. *IoT Security*: Edge devices such as routers and thermostats are increasingly being used by hackers to gain access to larger networks. Because of the current fascination with AI, hackers now have an easier time accessing larger systems such as home automation and edge devices such as "smart" switches. The majority of these IoT devices have questionable security capabilities. Blockchain may be used to protect such enormous systems or devices by decentralizing their administration. The procedure will allow the device to select its own security measures. Edge devices become more secure by recognizing and responding to questionable requests from unknown networks rather than relying on the central admin or authority. When a device's central administration is penetrated, the systems and devices are immediately taken over by the hacker. Blockchain ensures that such attacks are more difficult to carry out by decentralizing such device authority mechanisms.

3. *Protecting DNS and DDoS*: When a DDoS attack is launched against a target resource, such as a network resource, server, or website, users of the target resource are denied access to or service from the target resource. These attacks degrade or render resource systems unworkable. A healthy DNS on the other hand is highly centralized, making it a great target for cybercriminals who break the link between an IP address and the name of a website. A website may become unavailable as a result of this assault, and viewers may be directed to other fake websites. Fortunately, by decentralizing DNS records, a blockchain can help to mitigate these assaults. By using decentralized means, hackers may have exploited flaws that a blockchain would have made impossible.

4. *Decentralizing Medium Storage*: Businesses are increasingly concerned about data breaches and theft. The great majority of businesses continue to rely on centralized storage. A hacker only needs to target one weakness in these systems to have access to all of the stored data. A criminal now has access to sensitive and confidential information, including corporate financial information. Sensitive data can be protected by using blockchains to provide decentralized data storage. Hackers would find it more difficult, if not impossible, to get access to data storage systems using this mitigation method. Many storage service providers are investigating the efficacy of blockchain in securing data from hackers. The Apollo Currency Team is a company that has already used blockchain technology (The Apollo Data Cloud).

5. *The Provenance of Computer Software*: A blockchain can be used to prevent tampering and to validate program downloads. Blockchain may be used to authenticate operations, such as firmware upgrades, installers, and patches, similar to how MD5 hashes are used today, to prevent the entry of malicious software into workstations. In the MD5 scenario, the identities of new software are compared to hashes from vendor websites. This method is not totally secure because the hashes available on the supplier's platform may have already been updated. When adopting blockchain technology, however, the hashes are retained in the chain. Because the information recorded in technology is irreversible and unchangeable, blockchains may be more successful in confirming the correctness of software by comparing its hashes to those on the network.

6. ***Cyber-physical infrastructure verification***: Data tampering, system misconfiguration, and component failure have all affected cyber-physical system information. However, any cyber-physical infrastructure's status can be confirmed by utilizing blockchain technology's information integrity and verification capabilities. Blockchain data created on infrastructure components may be more trustworthy throughout the entire chain of custody.

7. ***Preventing Unauthorized Access to Data While in Transit***: Blockchain may be used in the future to restrict access to data while it is in motion. Data transport can be protected by leveraging the technology's full encryption capability, preventing hostile actors, whether individuals or organizations, from accessing it. This technique would dramatically improve the integrity and reliability of data transferred between blockchains. Data in transit is intercepted by malevolent hackers, who subsequently modify or remove it completely. This creates a significant vacuum for ineffective modes of communication, such as emails.

Human Safety Loss due to Cyberattacks' negative consequences: Unmanned military equipment and public transportation have both been introduced as a result of recent technology breakthroughs. These self-driving cars and weaponry are only conceivable because of the Internet, which allows data to travel from sensors to databases used for remote control. However, fraudsters have attempted to get access to and breach into networks such as the Car Area Network (CAN). Access to these networks allows hackers to take complete control of critical car systems. Such accidents would have a direct impact on human safety. These issues, however, might be prevented by doing blockchain data verification on every data that enters and exits such systems.

1.5 The application of artificial intelligence technologies in cyber security

- The attack surface for organizations is massive, and it is continually increasing and changing. Processing up to several hundred billion time-varying data points is required to accurately evaluate risk, depending on the size of your firm.
- Analyzing and enhancing cybersecurity posture on a human scale is no longer a challenge.
- In response to this unprecedented challenge, AI-based cybersecurity technologies have been developed to assist information security teams in lowering the risk of breaches and strengthening their security posture.
- AI and ML have emerged as critical information security technologies because they can rapidly analyze millions of events and identify a wide range of threats, including malware that exploits zero-day vulnerabilities and risky behavior that could lead to phishing attacks or the download of malicious code. These algorithms adapt over time and use historical data to identify new threats as they appear. AI can recognize and respond to

departures from the norm by constructing profiles for people, resources, and networks based on their behavioral histories.

- Cybersecurity is one of the most difficult problems we face, and AI is best positioned to handle it. With today's constantly developing cyberattacks and multitude of devices, ML and AI may be utilized to "keep up with the bad guys," automating threat identification and response more efficiently than traditional software-driven techniques.
- However, cybersecurity faces a number of unique obstacles, including enormous shortages of competent security workers, a vast attack surface, tens to hundreds of thousands of devices per firm, hundreds of attack paths, and massive amounts of data that go beyond the limits of a human problem.

Many of these issues should be addressed by a self-learning AI-based cybersecurity posture management system. A self-learning system can be technologically designed to collect data continuously and autonomously from all of your company's information systems. Patterns from millions to billions of signals relevant to the corporate attack surface are connected after data analysis. Human teams are therefore given unprecedented degrees of intelligence in numerous cybersecurity sectors, such as:

The process of generating a thorough, accurate list of all the hardware, software, and personnel who have access to information systems is known as IT asset inventory. Both business criticality measurement and inventory classification are critical.

Threat exposure: Hackers, like everyone else, are inspired by fashion, therefore, what they wear changes on a regular basis. AI-based cybersecurity solutions may provide up-to-date information on regional and industry-specific threats, allowing you to prioritize key tasks based on what could be used to attack your firm as well as what is likely to be used to attack your organization.

Control effectiveness: Understanding the impact of the various security instruments and security processes you have implemented is critical for maintaining a high level of security. AI can assist you in identifying the areas of your InfoSec program's strengths and flaws.

Breach risk prediction: AI-based solutions may estimate how and where you are most likely to have a breach based on your IT asset inventory, threat exposure, and control efficacy. This allows you to plan ahead of time and allocate resources and tools to your weakest points. You can more effectively boost your organization's cyber resilience by developing and improving policies and procedures based on prescriptive insights from AI analysis.

Incident response: AI-powered systems may provide more context for prioritizing and responding to security warnings, for rapid event response, discovering root causes to reduce vulnerabilities, and preventing future issues. To assist human InfoSec teams, AI must be understandable. Analyses and recommendations must be brief and easy to understand. Obtaining the support of all key internal stakeholders, comprehending the implications of various InfoSec initiatives, and providing critical data to all interested parties, including end users, security operations, the CISO, auditors, CIO, CEO, and board of directors, all rely on this [23–27].

1.6 The benefits of artificial intelligence in cybersecurity

Cybersecurity is one of the many domains where AI is valuable and has applications. AI and ML can assist in keeping up with hackers, automate threat identification, and respond more efficiently than outdated software-driven or manual procedures in today's context of rapidly changing cyberattacks and expanding gadgets [28–33].

1.7 Here are a few advantages and applications of artificial intelligence in cybersecurity

- *Identifying Fresh Threats*: AI can detect online risks and potentially illegal behavior. Because traditional software systems cannot handle the massive amount of new malware that is generated every week, AI can be highly effective in this case. AI systems are being trained to detect malware and ransomware attacks before they reach the system, discern patterns in them, and recognize even the smallest elements of these threats. AI enables higher predictive intelligence by utilizing natural language processing, which accumulates data on its own by reading news articles, publications, and cyber threat research. Details about new anomalies, cyberattacks, and defense techniques may be included. Hackers, as trend-followers, are continuously changing what is popular with them. AI-based cybersecurity solutions can provide up-to-date information on both general and industry-specific threats, allowing you to make more informed decisions about what is most likely to attack your systems and what methods may be used to do so.
- *Bots in combat*: Malicious bots now account for a sizable portion of internet traffic. The use of stolen passwords to access accounts, the establishment of fake accounts, and data fraud are all instances of how bots can pose a serious threat. Manual reactions cannot totally defeat automated threats. It is feasible to discern between individuals and website visitors, as well as good bots (such as search engine crawlers) and hazardous bots, using AI and ML. With the help of AI, we can evaluate massive amounts of data, allowing cybersecurity teams to adjust their methods in reaction to a changing environment. Businesses can learn the answers to the questions "what does an average user trip look like" and "what does a dangerous unusual journey look like" by examining behavioral patterns. According to Mark Greenwood, Chief Technical Architect and head of Data Science at Netacea, from this point on, we can understand the aim of their website visitors and get and stay ahead of dangerous bots.
- *Prediction of Breach Risk*: The IT asset inventory, which is an accurate and comprehensive record of all devices, users, and apps with varying levels of access to various systems, is created using AI algorithms. AI-based solutions may now analyze how and where you are most likely to be compromised based on your asset inventory and threat exposure (described above), allowing you to plan and allocate resources to regions with the highest risks. Prescriptive insights from AI-based analysis enable you to build and improve cyber resilience policies and practices.

- *Improved endpoint security*: AI is critical for safeguarding all endpoints utilized for remote work, which employs an increasing number of devices. Although antivirus software and VPNs can protect users against remote malware and ransomware attacks, these solutions mainly rely on signature-based operations. This implies that keeping up with signature definition changes is critical to be protected against the most recent threats. It may be alarming if antivirus software is not kept up to date or if the program's developer is unaware that the virus definitions are out of date. As a result, if a new type of malware assault emerges, signature protection may be rendered ineffective. Endpoint protection powered by AI provides a different method, employing repeated training to establish an endpoint's baseline behavior. AI is capable of detecting anomalies and, if necessary, taking appropriate action, such as informing a technician or restoring security following a ransomware assault. According to Tim Brown, vice president of security architecture at Solar Winds, this strategy provides proactive prevention against attacks rather than waiting for signature changes.

1.8 Conclusion

This study reveals how AI is significantly impacting every area of cybersecurity. CAPTCHA technology has begun to become obsolete and ineffective as AI methods for login security progress. AI approaches have shown enormous potential in the advancement of cybersecurity through the actual usage of these techniques in evaluating and identifying any cyberattack on a computer system. Cyberspace breaches are thought to drastically lower the cost of detection and response. Furthermore, introducing AI approaches into the traditional detection process has been shown to speed up the process overall by recognizing risks and irregularities more quickly.

AI algorithms that help with input augmentation provide an improved cybersecurity strategy, and other activities boost the detection process's accuracy and spontaneity. Intelligence systems may be built to notify users of potential dangers and assaults that their computer system may be vulnerable to, in addition to assisting in the detection process. Because it comprises scalable, trustworthy data encryption mechanisms; data integrity; and network resilience, the blockchain, on the other hand, provides numerous chances for maintaining a high level of data security. As a result, transitioning from a traditional system to a blockchain-based system may benefit organizations in practically every industry. However, as with any new technology, businesses must be prepared to deal with a number of disadvantages and obstacles when deploying a blockchain to improve the cybersecurity of their products. The main issues are reliance on private keys, adaptation difficulties, and a lack of knowledge.

References

[1] Y. Maleh, Y. Baddi, M. Alazab, L. Tawalbeh, I. Romdhani (Eds.), Artificial Intelligence and Blockchain for Future Cybersecurity Applications, Vol. 90, Springer Nature, 2021.

[2] M. Javaid, A. Haleem, R.P. Singh, S. Khan, R. Suman, Blockchain technology applications for Industry 4.0: A literature-based review, Blockchain: Res. Appl. (2021) 100027.

[3] A. Chang, N. El-Rayes, J. Shi, Blockchain technology for supply chain management: a comprehensive review, FinTech 1 (2) (2022) 191−205.

[4] X. Feng, M. Conrad, K. Hussein, NHS big data intelligence on blockchain applications, In Big Data Intelligence for Smart Applications, Springer, Cham, 2022, pp. 191−208.

[5] B. Naik, A. Mehta, H. Yagnik, M. Shah, The impacts of artificial intelligence techniques in augmentation of cybersecurity: a comprehensive review, Complex Intell. Syst. (2021) 1−18.

[6] A.F. Abbas, N.A. Qureshi, N. Khan, R. Chandio, J. Ali, The blockchain technologies in healthcare: prospects, obstacles, and future recommendations; lessons learned from digitalization, Int. J. Online Biomed. Eng. 18 (9) (2022).

[7] J. Singh, M. Sajid, S.K. Gupta, R.A. Haidri, Artificial intelligence and blockchain technologies for smart city, Intell. Green Technol. Sustain. Smart Cities (2022) 317−330.

[8] A.S. Tagliafico, C. Campi, B. Bianca, C. Bortolotto, D. Buccicardi, C. Francesca, et al., Blockchain in radiology research and clinical practice: current trends and future directions, La Radiologia Medica (2022) 1−7.

[9] A. Kuzior, M. Sira, A bibliometric analysis of blockchain technology research using VOSviewer, Sustainability 14 (13) (2022) 8206.

[10] F. Tao, M.S. Akhtar, Z. Jiayuan, The future of artificial intelligence in cybersecurity: a comprehensive survey, EAI Endorsed Trans. Creative Technol. 8 (28) (2021). e3-e3.

[11] H. Fatoum, S. Hanna, J.D. Halamka, D.C. Sicker, P. Spangenberg, S.K. Hashmi, Blockchain integration with digital technology and the future of health care ecosystems: systematic review, J. Med. Int. Res. 23 (11) (2021) e19846.

[12] M. Ghiasi, M. Dehghani, T. Niknam, A. Kavousi-Fard, P. Siano, H.H. Alhelou, Cyber-attack detection and cyber-security enhancement in smart DC-microgrid based on blockchain technology and Hilbert Huang transform, IEEE Access 9 (2021) 29429−29440.

[13] M. Gimenez-Aguilar, J.M. De Fuentes, L. Gonzalez-Manzano, D. Arroyo, Achieving cybersecurity in blockchain-based systems: a survey, Fut. Gen. Comput. Syst. 124 (2021) 91−118.

[14] Y.I.L. Lucio, K.M. Villalba, S.A. Donado, Adaptive blockchain technology for a cybersecurity framework in IIoT, IEEE Revista Iberoamericana de Tecnologias del Aprendizaje 17 (2) (2022) 178−184.

[15] O. Lage, M. Saiz-Santos, Blockchain and the decentralisation of the cybersecurity Industry, DYNA 96 (3) (2021) 239.

[16] A. Mittal, M.P. Gupta, M. Chaturvedi, S.R. Chansarkar, S. Gupta, Cybersecurity Enhancement through blockchain training (CEBT)−a serious game approach, Int. J. Inform. Manage. Data Insights 1 (1) (2021) 100001.

[17] A. Dwivedi, A. Mishra, D. Singh, Cybersecurity and privacy issues of blockchain technology, Blockchain for Information Security and Privacy, Auerbach Publications, 2021, pp. 69−94.

[18] M. Liu, W. Yeoh, F. Jiang, K.K.R. Choo, Blockchain for cybersecurity: systematic literature review and classification, J. Comput. Inform. Syst. (2021) 1−17.

[19] S.N.G. Gourisetti, Ü. Cali, K.K.R. Choo, E. Escobar, C. Gorog, A. Lee, et al., Standardization of the distributed ledger technology cybersecurity stack for power and energy applications, Sustain. Energy, Grids Network. 28 (2021) 100553.

[20] A.U. Nwosu, S.B. Goyal, P. Bedi, Blockchain transforming cyber-attacks: healthcare industry, International Conference on Innovations in Bio-Inspired Computing and Applications, Springer, Cham, 2021, pp. 258−266.

[21] V. Wylde, N. Rawindaran, J. Lawrence, R. Balasubramanian, E. Prakash, A. Jayal, et al., Cybersecurity, data privacy and blockchain: a review, SN Comput. Sci. 3 (2) (2022) 1−12.

[22] B. Chillakuri, V.P. Attili, Role of blockchain in HR's response to new-normal, Int. J. Organiz. Anal (2021).

[23] D. Ghillani, Deep learning and artificial intelligence framework to improve the cyber security, Authorea Preprints (2022).

[24] B. Alhayani, H.J. Mohammed, I.Z. Chaloob, J.S. Ahmed, Effectiveness of artificial intelligence techniques against cyber security risks apply of IT industry, Mater. Today: Proc (2021).

[25] C. Zhang, Intelligent internet of things service based on artificial intelligence technology, in 2021 IEEE 2nd International Conference on Big Data, Artificial Intelligence and Internet of Things Engineering (ICBAIE), IEEE, 2021, pp. 731−734.

[26] Z. Zhang, H. Ning, F. Shi, F. Farha, Y. Xu, J. Xu, et al., Artificial intelligence in cyber security: research advances, challenges, and opportunities, Artif. Intell. Rev. 55 (2) (2022) 1029−1053.

[27] T.M. Ghazal, Internet of things with artificial intelligence for health care security, Arabian J. Sci. Eng 48 (4) (2021) 400−425.

[28] F. AL-Turjman, R. Salama, Cyber security in mobile social networks, Security in Iot Social Networks, Academic Press, 2021, pp. 55−81.

[29] F. Al-Turjman, R. Salama, Security in social networks, Security in IoT Social Networks, Academic Press, 2021, pp. 1−27.

[30] R. Salama, F. Al-Turjman, AI in blockchain towards realizing cyber security, In 2022 International Conference on Artificial Intelligence in Everything (AIE), IEEE, 2022, pp. 471−475.

[31] F. Al-Turjman, R. Salama, An overview about the cyberattacks in grid and like systems, Smart Grid in IoT-Enabled Spaces (2020) 233−247.

[32] R. Salama, F. Al-Turjman, R. Culmone, AI-powered drone to address smart city security issues, in Proceedings of the 37th International Conference on Advanced Information Networking and Applications (AINA-2023), Vol. 3, Springer International Publishing, Cham., 2023, pp. 292−300.

[33] X. Raybon, G. Che, D. Burrows, E. Olsson, R. Tkach, Shaping lightwaves in time and frequency for optical fiber communication, Nat. Commun. 13 (1) (2022) 1−11.

2

A survey of issues, possibilities, and solutions for a blockchain and AI-powered Internet of things

Ramiz Salama, Sinem Alturjman, Fadi Al-Turjman

ARTIFICIAL INTELLIGENCE, SOFTWARE, AND INFORMATION SYSTEMS ENGINEERING DEPARTMENTS, RESEARCH CENTER FOR AI AND IOT, AI AND ROBOTICS INSTITUTE, NEAR EAST UNIVERSITY, NICOSIA, MERSIN10, TURKEY

2.1 Introduction

Following the massive commercial sending of 5G (and prior 5G) networks, there have been major advancements in flexible communication in the 6th era. It is anticipated that the introduction of 6G will significantly improve human productivity and manner of life. The Federal Communications Commission had an interesting conversation regarding 6G innovation in September 2018. It was mentioned that the 6G recurrence band would soon advance into the Tera-Hertz (THz) range. In Walk 2019, the FCC decided to allow 6G organization preliminary testing in the THz recurrence band between 95 and 3 THz. In January 2020, it was suggested that it was crucial to advance and take part in early research for vitally important and forward-thinking 6G advancements. It has been accepted that 6G normalization might take place around 2025 and that 6G prebusiness organizations would be implemented around 2030. 6G needs to provide omnipresent security to remain relevant. Additionally, this is the key area where innovations like the blockchain and circulating records are crucial. Initially, the blockchain was proposed for use with digital money. Whatever the case, it has currently found uses well outside that industry, such as in remote correspondences, brilliant lattices, and the Internet of Things (IoT). Reconfigurable smart surfaces, intelligent cells using artificial intelligence (AI), and possibly THz recurrence groups should all benefit from 6G. These advances will need to be implemented in a stable environment. This will be confusing because the organization's thickness intends to massively increase while simultaneously depleting its resources and maintenance budget.

There is growing consensus that blockchain, a well-known kind of distributed record technology, will play a crucial role in the future of mobile communication systems. In contrast, whether or not 5G organizations will be useful has become a well-known field of focus in just the previous few years. For the safe and complete robotization of the era of mobile businesses, notably,

Computational Intelligence and Blockchain in Complex Systems. DOI: https://doi.org/10.1016/B978-0-443-13268-1.00019-4
© 2024 Elsevier Inc. All rights reserved, including those for text and data mining, AI training, and similar technologies.

13

6G, which will be logically software-driven, decentralized, and a cross-section of open frameworks, blockchain innovation is seen as necessary. In particular, the use of blockchain technology is anticipated to benefit both the specialized aspects of 6G (such as security, network administration of the board, asset usage, and range of the executives) as well as the utilization of 6G (such as medical care, energy Internet, automated flying vehicles, independent vehicles, and expanded reality; some of these applications are thoroughly discussed in Segment 4). Experts are investigating how blockchain might affect 6G enterprises to better comprehend these applications. Understanding that decentralized procedures and means would be necessary is crucial. Blockchain technology has demonstrated value in terms of organizational security and transparency. The flexibility of the blockchain technology (as its appropriate components can be altered depending on the applications) is a key component.

A blockchain is a decentralized distributed ledger that is maintained by a fundamental peer-to-peer (P2P) network of nodes. As suggested by its name, a blockchain is made up of a number of exchange-related blocks that are legally linked to one another to form an electronic record. Then, a "block" is formed from all of the checked exchanges that occurred over a particular period. Each block consequently has a respectable number of exchanges. These blocks are logically related in the request for their age using cryptographic hashes. According to this, each block contains the hash value of the previous block in the "past block hash" field. The "beginning block"—the underlying block—has no ancestors. In this manner, all zeros are placed in the beginning block's earlier block hash field. The digital record is encoded and contains a sequential request of all prior trades. A distributed blockchain network's hubs all repeat this record as well. Since only attach mode is used to execute compose jobs, the transmitted record continues to grow over time.

Blockchain is viewed as a unique mechanical innovation from an inventive perspective that is a potent amalgam of concepts, methods, and developments. For instance, blockchain uses cryptographic techniques such as the Merkle tree, hashing, advanced markings, and public key infrastructure. Additionally, it connects hubs (also known as excavators) using P2P technology to create a blockchain network. The blockchain organization's hubs can agree on the current condition of the scattered record and remain in a state of harmony thanks to an agreement component. Blockchain promises to resolve problems like shared trades without involving outsiders controlling assembled tools. Blockchain helps establish confidence through pseudonymity, simple yet reliable record keeping, and managing fake duplicates of advanced resources (such as double spending).

Blockchain executions are anticipated to be transmitted and connected during the 6G era to pass via many organizational areas (i.e., center, transport, edge, and access organizations) and power a challenging 6G environment. Block-oriented 6G suggests a biological system in which blockchains will become integrated, essential to, and unbounded throughout the entire climate. This will give the 6G area a variety of extra benefits. The robotization of organization executives, the unique range the board of THz correspondence, computer-based intelligence-fueled edge figuring, and combined asset participation in trustless conditions, as well as the security of AI and combined learning models, are just a few examples of how blockchain has a significant amount of potential to enable and improve numerous key 6G functionalities. The blockchain-focused version of 6G may also help with the development of new 6G applications, such as associated autonomous vehicles, the energy Internet, expanded reality, numerous automated aircraft, digital twins, industry 5.0, and smart medical services due to the smart Internet of clinical things. The growth of the IoT involves detecting abilities, invitation, and over-the-Internet communications, providing a new method for handling a variety of business, governmental, and public/confidential area concerns and challenges. IoT devices come in all sizes, from tiny wearable sensors to massive equipment stages. IoT frameworks have numerous important applications in diverse industries. In any event, they also stand for a variety of challenges. To improve IoT mix and eliminate vertical storehouses, standard conventions are required due to the variety of devices and organizations. IoT information clarity is yet another formidable obstacle. The vast amounts of developed information should be obtained and should not be manipulated, misrepresented, or changed in any other way. A weak link can cause a few components of an integrated IoT design to malfunction. Conveyed administrations, which guarantee that information will not change for all of its participants, are a promising solution for providing dependability in IoT information. Blockchain-based innovation plays a key role in building distributed and secure companies. A blockchain is a distributed, permanent record that is transmitted across a P2P network. Blockchain collects transactions during registration and then updates them in a distributed manner. Blockchain technology could be accessed by IoT frameworks and devices.

The goal of this research is to fully understand the benefits that might be realized in the 6G era by dissecting the integration of blockchain technology. The idea is to specifically introduce the key research questions pertaining to the use of blockchain technology for 6G and bring them to the attention of interested professionals. The momentum research patterns demonstrate that the local area has picked up speed in its pursuit of 6G development and its integration with blockchain innovation. This study provides a thorough analysis of pertinent and recent examination trends in this manner. This exploratory essay looks at the trends influencing the future growth of 6G and its powerful innovations. The patterns and applications that the combination of 6G-enabled IoT and blockchain can introduce are investigated from top to bottom, which aids in understanding the explicit requirements of 6G and prepares for a thorough investigation regarding the reconciliation of blockchain in the 6G biological system. The following are the commitments of this work:

1. A comprehensive discussion on the fusion of blockchain innovation and 6G-enabled IoT has been introduced. These innovations are discussed separately in the new writing, but we acknowledge that their combination has additional benefits and provides examples of novel applications that will be thoroughly discussed later in the composition.
2. Of utmost importance is the security of IoT-based applications. This review outlines the inherent security benefits of combining blockchain technology with 6G-enabled IoT. This serves as a credible beginning point for study on Industry 5.0.

Together, 6G communications and AI have the power to alter our mechanical reasoning viewpoints and upend the modern way of life. In this way, 6G correspondence innovation will flourish in the market later, between 2030 and 2040. Similar to many innovations, it will take some time for the market to take off. Many analysts have proactively identified both the favorable and unfavorable effects of the new organizational innovation. Full AI will be incorporated with 6G correspondence innovation. Man-made intelligence will play a crucial role in the 6G correspondence organization's communication frameworks. Helping the extended reality (AR) and lengthened reality (XR) is also acceptable. These innovations are sufficient to upgrade the organizational framework. All of that will, therefore, be cloud-based engineering, such as edge processing. The client only needs a rapid Internet connection and does not need to worry about any server, programming, or equipment execution. A continuously information-driven biological system will be provided by cloud innovation, which will improve all organization networks and adaptability. With its high limit and extremely low dormancy, 6G will actually need to manage extremely long network architectures with very little inactivity and power consumption. The global media communications sector is undergoing a striking transformation. It becomes even more striking when a decentralized organizational framework is used. The developing organizational framework aims to achieve continuous success for enhanced portable broadband, extremely reliable low-dormancy correspondences, and extensive machine-type cross-association. Many of the new pieces of technology can also handle large-scale information fusion. To increase availability, cell-distant enterprises use innovative techniques including virtualization, heterogeneous organizations, and programming-driven organizing. Network executives were enabled to govern the quick checking framework by AI. Using a few network virtualization techniques, cloud administrations, and other individual components may be effective in some situations. However, it eventually leads to increased fracture and a greater demand for control tools. 6G will help us create and modify that remarkable toolkit. Edge AI would handle the complex reconciliation in a variety of tiered requests over the administration framework.

The current structure for managing correspondence is cleverly being advanced by 6G communication. While 5G is the foundation for constructing the upcoming age of connectivity innovation, Nayak and Patgiri envision the various future applications of 6G in various locations, such as smart cities, the IoT, and connected automobiles. Scientists stand out enough to be detected by the 6G correspondence system, despite the fact that 5G still does not seem to be able to relay information broadly and provide insight. To provide ubiquitous and reliable communication, analysts have also started making progress in fusing the capabilities of computer-based intelligence with the 6G communication networks. As a result, it is evolving into the cornerstone of society's computerized change. By merging various innovations and applications, 6G correspondence technology streamlines the connection with all of that. Additionally, it supports haptic, submerged, and holographic advancements. The Internet of everything, including the Internet of modern things, the Internet of medical things, the Internet of nanothings, and other networks, will be strengthened. This will enable the 6G correspondence innovation to fulfill its obligations with the aid of cutting-edge AI. The main focus of our analysis paper is the thorough assessment of the 6G correspondence organization. To execute the simulated intelligence constraints to each product framework, we have discovered comparative degrees for the smart medical care framework. Chen also describes the crucial advancement of excellent systems management frameworks. Sun and Ali both scored zero. Pay attention to the different systems management framework layers.

In contrast, our analysis piece reveals the high-level additions that support the high-design organizing framework, such as quantum AI, deep learning, and discovery methodologies. The 6G organization will largely rely on the cloud, and the serverless cloud framework will deliver and maintain the entire systems administration atmosphere, according to another key viewpoint that we have discovered that differs from our own. The coordination of AI with smart organizations is emphasized in both articles. However, the focus of our investigation is the computerized reasoning interaction's full life cycle. Additionally, it illustrates usage scenarios for creating and verifying precise information pieces. In addition, we have carried out a thorough security analysis and protection requirements in comparison to the items. Our in-depth analysis focuses on the requirements for security, mystery, and protection in system management frameworks with the legal application of cutting-edge computerized reasoning techniques [1−5]. The clever organization needs a low-dormancy network relationship to increase the speed at which information moves.

2.2 The volume of prior work

The support for device expansion and diverse information dealing is the inspiration behind the 6G innovation. The move to 6G entails upgrading availability for everyone and everything from everywhere through a structure of the organization that is incredibly flexible and adaptable. The new design requirements include a greater information rate, little idle time, low cost, and an energy reduction. Numerous contemporary applications, such as smart energy organizations, dazzling portable applications, modern IoT, smart health, and AR/VR-improved customer services, will be made possible by the extensive 6G network. The mechanical headway presented by various cell ages is examined. It is predicted that 6G will provide a significant increase in information rate (approximately 1000 times more than 4G), is expected to be several times faster than 5G, and is likely to offer improved reliability and wider organization inclusion. It will also support higher edge speeds of up to very nearly 1 Gbps. It is important to note that the edge rate is influenced by the size and weight of the cell. The peak rate is a highlighting component and typically reaches around 10 Gbps. A complete cycle idleness of roughly 1 Ms is required for just a select few 6G applications, such as computer-generated reality, machine-to-machine communication, cloud-based innovations, two-way gaming, and so on. The improvements associated with 6G, such as the use of the mmWave spectrum (with frequencies up to the sub-THz region of 300 GHz), new base stations, and small cells, give reasonable cost and power scaling capability. Despite the protection offered by encryption technology, a higher level of security should be provided by strengthening the actual layer security structure. This should be used with a variety of PCs and gadgets. It is typical for the general abilities of 6G to be somewhere between 10 and several times greater than those of 5G. When combined with earthly remote mobile, short-range direct, and medium/low circle satellite correspondence developments along with large resources, it will be capable of providing full inclusion and super remote connectivity. Additionally, 6G will combine a wide range of improvements, including imaging, computerized reasoning, calculation, route, area, insight, control, and buffering, among others.

The THz band exchanges, inertial estimation frameworks (IMSs), holographic beamforming, orbital precise energy multiplexing, noticeable light interchanges, blockchain-based range sharing, nanoweb, and other fundamental innovations are a few of the innovations that will be used in 6G organizations. High-end 5G communication networks provide three different help options that are selected based on the type of use being made. These include low dormancy correspondences (URLLC), enormous machine-type correspondences (mMTC), and improved versatile broadband (eMBB) [6]. The first one, called mMTC, increases the number of supported devices and provides assistance for low-cost devices, while the second, called eMBB, focuses on simulated proficiency and maximum throughput. Finally, URLLC aims to increase information transfer efficiency and reduce start-to-end inertness. Despite this, such a decision strategy is definitely insufficient for 6G, where the numerous nature and complexity of the assignments and cycles would lead to varying and, shockingly, conflicting requirements. Network thickness, availability of various correspondence organizations, intermixing of communication, reserving, calculation, control, detecting, and confinement, progress to organize knowledge, and the switch from centralization to dispersal and circulated courses of action are some of the 6G-related advancements that have started to emerge.

Therefore, 6G must be able to connect a large number of devices and applications while still providing guaranteed performance. Therefore, 6G will play a crucial role in meeting the Web of Things' extreme interconnectivity and significantly increased support requirements, resulting in the so-called 6G-empowered IoT (or simply 6G-IoT) [7–11]. With its new organizational structure and technological advancements, 6G will make it possible for a huge number of IoT devices to work together. With enhanced mobile broadband and eMBB, it is entirely anticipated that 6G would use enormous communications (BigCom), secure super dependable low-idleness correspondences, three-layered integrated correspondences (3D-InteCom), and unpredictable information correspondences (UCDC).

2.3 Internet of things driven by 6G

With information speeds of 100 Gbps or more and inactive seasons of milliseconds or less, THz interchanges are expected to be a key innovation for 6G-IoT. Additionally, it is projected that the THz band of 0.1–10 THz will need to fulfill the requirements of the 6G-IoT application, including picosecond level picture perseverance, incorporation of hundreds of submillimeter-long receiving wires, and weak impedance without full inheritance control [12]. A platform for connecting billions of smart devices will be provided by 6G. Massive IoTs introduce omnipresent smart devices that can connect and exchange information with one another without human interference. Different remote technologies are used by current IoT frameworks, including sensor networks, ZigBee, close-field communication, low-energy Bluetooth, and radio frequency identification. Tragically, these advancements might not be sufficient for fresh, expert IoT framework implementations focusing on brand-new contemporary applications. Security issues, protection needs, dormancy, and the requirement for rules and principles are the boundaries of these advancements. High data transfer capacity from new technology is anticipated to be able to transport the massive amount of information generated by the numerous smart devices in the IoT framework. Additionally, greater innovation is anticipated to fulfill the key requirements of the upcoming IoT device era, including increased information rate, increased data transfer limit, and decreased inertness. The omnipresent IoT calculating applications' requirements for greater accessibility, increased adaptability, decreased idleness, expanded information rates, lower energy consumption, etc. are all met by 6G technology.

With device-to-device and machine-to-machine communications, the 6G-IoT cooperation transforms the business landscape for many industries. It also functions with the expansion of intelligent devices with IoT capabilities. The rise in the number of dispersed and heterogeneous devices and the swift development of IoT frameworks benefit end users, businesses, state-run institutions, and public workers. Recent years have seen a fundamental increase in portable availability, largely due to the proliferation of innovative devices and the rapid advancement of distant communication technology. In 2030, it is predicted that global mobile traffic will increase and reach more than 5000 exabytes. Networks powered by low-Earth orbit satellites and broadband access points will support developing communications, including future bright devices. Additionally, the use of flying platforms will be required in situations where stationary base stations are unable to guarantee consistent and reliable device communications to provide consistent availability across future large-scale IoT organizations [13–15].

Based on 5G, the URLLC technology was developed and applied in real IoT systems. Whatever the case, it really has to be enhanced to make 6G-IoT networks more useful for applications such as fully independent IoT frameworks and flying IoT frameworks. Future clever businesses (such as those providing autonomous driving and e-medical services, e.g.) can be expected to introduce new vertical IoT applications as critical building alterations of existing flexible organizations take place. In this situation, as 6G-IoT biological systems interact with key figuring (e.g., edge, cloud) and remote administrations, the organization correspondence norms and conventions become crucial to the huge scope arrangement of 6G-IoT biological systems. Future 6G-IoT networks are expected to rely on cutting-edge devices that can fully comprehend registration and edge knowledge. Without the requirement for an integrated regulator, each IoT intelligent device would have the potential to serve as an end-client terminal, while providing availability and services (such as insightful control, reserving, and network motioning toward) to various devices at the organization's edge. This could be expanded to include demand-driven creative organizing that adapts to various clients, services, or organizational requirements, such as energy cost reduction or range proficiency enhancement.

2.4 What is blockchain, anyway?

Satoshi Nakamoto created the decentralized digital currency known as Bitcoin in 2009. A "blockchain" is the promised underlying technological advancement that underlies electronic money. A network that has been obtained through cryptography consists of dishonest buddies interacting remotely. The blockchain is portrayed as a recorded ledger that is constantly updated and contains unchangeable transactions. A chain is created by connecting blocks that have been timestamped using cryptographic hashes. All connections are verified by cryptographic techniques (such as symmetric and lopsided calculations). Blockchain technology does not require outside influence to maintain network control. A duplicate of the blockchain record as well as exchanges is stored by each hub and member. A proof of work is used as a calculation for the following and ownership management of resources (coins), and it makes use of public-key cryptography. The agreement calculation evaluates the authenticity and dependability of all exchanges made when a new block is added to an existing one. When 51% of the hubs are truthful, the hubs will reach a consensus. The Merkle tree (a double hash tree in which each leaf addresses the information hash) is used to bundle trades into blocks in the blockchain [16−18]. The core characteristics of the blockchain architecture are respectability, changelessness, clarity, nondisavowal, and equal liberties.

2.5 Blockchain with artificial intelligence: challenges, opportunities, and solutions for the 6G internet of things

With additional strict requirements for a high information rate; high energy productivity; enormous low-idleness control; high dependability; associated knowledge with AI, machine learning (ML), and profound learning (DL); and extremely wide recurrence groups, the 6th era (6G) innovation was imagined in 2019−20 to transform the "Web of Everything" into a "Canny Web of Everything" [19]. Calculation Situated Correspondences (COC), Logically Dexterous eMBB Interchanges (CAeC), and Occasion Characterized uRLLC (EDuRLLC) are three novel application administrations that are suggested [19]. According to the available correspondence resources, COC will enable the flexible selection of resources from the rate-inertness unwavering quality space to achieve a certain level of computational accuracy for learning approaches. With regard to organizational blockages, traffic, location, client portability, and long-distance interpersonal contact settings, CAeC will arrange eMBB administrations that are flexible. The 5G-URLLC applications that will function in emergency or outlandish situations with spatially transitory device densities, traffic examples, and foundation accessibility are the focus of 6G-EDuRLLC. A major driver for 6G has been the challenging development of highly distributed smart city mobile applications such as the IoV, IoMTs, IoD, IoRT, IIoT, and 3D computer-generated simulation, as well as their stringent QoS requirements and demand for expert coops to meet SLAs. Furthermore, a significant portion of those applications is driven by AI and enormous amounts of data, making it difficult to say with certainty if 5G will be able to meet those demands. As a result, 6G should provide beyond what 5G LTE can, including ubiquitous broadband-global organization inclusion, extremely high information rates, high energy efficiency, enormous low-dormancy control, and exceptionally expansive recurrence groups. Instead of using 5G, 6G should be equipped with careful calculations that develop its engineering, conventions, and operations to achieve that level of productivity. As a result, from the edges to the cloud and core system, 6G will integrate related knowledge into its design in a coordinating correspondence, figure, and capacity foundation. A computer-based intelligence-enabled improvement for 6G is necessary to support a large number of applications that are demanding reduced inactivity, high unchanging quality, security, and execution time. Due to the lapsed time from examination to navigation, conventional procedures that involve factual inquiry based on prior knowledge and experiences through the transmission of the Product Characterized Organization (SDN) will not be any more persuasive. As a result, ML and DL calculations are used to address a few challenges in system management, such as information offloading and reserving.

Different tweak approaches are used in a correspondence framework for effective and successful information transmission by regulating the transmitted sign in light of the increasing information traffic in sophisticated urban areas. To distinguish the adjusted information of the indications, in this particular scenario, when dealing with a loud obstructed environment is known as regulation acknowledgment. For applications such as obstruction ID, range checking, mental radio, hazard assessment, and transmission acknowledgment, tweak acknowledgment supports signal demodulation and decoding. For applications in dazzling cities, the conventional choice hypothesis- and measurable example-based balance acknowledgment procedures become laborious and expensive to compute. Yang suggested using CNN and Intermittent Brain Organizations (RNNs) for balancing acknowledgment as opposed to more content-light Rayleigh blurring channels and white Gaussian noise. The researchers discovered that when compared to ML calculations such as the help vector machine (SVM), DL computations modify acknowledgment much more precisely. Shi 0 proposed a CNN-based unified learning strategy with differential security for modified acknowledgment to ensure the safety and security of the conveyed information.

2.6 Discussion

The "Internet of Everything" was predicted to transform into a "Vigilant Trap of Everything" under the sixth period (6G) development in 2019–20, with more rigid requirements for a high data rate, high energy efficiency, tremendous low-inactivity control, high constancy, related information with computer-based intelligence (ML) and significant learning (DL), and very wide repeat bunches [20]. Estimation Arranged Correspondences (COC), Intelligently Capable eMBB Exchanges (CAeC), and Event Portrayed uRLLC (EDuRLLC) are three brand-new application organizations that are suggested [21]. To reach a certain level of computational accuracy for learning moves close, COC will make use of the flexible assurance of resources from the rate-idleness steady quality space dependent upon the open correspondence resources. The eMBB organizations that CAeC will direct will be flexible enough to react to association blockages, traffic, geology, customers' abilities to send messages, and long-distance relational correspondence settings. The 5G-URLLC applications that will function in emergency or absurd settings with spatial-transient device densities, traffic models, and establishment availability are the focus of 6G-EDuRLLC. A major driving force behind the development of 6G has been the challenging development of highly distributed smart city flexible applications such as the IoV, IoMTs, IoD, IoRT, IIoT, and 3D PC-produced reproduction, as well as their rigid requirements for QoS and the requirement for professional centers to meet SLAs. Furthermore, a significant portion of those applications rely on man-made knowledge and enormous amounts of data, making it challenging—if not impossible—for 5G to meet those needs. Therefore, 6G should provide above what 5G LTE can, without battery device limitations, extremely high data rates, a particularly high energy sufficiency, enormous low-lethargy control, exceptionally far-reaching repeat gatherings, and unavoidable broadband-overall association integration. Instead of using 5G, 6G should be equipped with thorough estimations to drive its design, shows, and activities if it wants to operate at that degree of efficiency. Therefore, 6G will incorporate pertinent data into its configuration in the form of a planned correspondence, figure, and limit establishment from the edges to the cloud and focus structure. A PC-based knowledge-engaged improvement for 6G is necessary to support a huge variety of purposes that address low latency, high unrelenting quality, security, and execution speed. As a result of the snuck past time from evaluation to route, conventional theories applying sincere examination taking into account prior information and experiences through the transmission of the Item Portrayed Association (SDN) will not be any more convincing. Then, ML and DL estimations are employed to address a few organizational problems using frameworks, such as saving and data offloading. In this section, we exhibit 6G association shows and segments that leverage mimicked knowledge along with self-learning ML/DL models.

Different change techniques are utilized in a correspondence structure for efficient and effective data transmission by directing the sent sign as a result of the increasing data traffic in clever metropolitan networks.

2.7 Conclusion

Blockchain and the Internet of Things (IoT) together play a crucial role in the 6G era. This article discusses several opportunities and current uses for 6G-enabled IoT devices, including inventory networks, electronic voting, industrial 6.0, smart homes, and so forth. The study also lists some of the major challenges involved in integrating blockchain with Web of Things devices, such as capacity and throughput flexibility, network adaptation, and security. The suggested method used pontoon agreement to address the slow throughput issue and Blockchain Disseminated Organization to address network adaptability difficulties. We discussed all the certain solutions that are currently available to overcome the challenges associated with combining the two technological advances. The suggested method uses a record (ZK Record) in light of zero-information confirmation to avoid security issues in blockchain and IoT, which is another important issue with blockchain. One of the emerging areas in software engineering is zero-information, and this invention is still being studied to address a few odd exploratory problems.

References

[1] F. Al-Turjman, R. Salama, Cyber security in mobile social networks, in, Security in IoT Social Networks, Academic Press, 2021, pp. 55–81.

[2] R. Salama, F. Al-Turjman, AI in blockchain towards realizing cyber security, In 2022 International Conference on Artificial Intelligence in Everything (AIE), IEEE, 2022, pp. 471–475. August.

[3] R. Salama, F. Al-Turjman, Cyber-security countermeasures and vulnerabilities to prevent social-engineering attacks, In Artificial Intelligence of Health-Enabled Spaces, CRC Press, 2023, pp. 133–144.

[4] F. Al-Turjman, R. Salama, An overview about the cyberattacks in grid and like systems, Smart Grid IoT-Enabled Spaces (2020) 233–247.

[5] R. Salama, F. Al-Turjman, R. Culmone, AI-powered drone to address smart city security issues, International Conference on Advanced Information Networking and Applications, Springer International Publishing, Cham, 2023, pp. 292–300. March.

[6] R. Salama, C. Altrjman, F. Al-Turjman, A survey of the architectures and protocols for wireless sensor networks and wireless multimedia sensor networks, NEU J. Artif. Intell. Internet Things 2 (3) (2023).

[7] R. Salama, F. Al-Turjman, C. Altrjman, D. Bordoloi, The ways in which artificial intelligence improves several facets of cyber security—a survey, in 2023 International Conference on Computational Intelligence, Communication Technology and Networking (CICTN), IEEE, 2023, pp. 825–829.

[8] R. Salama, F. Al-Turjman, S. Bhatla, D. Mishra, Mobile edge fog, blockchain networking and computing—a survey, in 2023 International Conference on Computational Intelligence, Communication Technology and Networking (CICTN), IEEE, 2023, pp. 808–811.

[9] R. Salama, F. Al-Turjman, P. Chaudhary, L. Banda, Future communication technology using huge milli-meter waves—an overview, in 2023 International Conference on Computational Intelligence, Communication Technology and Networking (CICTN), IEEE, 2023, pp. 785–790.

[10] R. Salama, F. Al-Turjman, M. Aeri, S.P. Yadav, Internet of intelligent things (IoT)—an overview, in 2023 International Conference on Computational Intelligence, Communication Technology and Networking (CICTN), IEEE, 2023, pp. 801–805.

[11] R. Salama, F. Al-Turjman, P. Chaudhary, S.P. Yadav, Benefits of internet of things (IoT) applications in health care—an overview, in 2023 International Conference on Computational Intelligence, Communication Technology and Networking (CICTN), IEEE, 2023, pp. 778–784.

[12] F. Al-Turjman, R. Salama, C. Altrjman, Overview of IoT solutions for sustainable transportation systems, NEU J. Artif. Intell. Internet Things 2 (3) (2023).

[13] R. Salama, F. Al-Turjman, C. Altrjman, R. Gupta, Machine learning in sustainable development—an overview, in 2023 International Conference on Computational Intelligence, Communication Technology and Networking (CICTN), IEEE, 2023, pp. 806–807.

[14] R. Salama, F. Al-Turjman, C. Altrjman, S. Kumar, P. Chaudhary, A comprehensive survey of blockchain-powered cybersecurity—a survey, in 2023 International Conference on Computational Intelligence, Communication Technology and Networking (CICTN), IEEE, 2023, pp. 774–777.

[15] R. Salama, F. Al-Turjman, D. Bordoloi, S.P. Yadav, Wireless sensor networks and green networking for 6G communication—an overview, in 2023 International Conference on Computational Intelligence, Communication Technology and Networking (CICTN), IEEE, 2023, pp. 830–834.

[16] R. Salama, F. Al-Turjman, S. Bhatia, S.P. Yadav, Social engineering attack types and prevention techniques—a survey, in 2023 International Conference on Computational Intelligence, Communication Technology and Networking (CICTN), IEEE, 2023, pp. 817–820.

[17] F. Al-Turjman, R. Salama, Security in social networks. In, Security in IoT Social Networks, Academic Press, 2021, pp. 1–27.

[18] R. Salama, C. Altrjman, F. Al-Turjman, A survey of machine learning (ML) in sustainable systems, NEU J. Artif. Intell. Internet Things 2 (3) (2023).

[19] R. Salama, C. Altrjman, F. Al-Turjman, An overview of the internet of things (IoT) and machine to machine (M2M) Communications, NEU J. Artif. Intell. Internet Things 2 (3) (2023).

[20] J. Subramani, M. Azees, A.S. Rajasekaran, F. Al-Turjman, EPF-FDA: Efficient pairing free and confidentiality preserving fog-based data aggregation scheme for WBANs. IEEE Instrumentation & Measurement Magazine, 26(8) (2023), 10−16

[21] R. Salama, F. Al-Turjman, C. Altrjman, D. Bordoloi, The use of machine learning (ML) in sustainable systems—an overview, in 2023 International Conference on Computational Intelligence, Communication Technology and Networking (CICTN), IEEE, 2023, pp. 821−824.

3

A simple online payment system using blockchain technology

Hasan Kuren, Fadi Al-Turjman

ARTIFICIAL INTELLIGENCE, SOFTWARE, AND INFORMATION SYSTEMS ENGINEERING DEPARTMENTS, RESEARCH CENTER FOR AI AND IOT, AI AND ROBOTICS INSTITUTE, NEAR EAST UNIVERSITY, NICOSIA, MERSIN10, TURKEY

3.1 Introduction

Online payments are becoming more common. Many businesses are adopting online payment systems for their systems. However, these systems have challenges with security being a major concern. Blockchain technology has provided a more secure and transparent way to conduct online transactions. Blockchain technology is a decentralized system. Therefore, it stores information securely and transparently. Transactions are recorded in a digital ledger. They are distributed in a computer network. For this reason, the information will be made nearly impossible to change or mess with. On the other hand, Metamask is a well-known cryptocurrency wallet that allows users to send and receive ether and other Ethereum-based tokens [1,2] by interacting with the Ethereum blockchain.

3.1.1 Objectives

The main purpose of this offer is to use blockchain technologies in a simple online payment system and Metamask API. This system will be designed to provide a secure and transparent environment for a business and an individual to conduct their online transactions [3].

- **Improved security:** One of the benefits of using blockchain technology is to ensure that there are secure and transparent transactions. At the same time, it is to reduce the risk of fraud.
- **Fast and efficient transactions:** the transactions will take place in real-time. Therefore, as the need for intermediaries will disappear, faster and more efficient transactions will be realized.
- **Cost-effective:** Blockchain technology is used to provide cost savings for businesses and individuals as it eliminates the need for intermediaries.
- **User-friendly:** The system should be designed with a user-friendly interface that makes it easy for users to navigate. Thus, the complexity of the transactions is eliminated.

Computational Intelligence and Blockchain in Complex Systems. DOI: https://doi.org/10.1016/B978-0-443-13268-1.00026-1
© 2024 Elsevier Inc. All rights are reserved, including those for text and data mining, AI training, and similar technologies.

3.2 Research and design

3.2.1 Blockchain technology and its application on online payment systems

Blockchain technology is a decentralized system that stores information securely and transparently. The use of blockchain technology in online payment systems offers several advantages, including improved security, faster and more efficient transactions, and cost-effectiveness [4]. Below are some of the key features of blockchain technology and how they can be applied to online payment systems [5–7].

- **Decentralization:** Blockchain technology operates on a decentralized network, meaning that there is no single point of failure. This makes it more secure than centralized payment systems, as there is no central database that can be hacked or compromised.
- **Transparency:** Transactions on the blockchain are transparent and immutable, meaning that they cannot be altered or deleted. This transparency ensures that transactions are accurate and that there is no room for fraud.
- **Smart contracts:** Smart contracts are self-executing contracts that are stored on the blockchain. They can be used to automate the payment process, ensuring that payments are made automatically once certain conditions are met.
- **Cryptography:** Blockchain technology uses cryptography to secure transactions. Cryptography ensures that transactions are secure and that data cannot be intercepted or altered.
- **Speed and efficiency:** Transactions on the blockchain can be processed in real time, eliminating the need for intermediaries and reducing transaction times.
- **Cost-effectiveness:** The use of blockchain technology eliminates the need for intermediaries, resulting in lower transaction fees and cost savings for businesses and individuals.

3.2.2 Designing the architecture of the online payment system

Online payment system design has been developed by a lot of researchers [8,9]. This architecture has three levels, which are transactions, acceptances, and oversight as shown in Fig. 3–1 [10,11].

All blocks are being implemented as a chain of the previous block to the next block. These blocks have been connected with the previous block hash value, which is to get the root tree of the blockchain [10]. Fig. 3–2 shows the architecture of the blockchain. Transferring money process needs to be in a secure way to send money from users. Blockchain technology has been implemented in the following way to keep secure money transfers from user to company. Fig. 3–3 shows that how to transfer money from user to company.

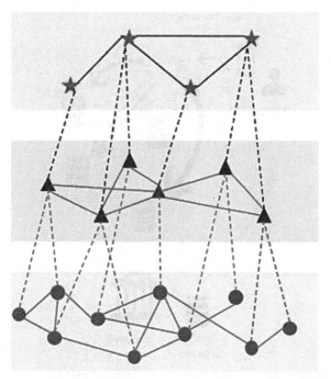

FIGURE 3–1 Architecture of the blockchain system.

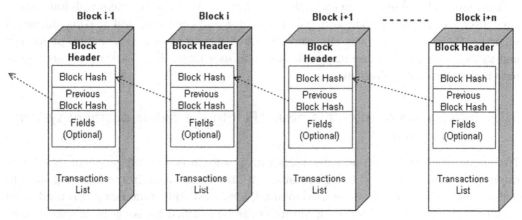

FIGURE 3–2 Architecture of the blockchain.

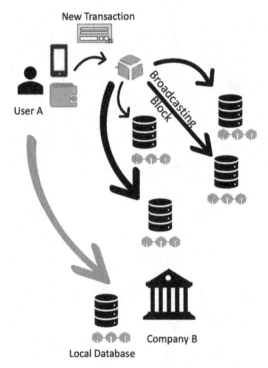

FIGURE 3–3 Transferring money from user A to company B and broadcasting block.

The system that transfers money from user to company. Algorithm 3−1 shows transfer money from user to company.

Database tables design has been implemented for the blockchain system with four tables. Each user has unique private and public keys for authenticating and making payments securely. The system generates automatically when the user registers a unique public key and saves it into the database user auth table and user table. Fig. 3−4 shows system database tables relationship diagram.

3.2.3 Integration of the Metamask API into the online payment system using Python

The online payment system provides users with a smooth and secure payment experience using blockchain technology. Using Metamask API has been shown in the following steps in Python. The Pip command can be used to install Metamask API. Metamask API is used as an e-wallet for payment. The Metamask API web3 can be installed by using the following commands in Python project.

Algorithm 3–1   Transfer money from user to company.

1: Procedure UserTOCompanyTransfer (Public Key, Amount)
2: Begin
3: init Transaction ↤ tx
4: **if** (!Verification(Tx)) **then**
5:        out put ↤ TransactionFailed
6:        Return -1
7: end if
8: Validator Nodes ← tx if block is committed then
9: **if** (Commit(Block)) **then**
10:       **if** (Validate(tx)) **then**
11:              Update wallets of user and receiver
12:              return 0 // Terminated succesfuly
13:       end if
14:       Return 1 // not commited
15: end if
16: End Procedure

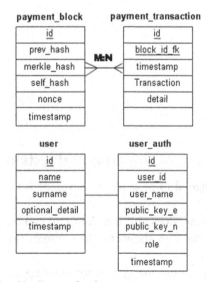

FIGURE 3–4 Database tables relationship diagram for the system.

pip install web3

The Metamask API used in the process of connecting to the Ethereum network allows the online payment system to be connected to the Ethereum network. The Web3 object, on the other hand, can be provided by creating an instance where we can perform this operation and use the Metamask provider.

```
from web3 import Web3
from web3 . autoimport w3
web3 = Web3 ( Web3 . HTTPProvider ( ' h t t p s : / / mainnet . i n f u r a . i o / v3 / { PROJECT ID } '))
```

Connecting to e-wallet, the following code should be used. This code allows to use of API to link via websocketprovider.

```
web3 = Web3(Web3 . W e bs o c k etPr o vi d er ( ' wss : / / mainn et . i n f u r a . i o / ws / v3 / { PROJECT ID } ' ) )
if web3 . isConnected ( ) :
account = w3 . et h . a c c o u n t s [ 0 ] web3 . et h. d e f a u l t A c c o u n t = a c c o u n t p r i n t ( " Conn e ct ed
to account : " , a c c o u n t )
else :
print ( " Unable t o
connect to t h e Ethereum n etwork . " )
```

In the next step, after connecting, the online payment system uses the Metamask API to send transactions. In the proposed model, Metamask transactions are also recorded in the local database.

```
from web3 im p ort Web3 , e t h
web3 = Web3(Web3 . HTTPProvider ( ' h t t p s : / / m ainn et . i n f u r a . i o / v3 / { PROJECT ID }' ) )
t x h a s h = web3 . e t h . s e n d T r a n s a c t i o n ({
' from ' : ' 0 x . . . ' ,
' to ' : ' 0 x . . . ' ,
' v alu e ' : web3 . toWei ( 1 , ' e t h er ' )
})
print ( " T r a n s a c t i o n h ash : " ,
t x h a s h . hex ( ) )
```

3.2.4 User interface design of the proposed system

This project case study is designed to be a secure payment system for students at Near East University in Cyprus.

The system works with API services and the front end can be easily redesigned for other Universities and Companies. Fig. 3–5 shows the first system splash form and give information to the user about the system.

The login form allows users to use the system for entering and also gives terms and conditions acceptance about using this application. Fig. 3–6 shows the student login UI form with his or her student number and other criteria if needed.

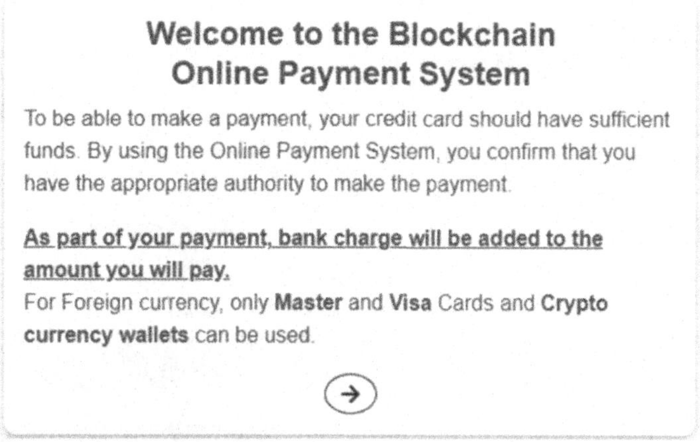

FIGURE 3–5 Splash form UI payment information.

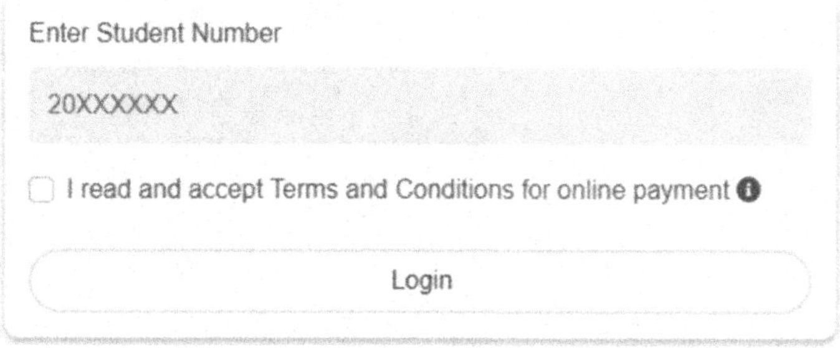

FIGURE 3–6 Terms and conditions acceptance and login into the system.

Payment main page of the payment system is the main UI for the system. This page allows to user select any payment method and currency and pay by the system. Fig. 3−7 shows the selection of the payment methods.

Fig. 3−8 below illustrates the filled form of the payment details. The system has multicurrency types from which the user can select any of them. After selecting the currency type, the user should write the amount of payment. The total amount of payment has been calculated with added bank charge.

The system checks all given information and validates them. If there is any problem with validation, it gives the message about the problems to the user. Fig. 3−9 shows invalid card number alert. Also, the system knows which type of card the user uses.

After the "Make Payment" button is clicked, confirmation page is shown. When the user clicks the "Confirm" button, which is shown in Fig. 3−10, the system prepares the block and

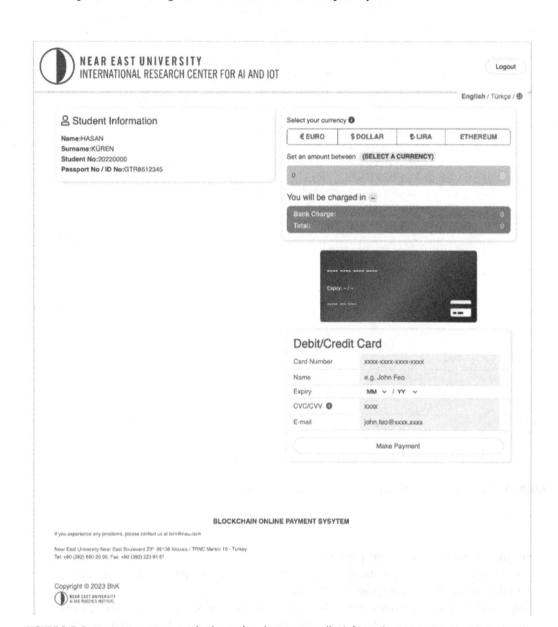

FIGURE 3–7 Payment page currency selection and card or crypto wallet information entrance page.

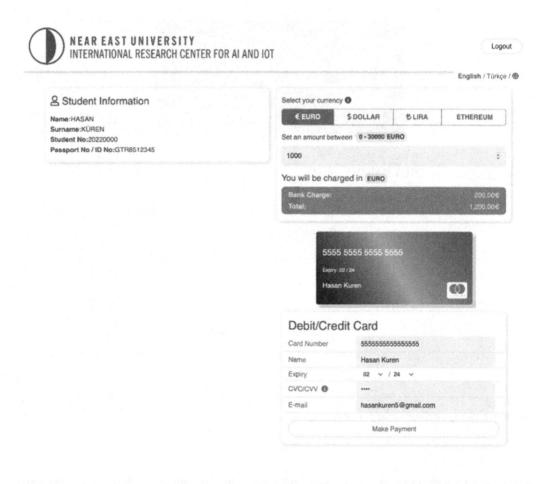

FIGURE 3–8 The detail of the payment bank card info.

FIGURE 3–9 Wrong card number and error message alert.

sends the payment transactions to nodes and saves it into the database. Validated blocks are added to secure transactions via blockchain technology. All blocks are saved as JSON data into databases.

After payment has been accepted and approved, the system gets a response from the status of the payment from user accounts. This result comes from the user accounts service. Fig. 3–11 is the result page of the system, which means the payment has been successfully done.

Fig. 3–12 presents that the test block has been created and blockchain listed which comes from the API via Postman. Therefore, these data blocks after the users have been accepted then all transactions have been saved into the database accordingly.

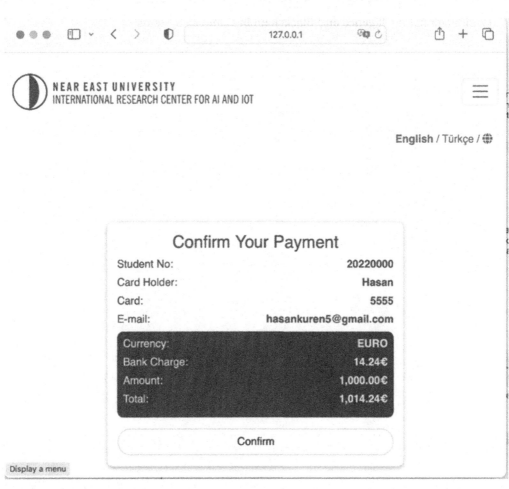

FIGURE 3–10 Payment confirm page.

FIGURE 3–11 Result page of the system.

FIGURE 3–12 Postman application output of the blockchain testing.

3.3 Conclusions

Blockchain technology has the potential to revolutionize online payment systems by providing a secure, transparent, and efficient way for businesses and individuals to conduct transactions. Its use can reduce the risk of fraud, increase transaction speed, and provide cost-effective solutions for businesses and individuals. The development and implementation of a simple online payment system using blockchain technology and the Metamask API will provide a secure, transparent, and efficient way for businesses and individuals to conduct online transactions. The system will be designed to meet the needs of users while providing cost-effective solutions.

References

[1] M.R. Ahmed, K. Meenakshi, M.S. Obaidat, R. Amin, P. Vijayakumar, Blockchain based architecture and solution for secure digital payment system, in ICC 2021-IEEE International Conference on Communications, IEEE, 2021, pp. 1–6.

[2] A.S. Rajasekaran, M. Azees, F. Al-Turjman, A comprehensive survey on blockchain technology, Sustain. Energy Technol. Assess. 52 (2022) 102039.

[3] S.-I. Kim, S.-H. Kim, E-commerce payment model using blockchain, J. Ambient. Intell. Humanized Comput. 13 (3) (2022) 1673–1685.

[4] K. Thanapal, D. Mehta, K. Mudaliar, B. Shaikh, Online payment using blockchain, in ITM Web of Conferences, vol. 32, EDP Sciences, 2020, p. 03007.

[5] G. Goodell, Tokens and distributed ledgers in digital payment systems, arXiv preprint arXiv:2207.07530, 2022.

[6] J. Lovejoy, C. Fields, M. Virza, T. Frederick, D. Urness, K. Karwaski, et al., A high performance payment processing system designed for central bank digital currencies, Cryptol. ePrint Archive (2022) 2022.

[7] F. Al-Turjman, Artificial Intelligence in IoT, Springer, 2019, p. 2019.

[8] D. Ghelani, T.K. Hua, S.K.R. Koduru, A model-driven approach for online banking application using angularJS framework, Am. J. Inf. Sci. Technol. 6 (3) (2022) 52–63.

[9] S. Sekar, A. Solayappan, J. Srimathi, S. Raja, S. Durga, P. Manoharan, et al., Autonomous transaction model for e-commerce management using blockchain technology, Int. J. Inf. Technol. Web Eng. (IJITWE) 17 (1) (2022) 1–14.

[10] B. Shrimali, H.B. Patel, Blockchain state-of-the-art: architecture, use cases, consensus, challenges and opportunities, J. King Saud. Univ.-Comput. Inf. Sci. 34 (9) (2022) 6793–6807.

[11] R. Ali, Y.A. Qadri, Y.B. Zikria, F. Al-Turjman, B.-S. Kim, S.W. Kim, A blockchain model for trustworthiness in the internet of things (IoT)-based smart-cities, Trends Cloud-based IoT 2020 (2020) 1–19.

4

Efficient spam email classification logistic regression model trained by modified social network search algorithm

Branislav Radomirovic, Aleksandar Petrovic, Miodrag Zivkovic, Angelina Njegus, Nebojsa Budimirovic, Nebojsa Bacanin

SINGIDUNUM UNIVERSITY, DANIJELOVA, BELGRADE, SERBIA

4.1 Introduction

Modern spam filtering systems generally use a machine learning (ML) model to categorize spam. The two ML models most typically employed in this context are logistic regression (LR) and extreme learning machine. The logistic function presumes that each pair of elements in an attribute array is independent and serves as the basis for LR classifiers [1]. Due to its clarity and capability to swiftly converge, LR is one of the most frequently encountered models used for filtering spam mail. A nonlinear transform is applied to the output of this linear algorithm.

According to Dedeturk et al. [2], the LR reaches desirable weight and bias rates that may converge to local optima and is reactive to equally weighted features. Once a dataset has undergone feature reduction preprocessing, the LR classifier acts steadily following the tf-idf feature selection and provides high accuracy. Only LR was able to obtain the same percentages for all three metrics when evaluating all classifiers in another study [3]. This research tested the performance of several classifier systems. The implementation of an online gradient descent approach to improve a simplistic LR model was shown by Goodman and Yih in their paper [4]. They asserted that their model can provide results that are competitive with the best-reported generative strategy.

Even though the aforementioned LR-based classifiers are fairly effective, they have a tendency to over-fit or get stuck in the local minimum, produce significant computational expenses, exhibit future weight responsiveness problems, and have low operating speeds for practical applications [2]. A common choice to improve ML models is to apply swarm intelligence metaheuristics algorithms to optimize the training process. The approach presented in

Computational Intelligence and Blockchain in Complex Systems. DOI: https://doi.org/10.1016/B978-0-443-13268-1.00010-8
© 2024 Elsevier Inc. All rights reserved, including those for text and data mining, AI training, and similar technologies.

this research proposes an improved rendition of the social network search (SNS) method to train the LR model. The proposed method has been evaluated on the CMDCS2010 spam classification dataset, where the extensive array of attributes makes this dataset a part of large-scale global optimization issues.

Therefore, the main contribution of this study is the efficacy of the proposed method for different spam datasets, be it linear or nonlinear, class balanced or class imbalanced. The method is also effective when data is characterized by distinct nonlinearity and a great number of dimensions due to its training methodology, which executes local and global explorations in the solution space. It tackles complexities and linguistic disparities in publicly available data and allows the learning of extremely complicated features from data.

The manuscript is structured in the following way. Section 4.2 brings a brief review of LR and swarm intelligence algorithms. Next, the proposed modified algorithm is discussed in Section 4.3. The simulation setup and experimental outcomes are presented in Section 4.4. Lastly, Section 4.5 gives a summary of the presented work and discusses future research topics.

4.2 Background and literature review

4.2.1 Logistic regression

A probability-based method known as LR [5] is commonly used for classification problems because it is particularly effective at identifying relationships between features and certain outputs. LR determines the probability of an event occurring from a collection of independent variables and data. The result is given in probabilistic terms; therefore, the dependent variable's span is restricted to values between 0 and 1. Because the goal of the logistic model is to estimate the parameters, it falls within the scope of regression analysis. It is regarded as the fundamental ML technique for processing natural language. LR may be applied to problems requiring binary or multiple-class categorizations. LR has been widely applied in spam filtering assignments; it is a highly simple and trustworthy ML tactic that permits quick classification and is particularly useful when instantaneous response is needed [6]. While independent variables in LR may either take on a binary or a continuous form, dependent variables always have a single binary class, where the values are designated as true/false or 1/0. In LR, certain points from the classes experience random decisions because identifying the exact boundary diverging the two classes in a linear model is difficult.

Eq. (4−1) represents the logistic function.

$$p(x) = \frac{1}{1 + e^{-\frac{(x-\mu)}{s}}} \qquad (4-1)$$

Here, a position variable (the midsection on the curve, with $p(\mu) = \frac{1}{2}$), denoted by μ and s, signifies a scaling factor. This equation may be transformed into Eq. (4−2), with $\beta_0 = \frac{-\mu}{s}$ representing the y-intercept of the line $y = \beta_0 + \beta_1 x$, and $\beta_1 = \frac{1}{s}$ being the inverse value of the rate variable. Together, they signify the y-intercept and gradient of the logarithm of the odds as a function of x. Furthermore, $\mu = \frac{-\beta_0}{\beta_1}$ and $s = \frac{1}{\beta_1}$.

$$p(x) = \frac{1}{1 + e^{-(\beta_0 + \beta_1 x)}} \tag{4-2}$$

In order to determine the odds (ratio of success and failure probability), logistic formulae (3) and (2.1), also known as the natural logarithm of the odds, are employed.

$$logit\,p = \sigma^{-1}(p) = ln\frac{p}{1-p} \quad for \ \ p \in (0, 1) \tag{4-3}$$

$$P_i = Prob(y_i = 1)$$

$$= \frac{1}{1 + e^{(-(\beta_0 + \beta_1 x_1 + \ldots \beta_k x_k + \varepsilon))}} = >$$

$$ln\left(\frac{P_i}{1 - P_i}\right) = \beta_0 + \beta_1 x_1 + \ldots \beta_k x_k + \varepsilon \tag{4-4}$$

Despite the LR's evident benefits, this strategy has a limitation in that it frequently uses stochastic gradient descent for training, which might cause an early convergence to subpar local optima. In line with the suggestion made in [2], this research demonstrates training with a metaheuristic method to circumvent the issue.

4.2.2 Metaheuristic optimization

While conventional, deterministic algorithms fail to produce satisfactory results when confronted with NP-hard problems, metaheuristic algorithms address these tasks exceptionally well, consuming a reasonable amount of time and resources. The most notable class within the metaheuristic family is swarm intelligence algorithms, inspired by phenomena and dynamics encountered in the natural world. The most well-known method, Particle Swarm Optimization, was first created to model social interactions observed in nature [7]. This stochastic population-based optimization algorithm was created to address challenges involving continuous optimization. The artificial bee colony (ABC) metaheuristics [8], which are often used to optimize the performance of neural networks [9], is one of the most well-known approaches that draw inspiration from wildlife. Another noteworthy illustration is the whale optimization algorithm (WOA) [10], which simulates the distinctive fishing strategy of humpback whales. Due to its fascinating search patterns, WOA is quite well-known and has been successfully applied to tackle several real-world problems [11].

Initiatives to combine population-based metaheuristics with ML are now one of the most prominent research fields. The effective integration of artificial neural networks with swarm intelligence algorithms is demonstrated in a number of recent papers. The most prominent applications are the classification and severity assessment [12–14], forecast of COVID-19 cases [15], the estimation of virtual currency trends [16], intrusion and fraud detection

[1–22], computer-assisted diagnostics and tumor identification [23–25], cloud computing schedule optimization [26–28], sensor networks enhancements [29–32], plant classification [33], neural networks tuning [9,34,35], and feature selection task [36,37], among others.

The renowned no-free lunch theorem states that it is impossible to demonstrate the existence of a single ideal solution that is the right choice for all optimization issues. The introduction of new, more effective choices as well as modification and hybridization of current algorithms are the main topics of contemporary studies.

4.3 Proposed hybrid metaheuristics

4.3.1 Introduced social network search algorithm

Humans naturally engage in social activities, which have evolved to accommodate information technology in the current era of communication. Individuals modified social behaviors to fit technological innovations, creating strategies for social networking, much like technology had to conform to human nature. The SNS algorithm [38] mimics the strategies used by individuals on social media to increase their popularity. This is accomplished by factoring the user's sentiments into the algorithm. These emotions influence how the simulated users behave, which in turn affects how the algorithm operates.

The attitude of others around them has an impact on the simulated user behavior in the concept of the algorithm. These emotions, which include imitation, conversation, disputation, and innovation, are reduced versions of those experienced in daily life.

One of the key aspects of social media is imitation paradigms. Users follow people they admire as well as their friends and relatives. When a person publishes a new post, others who are following them are made aware of it and given the chance to share it further. Users will attempt to mimic the thoughts stated in this post and remark on related subjects if they provide complex ideas. Eq. (4–5) provides a mathematical expression for this paradigm.

$$U_{i\ new} = U_j + random(-1, 1) \times S$$
$$S = random(0, 1) \times s \qquad\qquad (4-5)$$
$$s = U_j - U_i,$$

where U_j denotes the j th user's view vector chosen randomly having $i \neq j$. Correspondingly, the i th user's view vector is signified by U_i. Indicators for random value selection include $random(-1, 1)$ and $random(0, 1)$, denoting the segments of random values $[-1, 1]$ and $[0, 1]$, respectively. By combining shock and popularity, new solutions will be generated in the imitation domain. The j th user's impact determines the shock's radius S, and s is multiplied by this radius to determine the shock's magnitude. The popularity of the j th user impacts the s value, which is computed based on the divergences in these users' viewpoints. Multiplying the random vector value $[-1, 1]$ with positive component values in the case of a match in shared beliefs, and negative component values in the absence of a match yields the shock's ultimate effect.

Social networks promote discussion among members regarding a variety of topics. The algorithm for the conversation mood reflects this. In this state, the simulated users share ideas confidentially and learn from each other. Users gain insight into disparities in their viewpoints through conversations. They can then provide a unique viewpoint on the situation Eq. (4−6) is used to describe this phenomenon.

$$U_{i\ new} = U_k + S$$
$$S = random(0, 1) \times I$$
$$Q = sign(f_i - f_j) \times (U_j - U_i),$$

(4−6)

where U_k is the randomized conversation topic vector, S is the conversational effect based on the disparity in perspectives and indicates the opinion inclination toward K_k. Q stands for inconsistency, i.e., disparity in viewpoints. A random number within the segment $[0, 1]$ is denoted by $random(0, 1)$. Moreover, U_i and U_j correspondingly represent the chat arrays of the users i and j who were chosen at random. It is noteworthy that while identifying users $j \neq i \neq k$. By comparison, $sign(f_i - f_j)$ establishes the direction of U_k. If a user's viewpoint changes as a result of interaction, it is treated as a novel perspective and is shared as such.

Users who are in a disputation mood expand and justify their positions to one another. This is typically done on social media platforms through a discussion in the comment or group chat areas, where people with divergent opinions may be persuaded by the arguments of others. Users may also become acquainted with one another and create new discussion groups as a result. By designating a random sample of users as cementers or group members, the algorithm simulates this attitude. Eq. (4−7) illustrates how views are constructed throughout this phase.

$$U_{i\ new} = U_i + random(0, 1) \times (M - AF \times U_i)$$
$$M = \frac{\sum_t^{N_r} U_t}{Nr}$$

(4−7)

$$AF = 1 + round(rnd),$$

where ith user's view vector is designated by U_i, $random(0, 1)$ denotes a randomized array within the segment $[0, 1]$, and M represents the mean value of views. The admission factor, AF, reflects users who have their own viewpoints debated among peers and has a random value of 1 or 2. The $round()$ function, as the name implies, rounds the input to the closest integer, rnd denoting an arbitrarily chosen value in the range $[0, 1]$. An arbitrary integer N_r ranging between 1 and N_{user}, where N_{user} signifies the total number of users in the social network, is used to denote the number of comments or participants in a discussion group.

Individuals occasionally contribute novel ideas while contemplating a topic when they have a different understanding of the issue's origins. The innovation mood provides a representation of this process. There are instances when a certain topic presents a variety of aspects, each of which has an impact on the overall problem. By challenging the underlying assumptions of the accepted norm, one may shift their core understanding and arrive at a unique perspective. This strategy may be quantitatively described using Eq. (4−8) and is reflected by the algorithm in the innovation state.

$$U^q_{i\ new} = t \times u^q_j + (1 - t) \times n^q_{new}$$
$$n^q_{new} = lb_q + rnd_1 \times (ub_q - lb_q) \qquad (4-8)$$
$$t = rnd_2,$$

with Q denoting the number of variables accessible for the current issue, and q denotes the q th randomly selected variable inside the [1,Q] segment. The random numbers rnd_1 and rnd_2 indicate additional values in the range of [0, 1]. The q th value of n^q_{new} has minimum and maximum values, which are symbolized, respectively, by ub_q and lb_q. The j user is chosen at random so that $j \neq i$, and U^q_j signifies the current idea for the q th one. If the i th user alters their viewpoint, a new idea is generated and thus transforms into n^q_{new}. Eventually, a new interpolation of the present idea, u^q_{new}, is generated on the q th dimension.

It is reasonable to perceive the dimension fluctuation u^q_{new} as a new perspective to share because it creates a general concept switch. Eq. (4−9) is used to model this process.

$$U_{i\ new} = [u_1, u_2, u_3, \ldots, u^q_{i\ new}, \ldots, u_Q], \qquad (4-9)$$

where, as stated previously, $u^q_{i\ new}$ denotes a new understanding of a problem from the q th perspective, which is substituted via the existing one u^q_i.

Limits are imposed on user count, iteration count, and other factors before building the initial network. Eq. (4−10) is applied to build each original view.

$$U_0 = lb + random(0, 1) \times (ub - lb) \qquad (4-10)$$

where U_0 stands for individual user's starting view array, $random(0, 1)$ denotes a random value in the range [0, 1], and the upper and lower bounds of each parameter are indicated by ub and lb, respectively.

Eq. (4−11) is utilized by the algorithm to constrain views while tackling maximizing issues.

$$U_i = \begin{cases} U_i, & f(U_i) < f(U_{i\ new}) \\ U_{i\ new}, & f(U_{i\ new}) \geq f(U_i)) \end{cases} \qquad (4-11)$$

4.3.2 Novel initialization scheme

The suggested approach employs the usual initialization procedure represented by the next equation:

$$U_{i,j} = lb_j + \alpha \cdot (ub_j - lb_j), \qquad (4-12)$$

where $U_{i,j}$ represents the i th individual's j th component, with lb_j and ub_j being the lower and upper bounds of the parameter j, respectively. Pseudo-arbitrary value α is generated by the normal distribution within segment $[0, 1]$. However, as demonstrated in [39], employing quasireflection-based learning (QRL) for the Eq. $(4-12)$ broadens the search area's scope as a consequence. For each distinct argument j (U_j), this produces a quasi-reflexive-opposite element (U_j^{qr}).

$$U_j^{qr} = \text{rnd}\left(\frac{lb_j + ub_j}{2}, u_j\right), \qquad (4-13)$$

Here, the *rnd* function is employed to select a pseudo-random value in the closed interval $\left[\frac{lb_j + ub_j}{2}, u_j\right]$. The provided initialization technique begins by initializing just $NP/2$ when the QRL is accounted for because doing so does not cause the algorithm to execute more sluggishly when the *FFEs* are factored in. The algorithm provides the used strategy. 1.

4.3.3 Strategy for preserving population heterogeneity

According to ref. [40], population diversification is a method for keeping track of how the algorithm's searching procedure converges or diverges. The study that is being presented makes use of the $L1$ population diversity metric, where diversity is acquired through individuals and dimensionality components. The aforementioned study advises using the dimensionality component of the $L1$ norm to assess how well the algorithm performs.

The $L1$ norm has the following structure, as indicated in Eqs. $(4-14)-(4-16)$, where m is properly considered as the population's number of units with n representing the dimensionality problem.

$$\bar{u} = \frac{1}{m}\sum_{i=1}^{m} u_{ij} \qquad (4-14)$$

$$Q_j^p = \frac{1}{m}\sum_{i=1}^{m} |u_{ij} - \bar{u}_j| \qquad (4-15)$$

$$Q^p = \frac{1}{n}\sum_{i=1}^{n} Q_j^p, \qquad (4-16)$$

where $\bar{u}$ denotes a particular dimension vector's mean solution placement, $L1$ norm represents the diversity vector of solutions' positions Q_j^p, with Q^p being a scalar value describing the total population's diversity.

The diversity needs to be of excellent quality throughout the early rounds of the algorithm's operation, during which the shared initialization formula is used $(4-12)$. However, it is anticipated that the quality may deteriorate in subsequent iterations. The enhanced algorithm uses the dynamic diversity threshold (Q_t) parameter's $L1$ norm to address this issue.

The following procedure is used for population diversity framework: First, the Q_t (Q_{t0}) is retrieved; then, during each iteration, the $Q^p < Qt$ criterion is taken into account, where the

Q^P represents the current population's diversity; if the criterion's result is true, indicating poor diversity, equivalently produced random solutions are substituted for the nrs of the most undesirable individuals. The supplementary control factor is denoted by nrs (count of substituted solutions). The equation for deriving Q_{t0} that results from taking into account conceptual research and practical simulations may be applied as follows:

$$Q_{t0} = \sum_{j=1}^{NP} \frac{(ub_j - lb_j)}{2 \cdot NP} \qquad (4-17)$$

According to Eq. (4−12) and Algorithm 4−1, the major part of the elements are produced at the mean of the lower and upper parameter bounds, which is the basis for Eq. (4−17). As seen in the following equation, Q_t is meant to decrease from its original value of $Q_t = Q_{t0}$, assuming that the process is operating as anticipated and the algorithm is advancing toward the optimum area:

$$Q_{t+1} = Q_t - Q_t \cdot \frac{t}{T}, \qquad (4-18)$$

where T is the maximum limit of cycles that may be completed in a single run, and t and $t+1$ stand for the current and next iterations, correspondingly. In conclusion, because Q_t is dynamically declining, the aforementioned procedure will not be engaged regardless of the value Q^P.

4.3.4 Inner functioning and complexity of the proposed algorithm

The novel model, which was dubbed diversity-oriented SNS (DOSNS), was introduced taking into account the algorithmic modifications. The revised SNS approach does not yield a higher computational complexity when $FFEs$ are factored in. That being said, the enhanced initialization method does not call for further $FFEs$. As it generates new solutions, whether they are superior or inferior to the nrs weakest ones, it does not confirm the population diversity mechanism's validity. The final equation for defining the DOSNS's complexity in the context of $FFEs$ is as follows: $O(DOSNS) = O(NP) + O(T \cdot NP)$.

Algorithm 4−2 provides the pseudocode for this enhanced approach.

Algorithm 4−1   QRL-based initialization mechanism pseudocode.

Notch 1: Produce population P^{init} of $NP/2$ elements as per Eq. (4−12).
Notch 2: Produce QRL population P^{qr} using P^{init} as per Eq. (4−13).
Notch 3: Generate initial population P through the union of P^{init} and P^{qr} ($P \cup P^{qr}$).
Notch 4: Acquire the error rate for each element within P.
Notch 5: Arrange all solutions in P with regard to an error rate.

Algorithm 4–2   DOSNS method pseudocode.

Set user number, T, lb, ub, $t = 0$
Initialize population P with NP solutions as per Algorithm 4.1
Establish values of Q_{t0} and Q_t
Evaluate each user in accordance with the objective function $i = 0$
while
   If **thendo** $(!(i < N))$
     $t = t + 1$
     $i = 0$
   end if
   $i = i + 1$
   $Mood = random(1, 4)$
   if $(Mood == 1)$ **then**
     Generate novel views as per Eq. (4–5)
   else if $(Mood == 2)$ **then**
     Generate novel views as per Eq. (4–6)
   else if $(Mood == 3)$ **then**
     Generate novel views as per Eq. (4–7)
   else if $(Mood == 4)$ **then**
     Generate novel views as per Eq. (4–8)
   end if
   Limit novel views As per Eq. (4–11)
   Assess novel view according to the objective function
   If (Novel view superior to latest view) **then**
     Retain legacy view, do not share novel view
   else
     Substitute the legacy view with the novel one and share it
   else if
   Compute Q^P
   If $(Q^P < Q_t)$ **then**
     Substitute worst nrs with solutions generated as in (4–12)
   end if
   Evaluate the population
   Locate the latest best
   Update Q_t using formula (4–18)
end while $(t \le T)$
Return Optimal Solution
Return General, comprehensive optimization statistics including visualization

4.4 Experiments and comparative analysis

4.4.1 Dataset and preprocessing

With regard to both datasets, we offer investigative study. The CSDMC2010 dataset contains 82,148 distinct words, as determined using unique term enumeration. The examination of sparsity and imbalance is a further approach to exploratory investigation. Imbalance is frequently displayed using an imbalance ratio. Dividing the overall quantity of emails by the grand total of spam emails is the equation for computing this ratio. The imbalance ratio for the CSDMC2010 datasets is 2.14.

The CSDMC2010 datasets' degrees of sparsity are 90.48. This is a succinct description of the CSDMC2010 dataset's factual condition. The primary frequency metrics of the trained bundles are shown by exploratory investigation in Table 4–1.

Porter Stemmer is used as a stemmer for the CSDMC2010 dataset because it is a typical python routine for this kind of data. The fraction of borderline points has been employed as a complexity assessment. Friedman suggested using this metric to determine whether two multivariate samples originated from the same distribution. While linking opposing classes from the training samples, a percentage of points is awarded. Each border point that is recorded in this measurement corresponds to a case pertaining to a different class. Being that the outcome ranges from 0 to 1, the final figure is normalized. A result close to 0 suggests that the data can be segregated, whereas a result close to 1 suggests that they cannot. The measurement is susceptible to unbalanced data as well as class separability.

4.4.2 Experimental setup

The experimental setup for LR tests is described in this subsection. The results of the experiment are presented and analyzed subsequently.

Each solution in the DOSNS training encodes the LR coefficients and intercept, hence the solution dimensionality L is calculated as $L = nf + 1$, with nf denoting the total quantity of features of unit length. When the English datasets containing 500 and 1000 attributes, correspondingly, are considered, the limits of the coefficients are established experimentally. A thorough explanation of the English dataset is provided in Section (4.4.1). The limits in the cited work [2] were adjusted to $[-8, 8]$, but these experiments were used $[-6, 6]$. Although

Table 4–1 Frequency statistics of both datasets.

	CSDMC2010 dataset
len(tokens)	1,574,504
len(distinct tokens)	90,392
len(not stopwords)	47,385
len(tokens when string is alphabetic)	47,533
len(stemming)	35,652
len(dictionary tf-idf for vectorization)	35,617
Shape(data frame)	(4327, 35,617)

not divulged in ref. [2], intercept limits were determined experimentally for the sake of this study through a trial and error method and they had been calibrated to $[0, 1]$ for the English dataset. In this situation, every reported variable is continuous.

Because the purpose of this research is model training, particular LR parameters (including C, regularization, etc.) were adjusted to the predefined configuration from the scikit-learn package in the context of LR trials. These algorithms were evaluated on a sample of 40 users, with a maximum iteration count of $T = 500$. The publication [2] that served as the basis for the LR experiments makes use of more iterations and outcomes. As a result, regarding fitness function evaluations (FFEs), $N + N \cdot T$, all methods were considered identical. Firefly algorithms (FA) was analyzed with a twenty-solution population, with the complexity of FA's worst-case being $N^2 \cdot T$ and its average being $N/2 \cdot T$. Individual methods were run 15 times in distinct iterations ($R = 15$).

A swarm individual's fitness computation is dependent on the training set in carried-out trials. The most desirable element (the one with the best fitness result within the training set) is authenticated against the testing set when all iterations in a run are concluded, and this serves as the run's outcome.

The performance of the recommended DOSNS model was assessed with respect to its general optimization prowess and convergence rate. The findings of the experiment were compared to those of seven additional state-of-the-art metaheuristic optimizers that were used in the same empirical setting. The initial versions of sine cosine algorithm (SCA) [41], ABC [8], FA [42], BA [43], harris hawks optimization (HHO) [44], SNS [45], and teacher learning-based (TLB) [46] were these rival methods. The configuration of the control parameters was obtained from the original papers, and these comparative metaheuristics were autonomously created by the authors. The following abbreviations were employed to facilitate results monitoring: All optimizers were prefixed with "LR" (e.g., LR-DOSNS, LR-ABC, etc.).

4.4.3 Obtained simulation outcomes and comparative analysis

In all results' tables, best obtained metrics for each category are denoted with bold style. The aggregate metrics for LR trials on English 500 and 1000 that were attained by all metaheuristic algorithms are shown in Table 4−2. As may be observed, the experiment's recommended LR-DOSNS metaheuristic technique generated the most favorable results. Table 4−3 provides specific metrics for the best run for English datasets. The LR-DOSNS model's advantages may be seen in this situation. The results for English 500 dataset show that the proposed model obtained the best accuracy with approximately 97.00%, while linear regression-bat algorithm (LR-BA) finished second, with 96.77%. LR-DOSNS managed to obtain superior results for 6 out of 10 metrics observed with this experiment.

The advantages of LR-DOSNS are even more evident when English 1000 dataset is considered, where the approach obtained 97.46% accuracy, in front of LR-ABC, LR-BA, and LR-TLB that all achieved 96.54% accuracy, meaning that the difference between the proposed model and the second best is almost 1%. In this scenario, LR-DOSNS was superior in all observed metrics, achieving the best results for all 10 indicators.

Table 4–2 General logistic regression performance metrics regarding classification error.

Method	LR-DOSNS	LR-SCA	LR-ABC	LR-FA	LR-BA	LR-HHO	LR-SNS	LR-TLB
English 500								
Best	**0.030019**	0.036953	0.039261	0.036953	0.032334	0.039261	0.034641	0.036953
Worst	0.043881	0.046192	0.043878	**0.041568**	0.043877	0.043877	0.053121	0.046190
Mean	0.036949	0.041568	0.041568	0.039259	**0.036372**	0.040995	0.043305	0.040997
Median	0.036949	0.041569	0.041569	0.039259	**0.034641**	0.040415	0.042726	0.040417
Std	0.005163	0.003654	0.002311	**0.001631**	0.004728	0.001914	0.007001	0.003416
Var	0.000026	0.000012	0.000006	**0.000003**	0.000019	0.000005	0.000050	0.000011
English 1000								
Best	**0.025402**	0.041571	0.034643	0.034643	0.039259	0.036951	0.039259	0.034643
Worst	0.050811	0.046192	0.055431	0.050812	0.048501	0.046193	0.046193	**0.041572**
Mean	0.040418	0.043304	0.043304	0.042150	0.044458	0.042150	0.043304	**0.039259**
Median	0.042726	0.042726	0.041572	0.041572	0.045036	0.042726	0.043879	**0.040414**
Std	0.009311	**0.001914**	0.008223	0.005746	0.004125	0.004125	0.002518	0.002831
Var	0.000084	**0.000004**	0.000070	0.000035	0.000018	0.000018	0.000007	0.000009

Table 4–3 Detailed metrics for logistic regression results and English dataset.

	LR-DOSNS	LR-SCA	LR-ABC	LR-FA	LR-BA	LR-HHO	LR-SNS	LR-TLB
English 500								
Accuracy (%)	**96.9974**	96.3051	96.0742	96.3051	96.7668	96.0742	96.5360	96.3051
Precision 0	0.970000	0.957379	0.966441	0.963457	0.966779	**0.976025**	0.963578	0.963457
Precision 1	0.969927	**0.976562**	0.948151	0.962122	0.969696	0.929082	0.969463	0.962122
M. Avg. Precision	**0.969977**	0.963489	0.960608	0.963029	0.967711	0.961067	0.965451	0.963029
Recall 0	0.986443	**0.989832**	0.976269	0.983048	0.986443	0.966104	0.986443	0.983048
Recall 1	0.934781	0.905794	0.927538	0.920289	0.927533	**0.949278**	0.920289	0.920289
M. Avg. Recall	**0.969974**	0.963051	0.960742	0.963051	0.967668	0.960742	0.965360	0.963051
F1 Score 0	**0.978149**	0.973334	0.971331	0.973155	0.976509	0.971042	0.974876	0.973153
F1 Score 1	**0.952028**	0.939847	0.937731	0.940743	0.948151	0.939064	0.944242	0.940739
M. Avg. F1 Score	**0.969825**	0.962664	0.960625	0.962823	0.967473	0.960848	0.965109	0.962823
English 1000								
Accuracy (%)	**97.4592**	95.8429	96.5361	96.5361	96.0742	96.3053	96.0742	96.5361
Precision 0	**0.973333**	0.960131	0.969802	0.963574	0.957235	0.966558	0.960266	0.963573
Precision 1	**0.977446**	0.954545	0.955555	0.969468	0.968989	0.955221	0.961834	0.969468
M. Avg. Precision	**0.974641**	0.958349	0.965261	0.965455	0.960982	0.962946	0.960762	0.965451
Recall 0	**0.989829**	0.979658	0.979658	0.986443	0.986443	0.979658	0.983049	0.986443
Recall 1	**0.942026**	0.913041	0.934782	0.920288	0.905796	0.927533	0.913041	0.920288
M. Avg. Recall	**0.974592**	0.958429	0.965361	0.965361	0.960742	0.963053	0.960742	0.9653561
F1 Score 0	**0.981512**	0.969795	0.974703	0.974871	0.971616	0.973062	0.971525	0.974872
F1 Score 1	**0.959408**	0.933333	0.945053	0.944241	0.936329	0.941173	0.936801	0.944242
M. Avg. F1 Score	**0.974463**	0.958175	0.965253	0.965108	0.960369	0.962898	0.960454	0.965108

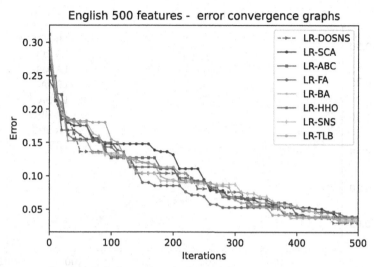

FIGURE 4–1 Convergence diagram of all observed methods on English 500 dataset. Please check the online version to view the color image of the figure.

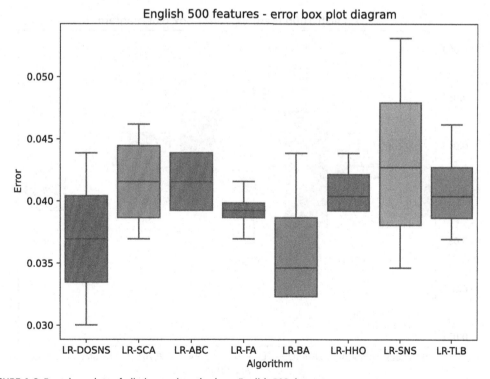

FIGURE 4–2 Error box plots of all observed methods on English 500 dataset.

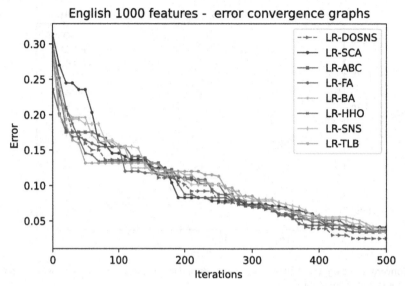

FIGURE 4–3 Convergence diagram of all observed methods on English 500 dataset. Please check the online version to view the color image of the figure.

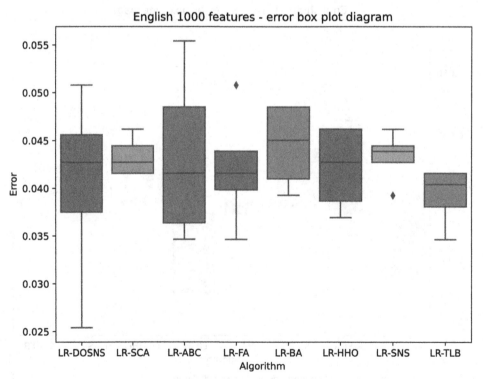

FIGURE 4–4 Error box plots of all observed methods on English 500 dataset.

For visualization purposes of the superiority of LR-DOSNS model over the competitor models, the convergence graphs and error box plots diagrams of all observed methods for English 500 are given in Figs. 4−1 and 4−2 and for the English 1000 dataset are shown in Figs. 4−3 and 4−4, respectively.

4.5 Conclusion

This work provided a unique implementation of the SNS optimizers to overcome the inadequacies of the classic SNS variant. DOSNS, the term given to the new method, was utilized to include it into the ML framework. For LR training, the proposed DOSNS was used. The study aims to improve intelligent algorithm-based spam email filtering solutions even more. As a result, the suggested model was assessed using the English-language CSDMC2010 benchmark spam email dataset.

Seven alternative metaheuristics that were employed in the same empirical context as the DOSNS algorithm were compared to the experimental results of the latter. The acquired simulation outcomes unmistakably indicate that, when compared to other techniques that were taken into consideration for the comparison study, LR-DOSCA obtained a greater accuracy level.

Prior to considering their implementation in actual systems that are concerned with spam screening and general cybersecurity as well as the protection of other networks that involve email service, further research in this area will aim to strengthen the algorithms' robustness by further validating the proposed architectures on other datasets obtained in the real world.

References

[1] D. Maulud, A.M. Abdulazeez, A review on linear regression comprehensive in machine learning, J. Appl. Sci. Technol. Trends 1 (4) (2020) 140−147.

[2] B.K. Dedeturk, B. Akay, Spam filtering using a logistic regression model trained by an artificial bee colony algorithm, Appl. Soft Comput. 91 (2020) 106229.

[3] P. Vanaja, M.V. Kumari, Machine learning based optimization for efficient detection of email spam.

[4] J. Goodman, W.-T. Yih, Online discriminative spam filter training, in: CEAS, Citeseer, 2006, pp. 1−4.

[5] D. Jurafsky, J.H. Martin, Speech and Language Processing, 3, Prentice Hall, US, 2014.

[6] Y. Han, M. Yang, H. Qi, X. He, S. Li, The improved logistic regression models for spam filtering, 2009 International Conference on Asian Language Processing, IEEE, 2009, pp. 314−317.

[7] J. Kennedy, The particle swarm: social adaptation of knowledge, in: Proceedings of 1997 IEEE Int. Conf. Evol. Comput. (ICEC '97), 1997, pp. 303−308.

[8] D. Karaboga, Artificial bee colony algorithm, Scholarpedia 5 (3) (2010) 6915.

[9] N. Bacanin, T. Bezdan, K. Venkatachalam, M. Zivkovic, I. Strumberger, M. Abouhawwash, et al., Artificial neural networks hidden unit and weight connection optimization by quasi-refection-based learning artificial bee colony algorithm, IEEE Access 9 (2021) 169135−169155.

[10] S. Mirjalili, A. Lewis, The whale optimization algorithm, Adv. Eng. Softw. 95 (2016) 51−67.

[11] N. Bacanin, E. Tuba, M. Zivkovic, I. Strumberger, M. Tuba, Whale optimization algorithm with exploratory move for wireless sensor networks localization, International Conference on Hybrid Intelligent Systems, Springer, 2019, pp. 328−338.

[12] T. Bezdan, M. Zivkovic, N. Bacanin, A. Chhabra, M. Suresh, Feature selection by hybrid brain storm optimization algorithm for COVID-19 classification, J. Comput. Biol. (2022).

[13] N. Budimirovic, E. Prabhu, M. Antonijevic, M. Zivkovic, N. Bacanin, I. Strumberger, et al., COVID-19 severity prediction using enhanced whale with salp swarm feature classification, Comput., Mater. Continua (2022) 1685–1698.

[14] M. Zivkovic, A. Petrovic, N. Bacanin, S. Milosevic, V. Veljic, A. Vesic, The COVID-19 images classification by mobilenetv3 and enhanced sine cosine metaheuristics, Mobile Comput. Sustain. Inform, Springer, 2022, pp. 937–950.

[15] M. Zivkovic, N. Bacanin, K. Venkatachalam, A. Nayyar, A. Djordjevic, I. Strumberger, et al., Covid-19 cases prediction by using hybrid machine learning and beetle antennae search approach, Sustain. Cities Soc. 66 (2021) 102669.

[16] M. Salb, M. Zivkovic, N. Bacanin, A. Chhabra, M. Suresh, Support vector machine performance improvements for cryptocurrency value forecasting by enhanced sine cosine algorithm, Comput. Vis. Robot, Springer, 2022, pp. 527–536.

[17] N. AlHosni, L. Jovanovic, M. Antonijevic, M. Bukumira, M. Zivkovic, I. Strumberger, et al., The xgboost model for network intrusion detection boosted by enhanced sine cosine algorithm, International Conference on Image Processing and Capsule Networks, Springer, 2022, pp. 213–228.

[18] M. Tair, N. Bacanin, M. Zivkovic, K. Venkatachalam, I. Strumberger, Xgboost design by multi-verse optimiser: an application for network intrusion detection, Mobile Computing and Sustainable Informatics, Springer, 2022, pp. 1–16.

[19] M. Zivkovic, N. Bacanin, J. Arandjelovic, A. Rakic, I. Strumberger, K. Venkatachalam, et al., Novel harris hawks optimization and deep neural network approach for intrusion detection, Proceedings of International Joint Conference on Advances in Computational Intelligence, Springer, 2022, pp. 239–250.

[20] M. Zivkovic, L. Jovanovic, M. Ivanovic, N. Bacanin, I. Strumberger, P.M. Joseph, Xgboost hyperparameters tuning by fitness-dependent optimizer for network intrusion detection, Communication and Intelligent Systems, Springer, 2022, pp. 947–962.

[21] D. Jovanovic, M. Antonijevic, M. Stankovic, M. Zivkovic, M. Tanaskovic, N. Bacanin, Tuning machine learning models using a group search firefly algorithm for credit card fraud detection, Mathematics 10 (13) (2022) 2272.

[22] A. Petrovic, N. Bacanin, M. Zivkovic, M. Marjanovic, M. Antonijevic, I. Strumberger, The adaboost approach tuned by firefly metaheuristics for fraud detection, 2022 IEEE World Conference on Applied Intelligence and Computing (AIC), IEEE, 2022, pp. 834–839.

[23] T. Bezdan, M. Zivkovic, E. Tuba, I. Strumberger, N. Bacanin, M. Tuba, Glioma brain tumor grade classification from mri using convolutional neural networks designed by modified fa, International Conference on Intelligent and Fuzzy Systems, Springer, 2020, pp. 955–963.

[24] N. Bacanin, M. Zivkovic, F. Al-Turjman, K. Venkatachalam, P. Trojovsky, I. Strumberger, et al., Hybridized sine cosine algorithm with convolutional neural networks dropout regularization application, Sci. Rep. 12 (1) (2022) 1–20.

[25] L. Jovanovic, M. Zivkovic, M. Antonijevic, D. Jovanovic, M. Ivanovic, H.S. Jassim, An emperor penguin optimizer application for medical diagnostics, 2022 IEEE Zooming Innovation in Consumer Technologies Conference (ZINC), IEEE, 2022, pp. 191–196.

[26] N. Bacanin, M. Zivkovic, T. Bezdan, K. Venkatachalam, M. Abouhawwash, Modified firefly algorithm for workflow scheduling in cloud-edge environment, Neur. Comput. Appl. 34 (11) (2022) 9043–9068.

[27] T. Bezdan, M. Zivkovic, N. Bacanin, I. Strumberger, E. Tuba, M. Tuba, Multi-objective task scheduling in cloud computing environment by hybridized bat algorithm, J. Intell. Fuzzy Syst. 42 (1) (2022) 411–423.

[28] M. Zivkovic, T. Bezdan, I. Strumberger, N. Bacanin, K. Venkatachalam, Improved harris hawks optimization algorithm for workflow scheduling challenge in cloud–edge environment, Computer Networks, Big Data and IoT, Springer, 2021, pp. 87–102.

[29] I. Strumberger, T. Bezdan, M. Ivanovic, L. Jovanovic, Improving energy usage in wireless sensor networks by whale optimization algorithm, 2021 29th Telecommunications Forum (TELFOR), IEEE, 2021, pp. 1–4.

[30] M. Zivkovic, T. Zivkovic, K. Venkatachalam, N. Bacanin, Enhanced dragonfly algorithm adapted for wireless sensor network lifetime optimization, Data Intelligence and Cognitive Informatics, Springer, 2021, pp. 803–817.

[31] N. Bacanin, M. Sarac, N. Budimirovic, M. Zivkovic, A.A. AlZubi, A.K. Bashir, Smart wireless health care system using graph lstm pollution prediction and dragonfly node localization, Sustain. Comput.: Inform. Syst. 35 (2022) 100711.

[32] N. Bacanin, M. Antonijevic, T. Bezdan, M. Zivkovic, T.A. Rashid, Wireless sensor networks localization by improved whale optimization algorithm, Proceedings of 2nd International Conference on Artificial Intelligence: Advances and Applications, Springer, 2022, pp. 769–783.

[33] N. Bacanin, M. Zivkovic, M. Sarac, A. Petrovic, I. Strumberger, M. Antonijevic, et al., A novel multiswarm firefly algorithm: an application for plant classification, International Conference on Intelligent and Fuzzy Systems, Springer, 2022, pp. 1007–1016.

[34] M. Salb, N. Bacanin, M. Zivkovic, M. Antonijevic, M. Marjanovic, I. Strumberger, Extreme learning machine tuning by original sine cosine algorithm, 2022 IEEE World Conference on Applied Intelligence and Computing (AIC), IEEE, 2022, pp. 143–148.

[35] M. Zivkovic, M. Tair, K. Venkatachalam, N. Bacanin, Š. Hubálovsky, P. Trojovsky, Novel hybrid firefly algorithm: an application to enhance xgboost tuning for intrusion detection classification, PeerJ Comput. Sci. 8 (2022) e956.

[36] M. Zivkovic, C. Stoean, A. Chhabra, N. Budimirovic, A. Petrovic, N. Bacanin, Novel improved salp swarm algorithm: An application for feature selection, Sensors 22 (5) (2022) 1711.

[37] R. Latha, B. Saravana Balaji, N. Bacanin, I. Strumberger, M. Zivkovic, M. Kabiljo, Feature selection using grey wolf optimization with random differential grouping, Comput. Syst. Sci. Eng. 43 (1) (2022) 317–332.

[38] S. Talatahari, H. Bayzidi, M. Saraee, Social network search for global optimization, IEEE Access 6 (2021) 92815–92863.

[39] S. Rahnamayan, H.R. Tizhoosh, M.M.A. Salama, Quasi-oppositional differential evolution, in: 2007 IEEE Congr. Evol. Comput., 2007, pp. 2229–2236.

[40] S. Cheng, Y. Shi, Diversity control in particle swarm optimization, 2011 IEEE Symposium on Swarm Intelligence, IEEE, 2011, pp. 1–9.

[41] S. Mirjalili, Sca: a sine cosine algorithm for solving optimization problems, Knowledge-Based Systems 96 (2016) 120–133.

[42] X.-S. Yang, Firefly algorithms for multimodal optimization, International Symposium on Stochastic Algorithms, Springer, 2009, pp. 169–178.

[43] X.-S. Yang, Bat algorithm for multi-objective optimisation, International Journal of Bio-Inspired Computation 3 (5) (2011) 267–274.

[44] A.A. Heidari, S. Mirjalili, H. Faris, I. Aljarah, M. Mafarja, H. Chen, Harris hawks optimization: algorithm and applications, Future generation computer systems 97 (2019) 849–872.

[45] S. Talatahari, H. Bayzidi, M. Saraee, Social network search for global optimization, IEEE Access 9 (2021) 92015–92863.

[46] R.V. Rao, V.J. Savsani, D. Vakharia, Teaching–learning-based optimization: a novel method for constrained mechanical design optimization problems, Computer-aided Design 43 (3) (2011) 303–315.

5 ▪▪▪
▪▪▪
▪▪▪

Reviewing artificial intelligence and blockchain innovations: transformative applications in the energy sector

Olukayode Akanni[1], M. Vubangsi[1], Sarumi Usman Abidemi[1], Odunlami EriOluwa[1], Fadi Al-Turjman[2]

[1]ARTIFIICAL INTELLIGENCE ENGINEERING DEPARTMENT, RESEARCH CENTER FOR AI AND IOT, AI AND ROBOTICS INSTITUTE, NEAR EAST UNIVERSITY, NICOSIA, MERSIN, TURKEY
[2]ARTIFICIAL INTELLIGENCE, SOFTWARE, AND INFORMATION SYSTEMS ENGINEERING DEPARTMENTS, RESEARCH CENTER FOR AI AND IOT, AI AND ROBOTICS INSTITUTE, NEAR EAST UNIVERSITY, NICOSIA, MERSIN10, TURKEY

5.1 Introduction

AI and blockchain applications are required in the decarbonization of the energy business. Despite the critical need to shift away from these fuels, over 85% of the world's energy is produced using fossil fuels [1]. Furthermore, energy output surged by 70% between 2010 and 2017 [2,3], and it is predicted to expand by the same amount by 2050 [4,5]. As a result, we must define a route for transitioning from thermal energy to renewable energy without unnecessarily pressuring the world's infrastructure [4].

According to a Boston Consulting Group assessment [5] using artificial intelligence (AI) can cut greenhouse gas emissions by 5% to 10% by 2030. AI uses data such as historical/weather patterns, consumer demands, and market prices to train machines to learn and behave in ways that mimic the human mind in order to perform intelligent tasks. Because this is done in real-time, the energy system will be smoother and more engaging, while also being able to automatically correct irregularities. This would result in a long-term decrease in generated loss, requiring less energy to be produced and achieving the industry's lofty emission reduction targets.

Blockchains are decentralized systems, by doing away with the intermediary from the central for verifying transactions, it saves money and time while delivering a high level of security [6].

Peer-to-peer (P2P) energy trading became feasible with the advent of Ethereum in 2015, which enabled the use of smart contracts in conjunction with blockchain technology. This would enable energy to be redistributed on a grid in combination with AI prediction [7]. Blockchain technology, with its transparency and data traceability, has the potential to totally

Computational Intelligence and Blockchain in Complex Systems. DOI: https://doi.org/10.1016/B978-0-443-13268-1.00023-6
© 2024 Elsevier Inc. All rights reserved, including those for text and data mining, AI training, and similar technologies.

alter the energy sector by enabling decentralized energy trade, the usage of smart meters and invoices, and improved grid and smart contract management.

For example, an Internet of Things-enabled device such as a washing machine will continually look for and run when cheap electricity windows are identified. If the Telsa battery is completely charged, it may sell energy back to the grid and deposit tokens into the energy wallet [8].

Our main contribution is to highlight, via the perspective of today's markets and power networks, a study of AI and blockchain applications in the Energy business, compare consensus algorithms, and compare Ethereum with Solana in blockchain implementation.

5.2 Literature review

Two of the most disruptive technologies are AI and blockchain. The term "artificial intelligence" refers to a large family of innovations, including machine learning (ML), data science, and deep learning, which are the driving forces behind developments like self-driving cars and delivery robots [9].

AI has caused several unanticipated damages and concerns, including the production of fake news, voice, photos that look real but are not, deceptive use of AI in elections, adult films [10], invasion of privacy, and need to protect citizens' digital rights [11]. Concerns about the decolonization of AI power and Big Tech's monopoly on AI power are also present. These issues are related to the high upfront costs of computer resources, data, and talent, as well as the high entry barriers they entail.

5.2.1 Background of blockchain technology

A blockchain is an electronic data structure, composed of a chronological history of transactions and a continuously expanding log of transactions. It allows peers to use and store data in such a distributed network with links that allow communication in either a private or public environment. It is a decentralized registration system that encourages openness and data integrity. It is made up of data "blocks" (such as hashes, scripts, timestamps, and transactions) that are transferred to each shared node. There are three sorts of blockchain systems: private (not completely distributed high-efficiency systems, in which only a small number of carefully verified users who have been tested are eligible to validate, read, and participate in publishing extra new blocks), public (totally distributed, less efficient systems than private ones, needing a mandatory consensus process for data integrity and security, and with a public ledger allowing open participation), and open source systems [12–20].

Blockchain technology improves resilience, trust, security, and immutability while simultaneously cutting costs and complexity and empowering users. Furthermore, it lowers the possibility of data duplication and may significantly reduce the cost of maintaining IT infrastructure. Blockchain technology has the promise of enhancing company procedures, supplying data traceability and transparency, and enabling AI for smart contracts. It is particularly relevant for manufacturers migrating to new business models based on servitization and digital transformation. It can also help to eliminate delays caused by mistakes in the logistics and supply chain sectors, provide more transparent and secure transaction tracking, and reduce costs associated with trade documentation and processing [21].

The new energy market paradigm for smart communities is posing new issues for distribution network regulation of bidirectional energy flows. Prosumers may create, utilize, and trade energy over the present grid infrastructure without constraints, thanks to blockchain technology that enables P2P energy transactions to be formed without the need for third-party middlemen. Furthermore, by 2025, when electric cars are expected to be priced similarly to gasoline-powered vehicles, self-generation and supply from distributed renewable generation are expected to be grid-parity and more effective and efficient than relying on the network. Smart contracts and blockchain technology enable an automated and decentralized energy exchange, making the energy microgeneration market more lively and competitive.

As a result, load scheduling may vary more, transactions may be more frequent, and power settlements may increase. Furthermore, it allows cutting-edge transactive applications and can provide transparent, egalitarian, reliable, environmentally sustainable, and cost-effective trading platforms for virtual power plants.

5.2.2 Distributed energy resources, a new paradigm

A complex web of producers and consumers, blockchain, and tokenomics exists. The blockchain in distributed energy is the future paradigm [22] that will benefit from AI. Balancing all the loads from multiple inputs and outputs is substantially more difficult in a distributed system and necessitates a high level of AI, data analytics, and some form of open, transparent, dependable, and irreversible accounting system (Fig. 5-1).

The electricity system may be made greener by employing digital agents to trade for individuals, homes, big enterprises, and machines as consumers who make, stop, buy, sell, and store energy online, and extract is explicitly open. By combining blockchain, energy audits, algorithm trading, data engineering, and data science, it is possible to create a decentralized business solution. It ensures that transactions are secure, fair, transparent, and reconciled—all of which are critical in traditional energy trading. The blockchain reduces the cost of managing micro transactions. Blockchain technology allows safe trade and decreases settlement risk by providing a verifiable and immutable audit trail. Shore power, microgrids, and industrial port facilities are all alternatives. Docked ships require variable power, which is typically provided by diesel generators. To address this issue, Distro can seek to increase access to clean energy and renewable resources. For example, Africa/Cyprus might change its legislation to enable limited P2P trade in Northern Cyprus for electric vehicle batteries and rooftop solar energy. In essence, without the need for government subsidies, the future energy system may be provided through market mechanisms enabled by blockchain technology.

5.2.3 Consensus algorithms

Consensus algorithms are critical to the operation of blockchain networks, although not all blockchains can use them owing to privacy and performance problems. The two most used consensus algorithms are Proof-of-Work and Proof-of-Stake. Proof-of-Labor is the most widely used consensus technique, whereas Proof-of-Stake is a version that requires

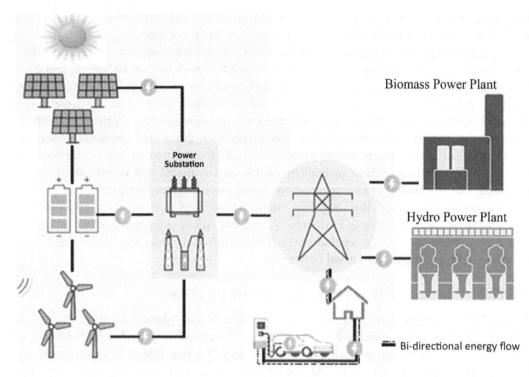

FIGURE 5-1 Distributed energy resources.

significantly less CPU processing power and energy for mining rather than a substantial amount of calculation labor solving cryptographic riddles [23].

We advocate the Proof-of-History (PoH) consensus method for the energy business because it operates like a clock before consensus. Proof-of-History is a scalable strategy for establishing and protecting portable blockchain with a traceable past. PoH is suggested for the energy industry because Proof-of-Job is basically PoH, just as a business entity may demonstrate Proof-of-Work is actually done on the field (like PoW) with photographs acquired by a camera on the field demonstrating the job done with a time stamp (like PoH) (Table 5-1).

5.3 Applications of artificial intelligence and blockchain in the energy industry

5.3.1 Artificial intelligence in solar energy: yield performance predictions

Artificial neural networks (ANNs), a subset of AI, are critical in anticipating performance in solar energy systems. ANNs are multilayer linked nodes that are trained to operate as

Table 5-1 Blockchain consensus algorithms comparison frameworks.

Consensus algorithm	Consensus approach	Pros	Cons
Proof-of-Work (PoW) [12,24–27]	By resolving the cryptographic challenge to obtain the hash value, validators dispute among themselves for a new block to be added to blockchain that existed previously. It also inserts a nonce after computing the block header's hash result.	The blockchain is faster. There is significantly less of a chance of a 51% attack because much less power is needed.	Finality and transaction costs might not be fit for all instances. Low throughput, a long latency, and excessive energy usage.
Proof-of-Stake (PoS) [26,28–30]	PoS replaces computation-based work with a random selection process, and mining success is intimately related to the wealth of validators. The financial commitment of stake nodes to the system, or their ownership of coins, influences their chance of creating a block.	Blockchains are faster. Because much less power is needed, the possibility of a 51% assault is reduced.	"Nothing is at stake" argument, or, more specifically, the cheap cost of voting or gaining rewards from multiple chains.
Practical Byzantine fault tolerance [26,31–33]	PBFT algorithms are better suitable for trustworthy scenarios due to independent checks and validator node signatures.	Because globally certified blocks cannot be reversed, PBFT provides instant. finality.	Increased message overhead derives from the algorithm's necessity that at least 2/3 of the network act ethically.
Delegated Proof-of-Stake (DPoS) [34–36]	DPOS is a kind of PoS that allows for quick transaction confirmation by choosing delegates to construct and validate blocks. An asynchronous network design maximizes transaction throughput and minimizes Delegate co-dependency, enhancing network security.	DPoS can withstand Byzantine faults up to 49% of the time. Members of the network may all choose whom to believe, and the members with the most resources are not the only ones who can do so.	Because limited node participation in the voting/election process is allowed, there is a risk of centralization.
Proof-of-History (PoH) [37,38]	It is a collection of computations that may be used to verify the amount of time that has safely passed between two occurrences. It employs a cryptographically safe function that requires complete execution to yield the output, rendering prediction impossible. Proof-of-History (PoH), a scalable consensus technique, validates the time and sequence of events. It may be used in conjunction with Proof-of-Stake to penalize any verifier who goes against the network's goal.	PoH allows for decentralized security while also making a Blockchain extremely fast and energy-efficient. It enables millions of transactions to be completed almost instantly per second.	If your hardware did not meet tight specifications, you were not able to participate in Solana or be counted in the consensus. It generates a massive amount of data that many corporations, let alone regular people, are unable to keep up with.

(Continued)

Table 5-1 (Continued)

Consensus algorithm	Consensus approach	Pros	Cons
Federated Byzantine Agreement (FBA) [39]	Participants place their faith in a small number of validators, all of whom are regarded as trustworthy. A block is considered authentic if the requisite number of validators sign it or if users create and distribute a "candidate set" of transactions.	A Byzantine fault tolerance system in which each Byzantine general is in control of their own Blockchain. A Federated Byzantine Agreement (FBA) is popular because of its high throughput, network scalability, and low transaction costs.	Other nodes vote on the transactions, and when a node changes its candidate list, the majority of the votes are considered.
Proof-of-Authority (PoAu) [12,28]	Users generate and disseminate a "candidate set" of transactions throughout the network. When a node changes its candidate list, the majority of votes are taken into account. Other nodes decide on the transactions.	When security and integrity cannot be compromised, this may be advantageous. Users on the network place their faith in authorized nodes, and a block is validated if voting can be used to bring in more validators.	Energy utility businesses are realizing that the notion is popular, despite the fact that it is a more centralized manner best suited for governing or regulating agencies.
Proof-of-Elapsed Time (PoET) [35,40,41]	PoET implements a randomized timer object to prevent unethical users from always receiving the shortest timer.	It is necessary to wait till the waiting period has expired before publishing a new block. The public has come to trust the time-keeping devices.	The fundamental critique of this strategy is that it requires the environment built by Intel, implying that faith in a single authority is still required.
Proof-of-Activity (PoAc) [12,28]	Proof-of-Stake and Proof-of-Work are combined in the hybrid PoAc system.	Block validation is deemed complete if all validators in the group have collected their signatures. If no nodes are found, a new group is formed.	PoA combines the advantages and disadvantages of PoW and PoS, such as resource waste and validators that double-sign documents.
Proof-of-Burn (PoB) [42]	To imitate the cost of PoW validation, PoB charges validator nodes, who get money in the form of coins in exchange for the privilege of validating blocks. Validator nodes commit coins that can never be retrieved, increasing the risk of their being chosen at random.	Because validation is based on the desire to squander money, PoB wastes a lot of resources.	Centralization risks, in contrast to PoW, are hardware-independent.
Proof-of-Capacity (PoC) [42]	Validator nodes in proofs of space or proofs of storage must allocate hard drive space to increase their chances of forging new blocks.	It makes use of free disk space as a resource and is efficient, distributed, and cost-effective.	PoC generates massive datasets known as "plots" that consume storage space.
Lease POS [12]	Allows for the leasing of node resources to third parties.	The primary aims of this lease are to increase the chance of validators, increase the number of participants who are qualified to vote, and decrease the likelihood of a small number of nodes gaining control of the blockchain network.	Prizes are usually distributed equitably.

Protocol	Description	Advantages	Disadvantages
Hyperledger Fabric Ordering Service-variants of byzantine fault tolerance (BFT)-based protocols [43]	Voting by permission. The commands are given by the leader. Only synchronized clones.	Provides crash fault tolerance. Finality arrives in a matter of seconds.	While Kafka is crash fault tolerant, it is not byzantine fault tolerant, which means that the system cannot reach a consensus if some nodes are malevolent or malfunctioning.
RBFT in Hyperledger Indy-variants of BFT-based protocols [43]	The pluggable election technique is preset to employ a permissioned voting mechanism. Even if all instances order, only the requests that the master instance orders are really fulfilled.	Byzantine fault tolerance is available. Finality happens in a matter of seconds.	The node density of the network influences how long it takes to reach an agreement. The nodes of the network are known and require perfect connection.
Sumeragi in Hyperledger Iroha-variants of BFT-based protocols [43]	Permission-based server reputation system.	Byzantine fault tolerance is available. Finality arrives in a matter of seconds. Petabytes of data are spread over several clusters.	The node density of the network influences how long it takes to reach an agreement. The network's nodes are known and must be completely connected.
PoET in Hyperledger Sawtooth-variants of BFT-based protocols [43,44]	The pluggable election technique's default option is a permission, lottery-based approach.	There is scalability and Byzantine fault tolerance.	Finality may be delayed due to the necessity to reconcile forks.
Algorand [45].	Verifies transactions in a minute or less while scalable to many users. Algorand ensures that users' perspectives on verified transactions are never contradictory.	Verifiable Random Functions to scale consensus among a large number of users.	To defend against targeted assaults, users can immediately swap out participants after sending a message.
Proof-of-Retrievability (PoR) [35,46]	PoR allows for distributed archival data storage, making it suitable for cloud computing.	Efficient	Increasing the number of requests is challenging.
Proof-of-Publication (PoP) [35,47]	Even if the clocks are off, the overall order of the records can be assured by utilizing hashed and signed timestamps.	Can be used for cryptocurrencies as well as noncrypto purposes.	Inability to conserve energy.
Proof-of-Luck (PoL) [48]	PoW tries to increase transaction throughput while utilizing fewer processing resources by assigning each block a "luck value" derived by adding all of the values of each block beginning with the genesis. A higher luck value results in less delay and better communication.	Transaction validation is decentralized, low latency, and power-safe.	Revision is a viable option. Unfair and forking.

(Continued)

Table 5-1 (Continued)

Consensus algorithm	Consensus approach	Pros	Cons
Tendermint [33,35,49]	Tendermint, a permissioned consensus technique, accepts one-third of malicious nodes.	It does not call for mining.	Unfair.
Proof-of-Vote [50]	PoV is a proposed consensus technique for consortium blockchains, in which firms create partnerships and each enterprise represents an officer. The authority within the partnership committee is decentralized because the team develops the blocks and delivers them to the companies for verification and voting.	Continuity, accessibility, and partition tolerance.	Problems with concurrent processing and modular design.
Proof-of-Human Work [51]	Human-work puzzles should be challenging for humans and difficult for machines, not simple for robots.	Reasonable.	It requires an initial trustworthy configuration and is vulnerable to malicious assault.
Simplified Byzantine Fault Tolerance [52]	SBFT, a condensed byzantine fault tolerance protocol, beats PoW by using a realistic PBFT consensus process. When a certain number of nodes approve a block, consensus is attained. A block signer validates transactions and signs them.	Signature verification and excellent security.	No public blockchain is permitted.
Raft [53–55]	The first and second phases of the voting-based consensus approach. Raft is a leader election and log replication system. It has high throughput and low latency, but its lack of security and limited capacity makes it unsuitable for the Internet of things.	Allows for configuration changes; simpler and more basic than Paxos. It assures coherence, deconstructs key components of consensus, and introduces a brand-new mechanism for changing cluster membership.	Centrally managed
Proof-of-Proof [56]	Evidence that is suggestive. Other blockchains can borrow security from one another and form a security ecosystem by leveraging proof of work and consensus.	Security transmission.	Vectors of attack are a possibility.
Proof-of-Believability (PoB) [57]	Internet of services token (IOST) developed the PoB protocol to improve the blockchain's fairness and decentralization.	Scalability, speed of completion, and a more decentralized governance model than PoS.	Not yet determined.

Proof-of-Property [58]	New participants can validate transactions without downloading a blockchain by accessing the root hash of the Patricia tree system state of the new block.	It is scalable and saves a lot of space locally.	Forking might pose issues.
Proof-of-Ownership (PoO) [35,59]	Because the owner epoch register for PoW is vulnerable to the Sybil attack, different pseudonyms are generated using a trusted execution environment (TEE) signature.	Using different pseudonyms makes multiple assaults difficult.	It is not known.
Stellar Consensus Protocol (SCP) [35,60]	A decentralized consensus technique in which nodes may choose which nodes to trust and in which quorum slices create a consensus. Each node uses a "nomination protocol" and a "ballot protocol" to propose new candidate values for agreement. If the quorum slice cannot reach an agreement, the value is shifted to a ballot with a higher value, and a fresh vote is taken.	Transfers are cheap and rapid.	Ineffective in terms of message volume transmitted.
Proof-of-Space-time [35,61]	PoST saves energy by extending the lifetime of data storage rather than increasing processing costs.	Low computational cost.	More discussion is required.
Proof-of-Importance (PoI) [35,59]	To qualify for "Importance Calculation," which is based on the difference between the account's vested and unvested XEM balances, a balance of 10,000 XEM must be retained in the account's vested component. To maintain ranking, the NCDawareRank algorithm and NEM network selected two acceptable constants.	Encourages active participation and contributions within the network.	Decentralization problem.
Proof-of-Exercise (PoX) [35,60]	Uses computational power to address scientific problems. Employers provide matrix-based tasks to miners, and a "hostage credit" approach is used to ensure that the data is freely available. When a problem is solved successfully, miners bid on it and deposit the money. If many miners win at the same time, the monetary award is shared.	Reduce the consumption of computational resources.	Focused research is necessary for implementation in practice.

(Continued)

Table 5-1 (Continued)

Consensus algorithm	Consensus approach	Pros	Cons
Proof-of-Inclusion (PoI) [12,62,63]	The Merkle tree root in the block may be viewed as a point of interest for records, allowing nodes to validate certain records without having to examine and compare the entire chain. If two nodes' copies of the blockchain have the same Merkel tree root for a given block, then those copies are said to be verified and consistent.	This PoI is built on the Ethereum blockchain using smart contracts.	It is not known.

computer operational nodes, gather data, and learn how to carry out tasks in order to solve issues in many domains of solar energy yield analysis.

The performance of Concentrating Solar Power generators is evaluated using ANNs to determine the efficiency of a solar steam generator while utilizing concentrating collectors.

The varied incidence angles and normal incidence angles are difficult to achieve due to the size of the collectors and the complexities of the parabolic geometry. ANNs are used to anticipate radiation angles and temperature profiles for heat-up periods and to aid in the more efficient start-up of generators [64,65].

5.3.2 Using artificial intelligence to improve energy performance

The challenge for the urban industry is that more and more countries are enacting smart rules to improve building energy performance and reduce costs and outages. These goals are easier to achieve because of AI and IoT [64,65].

5.3.3 Artificial intelligence in grid management

Modern networks collect energy from several sources, including coal, wind, and solar. The operation and management of huge power grid networks have become more difficult. AI increases the efficiency and reliability of various energy sources via its ability to examine massive datasets in a short period. As a result, smart grids were developed to efficiently handle a variety of energy sources (including traditional gas and renewables).

For example, Siemens' active network management (ANM) software manages grids on its own. It monitors how a grid responds to changing energy demands and modifies the grid as needed to increase efficiency. Previously, manual alterations were utilized; however, ANM now makes power grids proactive by adjusting its components whenever new energy sources become available.

5.3.4 Solar coin use on blockchain for renewables

This technology provides an opportunity to change how energy is distributed across the grid in terms of how it is generated, utilized, and input into it.

SolarCoin created a blockchain-based coin to reward freshly generated KWh (by the solar power plant's operator).

SolarCoin, a blockchain-based digital asset and money, is meant to promote and stimulate the transition to renewable energy systems. This is how the energy-related cryptocurrency wants to enhance global solar energy generation. One SolarCoin (SLR) is equal to one MWh of solar-generated electricity [66].

5.3.5 Trading in energy (blockchain using peer-to-peer and artificial intelligence technologies)

Blockchain technology, with its secure distributed accounting system and method of data recording, has the potential to create a new "digital ledger" of economic transactions, agreements, and contracts. The data is kept in tens of thousands of computers throughout the world [38].

5.3.6 Intelligent grids

Grids can now be made "smart" by integrating them with IoT, sensors, and other energy technology, allowing power providers to collect data on energy consumption from every grid device by deploying smart grids, use data to create efficient energy programs for their customers, and track the use and flow of energy in near real-time [67].

5.3.7 Grid security

The electrical grid is a complex technology that is vulnerable to hackers. Energy grid security may be improved by employing AI and machine learning (ML) to detect and prevent attacks using pattern recognition [68].

5.3.8 Grid administration and efficiency

AI manages energy flows between buildings, commercial buildings, DER, energy storage batteries, and the grid to improve energy systems. As a consequence, less energy is wasted and consumers are more involved in energy consumption.

Even when DER become more popular, they are only accessible for a limited time. As a result, these energy sources are not always available to produce the needed energy, hence AI is employed to forecast their availability and grid management [69].

Robots are used in energy installations and grid maintenance, energy generation and consumption, and repairs to wind turbines, pipelines, and other energy infrastructure.

5.3.9 Increased productivity

Furthermore, the energy business is utilizing AI and machine intelligence to boost output. For example, using ML algorithms to analyze seismic data and other data sources can lead to better well placement and drilling for oil and gas, resulting in increased output. In addition to increasing energy efficiency, this will result in a system that is simpler and more effective for energy companies to maintain [67].

5.3.10 Predictive analytics

Predictive analytics is used to estimate the future trajectory of energy consumption, allowing for future planning and development of equipment to meet the world's energy demands.

Predictive analytics may be used to predict the possibility of a machine or piece of equipment failing. This assists firms in scheduling maintenance and avoiding unforeseen outages, saving money, providing improved performance, and preparing for capital-intensive and critical equipment [70].

5.3.11 Storage of energy

The energy storage industry will have grown 20 times by 2030. Smart energy storage devices, for example, can be integrated into the grid to increase the efficiency of energy management. Energy storage is being used to build virtual power plants, allowing energy suppliers to offer electricity when it is needed even if their current energy supply is insufficient. As a consequence, energy companies will not need to build as many new power plants [8].

5.3.12 Trading in energy

Because of the necessity for quick delivery, energy trading must be near real-time, which presents a challenge for traders. However, there is also an opportunity due to the increased liquidity of the energy markets.

AL and ML are used to boost the efficiency of the energy trading market by forecasting energy demand and providing dealers with real-time pricing data. By forecasting energy demand and providing traders with real-time price data, traders may determine when to sell and purchase electricity. Power purchase agreement (PPA) has been established utilizing blockchain technology, which is less expensive to operate than traditional PPA platforms and speeds up transactions, making these contracts more efficient [38].

5.3.13 Power theft and energy fraud detection

The global cost of power theft and fraud to the energy and utilities sectors is up to $96 billion a year, with losses of up to $6 billion in the United States alone [71]. Power theft is the illegal exploitation of grid electricity. Energy fraud is the intentional misrepresentation of energy information or energy use. AI and ML can detect these irregularities automatically and flag them for resolution by energy companies. This allows energy companies to protect their resources, reduce energy waste, and save money.

5.3.14 Microgrids

Microgrid control systems combine AI and ML to monitor energy flow and optimize energy utilization. Microgrids are gaining popularity because they may provide energy security in times of crisis and can incorporate DER into the main energy grid more rapidly than traditional energy networks [72].

5.3.15 Customer engagement

For client contact, the energy industry is now utilizing AI and ML. Using AI and ML, energy companies may give their customers information that is suited to their specific needs. Data analytics is used to monitor consumer energy consumption and customers are then provided advice on how to improve their usage patterns and spend less energy [73].

5.4 Use cases

5.4.1 Powerledger

The Powerledger platform is one such example. It interfaces with smart meter systems and allows homes to set prices, monitor energy trading in real-time, and settle transactions involving extra solar energy in real-time using blockchain smart contracts. Powerledger platform is scalable and modular. Their items can be acquired individually to satisfy specific demands. Powerledger's three product areas are trading in environmental commodities, flexibility trading, and energy trading and traceability [38].

5.4.2 Energy web foundation

Customer investments in renewable energy, DERs, and electric vehicles will outnumber utility investments in production, transmission, and distribution by 2030. However, today's electricity markets and networks are not suited for a society where customers' needs come first.

At the distribution level, batteries, solar panels, electric vehicles, and water heaters may all interact with one another. The Energy Web Foundation, a scalable blockchain and open-source platform, promotes the use of blockchain in the energy management business.

Their objective is to create and deploy open-source, distributed technologies and standards to address the identification, enforcement, and transaction needs of billions of DERs, service providers, utilities, grid operators, and customers throughout the world [74].

5.4.3 Verv

Verv is a blockchain-based P2P energy smart application that analyzes electricity via smart meters using AI and ML algorithms. This website allows prosumers (homeowners who consume energy generated by their own renewable energy systems, often solar panels) to measure production and sell any extra kWh in a single transaction. Thanks to ML algorithms and blockchain technology incorporated into its platform, increased networked microgrids will be able to control directly the production of renewable energy and sell the surplus to their neighbors. The advantages include a more accountable, democratic, and deliberate use of energy, reducing the cost of power. It will encourage everyone to have access to green energy and promote knowledge of IoT, smart metering, and renewable technologies [73].

5.5 Discussions

5.5.1 Comparison between Solana and the Ethereum network

The Solana design is faster, consumes less energy, and is more ecologically friendly than blockchains because it uses Proof-of-History and Proof-of-Stake consensus processes.

Solana's architecture's incredible scalability demonstrates a big innovation. Solana blockchain uses synchronized clocks across the network, reducing the time it takes for transactions to be verified. This synchronization optimizes the network for speed and security, enabling higher energy efficiency and security. Solana's built-in mechanism for synchronizing time across nodes, with 200 nodes can process 50,000 transactions per second, much above Ethereum's 20 transactions per second and Bitcoin's 7 transactions per second. It even outperforms Visa's predicted transaction rate of 1700 transactions per second. The protocol is designed to scale with Moore's Law, doubling in capacity every two years with hardware and bandwidth improvements. Solana's accomplishments speak for themselves.

This Proof-of-Work functionality is built into the Proof-of-History consensus process, which is at the heart of the Solana blockchain. The Proof-of-History algorithm determines the hash of a random integer using a cryptographic technique. The procedure is performed iteratively, with the initial hash result serving as the new input to construct the hash.

The Solana network is made possible by eight significant inventions, including PoH, Tower byzantine fault tolerance (BFT), Turbine, Gulf Stream, Sealevel, Cloudbreak, and Replicators. PoH is a cryptographic method that permits instant finality for transactions and generates a trustworthy ordering of transactions and events to address the issue of time agreement. In PoH-based blockchain, a verifiable delay function is employed to keep track of time, the result of which cryptographically certifies that real-time occurred during the production of that output. This is a hash function that is resistant to preimages. It takes a big quantity of input and makes a little fixed-size output.

Although it is impossible to predict the exact outcome, the security of these functions is where their value lies. We can always know whether data or messages have to arrive before or after other "blocks" by utilizing upper and lower time limits, no matter how rapidly or how many bits of data are added to the increasing PoH-based data structure. As a consequence, a decentralized network may accept and believe the instructions of the structure without having to confirm them again. To back to our analogy, each node on the decentralized network receives a snapshot of an old water clock with a cryptographic ledger. This ledger contains the most current and validated data of objects added to the blockchain, including messages, data, and transactions. Solana is distinguished by its short block durations and high throughput of more than 50,000 pieces per hour.

5.5.1.1 Tesla power and Powerlegder

Powerledger is supposed to support Tesla and other EV chargers, allowing clients to sell excess energy to these devices.

Tesla also uses the Ethereum network and ECR-20 protocols to provide consumers and investors with the most secure, dependable, and cost-effective transfer settings. The primary reason for decentralizing decision-making is to increase accountability and reliability.

Powerlegder retains flexibility and capabilities that would otherwise be unreachable by retaining the primary token powerledger (POWR) on the Ethereum blockchain. Because the Solana-based blockchain does not yet enable native coins, this is the case [38,75].

5.6 Conclusion

Although it is natural for people to be suspicious of new technology, blockchain is the foundation of a whole new internet. It is a new era in which sunshine may be swapped for money.

These projects offer immense promise for the developing world, perhaps, in the same way, that smartphone banking apps bypassed the Western concept of main street banks and went straight to mobile consumers in Africa and Asia.

Adoption of blockchain in the energy and resources industry might increase transparency, improve operational efficiency, and simplify regulatory reporting, but it would need significant time, money, and effort. AI and blockchain offer exciting potential to accelerate global decarbonization. The use of AI and blockchain in large-scale energy efficiency and orchestration has increased privacy concerns. The requirement for AI systems to collect and process data is an example of a conflict. To identify complicated patterns and make reliable predictions, an AI system would need as much user-specific data as feasible. In an optimized energy economy, P2P trading runs the danger of disclosing a householder's behavior patterns, particularly absence patterns. As a result, firms must consider potential privacy, risk, and security risks when deciding how to handle consumer response data. Similarly, before embracing AI and blockchain, consumers must educate themselves on data privacy, particularly when submitting personal or sensitive information.

References

[1] Transforming our world: the 2030 agenda for sustainable development, UN General Assembly. <https://sdgs.un.org/2030agenda>, 2015.

[2] Global energy & CO_2 status report, Emissions. <https://www.iea.org/reports/global-energy-co2-status-report-2019/emissions>, 2019 (accessed 21.11.22).

[3] Projected electricity generation worldwide from 2020 to 2050, by energy source. <https://www.statista.com/statistics/238610/projected-world-electricity-generation-by-energy-source/> (accessed 21.11.22).

[4] S. Sterl, A grid for all seasons: enhancing the integration of variable solar and wind power in electricity systems across Africa, Curr. Sustain. Renew. Energy Rep. 8 (2021) 274–281. Available from: https://doi.org/10.1007/s40518-021-00192-6.

[5] BGC, 2021 report-, reduce carbon and costs with the power of AI <https://www.bcg.com/publications/2021/ai-to-reduce-carbon-emissions> (accessed 21.11.22).

[6] Blockchain technology in the energy sector: a systematic review of challenges and opportunities. Renew. Sustain. Energy Rev. 100 (2018) 143–174. <https://www.researchgate.net/publication/328760651_Blockchain_technology_in_the_energy_sector_A_systematic_review_of_challenges_and_opportunities>.

[7] T. Dinh, M. Thai, AI and blockchain: a disruptive integration, Computer 51 (2018) 48–53. Available from: https://doi.org/10.1109/MC.2018.3620971, https://www.researchgate.net/publication/328085550_AI_and_Blockchain_A_Disruptive_Integration.

[8] M. Michael, Author at RenewEconomy - Page 180. Renew economy why storage is key to NSW government plans, in race to clean energy (14 June 2019). From [CrossRef] (assessed 20.04.23).

[9] Y. Leviathan, Google duplex: an AI system for accomplishing realworld tasks over the phone, Google AI Blog. <https://ai.googleblog.com/2018/05/duplex-ai-system-for-natural-conversation.html>, 2018.

[10] A. Hern, AI used to face-swap hollywood stars into pornography films, The Guardian. <http://www.theguardian.com/technology/2018/jan/25/ai-face-swap-pornography-emma-watson-scarlett-johansson-taylor-swift-daisy-ridley-sophie-turner-maisie-williams>, 2018.

[11] I. Calzada, Technological sovereignty: protecting citizens' digital rights in the AI-driven and post-GDPR algorithmic and city-regional European realm, Regions eZine (4) (2019). doi:10.1080/13673882.2018.00001038.

[12] M.B. Mollah, J. Zhao, D. Niyato, K.-Y. Lam, X. Zhang, A.M.Y.M. Ghias, et al., Blockchain for future smart grid: a comprehensive survey, IEEE Internet Things J. 8 (1) (2021) 18−43. Google Scholar.

[13] C. Burger, A. Kuhlman, P. Richard, J. Weinmann, Blockchain in the energy transition a survey among decision-makers in the German energy industry, Google Scholar, 60, 2015.

[14] M. Rauchs, A. Glidden, B. Gordon, G.C. Pieters, M. Recanatini, F. Rostand, et al., Distributed ledger technology systems: a conceptual framework, Google Scholar, 2018.

[15] A.M. Alonso, E. Martin, A. Mateo, F.J. Nogales, C. Ruiz, A. Veiga, Clustering electricity consumers: challenges and applications for operating smart grids, IEEE Power Energy Mag. 20 (3) (2022) 54−63. Google Scholar.

[16] S. Nakamoto, Bitcoin: a peer-to-peer electronic cash system, Decentralized Bus. Rev. (2008) 21260. Google Scholar.

[17] K. Ioannis, G. Raimondo, G. Dimitrios, D. Gioia, K. Georgios, N. Ricardo, et al., Blockchain in energy communities, Cent. Comum de. Investigação da Comissão Europeia 344003 (2017) 62. Google Scholar.

[18] I. Bashir, Mastering Blockchain: Distributed Ledger Technology Decentralization and Smart Contracts Explained, Packt Publishing, Birmingham, U.K., 2018. Google Scholar.

[19] B. Marchi, S. Zanoni, I. Ferretti, L.E. Zavanella, M. Pasetti, The disruptive potential of Blockchain technologies in the energy sector, in Proceedings of the ECEEE Summer Study, 2019, pp. 899−906. [Google Scholar].

[20] M. Andoni, V. Robu, D. Flynn, S. Abram, D. Geach, D. Jenkins, et al., Blockchain technology in the energy sector: a systematic review of challenges and opportunities, Renew. Sustain. Energy Rev. 100 (2018) 143−174 [Google Scholar]. Available from: https://doi.org/10.1016/j.rser.2018.10.014.

[21] B. Marchi, I. Ferretti, M. Pasetti, S. Zanoni, L. Zavanella, The disruptive potential of Blockchain technologies in the energy sector, Eceee Summer Study Proc. (2019) 899−906. Available from: https://doi.org/10.1016/j.rser.2019.109585.

[22] Q. Yang, H. Wang, T. Wang, S. Zhang, X. Wu, H. Wang, Blockchain-based decentralized energy management platform for residential distributed energy resources in a virtual power plant, Appl. Energy 294 (2021)117026 [Google Scholar]. Available from: https://arxiv.org/abs/2105.00174.

[23] J.I. Wong, Every cryptocurrency's nightmare scenario is happening to bitcoin gold, Quartz. <https://qz.com/1287701/bitcoin-golds-51-attack-is-every-cryptocurrencys-nightmare-scenario>, 2018.

[24] A. Back, Hash cash—a denial of service counter-measure. <http://www.hashcash>.

[25] G. Xethalis, K. Moriarty, R. Claassen, J. Levy, An introduction to bitcoin and blockchain technology. <https://files.arnoldporter.com//docs/introtobitcoinandblockchaintechnology.pdf> (accessed 11.11.22).

[26] M. Vukolic, The quest for scalable blockchain fabric: proof-of work vs. BFT replication, International Workshop on Open Problems in Network Security, Springer, 2015, pp. 112−125.

[27] Blockchain, Transactions per block. <https://blockchain.info/charts/ntransactions-per-block> (accessed 02.11.22).

[28] Castor A.A. (Short)Guide to blockchain consensus protocols. <https://www.coindesk.com/short-guide-Blockchain-consensus-protocols/> (accessed 05.11.22).

[29] Ethereum Wiki. Proof of stake FAQ. <https://github.com/ethereum/wiki/wiki/> (accessed 05.11.22).

[30] G. Ateniese, I. Bonacina, A. Faonio, N. Galesi, Proofs of space: when space is of the essence, in: International Conference on Security and Cryptography for Networks, Springer, Cham, 2014 [Google Scholar View in article].

[31] L. Lamport, R. Shostak, M. Pease, The byzantine general sproblem, ACMT Progr Lang. Sys(TOPLAS) 4 (3) (1982) 382−401.

[32] M. Castro, B. Liskov, Practical byzantine fault tolerance, OperSyst DesImplement (OSDI) 99 (1999) 173−186.

[33] Tender mint. <https://tendermint.readthedocs.io/en/master/> (accessed 05.11.22).

[34] M. Osadchuk, R. Oliynykov, Method of proof of work consensus algorithms comparison, PaДоⅢⅢ 198 (2019) 105–112 [Google Scholar] [CrossRef][Green Version].

[35] E. Buchman, Tendermint: byzantine fault tolerance in the age of blockchains, Ph.D. dissertation, Dept. Master Appl. Sci. Eng. Syst. Comput., Univ. Guelph, Guelph, ON, Can. (2016). Available from: https://doi.org/10.3390/app11146252.

[36] Bitshares, Delegated proof of stake. Available from: http://docs.bitshares.org/bitshares/dpos. (accessed 05.11.22).

[37] M. Pilkington, Blockchain technology: principles and applications (September 18, 2015), in: F. Xavier Olleros, M. Zhegu (Eds.), Research Handbook on Digital Transformations, Edward Elgar, 2016. Available at SSRN: https://ssrn.com/abstract = 2662660 (2016). [accessed 18th November 2022].

[38] Powerledger. <https://www.powerledger.io/> (accessed 24.05.22).

[39] J. Innerbichler, V. Damjanovic-Behrendt, Federated byzantine agreement to ensure trustworthiness of digital manufacturing platforms, in Proceedings of the 1st Workshop on Cryptocurrencies and Blockchains for Distributed Systems, Munich, Germany, 15 June 2018, pp. 111–116. [Google Scholar].

[40] L. Chen, L. Xu, N. Shah, Z. Gao, Y. Lu, W. Shi, On security analysis of proof-of-elapsed-time (PoET), in: P. Spirakis, P. Tsigas (Eds.), Lecture Notes in Computer Science, 10616, Springer, Cham, 2017. Stabilization, Safety, and Security of Distributed Systems. SSS 2017.

[41] J.P. Buntinx, What is proof of elapsed time? Available from: https://themerkle.com/what-isproof-of-elapsed-time/. (accessed 05.11.22).

[42] K. Karantias, A. Kiayias, D. Zindros, Proof-of-burn, International Conference on Financial Cryptography and Data Security, Springer, 2020, pp. 523–540. CrossRef Google Scholar.

[43] Hyperledger Architecture, Volume 1 <https://www.hyperledger.org/wp-content/uploads/2017/08/Hyperledger_Arch_WG_Paper_1_Consensus.pdf>.

[44] Intel Corporation, Saw tooth introduction. Available from: https://sawtooth.hyperledger.org/docs/core/releases/latest/introduction.html. (accessed 05.11.22).

[45] Y. Gilad, R. Hemo, S. Micali, G. Vlachos, N. Zeldovich, Algorand: scaling byzantine agreements for cryptocurrencies, in Proceedings of the 26th Symposium of Operations Systems Principles, 2017, pp. 51–68. https://dl.acm.org/doi/10.1145/3132747.3132757.

[46] A. Miller, A. Juels, E. Shi, B. Parno, J. Katz, Permacoin: repurposing bitcoin work for data preservation, in Proceedings of the IEEE Symposium on Security and Privacy, Berkeley, CA, USA, 18–21 May 2014, pp. 475–490. [Google Scholar].

[47] L. Bach, B. Mihaljevic, M. Zagar, Comparative analysis of blockchain consensus algorithms, in Proceedings of the 41st International Convention on Information and Communication Technology, Electronics and Microelectronics (MIPRO), Opatija, Croatia, 21–25 May 2018; pp. 1545–1550. [Google Scholar].

[48] M. Milutinovic, W. He, H. Wu, M. Kanwal, Proof of luck: an efficient blockchain consensus protocol, in Proceedings of the 1st Workshop on System Software for Trusted Execution, Trento, Italy, 12–16 December 2016, p. 2. [Google Scholar].

[49] E. Buchman, Tendermint: byzantine fault tolerance in the age of blockchains, Ph.D. Thesis, University of Guelph School of Engineering, Guelph, ON, Canada, 2016. [Google Scholar].

[50] Y. Chen, Proof of vote: a high-performance consensus protocol based on vote mechanism & consortium blockchain, in Proceedings of the IEEE 19th International Conference on High Performance Computing and Communications; IEEE 15th International Conference on Smart City; IEEE 3rd International Conference on Data Science and Systems (HPCC/SmartCity/DSS), Bangkok, Thailand, 18–20 December 2017, pp. 466–473. [Google Scholar].

[51] J. Blocki, H.S. Zhou, Designing proof of human-work puzzles for cryptocurrency and beyond, in Theory of Cryptography Conference, Springer, Berlin/Heidelberg, Germany, 2016, pp. 517–546. [Google Scholar].

[52] S. Namasudra, G.C. Deka, P. Johri, M. Hosseinpour, A.H. Gandomi, The revolution of Blockchain: State-of-the-art and research challenges, Arch. Comput. Meth. Eng. 28 (2020) 1497−1515 [Google Scholar] [CrossRef].

[53] D. Ongaro, J. Ousterhout, In search of an understandable consensus algorithm, in Proceedings of the USENIX Annual Technical Conference (USENIX ATC), 2014, pp. 305−320. <https://dl.acm.org/doi/10.5555/2643634.2643666>.

[54] M. Castro, B. Liskov, Practical Byzantine fault tolerance and proactive recovery, ACM Trans. Comput. Syst. 20 (2002) 398−461 [Google Scholar] [CrossRef].

[55] Ongaro, D.; Ousterhout, J. The Raft Consensus Algorithm; Stanford University: Stanford, CA, USA, 2015. [Google Scholar]

[56] Proof of proof. <https://medium.com/coinmonks/blockchain-consensus-algorithms-an-early-days-overview-2973f0cf49c6> (assessed 20.0323).

[57] Proof of believability. <https://www.btcwires.com/round-the-block/what-is-proof-of-believability/> (assessed 20.0323).

[58] D. Huang, X. Ma, S. Zhang, Performance analysis of the Raft consensus algorithm for private blockchains, IEEE Trans. Syst. Man. Cybern. Syst. 50 (2019) 172−181 [Google Scholar] [CrossRef][Green Version].

[59] S.M.H. Bamakan, A. Motavali, A.B. Bondarti, A survey of Blockchain consensus algorithms performance evaluation criteria, Expert. Syst. Appl. 154 (2020)113385 [Google Scholar] [CrossRef].

[60] V. Buterin, A next-generation smart contract and decentralized application platform, White Pap. 3 (2014) 1−36.

[61] T. Moran, I. Orlov, Proofs of space-time and rational proofs of storage, IACR Cryptol. ePrint Arch. 2016 (2016) 35 [Google Scholar].

[62] R.C. Merkle, A digital signature based on a conventional encryption functionin Proc. Conf. Theory Appl. Cryptograph. Techn. (1987) 369−378.

[63] G. Wood, Ethereum: a secure decentralised generalised transaction ledger, Ethereum, Zeughausgasse, Switzerland, Yellow Pap. 151 (2014) 1−32.

[64] <https://www.beebryte.com/news/> (assessed 20.0323)

[65] A.H. Elsheikh, S.W. Sharshir, M. Abd Elaziz, A.E. Kabeel, W. Guilan, Z. Haiou, Modeling of solar energy systems using artificial neural network: a comprehensive review, Sol. Energy 180 (2019) 622−639. ISSN 0038−092X. Available from: https://doi.org/10.1016/j.solener.2019.01.037.

[66] Solarcoin. <https://solarcoin.org/> (assessed 20.0323)

[67] A. Sircar, K. Yadav, K. Rayavarapu, N. Bist, H. Oza, Application of machine learning and artificial intelligence in oil and gas industry, Pet. Res. 6 (4) (2021) 379−391ISSN 2096−2495. Available from: https://doi.org/10.1016/j.ptlrs.2021.05.009.

[68] T. Mazhar, H.M. Irfan, S. Khan, I. Haq, I. Ullah, M. Iqbal, et al., Analysis of cyber security attacks and its solutions for the smart grid using machine learning and blockchain methods, Future Internet 15 (2023) 83. Available from: https://doi.org/10.3390/fi15020083.

[69] PSR and Kunumi (Brazil). From [CrossRef], 2019 (assessed 20.0323)

[70] Utilityx, McKinsey (United States). From [CrossRef], 2023 (assessed 20.0323)

[71] Energy theft and fraud reduction. Networked Energy Services. From [CrossRef], 2023 (assessed 20.0323)

[72] Harnessing the power of data: how machine learning is revolutionizing microgrid energy management, Grid-Scape. From [CrossRef], 2023 (assessed 20.0323)

[73] Verv. <https://verv.energy/> (assessed 20.0323).

[74] Energy web. <https://energyweb.org/blockchain/> (assessed 20.0323).

[75] Social Alpha Foundation, Blockchain for sustainable energy and climate in the Global south, use cases and opportunities. From [CrossRef], 2021 (assessed 20.0323).

6

Using artificial intelligence in education applications

Ramiz Salama, Fadi Al-Turjman

ARTIFICIAL INTELLIGENCE, SOFTWARE, AND INFORMATION SYSTEMS ENGINEERING DEPARTMENTS, RESEARCH CENTER FOR AI AND IOT, AI AND ROBOTICS INSTITUTE, NEAR EAST UNIVERSITY, NICOSIA, MERSIN10, TURKEY

6.1 Introduction

The use of technology in education has rapidly evolved in recent years, with the introduction of new tools and platforms that have the potential to transform the way we approach learning and teaching. One area that has gained significant attention is the integration of blockchain technology, artificial intelligence (AI), and big data into the educational system.

Blockchain technology, originally developed for the cryptocurrency industry, is a decentralized and secure way of storing and transferring data. In the context of education, blockchain can be used for a variety of purposes, such as creating secure and transparent records for grades, credentials, and transcripts.

AI, on the other hand, has the potential to personalize and optimize the learning experience for individual students. By analyzing data on students' learning preferences, progress, and performance, AI can provide personalized feedback and recommendations, adapt the curriculum to the needs of each student, and identify areas where additional support may be needed.

Big data, or the collection and analysis of large datasets, can also play a role in education by providing insights into various aspects of the educational process. For example, big data can be used to analyze student performance and identify trends and patterns that can inform curriculum design and resource allocation.

The integration of blockchain, AI, and big data into education has the potential to improve efficiency, fairness, and personalization in the educational system. However, there are also challenges to overcome, such as the need for appropriate infrastructure and the potential for data privacy concerns [1–6].

In this study, we aim to explore the current state of the use of blockchain, AI, and big data in education and to assess their potential impact on the educational system. To do so, we will conduct a literature review of previous research on the topic and analyze case studies of successful implementations of these technologies in education. We will also conduct

Computational Intelligence and Blockchain in Complex Systems. DOI: https://doi.org/10.1016/B978-0-443-13268-1.00012-1
© 2024 Elsevier Inc. All rights reserved, including those for text and data mining, AI training, and similar technologies.

interviews with educators and experts in the field to gather insights and perspectives on the challenges and opportunities of integrating blockchain, AI, and big data into education. Our findings will contribute to the understanding of the potential and limitations of using blockchain, AI, and big data in education and provide recommendations for future research and implementation.

6.2 Extent of past work

There has been a growing body of research on the use of blockchain, AI, and big data in education in recent years. In terms of blockchain, studies have focused on the potential benefits of using this technology for educational record-keeping and credentialing. The use of blockchain for creating secure and transparent records of grades, credentials, and transcripts has been examined in higher education. The study found that blockchain technology had the potential to improve the efficiency and fairness of the credentialing process, as well as to reduce the risk of fraud and errors. Other studies have also explored the use of blockchain for creating decentralized and secure platforms for online learning and for tracking and verifying the authenticity of educational resources.

AI has also been a topic of interest in the field of education, with studies focusing on its potential to personalize and optimize the learning experience for students. The use of AI-powered personalized learning platforms in primary and secondary education has been examined. The study found that these platforms had a positive impact on student learning outcomes and engagement and that they had the potential to address the needs of diverse learners. Other studies have also investigated the use of AI for providing personalized feedback and support to students and for identifying and addressing learning gaps.

In terms of big data, research has focused on the use of data analytics to improve various aspects of the educational process. The use of big data analytics in higher education to improve curriculum design and resource allocation has been examined. The study found that the use of big data had the potential to enhance the efficiency and effectiveness of the educational process by identifying trends and patterns in student performance and needs. Other studies have also explored the use of big data for predicting student performance and retention and for identifying best practices in teaching and learning.

Overall, the research on the use of blockchain, AI, and big data in education suggests that these technologies have the potential to bring significant benefits to the educational system, such as improved efficiency, fairness, and personalization. However, there are also challenges to overcome, such as the need for appropriate infrastructure and the potential for data privacy concerns [7−11].

6.3 Materials and methods

To explore the current state of the use of blockchain, AI, and big data in education and to assess their potential impact on the educational system, we conducted a literature review of previous research on the topic and analyzed case studies of successful implementations of these technologies in education. We also conducted interviews with educators and experts in the field to gather insights and perspectives on the challenges and opportunities of integrating blockchain, AI, and big data into education.

For the literature review, we searched for relevant articles and studies published in the last three years using a range of online databases, such as Google Scholar and the Education Resources Information Center. We used the keywords "blockchain," "artificial intelligence," "Big data," and "education" to identify relevant articles and studies. In total, we reviewed over 100 articles and studies, and we selected a sample of 15 that met our inclusion criteria, including a focus on the use of blockchain, AI, and big data in education and a publication date within the last three years. For the case studies, we identified a sample of five successful implementations of blockchain, AI, and big data in education. These case studies were selected based on their relevance to the research question and their demonstrated impact on the educational system. We gathered information on these case studies through online research, including articles, reports, and interviews with relevant stakeholders.

For the interviews, we conducted semistructured interviews with a sample of 10 educators and experts in the field of technology in education. The interviews were conducted via video conferencing and were recorded and transcribed for analysis. We used an interview guide to ensure consistency across interviews and to cover a range of topics, including the current state of the use of blockchain, AI, and big data in education, the benefits and challenges of implementing these technologies, and recommendations for future research and implementation. We analyzed the data from the literature review, case studies, and interviews using thematic analysis, a method that involves identifying and coding themes in the data. We used NVivo, a software tool for qualitative data analysis, to assist with the coding and analysis process [12−16].

One specific example of the use of blockchain in education that emerged from the literature and case studies was the use of blockchain for educational record-keeping and credentialing. A number of studies have examined the potential of using blockchain to create secure and transparent records of grades, credentials, and transcripts. These studies have found that blockchain technology can provide a decentralized and secure way of storing and transferring data, reducing the risk of errors and fraud and improving the efficiency and fairness of the credentialing process. In terms of the use of AI in education, the literature and case studies highlighted a number of potential benefits and challenges. On the one hand, the use of a powered personalized learning platform has been shown to have a positive impact on student learning outcomes and engagement. These platforms can provide customized feedback and support to students, adapting the curriculum to the needs and preferences of each student, and can address the needs of diverse learners. On the other hand, there are also challenges to the implementation of AI in education, such as the need for appropriate infrastructure and the potential for bias in the algorithms used. The use of big data in education has also been the subject of a number of studies, with a focus on the use of data analytics to improve various aspects of the educational process. These studies have found that the use of big data has the potential to enhance the efficiency and effectiveness of the educational process by identifying trends and patterns in student performance and needs, as well as by informing the design of curriculum and the allocation of resources. However, there are also challenges to the use of big data in education, such as the need for appropriate infrastructure and the potential for data privacy concerns.

In addition to the findings from the literature and case studies, the interviews with educators and experts in the field provided further insights and perspectives on the use of blockchain, AI, and big data in education. These interviews confirmed the potential benefits and challenges of these technologies, while also highlighting the need for more empirical research to assess their impact and the importance of ethical considerations in their implementation [17–23].

Overall, the results of the study suggest that the use of blockchain, AI, and big data in education has the potential to bring significant benefits to the educational system, but there are also challenges to overcome. To address these challenges and maximize the potential of these technologies, the study recommends a number of actions for future research and implementation, including the need for more empirical research and the consideration of ethical and social implications.

6.4 Result and discussion

The results of the study suggest that the use of blockchain, AI, and big data in education has the potential to bring significant benefits to the educational system, such as improved efficiency, fairness, and personalization. One of the main benefits identified in the literature and case studies was the potential of these technologies to improve the efficiency of the educational process. For example, the use of blockchain for educational record-keeping and credentialing can reduce the need for manual processes and reduce the risk of errors and fraud. The use of AI-powered personalized learning platforms can also optimize the learning experience for individual students, reducing the need for one-size-fits-all approaches and increasing the efficiency of the teaching process. The use of big data analytics can also inform the design of curriculum and the allocation of resources, leading to more efficient and effective use of resources.

Another benefit identified was the potential of these technologies to improve fairness in education. For example, the use of blockchain for educational record-keeping and credentialing can provide a transparent and secure way of storing and transferring data, reducing the risk of discrimination and bias. The use of AI-powered personalized learning platforms can also address the needs of diverse learners, ensuring that all students have access to an equitable learning experience. The use of big data analytics can also identify and address disparities in student performance and access to resources, leading to more equitable outcomes.

A third benefit identified was the potential of these technologies to personalize the learning experience for students. The use of AI-powered personalized learning platforms can provide customized feedback and support to students, adapting the curriculum to the needs and preferences of each student. The use of big data analytics can also inform the design of personalized learning paths and interventions, leading to more tailored and effective learning experiences.

However, the results of the study also highlighted a number of challenges to the implementation of these technologies in education. One challenge identified was the need for appropriate infrastructure to support the use of these technologies. This includes the need for robust and secure networks, as well as the need for trained personnel to manage and maintain the systems. Another challenge was the potential for data privacy concerns, with the need to ensure that personal data is collected, stored, and used in a responsible and ethical manner.

One specific example of the use of blockchain in education that emerged from the literature and case studies was the use of blockchain for educational record-keeping and credentialing. A number of studies have examined the potential of using blockchain to create secure and transparent records of grades, credentials, and transcripts. These studies have found that blockchain technology can provide a decentralized and secure way of storing and transferring data, reducing the risk of errors and fraud and improving the efficiency and fairness of the credentialing process. In terms of the use of AI in education, the literature and case studies highlighted a number of potential benefits and challenges. On the one hand, the use of AI-powered personalized learning platforms has been shown to have a positive impact on student learning outcomes and engagement. These platforms can provide customized feedback and support to students, adapting the curriculum to the needs and preferences of each student, and can address the needs of diverse learners. On the other hand, there are also challenges to the implementation of AI in education, such as the need for appropriate infrastructure and the potential for bias in the algorithms used. The use of big data in education has also been the subject of a number of studies, with a focus on the use of data analytics to improve various aspects of the educational process. These studies have found that the use of big data has the potential to enhance the efficiency and effectiveness of the educational process by identifying trends and patterns in student performance and needs, as well as by informing the design of curriculum and the allocation of resources. However, there are also challenges to the use of big data in education, such as the need for appropriate infrastructure and the potential for data privacy concerns.

In addition to the findings from the literature and case studies, the interviews with educators and experts in the field provided further insights and perspectives on the use of blockchain, AI, and big data in education. These interviews confirmed the potential benefits and challenges of these technologies, as well as highlighting the need for more empirical research to assess their impact and the importance of ethical considerations in their implementation [24−29].

Overall, the results of the study suggest that the use of blockchain, AI, and big data in education has the potential to bring significant benefits to the educational system, but there are also challenges to overcome. To address these challenges and maximize the potential of these technologies, the study recommends a number of actions for future research and implementation, including the need for more empirical research and the consideration of ethical and social implications.

6.5 Conclusion

In conclusion, the integration of blockchain technology, AI, and big data into the educational system has the potential to revolutionize the way we approach learning and teaching. These technologies have the potential to improve efficiency, fairness, and personalization in the educational system, by providing secure and transparent record-keeping, personalizing the learning experience for students, and informing the design of curriculum and the allocation of resources. However, the implementation of these technologies in education is not without challenges. There is a need for appropriate infrastructure to support their use, as well as for careful consideration of data privacy concerns. There is also a need for more empirical research to assess the impact of these technologies on student learning outcomes and the teaching process, as well as to identify best practices for their implementation.

Overall, the use of blockchain, AI, and big data in education has the potential to bring significant benefits, but it is important to carefully consider the challenges and implications of their use. Future research and implementation should aim to address these challenges and maximize the potential of these technologies to enhance the educational system.

References

[1] R.G.J. Pablo, D.P. Roberto, S.U. Victor, G.R. Isabel, C. Paul, O.R. Elizabeth, Big data in the healthcare system: a synergy with artificial intelligence and blockchain technology, Journal of Integrative Bioinformatics 19 (1) (2022).

[2] J. Park, From big data to blockchain: promises and challenges of an all-encompassing technology in education, Digital Communication and Learning (2022) 383−397.

[3] M. Zhou, C. Matsika, T.G. Zhou, W.I. Chawarura, Artificial intelligence and blockchain as disruptive technologies in adolescent lives, Impact and Role of Digital Technologies in Adolescent Lives, IGI Global, 2022, pp. 243−254.

[4] J. Jang, S. Kyun, An innovative career management platform empowered by AI, big data, and blockchain technologies: focusing on female engineers, Webology 19 (1) (2022) 4317−4334.

[5] R. Bucea-Manea-Țoniş, V. Kuleto, S.C.D. Gudei, C. Lianu, C. Lianu, M.P. Ilić, et al., Artificial Intelligence potential in higher education institutions enhanced learning environment in Romania and Serbia, Sustainability 14 (10) (2022) 5842.

[6] B.R. Rajagopal, B. Anjanadevi, M. Tahreem, S. Kumar, M. Debnath, K. Tongkachok, Comparative analysis of blockchain technology and artificial intelligence and its impact on open issues of automation in workplace, in 2022 2nd International Conference on Advance Computing and Innovative Technologies in Engineering (ICACITE), IEEE, 2022, pp. 288−292.

[7] J. Soldatos, D. Kyriazis, Big data and artificial intelligence in digital finance: increasing personalization and trust in digital finance using big data and AI, 2022.

[8] P. Sharma, J. Shah, R. Patel, Artificial intelligence framework for MSME sectors with focus on design and manufacturing industries, Mater. Today: Proc. (2022).

[9] Y. Ma, Accounting talent training reform in the era of artificial intelligence, 4th International Seminar on Education Research and Social Science (ISERSS 2021), Atlantis Press, 2022, pp. 282−286. January.

[10] F. Muheidat, D. Patel, S. Tammisetty, A.T. Lo'ai, M. Tawalbeh, Emerging concepts using blockchain and big data, Procedia Comput. Sci. 198 (2022) 15−22.

[11] L.K. Sahu, P.K. Vyas, V. Soni, A. Deshpande, Survey of recent studies on healthcare technologies and computational intelligence approaches and their applications, Computational Intelligence and Applications for Pandemics and Healthcare, IGI Global, 2022, pp. 282−307.

[12] V. Kuleto, R. Bucea-Manea-Ţoniş, R. Bucea-Manea-Ţoniş, M.P. Ilić, O.M. Martins, M. Ranković, et al., The potential of blockchain technology in higher education as perceived by students in Serbia, Romania, and Portugal, Sustainability 14 (2) (2022) 749.

[13] A. Kuzior, M. Sira, A bibliometric analysis of blockchain technology research using VOSviewer, Sustainability 14 (13) (2022) 8206.

[14] M. El Samad, S. El Nemar, H. El-Chaarani, Blockchain and big data for a smart healthcare model, Handbook of Research on Artificial Intelligence and Knowledge Management in Asia's Digital Economy, IGI Global, 2023, pp. 64−80.

[15] C. Chaka, Fourth industrial revolution—a review of applications, prospects, and challenges for artificial intelligence, robotics and blockchain in higher education, Res. Pract. Technol. Enhanced Learn. (2023) 18.

[16] J. Zhang, S. Haleem, Application of blockchain technology in the construction of MOOC digital communication platform, International Conference on Smart Technologies and Systems for Internet of Things, Springer, Singapore, 2023, pp. 564−573.

[17] Y. Liu, M. Chen, The knowledge structure and development trend in artificial intelligence based on latent feature topic model, IEEE Trans. Eng. Manage (2023).

[18] W. Liu, Research on the innovation and application of big data in higher education. In Third International Conference on Intelligent Computing and Human-Computer Interaction (ICHCI 2022), Vol. 12509, SPIE, 2023, pp. 259−264.

[19] S. Pu, J.S.L. Lam, The benefits of blockchain for digital certificates: a multiple case study analysis, Technology in Society 72 (2023) 102176.

[20] N. Su, Research on big data empower epidemic governance based on knowledge map, Proceedings of the World Conference on Intelligent and 3-D Technologies (WCI3DT 2022), Springer, Singapore, 2023, pp. 557−567.

[21] M. Andronie, G. Lăzăroiu, O.L. Karabolevski, R. Ştefănescu, I. Hurloiu, A. Dijmărescu, et al., Remote big data management tools, sensing and computing technologies, and visual perception and environment mapping algorithms in the internet of robotic things, Electronics 12 (1) (2023) 22.

[22] M.R.H. Polas, B. Ahamed, M.M. Rana, Artificial intelligence and blockchain technology in the 4.0 IR metaverse era: implications, opportunities, and future directions, Strategies and Opportunities for Technology in the Metaverse World, IGI Global, 2023, pp. 13−33.

[23] K.G. NALBANT, S. AYDIN, Development and transformation in digital marketing and branding with artificial intelligence and digital technologies dynamics in the metaverse universe, Journal of Metaverse 3 (1) (2023) 9−18.

[24] P. Tomar, H. Bhardwaj, U. Sharma, A. Sakalle, A. Bhardwaj, Transformation of higher education system using blockchain technology, Applications of Blockchain and Big Iot Systems, Apple Academic Press, 2023, pp. 499−524.

[25] M. Aseeri, K. Kang, Organisational culture and big data socio-technical systems on strategic decision making: case of Saudi Arabian higher education, Educat. Inform. Technol. (2023) 1−26.

[26] H. Zhang, S. Lee, Y. Lu, X. Yu, H. Lu, A survey on big data technologies and their applications to the metaverse: past, current and future, Mathematics 11 (1) (2023) 96.

[27]　A. Sasikumar, S. Vairavasundaram, K. Kotecha, V. Indragandhi, L. Ravi, G. Selvachandran, et al., Blockchain-based trust mechanism for digital twin empowered industrial internet of things, Fut. Gen. Comput. Syst. 141 (2023) 16−27.

[28]　K.P. Rao, S. Manvi, Survey on electronic health record management using amalgamation of artificial intelligence and blockchain technologies, Acta Informatica Pragensia 12 (1) (2023).

[29]　K. Lyytinen, H. Topi, J. Tang, MaCuDE IS task force phase II report: views of industry leaders on big data analytics and AI, Commun. Assoc. Inform. Syst. 52 (1) (2023) 18.

7

Performance measurements of 12 different machine learning algorithms that make personalized psoriasis treatment recommendations with a database of psoriasis patients responding to treatment

Hamit Altıparmak[1], Serkan Yazıcı[2], İzel Yılmaz[2], Emel Bülbül Başkan[2], Haluk Barbaros Oral[2], Kenan Aydoğan[2], Şehime Gulsun Temel[3], Mahmut Çerkez Ergören[4,5], Fadi Al-Turjman[6]

[1]DEPARTMENT OF COMPUTER ENGINEERING, NEAR EAST UNIVERSITY, NICOSIA, CYPRUS
[2]DEPARTMENT OF DERMATOLOGY, BURSA ULUDAG UNIVERSITY, NILÜFER, BURSA, TURKEY
[3]DEPARTMENT OF MEDICAL GENETICS, BURSA ULUDAG UNIVERSITY, NILÜFER, BURSA, TURKEY [4]DEPARTMENT OF MEDICAL GENETICS, NEAR EAST UNIVERSITY, NICOSIA, CYPRUS
[5]DESAM RESEARCH INSTITUTE, NEAR EAST UNIVERSITY, NICOSIA, CYPRUS [6]ARTIFICIAL INTELLIGENCE, SOFTWARE, AND INFORMATION SYSTEMS ENGINEERING DEPARTMENTS, RESEARCH CENTER FOR AI AND IOT, AI AND ROBOTICS INSTITUTE, NEAR EAST UNIVERSITY, NICOSIA, MERSIN10, TURKEY

7.1 Introduction and literature review

Autoimmune diseases are still a mystery to science. Even today, we still do not know the reasons why our immune system attacks the cells in our body. Such diseases are serious diseases such as multiple sclerosis, Crohn's disease, and rheumatoid arthritis. Genetic predisposition is a determining factor in autoimmune diseases, although it is also necessary to address environmental factors in many cases. The quality of life of people living with the daily reality of these diseases is greatly reduced.

Computational Intelligence and Blockchain in Complex Systems. DOI: https://doi.org/10.1016/B978-0-443-13268-1.00014-5
© 2024 Elsevier Inc. All rights are reserved, including those for text and data mining, AI training, and similar technologies.

Autoimmune diseases are those that tend to be chronic and can affect various parts of the body. An example of this is psoriasis disease, which we consider in this article. First of all, it is very important to remember that genes play an important role in these diseases. The interaction between the environment and some genes determines the occurrence of these situations. However, this relationship is not 100% directly proportional. This theory is based on intestinal permeability. Abnormalities in the gut allow some antigens to pass from the gut into the bloodstream. Thus, the response of the immune system changes and these antigens are perceived by some organs as "enemy tissues," which is one of the main causes of these autoimmune diseases.

We can define autoimmune diseases in two classes in general. These are systematic diseases and regional syndromes. Systematic diseases can attack multiple organs, not just one organ. Examples of these are celiac disease and amyotrophic lateral sclerosis. These regional syndromes are especially diseases of a single tissue. tissue can be dermatological, hematological, or endocrinological. Diseases among them are Hashimoto's thyroid and colitis. Many autoimmune diseases have no cure.

Psoriasis is a chronic disease. It is seen in approximately 1%−3% of the world. Although it often starts in the thirties, it can be seen from birth. In 30% of cases, there is a family history. In psoriasis, antigens are created by cells in the skin. These antigens activate the immune system. The activated cells return to the skin and cause cell proliferation in the skin and the formation of plaques specific to psoriasis. In other words, psoriasis is a disease developed by the body against its own tissues. Normally, the skin cell's cycle time is about 28 days, while in psoriasis, this period can decrease to 3−4 days. Because the cells cannot fully mature, they cannot be poured and accumulate on top of each other without us noticing. The cause of psoriasis is not fully known. However, there are strong indications that it is genetic. Figs. 7−1 and 7−2 show skin wounds caused by psoriasis.

The most important factor that triggers the disease is the stress factor. According to research, it is known that the immune system is stimulated and this causes skin cells to grow. The disease is diagnosed mostly with the appearance of skin lesions. Having a family

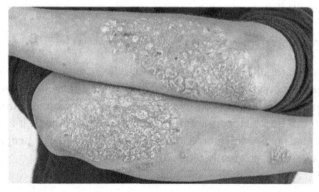

FIGURE 7−1 Psoriasis on the arms.

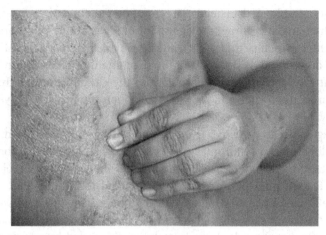

FIGURE 7–2 Psoriasis all over the body.

history of psoriasis helps with diagnosis. In suspicious cases, a skin biopsy is performed. In some cases, obesity, hypertension, and hyperlipidemia may accompany the picture.

The main factors that trigger psoriasis disease are:

- Hormonal changes such as infection, pregnancy, and menopause.
- Psychological problems and stress.
- Mechanical traumas that will cause injury such as sunburn, sac, and waxing.
- Smoking and alcohol consumption.
- Throat infection called beta microbe.
- Powerful painkillers and heart and malaria medications.
- Irregular nutrition.
- Dry and cold air.

Artificial intelligence (AI) practices in the detection of autoimmune diseases have started to increase today. The detection of diseases can be done faster with AI applications. Many AI assistants, which are used by nurses for preliminary detection when doctors are not available, are used today. The ability of AI algorithms to imitate human abilities makes people's jobs easier.

Nowadays, AI algorithms have been developed, which have the ability to solve all problems. It is surprising to scientists that AI detects genetic diseases in a very short time and early. While the technology developed in the USA enables the detection of diseases such as autism and Alzheimer's at a very early age, it makes it possible to easily understand even rare syndromes. It is useful to highlight the difference between the two terms that are frequently used to understand how AI accomplishes this. These are machine learning and AI. Machine learning refers to an algorithm capable of learning. This algorithm, also called deep learning, learns thousands of times in a given subject by identifying them successively. For example, to teach the computer about four legs, fur, etc. of a cat, thousands of cat pictures are being uploaded instead. The computer defines a new feature from every cat, and just like humans, over time, they get a lot of ideas about variations of the cat species. In this way, he can detect that a cat with hair or rashes has a problem compared to others. AI, on the other hand, is the state of the machine that takes action with what it has learned. If the software determines the problem of the cat and decides that the treatment is required, it informs the owner and arranges an appointment with the veterinarian, then AI comes into play.

Face2Gene, originating in America, is an AI application that uses the method in the cat sample to detect diseases and syndromes. Using facial recognition technology to understand different syndromes, the creators of Face2Gene are also the team that developed Facebook's facial recognition feature from photos. When you upload the photos you want to be diagnosed to the Face2Gene application, it starts to compare with thousands of photos in the database. It brings a list of diagnoses that can be made by comparing data such as how much the eyes are tilted to the side, how deep the eyelid is, and how far below the ears are. Deep learning technology, called The Right Eye Autism Test, enables diagnosis even for 12-month-old babies. The Right Eye detects the eye movements of infants with the help of infrared, watching the split screen. On the one half of the screen are people, and on the other, there are abstract geometric shapes. Infants without autism are expected to focus on human faces instead of abstract shapes at that age. The system was tried on more than 400 children in this way and made the correct diagnosis of 86%. There are numerous studies in the literature to assist in the diagnosis and diagnosis of many different diseases. In the diagnosis of a disease, the symptoms of which are visible and illustrated, we can come across many studies in which machine learning methods have been applied successfully.

Many studies in the literature have AI-assisted health solutions. If we give an example of these, the authors were able to classify skin diseases with a fuzzy logic method with 90.1% success. In this study, the algorithm made with images from red, green and blue space was tested. Doctors were consulted to develop the algorithm and establish the information system [1]. Fuzzy logic systems consist of fuzzy sets and subsets. In classical logic, an element is included or not included in a cluster, while in fuzzy logic, an element can be included in more than one cluster with a degree of membership. In fuzzy sets, the degree of membership of the elements can be infinite between zero and one.

In another study in the literature, the authors were able to detect cancerous regions in cancerous tissues by image processing method. In this study, with the algorithm developed biopsy images containing cancerous regions, they were able to convert the cancerous areas to white and healthy areas to black with full accuracy. Only with the image processing algorithm, images could reach the result in six stages. Image processing is used to convert the image to digital form. The visuals that are converted into digital form are separated into their layers and they help us get the colors we want [2].

AI has helped many studies to diagnose diabetes. The authors developed an expert system consisting of 280 rules using the expert systems method in the study named "Rule-Based Intelligent Diabetes Diagnosis System." This expert system asks 8 questions to the user and can make a diagnosis by looking for 280 answers in return. In this study, the authors can diagnose type1 diabetes, type 2 diabetes, risk, healthy, and pregnant diabetes, or do more tests [3].

AI does not only help people in the field of health. In the article titled "Development of a Vision-Based Feral Vertebrate Identifier Using Fuzzy Type II," the author classified vertebrate animals with a type 2 fuzzy logic algorithm. The purpose of this classification has been advocated in order to prevent wild animals from consuming water stocks in their habitats [4].

Yoldaş et al. created a diagnostic model using an artificial neural network (ANN) in the diagnosis of acute appendicitis (AA), 156 patients (132 correct, 24 misdiagnosed) diagnosed with AA between 2009 and 2010 were studied. The parameters used for ANN in this study are gender, pain sensitivity, pain localization, pain in the lower right quadrant, body temperature, avoidance, intestinal sounds, vomiting, and rebound phenomenon. In addition, the number of WBC (white sphere number) has been added to the parameters. In the ANN study, the SPSS 19 method was used as a model and the classification was created by comparing it to the standard models [5].

The correct evaluation rate of endodontists was 76%, ANN was 96%, and the reliability rate in the results was 64.16%−87.54% by the endodontists and 90.57%−101.43% by the ANN. Finally, the accuracy rate of ANN was found to be higher than the endodontics in the measurements made with the steroid microscope and shed light for future studies [6].

In the study by Colak et al. of using different ANN models in the prediction of coronary artery disease, 8 different algorithms were used for ANN. In the retrospective case-control study of ANN models, 124 coronary artery patients diagnosed with angiography and 113 people with normal coronary arteries were used [7].

In the study of ANN using hand and wrist radiography in patients with arthritis performed by Duryea et al., the parts determined as localization are five of the carpometacarpal joints, radiocarpal joint, and scaphocapitate joint. The algorithm used in the software of ANN was trained by introducing the joints digitally and manually. Joint localizations were compared with manual measurements of radiologists [8].

In the ANN study, conducted by Çolak et al., for the prediction of atherosclerosis (ATS), 20 clinical parameters, consisting of 10 patients with ATS in their radial arteries and 15 patients that were not detected between June 2003 and November 2003, were obtained. In the first stage, 60% of the total data was used for education [9].

In Kuchimov's study of classifying gait disturbance through ANN, the neural network is trained to classify four different gait patterns. Supervised learning methods and error feedback algorithms are used to train multilayer sensors. In this study, an average of 77% classification success was achieved in distinguishing between normal and three different abnormal walking patterns. Up to 96% higher success was achieved in the classification of normal and abnormal gait patterns into two groups [10].

Authors of Ref. [11] classified healthy and diseased tissues using images obtained with a thermal handheld imaging device. The authors obtained 78.3% accuracy with the hybrid machine learning method.

Paper [12] applied multiple machine learning algorithms for the dataset of 450 patients in this study. In the present study, low, intermediate, and high-risk patients were classified.

The literature review shows us that AI is used in many fields. When we look at the literature review in the field of health, it is seen that AI methods are used in the detection of many different diseases. In the literature, an AI-supported system has not been seen regarding the methods that should be applied specifically to psoriasis patients. In this respect, the novelty of this study is an AI system that recommends personalized treatment.

7.2 Materials and methods

In this study, the dataset created to give personalized treatment advice to psoriasis patients was trained with 12 different machine learning algorithms. All machine learning algorithms presented in this study are coded in Anaconda cloud environment and Jupyter interactive computing notebook module. Python language was used as the coding language. Python is a fast and high-level programming language. Python language is frequently preferred in data processing and AI applications. Of the 100-sample dataset used in this study, 70% was used for the training set and 30% for the test set. Twelve different machine learning algorithms used in this article are described below.

7.2.1 Logistic regression

Logistic regression analysis is one of the statistical methods used to determine the relationship between the response variable and the explanatory variables when the response variable is binary or multinomial and the explanatory variables are categorical, sequential, or continuous [13].

7.2.2 Gaussian naive Bayes

The classifier can also be thought of as a Bayesian network where each attribute is conditionally independent from each other and the concept to be learned is conditionally dependent on all these attributes [14]. Naive Bayes classification is in the subclass of guided learning in machine learning. More precisely, it is evident which classes (clusters) require classification and to which classes the sample data belong.

7.2.3 *K*-Nearest neighbors

K-nearest neighbor (KNN) is one of the algorithms used for classification and regression in supervised learning. It is considered the simplest machine learning algorithm. Unlike other supervised learning algorithms, it does not have a training phase. With KNN, basically, the closest points to the new point are searched. K represents the amount of nearest neighbors of the unknown point. We choose k quantities (usually an odd number) of the algorithm to predict the results. In pattern recognition, the nearest neighbor algorithm (KNN) is a nonparametric method used for classification and regression [15]. In both cases, the input consists of the k closest training examples in the feature space. The output depends on whether the kNN will be used for classification or regression.

7.2.4 Support vector classification

The purpose of support vector classification is to create a model that assigns new invisible objects to a specific category. It tries to do this by creating a linear division of the feature space into two categories. It places a category "above" or "below" in the multiple separation plane, based on features in new unseen objects. This would be an example of a nonprobabilistic linear classifier. It is unlikely because the properties of new objects determine their exact location in the property space [16].

7.2.5 Radial basis function

In the field of mathematical modeling, a radial basis function (RBF) network is an ANN that uses RBFs as activation functions. The output of the network is a linear combination of the RBFs of the inputs and the neuron parameters [17].

7.2.6 Artificial neural network

ANN are computer systems developed with the aim of automatically performing the abilities of the human brain, such as deriving new information and creating and discovering new information through learning, without any help [15].

7.2.7 Cart algorithm

Classification and regression tree can work on numeric and nominal values. There are three basic steps in the algorithm.

- Creating maximum trees.
- To determine the depth of the tree.
- Applying test data to the tree.

The main goal in generating the maximum tree is to achieve the purest, best-split state. Two algorithms are used for this. These are GINI and Twoing algorithms. If we look at the GINI algorithm first, the goal is to get the largest dataset at each step. Thus, the best splitting condition will be obtained. In addition, after the division, the part that we are not interested in is isolated [18].

7.2.8 Random forest

The feature of the random forest model is that it gives us how important the attributes are. The significance of an attribute is related to how much that attribute contributes to the explanation of the variance in the dependent variable [19]. We can give the random forest algorithm x number of attributes and ask it to choose the y most useful ones, and if we want, we can use this information in any other model we want.

7.2.9 Gradient boosting machines

Boosting is a method of transforming weak learners into strong learners. It does this incrementally with iterations. The difference between boosting algorithms is often in how weak learners identify their shortcomings. Initially, the initial leaf is created in gradient boosting. Afterward, new trees are created by taking into account the estimation errors. This situation continues until the number of trees is decided or no further improvement can be made from the model [20].

7.2.10 XGBoost

It is formed by the combination of gradient descent and boosting concepts. XGBoost is faster than other collective learning models. It is written in C++ on the basis of XGBoost and works on the principle of parallel computation. This feature makes it the most useful model in large datasets. XGBoost often performs better than other collective learning models. XGBoost contains many hyperparameters to be optimized [21]. This means you have more chances to improve the model.

7.2.11 LightGBM

It is a decision tree-based learning algorithm and its most important advantages can be listed as its "high speed," which is also the reason for the word Light, its ability to process large datasets, less memory required to run the code, and higher accuracy in results [22].

7.2.12 CatBoost

CatBoost is a fast, scalable, high-performance gradient boosting library for decision tree used for classification and regression. It supports central processing unit and graphical processing unit computing. It is a category-based boost machine [23].

7.3 Experimental results

Before the experimental results, Table 7−1 shows the statistical results of the dataset used in this study. The mean and standard deviation values are presented for our eight input and output values. The mean is an "average" number divided by the sum of all data points in our dataset divided by the total data point. Standard deviation is the method that measures the closeness and agreement of observations in a dataset to each other. It allows us to understand how the numbers in the data group spread according to the arithmetic mean.

In this study, 12 different machine learning algorithms were applied to the dataset we created, presented in Table 7−1. The results obtained with all these algorithms are listed in Table 7−2. The results obtained for 12 different machine learning algorithms created with the Python programming language were obtained by testing many different parameters. All

Table 7–1   Mean and standard deviation values of input and output values of the dataset.

Attributes	Mean (average)	Standard deviation
Start age	0.514	0.376056
Type	0.290	0.456048
Family history	0.100	0.301511
Artrit	0.470	0.501614
Pitting	0.430	0.497570
Smoking	0.240	0.429235
Stress	0.270	0.446196
Gender	0.520	0.502117
Treatment (output)	1.270	0.736563

Table 7–2   Success metric criteria for model selection.

Method	Accuracy	Precision	Recall	F-1 score
Logistic regression	0,58	0,48	0,58	0,53
Gaussian naive Bayes	0,60	0,57	0,60	0,58
K-nearest neighbors	0,55	0,65	0,55	0,58
Support vector classification (SVC)	0,63	0,54	0,63	0,57
Radial basis function (RBF)	0,63	0,54	0,63	0,57
Artificial neural network (ANN)	0,58	0,35	0,59	0,44
Cart algorithm	0,64	0,54	0,50	0,50
Random forest	0,63	0,54	0,63	0,57
Gradient boosting machines	0,43	0,42	0,43	0,43
XGBoost	0,50	0,53	0,50	0,51
LightGBM	0,53	0,47	0,53	0,49
CatBoost	0,50	0,45	0,50	0,47

algorithms showed close success on average. In proportion to this, the training times of all algorithms are similar on average. There is no need for normalization in the dataset.

Accuracy, precision, recall, and F-1 score were used as success measurement metrics in this study. Accuracy is a metric that is widely used to measure the success of a model but does not appear to be sufficient on its own. The accuracy value is calculated by the ratio of the areas that we predict correctly in the model to the total dataset. Model accuracy alone is not sufficient, especially in unbiased datasets that are not evenly distributed. In some cases, we do not want false-negative results. Therefore, we should evaluate the results of other metrics together. Precision, on the other hand, shows how many of the values we estimated as positive are actually positive. The precision value is especially important when the cost of false-positive estimation is high. Recall, on the other hand, is a metric that shows how much of the operations we estimate as Positive. The F-1 score value shows us the harmonic average of precision and sensitivity values.

7.4 Conclusion and future work

Psoriasis is a chronic skin disorder that causes flakes and sores on the skin that the body develops against its own tissues. On average, two out of every 100 people in the world are thought to have psoriasis. The cure rate for psoriasis is very low. That is why the right treatment is so important. With the right treatment, there may be a chance to get rid of psoriasis, which has a low recovery rate. Treatment for psoriasis is individualized. Each treatment should be carried out individually. No AI model has been found in the literature that offers personalized treatment for psoriasis. The statement problem in this study was the creation of a system that advises psoriasis patients on which treatment method they should use. 70% of the dataset was used for training all machine learning algorithms presented in this study. To determine the accuracy of this study, 30% test data was separated from the dataset. In this study, when 12 different machine learning algorithms applied to the dataset were compared, the highest accuracy was obtained with the customer analysis and research tool (CART) algorithm at 64%. The next best accuracy of 63% was obtained with software capability verification, RBF, and Random Forest algorithms. All machine learning algorithms used in this study and the obtained accuracy, precision, recall, and F-1 score results are presented in Table 7.2. In this study, the lowest accuracy was obtained with the gradient boosting machines algorithm. 43% accuracy was achieved with the gradient boosting machines algorithm. The aim of presenting this study is not to achieve high accuracy, but to contribute to the literature on an incomplete subject. For this purpose, our study has shown that a highly successful system can be established with much more data in the future.

References

[1] I.J. Bush et al., Integrated artificial intelligence algorithm for skin detection, in: ITM Web of Conferences, EDP Sciences, 2018, p. 02004.

[2] H. Altiparmak, F.V. Nurçin, Segmentation of microscopic breast cancer images for cancer detection, in: Proceedings of the 2019 8th International Conference on Software and Computer Applications, 2019, pp. 268–271.

[3] E. Imanov, H. Altiparmak, G.E. Imanova, Rule based intelligent diabetes diagnosis system, in: International Conference on Theory and Applications of Fuzzy Systems and Soft Computing. Springer, Cham, 2018, pp. 137–145.

[4] H. Altiparmak, Development of a vision-based feral vertebrate identifier using fuzzy type II, in: International Conference on Theory and Application of Soft Computing, Computing with Words and Perceptions. Springer, Cham, 2019, pp. 479–486.

[5] Ömer Yoldaş, Mesut Tez, Turgut Karaca, Artificial neural networks in the diagnosis of acute appendicitis, Am. J. Emerg. Med. 30 (7) (2012) 1245–1247.

[6] Mohammad Ali Saghiri, et al., The reliability of artificial neural network in locating minor apical foramen: a cadaver study, J. Endod. 38 (8) (2012) 1130–1134.

[7] M.Cengiz Çolak, et al., Predicting coronary artery disease using different artificial neural network models/ Koroner arter hastaliginin degisik yapay sinir agi modelleri ile tahmini, Anadulu Kardiyol. Dergisi: AKD 8 (4) (2008) 249.

[8] J. Duryea, S. Zaim, F. Wolfe, Neural network based automated algorithm to identify joint locations on hand/wrist radiographs for arthritis assessment, Med. Phys. 29 (3) (2002) 403–411.

[9] Cemil Çolak, M.C. Çolak, M.A. Atici, Ateroskleroz'un tahmini için bir yapay sinir ağı, Ank. Üniversitesi Tıp Fakültesi Mecm. 58 (04) (2005) 159–162.

[10] Y.ücel Gönül, et al., Yapay sinir ağları ve klinik araştırmalarda kullanımı, Genel Tip. Derg. 25 (2015) 3.

[11] S. Umapathy, et al. Automated segmentation and classification of psoriasis hand thermal images using machine learning algorithm, in: Proceedings of the International e-Conference on Intelligent Systems and Signal Processing. Springer, Singapore, 2022, pp. 487–496.

[12] H. Lejla, et al. Machine learning techniques for prediction of psoriatic arthritis development in patients with psoriasis, in: International Conference on Medical and Biological Engineering. Springer, Cham, 2021, pp. 208–216.

[13] L. Ali, S.U. Khan, N.A. Golilarz, I. Yakubu, I. Qasim, A. Noor, et al., A feature-driven decision support system for heart failure prediction based on statistical model and Gaussian naive Bayes, Computational Math. Methods Med. (2019). Available from: https://doi.org/10.1155/2019/6314328.

[14] I.L. Kambi Beli, C. Guo, Enhancing face identification using local binary patterns and k-nearest neighbors, J. Imaging 3 (3) (2017) 37. Available from: https://doi.org/10.3390/jimaging3030037.

[15] H. Altıparmak, R. Salama, H. Gökçekus, D.U. Ozsahin, Predict future climate change using artificial neural networks, Application Multi-Criteria Decis. Anal. Environ. Civ. Eng. (2021) 57–63. Available from: https://doi.org/10.1007/978-3-030-64765-0_9.

[16] Z. Hao, H. Ge, T. Gu, Automatic image annotation based on particle swarm optimization and support vector clustering, Math. Probl. Eng. (2017). Available from: https://doi.org/10.1155/2017/8493267.

[17] A. Helwan, J.B. Idoko, R.H. Abiyev, Machine learning techniques for classification of breast tissue, Procedia Comput. Sci. 120 (2017) 402–410. Available from: https://doi.org/10.1016/j.procs.2017.11.256.

[18] B. Zhang, Z. Wei, J. Ren, Y. Cheng, Z. Zheng, An empirical study on predicting blood pressure using classification and regression trees, IEEE Access. 6 (2018) 21758–21768. Available from: https://doi.org/10.1109/ACCESS.2017.2787980.

[19] C. Iwendi, A.K. Bashir, A. Peshkar, R. Sujatha, J.M. Chatterjee, S. Pasupuleti, et al., COVID-19 patient health prediction using boosted random forest algorithm, Front. Public Health 8 (2020) 357. Available from: https://doi.org/10.3389/fpubh.2020.00357.

[20] K. Zvarevashe, O.O. Olugbara, Gender voice recognition using random forest recursive feature elimination with gradient boosting machines, in: International Conference on Advances in Big Data, Computing and Data Communication Systems (icABCD), IEEE, 2018, pp. 1–6. Available from: https://doi.org/10.1109/ICABCD.2018.8465466.

[21] W. Dong, et al., XGBoost algorithm-based prediction of concrete electrical resistivity for structural health monitoring, Autom. Constr. 114 (2020) 103155.

[22] M. Tang, et al., An improved lightGBM algorithm for online fault detection of wind turbine gearboxes, Energies 13 (4) (2020) 807.

[23] F. Zhou, et al., Fire prediction based on catboost algorithm, Math. Probl. Eng. (2021) 2021.

8

Healthcare cybersecurity challenges: a look at current and future trends

Ramiz Salama, Chadi Altrjman, Fadi Al-Turjman

ARTIFICIAL INTELLIGENCE, SOFTWARE, AND INFORMATION SYSTEMS ENGINEERING DEPARTMENTS, RESEARCH CENTER FOR AI AND IOT, AI AND ROBOTICS INSTITUTE, NEAR EAST UNIVERSITY, NICOSIA, MERSIN10, TURKEY

8.1 Introduction

Healthcare is a need that exists for everyone in society and is, therefore, a universal need. With other businesses, patients, and medical professionals, the healthcare sector is responsible for collecting, safeguarding, and sharing exceedingly private and sensitive information. For healthcare systems (HCSs) to keep up with technological changes, they must grow. The transition in healthcare from hospital-centered, specialist-focused systems to distributed, patient-centered care, which is universally regarded as both inevitable and important, has been made easier by the digitalization of health records. Cybersecurity breaches in the HCS that reveal personal information or data might have negative effects on patients and the healthcare facility, possibly with lethal results. Cybersecurity dangers in healthcare, including ransomware attacks, hacking of personal medical devices, and loss of personal medical data, are ever-present. Health data that have been stolen are more valuable than records from any other industry because personal information is so important. When bought and sold on the dark web, they can be used to fund illegal operations and enable identity theft, blackmail, extortion, and even murder. The US Office of Personnel Management and Anthem health, which provides healthcare to government employees, both had cyberattacks in 2015 that appeared to be the result of the same hacker. These incidents happened within a few months of one another. Accordingly, by linking personnel data with private health information for government employees, the hackers are able to specifically attack high-value individuals. Despite an increase in cyberattacks on healthcare institutions around the world, the healthcare sector is behind other sectors in terms of its ability to protect its sensitive data. Healthcare cybersecurity has been identified as a developing health security risk, despite the fact that there is a low level of knowledge of the threat. A healthcare cybersecurity capabilities strategy is required to counter the expanding cyber threats. The recently deployed My Health Record (MHR) in Australia, a national electronic medical record system, makes it easy to assess healthcare cybersecurity capacity. The term "cybersecurity capability" refers to

Computational Intelligence and Blockchain in Complex Systems. DOI: https://doi.org/10.1016/B978-0-443-13268-1.00003-0
© 2024 Elsevier Inc. All rights reserved, including those for text and data mining, AI training, and similar technologies.

a business or industry's capacity to deliver a specific outcome, such as proactive cyber-awareness and defense. Historically, healthcare companies have placed a higher priority on patient care than cybersecurity, viewing the electronic health record as the gold standard of the highest quality medical care. On the other hand, healthcare lags behind other sectors in terms of personnel cybersecurity training and data security. As the volume and value of patient information increase, health management must develop cybersecurity competence across businesses. The improvements of existing information technology, as well as the proactive identification and acquisition of new technology, cybersecurity professionals, and comprehensive organization training, are all components of developing cybersecurity capabilities. The COVID-19 outbreak has presented an unprecedented challenge to the global HCS. It has weakened the resilience of the health information system, limiting our ability to achieve the universal goal of health and well-being. The sector has turned into one of the main targets for specialized cybersecurity threats. The healthcare industry has placed itself in a perilous situation by focusing on its main function of providing healthcare to save lives in order to handle the pandemic and this unique condition, rather than the security of its systems and procedures. While capitalizing on the COVID-19 outbreak, attackers have launched many cyberattacks on healthcare organizations. Recent hacks have impacted the WHO, Gilead Sciences, Inc., hospitals in Romania, the US Department of Health and Human Services, Brno University Hospital, and the larger healthcare supply chain. The healthcare industry needs to be prepared to protect against cyberattacks to guarantee the accessibility of crucial healthcare services as well as the confidentiality and integrity of patient data. Cybercrime reacts to developments in the international environment quickly. At the outset of the COVID-19 pandemic's escalation, malware attackers identified widespread vulnerabilities and altered their attacks to exploit these flaws. The current conditions in the UK and around the world allow for various cyberattacks to flourish. The increase in remote work, the decrease in mobility, the shutting of international borders, and the increased demand for personal protective equipment like masks and gloves are all being exploited by cyber attackers. The complex healthcare supply chain is another point of interest. As a result, the general populace is experiencing increased fear, uncertainty, and mistrust. The literature on cybersecurity in the medical industry has been looked at in a study. Jalali et al. carried out a detailed analysis of the literature on cybersecurity response tactics in healthcare. Coventry et al. conducted a narrative review of cyber threat patterns and potential directions for the healthcare sector. Kruse et al. looked closely at cyber threats and changes in the healthcare sector. Offer et al. investigated the cyber threats that Australian healthcare organizations faced and their defense mechanisms. Sardi et al. have out a comprehensive analysis of cyber risk in healthcare organizations. However, there has not been any research on a comprehensive evaluation and analysis of the key cybersecurity concerns and solutions, especially in the health sector, in the context of a pandemic like COVID-19. This study intends to identify cybersecurity concerns, answers, and areas that need further improvement during the COVID-19 pandemic. It also aims to identify the most prominent and major attack and threat tactics that have harmed the health sector. This study analyzes security issues resulting from the COVID-19 pandemic as well as underlying security issues in health information systems that could be exploited by attackers during the COVID-19 pandemic. The rise in cybersecurity dangers, including phishing, ransomware, and distributed denial of service (DDoS) attacks, during the coronavirus crisis and over time has ramifications for the entire spectrum of the health industry. Information technologies must be able to store enormous amounts of electronic patient data across a variety of operating systems in order to support the paradigm shift toward digitalized healthcare. When new technologies are combined with out-of-date, unsupported, or obsolete operating systems, interoperability is compromised and cybersecurity vulnerability is increased. The widespread 2017 Winery ransomware assault serves as a compelling illustration of this. The malware was able to propagate throughout the UK's National Health Service (NHS) because of the widespread usage of outdated Windows XP software18 and disregard for cybersecurity advisories to perform system upgrades. Winery, the largest malware cyberattack in history, had a significant negative impact on the NHS's ability to provide patient care for a week between May 12 and May 17, 2017, spreading over 200,000 machines in over 100 countries 19. Due to poor cyber hygiene and a lack of understanding among healthcare executive management of the business risk implications of cyber breaches, Winery spread to 80 out of 236 NHS institutions and 603 primary care organizations across England despite not having targeted the healthcare sector specifically. Nearly 7000 medical appointments had to be canceled, ambulances had to be redirected, diagnostic tools were infected, pathology and radiography were rendered inoperable, and patient records were unavailable. Healthcare is known for having "low-security maturity" and, in comparison to other businesses, lacks sophisticated data security technologies. Budgetary restrictions, a lack of cybersecurity education and awareness among health management, a diverse healthcare information infrastructure, and an abundance of wirelessly linked devices are all to blame for this. The current cyber defense in healthcare is frequently reactive and implemented following a malicious attack. Cyber risk is increased by the retroactive nature of healthcare cybersecurity and the industry's reliance on perimeter defense (firewalls and antivirus) for security [1−5]. Such precautions are unlikely to lessen insider threats or defend against sophisticated and persistent attacks. Lack of qualified cybersecurity personnel working in the healthcare industry, continually evolving malware threats, and complicated network infrastructure are additional major obstacles to healthcare cybersecurity.

8.2 The amount of prior works

The Brno University Hospital, one of the main COVID-19 testing facilities in the Czech Republic, was attacked by ransomware, forcing the cancellation of treatments. After learning of the ransomware attack in the early morning hours, the hospital made the decision to turn off all computer networks. It was found that the various systems were having issues and that the ransomware infection was gradually spreading. The outcome was that every computer had to be shut down. According to reports, the facility is still restoring its powers because the attack left it partially functional. Because there were no database systems or mechanisms to store data, the attack had an impact on hospital operations because staff had to physically record and communicate notes. This delays operations and can potentially endanger lives in these hard circumstances. To hinder the US Department of Health and Human Services' response to the COVID-19 pandemic, a DDoS attack was conducted against the agency. The servers were the target of this attack, which bombarded them with millions of visitors for several hours. According to sources, a disruption campaign was focused on the targeted organization in an effort to obstruct the response to the coronavirus epidemic. The organization in question was responsible for safeguarding the public's health and offering essential human services. Despite the agency's claims that the attack was unsuccessful and that the attackers did not infiltrate the internal network or steal any data, this demonstrates how attacks like these can harm not only the services provided by health agencies but also the lives that depend on them, especially in times of crisis. Due to an upsurge in phishing website hacking efforts against the WHO and its partners, the WHO issued a warning to the general public urging them to exercise greater caution. Over 4000 coronavirus-related domains—that is, names with phrases like "corona" or "covid"—have reportedly been registered since the year 2020 began. These registered domains were used by attackers for phishing-related activities. As a result, hackers organized the WHO event to get credentials. According to a study, hackers created a fake website that impersonated the WHO staff's email login page in an effort to steal their login information. The WHO reports that the attempt was unsuccessful, but it nonetheless serves as an example of how medical institutions can be the subject of phishing scams. Additionally, hackers targeted Gilead Sciences, Inc., a business that makes coronavirus vaccinations. The employees of this pharmaceutical company were the subject of a fake email login page created with the goal of obtaining login information. The breach, according to reports, was an attempt to use phony journalistic correspondence to get access to firm employees' email accounts. Hospitals in Romania were another victim of ransomware attacks by hackers. To disseminate ransomware to these hospitals, the hackers planned to send emails with COVID-19 themes. They were protesting against the country's COVID-19 quarantine laws. The hackers had malware, such as remote access Trojans, ransomware, website defacements, and SQL injection tools, that could be used to compromise networks and steal data. In order to infect computers, encrypt files, and disrupt hospital operations, it was reportedly their intention to email hospitals with information about COVID-19. However, because the hackers were discovered and apprehended by Romanian law enforcement, the attack was not as successful. Interpol reportedly alerted law enforcement agencies around the globe to a dramatic rise in the frequency of ransomware attacks that target hospitals and other healthcare facilities specifically [6]. It was discovered that attempts to launch ransomware attacks against companies in the 194 member countries had increased. Significant healthcare organizations working on the coronavirus response in the US and the UK also issued a cyber-warning. According to a joint statement from the National Cyber Security Center of the UK and the Cybersecurity and Infrastructure Security Agency of the US, extensive "password spraying" campaigns aimed at medical research institutions and healthcare organizations in both countries have been found. Malware assaults on the healthcare supply chain were warned about by the US Federal Bureau of Investigation (FBI), demonstrating that these attacks are not just confined to one sector. A remote access Trojan's, known as Kampar, infection preys on network weaknesses of targeted companies in the Middle East,

Europe, Asia, and the United States. Healthcare industry cyber-physical system assets were among the weak links in the supply chain. The FBI advised the healthcare sector to be alert for potential attacks because Kwampirs have historically targeted healthcare organizations [6−10]. Examining the aforementioned incidents reveals that the healthcare sector has become a major target for cyberattacks. Attackers are using the COVID-19 pandemic to perform attacks, mostly ransomware, DDoS, phishing, and other kinds of malware. Particularly during pandemics, the healthcare supply chain may be a target of cyberattacks more frequently. Cyberattacks have had a negative impact on the accessibility of crucial healthcare services and have made it challenging for healthcare organizations to uphold the security and confidentiality of patient data.

8.3 Difficulties

8.3.1 Security assurance for remote work

Both remote desktop technologies and virtual private networks have recognized security issues. The healthcare industry has been known to be a target of malware and other attacks including DDoS attacks. Numerous pieces of wirelessly connected medical equipment are the subject of cyberattacks.

8.3.2 Endpoint device administration

An endpoint device may act as a gateway into a larger healthcare network. Interoperability is jeopardized and cybersecurity susceptibility is elevated when new endpoint devices are coupled with antiquated, unsupported, or outdated operating systems. The health sector mostly uses perimeter defense (firewalls and antivirus) to reduce cyber risk. The factor that has the biggest influence on hospital cybersecurity is endpoint complexity.

8.3.3 The role of humans in cybersecurity

Most information security incidents are caused by human mistakes. Statistics show a positive correlation between workload and the risk that a medical professional may click a link in a phishing email. Root cause is the healthcare sector's lack of analysis and cybersecurity incident prevention, especially for those brought on by unintentional human error. Although a lot of effort has been made to evaluate human error (using IS-CHECa, for instance), these techniques are not very popular.

8.3.4 A disregard for security

The hazards of cyberspace are not well-known in the health sector. The most frequent response to violations or assaults is to improve employee communication or training. The health staff is not very aware of the consequences of their activities, and there are not enough rules or procedures to enforce safe behavior. There are no formal cybersecurity regulations, training courses, or guidelines for the most recent methods of operation.

8.3.5 Ineffective risk assessment communication at the board level

It is necessary to create a matrix that can translate a HCS's strategic needs into the most urgent problems relating to cyber-improvement. There is a lack of knowledge regarding security threats and how they affect business risk management. The business risk implications of cyberattacks are not completely understood by executive management in the healthcare sector.

8.3.6 Poor business continuity strategies

Risks will keep rising if cybersecurity is not built into the product from the very beginning of the product or project life cycle. The biggest security challenges that endanger company continuity include vendor dependence, incorrect encryption configurations, and the inability to manage health information sharing and exchange with third-party and foreign partners. The health sector does not have as many cutting-edge data security technologies as other industries. Every health organization must embrace cybersecurity capabilities as well as the concepts of building organizational resilience and the ability to learn from mistakes.

8.3.7 Ineffective incident response coordination

In the health industry, there is typically a wait between an assault and the revelation of the breach. The healthcare industry's current cyber security measures are typically reactive and put in place in reaction to nefarious activities. The ongoing and evolving malware threats are difficult to successfully combat without a centralized incident response capability. Everyone should be held accountable for cybersecurity, from board members to front-line employees.

8.3.8 A tight budget and the requirement to provide healthcare services uninterrupted

There is a shortage of seasoned cybersecurity experts in the healthcare industry. There is a lack of a value-based framework for considering the benefits and drawbacks of security, privacy, and technology adoption.

8.3.9 Dangerous medical cyber-physical systems

Due to the constrained medical cyber-physical sysem (MCPS) capacity, the health sector is especially vulnerable to breaches. HCS' reliance on the internet exposes them to greater cybersecurity risks. The MCPS may be vulnerable to cyberattacks if there are weak IoTc devices.

8.4 A review of current and future trends in cybersecurity challenges in healthcare

The relevant literature and background information about global cybersecurity in health systems and digital medical records were evaluated systematically using the PRISMA criteria. Ten distinct databases, including Medline/PubMed, Embase, Emcare, CINAHL, PsycINFO, Web of Science, Scopus, Compendex, IEEE, and Google Scholar Advanced Search, were searched in order to locate gray literature. The two main concepts were cybersecurity and electronic health records [11−15]. The search phrases that were used are listed below:

- Digital health records OR computerized medical records OR electronic health records OR computerized medical records.
- Terrorism (crime OR attack OR security OR threat) Malware OR Ransomware OR Cyber adj4 OR Data security OR Medical identity theft.

"'Healthcare AND cybersecurity" was a keyword used in the Google Scholar advanced search to find gray literature, such as books of conference proceedings, conference papers, and thesis dissertations. Due to the developing nature of electronic health records, the ongoing social and political debate over privacy and security, and the most recent changes to MHR deployment, it was chosen to incorporate media coverage. We searched the Factiva database for relevant media reports.

8.5 Discussion

A total of 316 relevant documents were found. One hundred texts out of 316 talked of hacking against HCS. In 131 entries, mitigation strategies were found. In 29 additional contributions, a particular cyber threat or cyber risk was mentioned, along with a recommended mitigating strategy. Results from 27 recordings in total were pertinent to the Australian setting [16−20].

8.5.1 Cyber-physical medical systems

The Medical Internet of Things and wearable and implantable medical devices are included in this phrase. Hospitals are using MCPS more frequently to provide high-quality care because they have shown promise as platforms for controlling various aspects of patient health. There will probably be 20 billion connected devices by 2020, and 50 billion by 2028. The MCPS's inherent qualities raise their security weaknesses. These traits increase the diversity, mobility, heterogeneity, and regularity of MCPS. They routinely record private physiological data when unattended (as with implanted devices), but they only have rudimentary security mechanisms due to their restricted size, power, and memory. Due to their dependence on and access to the hospital network, MCPS features render them susceptible to hacking, significantly increasing the cybersecurity risk to the entire HCS. MCPS have considerably enhanced their potential as attack vectors in order to let hostile actors' infiltration, malware installation, and alteration of treatment delivery. Two examples of cybersecurity practices that are commonly unavailable or only available to manufacturers are vulnerability scanning and patch management. Regarding MCPS postsale ownership, software updates, and security rules, there is a lack of international agreement. Manufacturers could be reluctant to publish documentation explaining cybersecurity weaknesses in equipment or patching and upgrading methods because this information is regarded as confidential. Lack of healthcare standards to promote MCPS interoperability increases incompatibility between various HCS and medical devices, which creates a market for healthcare manufacturers to rush patient products to market before cybersecurity issues are addressed. The Australian Therapeutic Goods Administration has cited the lack of vendor and regulatory oversight as well as the medical devices' cybersecurity risk as a strategic problem.

8.5.2 Data privacy, confidentiality, and consent

The privacy of sensitive patient data and issues with the use of personal data were found to be the second subtheme. Risk to personal information concerns include those related to healthcare confidentiality, accessibility, and integrity. Confidentiality is in danger due to lost personal health records or data, as well as low customer confidence. Health data, software platforms, operating systems, and hardware can be difficult to access due to malware that performs a DoS or ransomware assaults. Their integrity is exposed if health data is falsified, altered, or deleted or if wireless connections to important devices or monitors are compromised.

The healthcare sector is a vulnerable and appealing target for cyberattacks because of its size, economy, and broad attack surface. The industry should place more attention on cybersecurity given the significance of the health sector and the types of user information included in health information systems. Both patients and healthcare providers, as well as identity fraudsters, place a high value on health information and medical data. Health information is reportedly ten to twenty times more profitable than banking or credit card information. If a credit card or financial information is taken, it can be updated. Health history or data that can be uniquely identified cannot be updated.

8.5.3 Cloud computing

Cybersecurity risks associated with cloud computing have been shown to affect data and information both during transit and storage. The massive amount of health data generated has made centralized data storage, encryption, deployment, and upkeep too expensive for individual organizations. The development of cloud computing made it possible to outsource data storage, processing, and analysis to a distant server. Because of the size and efficiency of cloud computing, it follows that any potential breach would disclose data to a far wider audience. Cloud computing models share the risks associated with cybersecurity as well as the costs of managing and administering data. Attacks on data at rest, which change or replace data, and attacks on data in motion, which take place during transmission to or from geographically scattered cloud servers, are the two potential attack vectors for cloud storage.

Data stored on cloud platforms and patient health data must be encrypted in order to be secure. Attackers may have access to client apps, hypervisor operations, and hardware or software that creates and runs virtual machines through the use of a host operating system that has been compromised.

8.5.4 Malware

The recordings for this subtheme either examined malware generally or used actual examples, such as the UK WannaCry attacks. In-depth descriptions are provided for threat classification and malware assault types.

8.5.5 Security of health application (or "app")

The networked HCS infrastructure's integrity and the confidentiality of personal data are both at risk due to the widespread use of health applications and their lack of security safeguards. Health applications may generate, store, and handle enormous volumes of personally identifying health data. WhatsApp's accessibility, ease of use, low cost, increasing encryption, ability to establish professional networks, and team communication make it suitable for telemedicine services in resource-constrained environments. Given how frequently professionals use WhatsApp, there is an urgent need for regulations to stop physicians from inadvertently breaching patient privacy or confidentiality. Applications for mental health are promoted by healthcare providers as a confidential, practical, and affordable alternative to in-person counseling. However, there is no research on the prevalence of apps for dementia and mental health or the security and safety of medical apps. A recent study conducted in Australia found that more than half of government-approved applications lack a privacy statement describing the collection, usage, and sharing of users' personal information. App developers commonly ignore patient confidentiality and safety as well as the security of communications because they are typically unmanaged in terms of content, authorship, and dependability. In a study on the confidentiality and security of wearable device health applications, it was discovered that respondents ($n = 106$) were uninformed of the apps' confidentiality and security policies, including what data was obtained and how it was communicated or preserved. These results, according to the author's theory, show that the general public is mostly unaware of the risks to data security and privacy. The fact that the government has authorized the use of these applications by those suffering from dementia and mental diseases is troubling. Without adequate security safeguards, health apps are vulnerable to active and passive attacks that might manipulate or steal data.

8.5.6 Insider danger

The final subtheme found ($n = 7$) was that healthcare cybersecurity systems do not sufficiently handle the issue of insider threat as the "entry point" for ransomware. Most data breaches, whether intentional or not, involve some insider help. Despite email being the most common attack method against healthcare organizations, it is still a big problem when people are unable to detect or respond to phishing emails. Ignorance of health information technology and cyber-hygiene poses a severe risk because insider problems are frequently brought on by ignorance rather than malicious intent, despite the fact that inadvertent error is equally as detrimental as a deliberate error. Studies show that respondents use weak or insecure passwords and are unaware of the procedure for managing data security infractions. Malicious intent in relation to cyberattacks is poorly understood, and human factors must be taken into account in cybersecurity risk assessment to adequately understand and characterize its influence on mitigation strategies. Information breaches will unavoidably continue to occur because of the multiple risks associated with cooperative sharing in intricate healthcare network systems.

8.6 Cybersecurity tools, defenses, and mitigation techniques

8.6.1 Cryptographic systems or other technological advances

According to data from both Australia and around the world, the promotion of cybersecurity solutions lays a strong emphasis on technological advancements and cutting-edge cryptology. The majority of records ($n = 63$) dealt with technical cybersecurity defensive architecture and the records' authors often produced them. It is outside the scope of this paper to compare and analyze the various cryptographic security mechanisms available to handle patient data sharing and storage across network systems, cloud settings, or remote patient monitoring devices. Two cryptographies, however, will be briefly addressed due to their widespread application and potential to assist with health-related issues. Homomorphic encryption (HE), the first choice, offers good security and privacy guarantees while permitting analysis of encrypted material, such as personal medical records. Fully HE is adaptable, but because of its high computational costs, processing is now significantly slowed. HE may also be used in mobile devices to transport and store medical data without first decrypting it, protecting privacy in the case that a node is compromised. Blockchain comes in second place. Blockchain, a peer-to-peer distributed ledger technology, was first used in the banking industry. Blockchain's decentralization, verifiability, and immutability properties make it suitable for the secure archiving of individual medical records. Due to immutability, any data that has been saved in a blockchain cannot be altered or deleted. Applications in the field of health include data integration and data aggregation for research. The names of the patients as well as the keywords are all public key encrypted on a blockchain with keyword search. Blockchain has issues with cost, security, and scalability. Blockchain is secure in and of itself, but it may still be accessed through stolen credentials and root privilege assaults. Prior to significant commercial deployments, more research on blockchain technology will be required.

8.6.2 Governance and risk assessment

Every day, there is at least one data breach in the expanding global healthcare industry. The total average cost of a healthcare data breach in 2019 was $6.45 million, compared to the average of $4.08 million for the years 2017–18. In every other industry, the average total cost of a data breach is 65% less than this. The average time to find (mean 236 days) and cure (93 days) a data breach is longer in the healthcare sector than in any other industry. The antici- pated cost rises, the longer a breach is undiscovered. Therefore, in order to proactively iden- tify vulnerabilities and detect attacks or systemic breaches, it is essential to undertake extensive cybersecurity risk assessments. The cybersecurity risk of every piece of hardware, piece of software, MCPS, vendor, and third-party partner agreement must be carefully evalu- ated. Frameworks for risk evaluations and cybersecurity plans for the healthcare sector should be consistent internationally and include obligations for vendor responsibility and compliance. The National eHealth Security and Access Framework (NESAF) v4.0, an Australian technique for assessing cybersecurity risks, was developed to set guidelines for the protection of patient data and eHealth security. Evaluating NESAF's applicability, practicabil- ity, and acceptance in real-world settings is difficult. It is possible to apply the National Institute of Standards and Technology (NIST) Framework, which was developed in the US as a cybersecurity assessment methodology specifically for the healthcare business, to the Australian healthcare environment. The NIST Framework is currently utilized in HCS in the US.

8.6.3 Laws or other regulations

Many patients decline to give their agreement for the use of their data in research because they have major concerns about the privacy of the information and data obtained. This right is directly related to the phrase "right of patients to choose when, how, and to what extent their health information is shared with others." The HIPAA Omnibus Rules 2013120, which restricted access to patient information by healthcare suppliers, demonstrates how regulatory and policy oversight may lower data and privacy breaches. A comprehensive approach will not guarantee cybersecurity if it ignores real healthcare practice, culture, or infrastructure limitations, as the NHS discovered with WannaCry. Furthermore, it will not entirely eliminate insider dangers.

8.6.4 A comprehensive strategy for proactive cybersecurity culture

According to the international literature, healthcare cybersecurity is a complicated socio- technical issue that calls for a comprehensive integrated plan to improve staff awareness, competence, and threat mitigation throughout the industry. The global statistics also high- light how important it is to foster a proactive cybersecurity environment where data protec- tion compliance is embedded. Notably, the Australian documents do not touch on this matter. There is also a realization that simply following security standards and procedures will not result in learning or cultural change. Healthcare leadership must embrace cyberse- curity and cultivate strong cultures of cyber-vigilance among businesses and their employees in order to develop a robust, proactive incident response. By fostering a culture of routinely and carefully analyzing an organization's cyber environment, vulnerabilities and threats can be uncovered.

8.6.5 Instruction and simulated settings

Employee cybersecurity training is the most important line of defense against data breaches however, this is not mentioned in the publicly available Australian records. In-depth personnel education and training are a critical prerequisite for risk detection and assessment, and the global records address this vital issue. Cybersecurity simulation models reveal that experienced managers make less accurate cybersecurity decisions than novices because they are more likely to seek the optimal option based on prior experiences. The unpredictable nature of "zero-day" cyberattacks and the dynamic nature of cyber threats frequently prevent the best potential response steps from being taken. Instead, the ability to make proactive and preventative decisions is essential. Employee behavioral skills training and education are required to raise privacy protection awareness and change automatic information technology decisions into conscious cybersecurity activities because employees commonly unwittingly facilitate security breaches. Staff will take part in cybersecurity training if treatments do not require a lot of time or effort and if active engagement boosts self-efficacy. Using simulation-based training to improve cybersecurity abilities may help with this. The degree of company cybersecurity capabilities and individual employee skills required to lower the risk of vulnerabilities and breaches cannot be overstated.

8.6.6 Cyber maturity and capability

It is recommended that all health organizations use cybersecurity capabilities, organizational resilience building, and the capacity to learn from failures as a competitive advantage. To recognize, minimize, and protect against threats, the workforce, business, industry, and country all require cybersecurity skills. It is well known that the Australian HCS lacks sophisticated cybersecurity capabilities. Because Australia does not have a model for healthcare cybersecurity, it is recognized as a severe security risk in a country that has accepted an opt-out digitalized health record with MHR.

8.6.7 Cyber-hygiene procedures

Organizational cyber-hygiene policies are recognized as crucial security precautions that must be adhered to. These practices include utilizing antivirus protection, upgrading software, encrypting email transmissions of patient data, and requiring at least two factors of authentication before sharing patient data on cloud platforms. By recognizing dubious emails and reporting them or by abiding by business policies governing the sharing and protection of information, employees can practice cyber hygiene.

8.7 Conclusion

This review evaluates the body of literature on global cyberattacks against the healthcare sector to classify the cyber threats to health and offer mitigating countermeasures or protective ways in connection with a universal electronic health record in Australia. Cyberattacks on the healthcare business have increased as a result of the availability of sensitive patient data in digitalized health systems and the industry's inadequate cybersecurity defenses and awareness. Some of the security measures that other countries, including the US, have, like the HIPAA law and the need to report breaches, are absent from Australia. The hospital industry's underinvestment in cybersecurity and outdated medical computer systems are further problems. If the lack of cybersecurity information in health management training is not addressed, health system vulnerability will continue. If healthcare managers are not provided with essential cybersecurity training, it is unlikely that they will be able to influence improvements in healthcare cybersecurity capability and resilience in the workplace. It is impossible to completely eliminate the risk of a cybersecurity incident or breach within the Australian or worldwide HCS. A proactive, cyber-savvy hospital culture can, nevertheless, help to reduce cybersecurity risk. The COVID-19 epidemic has put the healthcare information system to the test. This research was motivated by the urgent need to halt recent cyberattacks against hospitals, pharmaceutical companies, the US Department of Health and Human Services, the WHO and its partners, etc. We looked at the COVID-19 solutions and the security challenges the healthcare sector is experiencing. We identified the root causes of the security concerns that the healthcare sector faced during the COVID-19 pandemic, along with cybersecurity issues, solutions, and undeveloped regions. The results show that malware, DDoS attacks, phishing, and ransomware are the main reasons for the security issues that developed during the COVID-19 epidemic. Poor endpoint device management, a lack of security awareness, unsafe remote working conditions, inadequate business continuity plans, a lack of coordinated incident response, and difficulty striking a balance between security investment and service delivery quality are among the biggest issues faced by healthcare organizations. Of course, another big challenge is human error, which affects both those working in front-line healthcare and those working from home. As the COVID-19 pandemic has changed our goals, human error is more likely to occur when staff members are focused on saving lives, working in an unfamiliar setting, and utilizing new or different technologies. Healthcare workers who are unprepared to operate in such situations due to a lack of knowledge, experience, or training require more than just support and instruction. Additionally, they require enough time, established protocols, and guidance on the most recent techniques and technologies. Although the healthcare industry has made significant efforts to solve these problems by applying technological solutions, raising security awareness, enforcing legislation, and developing COVID-19-specific standards, further research is still required in several areas. Future research should focus on investigating enhanced technical controls through the adaptation of general cybersecurity practices (e.g., NIST guidelines); improving cyber resilience by developing a coordinated cybersecurity capability to systematically assess vulnerabilities of the complex healthcare supply chain and respond to cyber threats; decreasing human-related security incidents by researching human error reduction approaches and pandemic-themed alert systems. Several healthcare organizations are employing a temporary strategy to mitigate cyber risks during the COVID-19 pandemic. These businesses should develop long-term strategies, provide enough cybersecurity resources to manage quickly changing conditions, and offer the appropriate confidence within those changes. This report provides useful insights into the cybersecurity issues facing the health sector during the COVID-19 pandemic and any future epidemic or pandemic crisis. The health industry may also benefit from the cybersecurity know-how of other sectors.

References

[1] F. Al-Turjman, R. Salama, Cyber security in mobile social networks, Security in IoT Social Networks, Academic Press, 2021, pp. 55–81.

[2] R. Salama, F. Al-Turjman, C. Altrjman, R. Gupta, Machine learning in sustainable development—an overview, in: 2023 International Conference on Computational Intelligence, Communication Technology and Networking (CICTN), IEEE, 2023, pp. 806–807.

[3] R. Salama, F. Al-Turjman, C. Altrjman, S. Kumar, P. Chaudhary, A comprehensive survey of blockchain-powered cybersecurity—a survey, in: 2023 International Conference on Computational Intelligence, Communication Technology and Networking (CICTN), IEEE, 2023, pp. 774–777.

[4] R. Salama, F. Al-Turjman, D. Bordoloi, S.P. Yadav, Wireless sensor networks and green networking for 6 g communication—an overview, in: 2023 International Conference on Computational Intelligence, Communication Technology and Networking (CICTN), IEEE, 2023, pp. 830–834.

[5] R. Salama, F. Al-Turjman, S. Bhatia, S.P. Yadav, Social engineering attack types and prevention techniques—a survey, in: 2023 International Conference on Computational Intelligence, Communication Technology and Networking (CICTN), IEEE, 2023, pp. 817–820.

[6] R. Salama, C. Altrjman, F. Al-Turjman, A survey of the architectures and protocols for wireless sensor networks and wireless multimedia sensor networks, NEU J. Artif. Intell. Inter. Things 2 (3) (2023).

[7] F. Al-Turjman, R. Salama, Security in social networks, Security in IoT Social Networks, Academic Press, 2021, pp. 1–27.

[8] R. Salama, C. Altrjman, F. Al-Turjman, A survey of machine learning (ML) in sustainable systems, NEU J. Artif. Intell. Inter. Things 2 (3) (2023).

[9] F. Al-Turjman, R. Salama, C. Altrjman, Overview of IoT solutions for sustainable transportation systems, NEU J. Artif. Intell. Inter. Things 2 (3) (2023).

[10] R. Salama, C. Altrjman, F. Al-Turjman, An overview of the internet of things (IoT) and machine to machine (M2M) communications, NEU J. Artif. Intell. Inter. Things 2 (3) (2023).

[11] R. Salama, F. Al-Turjman, C. Altrjman, D. Bordoloi, The use of machine learning (ML) in sustainable systems—an overview, in: 2023 International Conference on Computational Intelligence, 2023.

[12] R. Salama, F. Al-Turjman, AI in blockchain towards realizing cyber security, in: 2022 International Conference on Artificial Intelligence in Everything (AIE), IEEE, 2022, pp. 471–475.

[13] R. Salama, F. Al-Turjman, Cyber-security countermeasures and vulnerabilities to prevent social-engineering attacks, Artificial Intelligence of Health-Enabled Spaces, CRC Press, 2023, pp. 133–144.

[14] F. Al-Turjman, R. Salama, An overview about the cyberattacks in grid and like systems, Smart Grid in IoT-Enabled Spaces (2020) 233–247.

[15] R. Salama, F. Al-Turjman, R. Culmone, AI-powered drone to address smart city security issues, in: International Conference on Advanced Information Networking and Applications, Springer International Publishing, Cham., 2023, pp. 292–300.

[16] R. Salama, F. Al-Turjman, C. Altrjman, D. Bordoloi, The ways in which artificial intelligence improves several facets of cyber security—a survey, in: 2023 International Conference on Computational Intelligence, Communication Technology and Networking (CICTN), IEEE, 2023, pp. 825–829.

[17] R. Salama, F. Al-Turjman, S. Bhatla, D. Mishra, Mobile edge fog, blockchain networking and computing —a survey, in: 2023 International Conference on Computational Intelligence, Communication Technology and Networking (CICTN), IEEE, 2023, pp. 808–811.

[18] R. Salama, F. Al-Turjman, P. Chaudhary, L. Banda, Future communication technology using huge milli-meter waves—an overview, in: 2023 International Conference on Computational Intelligence, Communication Technology and Networking (CICTN), IEEE, 2023, pp. 785–790.

[19] R. Salama, F. Al-Turjman, M. Aeri, S.P. Yadav, Internet of intelligent things (IoT)—an overview, in: 2023 International Conference on Computational Intelligence, Communication Technology and Networking (CICTN), IEEE, 2023, pp. 801–805.

[20] R. Salama, F. Al-Turjman, P. Chaudhary, S.P. Yadav, Benefits of internet of things (IoT) applications in health care—an overview, in: 2023 International Conference on Computational Intelligence, Communication Technology and Networking (CICTN), IEEE, 2023, pp. 778–784.

9

EU artificial intelligence regulation

Esra Ersoy

FACULTY OF LAW, DEPARTMENT OF INTERNATIONAL LAW, KYRENIA UNIVERSITY, KYRENIA, TRNC

9.1 Introduction

Most laws are referred to as local apart from the digital realm. With the European Union's (EU) initiative to regulate digital world, a global impact on regulating the digital world could spread rapidly. Global companies adopt typically strict rules for all their products and markets in order to avoid having to comply with multiple regimes whereas governments follow the EU's legislation to enhance competition in digital market. The textbook example of what has been dubbed the "Brussels effect" is the EU's General Data Protection Regulation (GDPR) [1] of 2018, which became a global standard.

9.2 Background of the regulation

On April 21st, the European Commission published proposed regulations on artificial intelligence (AI) [2], making it the first influential regulator to craft a big law on AI. The question remains, will these rules be as widely adopted as the GDPR?

On March 9, 2021, the Commission laid out its vision for Europe's digital transformation by 2030 in its digital compass: the European way for the Digital Decade Communication [1]. President Ursula von der Leyen, in her State of the Union address, in September 2021, put forward the path to the digital decade with a robust governance framework for reaching digital targets of the EU. Combined efforts and investments were called upon for the creation of a digital environment in Europe to empower people and their businesses in the EU. Finally, a political agreement by the European Parliament and the Council of the EU was reached in July 2022.

Simultaneously, the interinstitutional declaration on digital rights and principles, the EU's "digital DNA," was signed in December 2022 [3]. The Commission also provided an assessment of the implementation of the digital principles in the annual State of the Digital Decade report to ensure that the rights and freedoms embodied in the EU's legal framework are respected whether they are online or offline.

© 2024 Elsevier Inc. All rights reserved, including those for text and data mining, AI training, and similar technologies.

The Digital Decade policy program 2030, a monitoring and cooperation mechanism to achieve common targets for Europe's digital transformation by 2030, has entered into force and was announced on January 9, 2023 [4].

The European Parliament, member states, and the Commission have jointly set concrete objectives and targets for the first time in the four key areas, digital skills, infrastructure including connectivity, the digitalization of businesses, and online public services, in accordance with the declaration on the European Digital Rights and Principles. The objectives and targets are backed up with a cyclical cooperation process in order to reach 2030 declared targets. The program also creates a new framework for multicountry projects, which will bring member states to join forces on digital initiatives.

9.2.1 Digital Decade targets and objectives

EU member states, in collaboration with the European Parliament, the Council of the EU, and the Commission, will shape their digital policies to achieve targets in four areas to:

Improve citizens' basic and advanced digital skills;

Improve the take-up of new technologies, like AI, data, and cloud, in the EU businesses;

Further advance the EU's connectivity, computing, and data infrastructure; and transform public services and administration available online.

The EU ensures safe and secure cybersecurity practices, digital technology, a competitive online environment, and fair access to digital opportunities for all citizens, as well as the development of sustainable and resource-efficient innovations.

Digital Decade objectives and targets guide the actions of member states, which will be assessed by the Commission in an annual progress report, the State of the Digital Decade. A new high-level expert group, the Digital Decade Board, will also reinforce the cooperation between the Commission and the member states on digital transformation issues. A new forum will also be created to bring on board various stakeholders and discuss their views.

9.2.2 2030 Targets of European Union

The Commission, together with member states, will develop key performance indicators that will be used to monitor progress toward individual targets, within the framework of the annual Digital Economy and Society Index (DESI). In turn, member states will prepare their national strategic roadmaps within nine months from January 9th and describe the policies, measures, and actions they plan on the national level for reaching the program's targets. From June 2023 onwards, the Commission will publish its annual progress report, the State of the Digital Decade, in order to update and assess the progress and provide a recommendation.

9.2.3 Multicountry projects

To join efforts for large-scale impact, the policy program creates a process to identify and launch multicountry projects in areas such as 5G, quantum computers, and connected public administrations among others, therefore pooling investments between member states are only a necessity to achieve some of the ambitions of the Digital Decade objectives and targets.

9.2.4 Road map

The Commission will adopt an implementing act defining the key performance indicators for the digital targets in the coming months.

In June, the Commission will provide an update, assessment, and recommendation on progress toward the targets and objectives and publish the first-decade report.

In October, member states will submit their first national strategic roadmaps, on which the Commission will have published guidance to support them.

9.3 Scope of the regulation

9.3.1 What is the Artificial Intelligence Act?

The AI Act is a proposed European law on AI—the first law on AI by a major regulator anywhere. The law assigns applications of AI to three risk categories. First, applications and systems that create an unacceptable risk, such as government-run social scoring of the type used in China, are banned. Second, high-risk applications, such as a CV-scanning tool that ranks job applicants, are subject to specific legal requirements. Lastly, applications not explicitly banned or listed as high-risk are largely left unregulated.

AI applications influence what information you see online by predicting what content is engaging to you, capturing and analyzing data from faces to enforce laws or personalize advertisements, and are used to diagnose and treat cancer. In other words, AI affects many parts of your life.

Like the EU's GDPR in 2018, the EU AI Act could become a global standard, determining to what extent AI has a positive rather than negative effect on your life wherever you may be. The EU's AI regulation is already making waves internationally.

The Code defines AI systems as "software developed with one or more approaches and techniques that can produce, for a specific defined set of objectives, outputs such as content, predictions, recommendations, or decisions that affect the environments in which they interact [5]." Its aim is to create a wide network by covering not only AI systems offered as software products but also products and services that are directly or indirectly based on AI services.

As defined in the Regulation, for software to be defined as an AI system, it is expected to have the following qualifications [5]:

- Ability to perform machine learning (systems using supervised, unsupervised, and reinforcement learning methods, including deep learning).

- Ability to present logic and knowledge-based approaches [systems using methods such as knowledge representation, inductive (logic) programming, knowledge foundations, inference/deductive engines, and (symbolic) reasoning].
- To be able to use statistical approaches, estimation, search, and optimization methods.

In terms of AI manufacturers in third-party countries, it is foreseen that a conformity assessment procedure will be carried out for foreign suppliers.

The product to be supplied to Europe must have the qualifications required by the Regulation. In addition, suppliers must obtain a European Certificate of Conformity (CE) for AI systems. This document is characterized as a document showing that the AI system has the necessary qualifications and is in compliance with the legal framework stipulated in the Regulation.

9.3.2 Risk assessment

The regulation prohibits any application that violates EU values and fundamental rights and freedoms of individuals for all AI systems. If the banned AI systems are taken as an example, the regulation prohibits the use of systems and products that provide the following services:

- Distorting and manipulating one's behavior through subconscious use. For this purpose, to use methods that may harm the rights of a person,
- Age, physical or mental disabilities, etc. use systems that will harm or potentially harm the behavior of persons who are vulnerable for reasons, or
- Classifying natural persons (evaluating and discriminating against people based on their social behavior, ethnicity, or gender).

Obligations for high-risk AI system providers and users: The most important obligation brought by the regulation is to ensure that AI systems are used together with a risk management system. The risk management system to be developed should be able to eliminate or reduce risks, implement technical measures, provide information, and test the current practice.

The Regulation introduced another innovation in the classification of AI systems. The Regulation introduced risk classes defined in Table 9—1.

In addition, the regulation imposes comprehensive obligations on high-risk AI systems such as data governance; storing and keeping records of technical information; transparency and information provision; human surveillance; accuracy, robustness, and cybersecurity; and obligations regarding transparency.

However, some AI systems are positioned to be subject to additional transparency obligations including AI systems that aim to interact with real people, AI systems that can perform emotion identification or biometric categorization activities, and deep fake systems.

On the recent classification of high-risk applications, various options are considered, such as adoption of the Parliament's version without the notification of competent authorities or refining it with binding self-assessment criteria for AI providers. It is also considered under

Table 9–1 Risk-based approach to AI systems.

Unacceptable (i.e., contravening EU values, for instance by violating fundamental rights)	Exception: real-time remote biometric enforcement purposes subject to specific restrictions and safeguards
High (i.e., creating an adverse impact on people's safety or their fundamental rights)	Subject to mandatory requirements and obligations, whose compliance should be verified through ex-ante and ex-post enforcement tools
Limited risk	
Minimal (low).	Subject to limited transparency obligations.
	May consider to voluntarily comply with the mandatory requirements for high-risk AI systems and adhere to voluntary codes of conduct

the presidency of Spain if the AI Act is the right place to address European concepts and fundamental principles such as democracy, the rule of law, and sustainability.

9.3.3 Innovation and implementation

In addition to the comprehensive obligations imposed on the development and use of AI systems, the Regulation contains a number of provisions to support innovation and further development in the digital field such as legal sandbox programs, reducing regulatory burdens for small and medium businesses and startups, and the creation of digital centers and testing facilities [4].

The Regulation significantly establishes a regulation and enforcement regime, which will be monitored by a European AI Board. National supervisory authorities will be tasked to ensure the uniformity in the application of the Regulation by member states.

The high-tech executives also called for the EU to establish a regulatory body of industry experts to monitor the implementation of the law as technology advances. EU regulators are in contact with Google regarding the AI Act. The company is purportedly working on tools to address a number of concerns by the EU regarding AI, including the difficulty in distinguishing between human and AI-generated content, welcoming regulation, and collaborating with governments to ensure the adoption of AI in the right way.

Finally, the regulation also provides a publicly available EU database for high-risk artificial systems. Provisions are also made for high-risk AI system providers to set up postmarket monitoring systems to collect, document, and analyze data on the performance and regulatory compliance of high-risk AI systems [5]. Current discussions and concerns are also on the points of market balance; the Spanish presidency highlights some concerns including losing control over the compliance process and causing a possible negative impact on competition.

9.3.4 The harm requirement

Harm can accumulate without a single event triggering a threshold of seriousness, making it difficult to prove [6]. Manipulative AI systems have been permitted on the fact that they are likely to an individual rather than a collective "harm," which entails a range of problematic loopholes. The result of the regulation might have little impact in practice. These "cumulative" harms are reinforced over time by their impact on individuals' environments, with hyperpersonalization, engagement, and "dwell" metrics and impact on children often called out in this regard [7]. Law in intimate partner violence increasingly considers underlying dynamics rather than one-off events [8]. Moreover, the Draft AI Act explicitly excludes systems where distortion or harm arises from the dynamics of the user base entwined with an AI system [5].

Upstream classification with both useful and harmful potency is a difficult-to-govern "dual use" artifact familiar in technology policy [9]. Accuracy of the AI Act with this challenge must be monitored closely for an effective result.

9.3.5 Current European Union legislation comparison

The regulation resembles the unfair commercial practices directive, which prohibits commercial practices if they "materially [distort] or [are] likely to materially distort the economic behavior with regard to the product of the average consumer [. . .] or of the average member of the group." What the regulation added to the existing EU legislation is found limited [9].

However, the importance of the AI Act's expansion beyond the Unfair Commercial Practices Directive to noneconomic decision-making is on the harm requirements and definition of AI. Legislators also wished to not only govern and regulate the digital market they also aimed to further developments and innovations. An EU board mechanism's existence also strengthens the importance of a unified approach toward this nonlocal market that the EU will dominate globally.

9.4 Conclusion

At the core of the framework, high-risk AI systems would be prohibited, however, with conformity assessments together with a requirement check, AI systems would be not only applied but also encouraged on a community level even for public services. The proposed regulation would establish governance systems at a national and an EU level through a new European AI Board, imposing rules on postmarket monitoring and penalties for noncompliance.

On a global scale, the regulation process of AI together with its worldwide impact would establish a role for the EU globally as a norm setter because The EU's member states have developed agreement on these principles to the point that they are legally binding commitments [10].

References

[1] <https://digital-strategy.ec.europa.eu/en/policies/data-governance-act>.

[2] <https://eurlex.europa.eu/legalcontent/EN/TXT/?uri = celex/3A52021PC0206>.

[3] <https://ec.europa.eu/commission/presscorner/detail/en/ip_22_7683>.

[4]   <https://commission.europa.eu/strategy-and-policy/priorities-2019-2024/europe-fit-digital-age/eur-opes-digital-decade-digital-targets-2030_en>.

[5]   Artificial Intelligence Regulation. <https://artificialintelligenceact.eu> (accessed 20.01.23).

[6]   O.H. Gandy, Coming to Terms with Chance: Engaging Rational Discrimination and Cumulative Disadvantage, Routledge, 2009.

[7]   N. Seaver, Captivating algorithms: recommender systems as traps, J. Mater. Cult. 24 (2019) 421. Harms are identified especially in relation to children, see, e.g., Beeban Kidron and others, 'The Cost of Persuasive Design' (5 Rights Foundation, June 2018). <https://5rightsfoundation.com/uploads/5rights-disrupted-childhood-digital-version.pdf>.

[8]   E. Stark, M. Hester, Coercive control: update and review, Violence Against Women 25 (2019) 81 (on how the concept of coercive control entered English law due to how 'discrete, injurious assaults [were] too narrow to capture [patterns] of coercion').

[9]   M. Veale, F. Zuiderveen Borgesius, Demystifying the Draft EU Artificial Intelligence Act, p. 99.

[10]   Dunne, Good Citizen Europe, International Affairs, 2008, p 22.

10

The issue of personality rights and artificial intelligence

Gökçe Maraşlı

FACULTY OF LAW, UNIVERSITY OF KYRENIA, KYRENIA, NORTHERN CYPRUS

10.1 Introduction

It has been a very long time since people created their own history. The concept of civilization arose with the development of the wheel, the discovery of fire, private property rights, etc. As human connections evolved under the influence of civilization, the law was always there. Law is nourished, influenced, and affected by human relationships because law exists everywhere humans are present. The law has been assigned a crucial role in resolving conflicts and preventing uncertainty with each new discovery. In the last century, all disputes and uncertainties have changed shape and become more complex due to the speed of development of technology. The debates among lawyers have also changed accordingly.

It is no longer important to argue over who should pay for damages or even who owns a residence. Obviously, these are still vital, but other topics are more "trendy" in the contemporary world. For example, taxing the revenues of cryptocurrencies and social media influencers, or the AI's personality and responsibilities.

Fifty years ago, it was unfathomable that software developers would be able to create such an intellect, yet now they are attempting to adapt artificial intelligence (AI) to everyday life. In 50 years from now, perhaps many professional groups and human relations will be determined and shaped according to AI. While artificial intelligence is in such an effective position, it is also debatable whether it is more competent than people. Some contend that a well-programmed AI may make near-perfect decisions simplifying life by handling numerous tasks without the need for human intervention [1].

There are other unsolved questions regarding AI, in addition to all these benefits. The most prevalent of them is the question of whether or not AI can attain consciousness on its own. This question cannot be answered at this time; however, the current consensus is that AI will not have a distinct consciousness [2] because an external "intermediary" transfers the data to AI. Therefore, it is inferred that data input is required for operation. As such, it is concluded that it needs data input for processing.

© 2024 Elsevier Inc. All rights reserved, including those for text and data mining, AI training, and similar technologies.

Even if AI requires external data input in order to complete transactions, the responsibility assumed by AI raises the question of who is responsible for the transactions it does and to whom it might appeal in the event of a dispute, bringing forth "personality" discussions.

10.2 Person and personality

Before addressing the question of whether AI may be recognized as a person, it is crucial to examine what constitutes a person and what constitutes personality. A person is the most general concept pertaining to the human species. At birth, each individual is recognized as a person. However, the law considers personhood as a much broader concept and recognizes personhood also for nonhuman beings.

Persons are categorized into two groups, real and legal persons, in terms of law. In general, this is the difference between a "natural person" and a "legal person." Consequently, while humans are natural people, the legal order also enables and recognizes the existence of organizations as legal entities [3]. However, there are significant differences in rights and obligations between natural individuals and legal corporations. A legal person is not a person in the same sense as a natural person, although being able to carry out the actions authorized by the document allows its existence. No right to marriage and no pension, for instance. In addition, the legal person carries out these specified transactions through and for the benefit of natural persons [4] Actually, legal persons are a collection of specialized, purpose-built assets [5].

Personality, from a legal standpoint, is the product of natural or legal personality [6]. Personality is a much broader term that includes the rights and personal assets of persons who are recognized as persons by the legal system [7].

10.2.1 Capacity to have right and capacity to act

There are also differences in rights and the capacity to act. In many legal systems, the capacity to exercise rights is obtained at birth, when the fetus leaves the body alive, and the capacity to act is acquired at puberty for natural persons.

Capacity to right is still widely used as a term in the Continental European legal system and is protected in the laws and constitutions of the countries that are part of this system. For instance, Article 8 of the Turkish Civil Code stipulates that every human being has the capacity of rights and has this ability in equal measure [8]. In common law systems, on the other hand, the concept of legal capacity is not used separately based on the idea that human beings have rights by nature [9]. Whoever is recognized as a person by the law also has the capacity of rights as a consequence of this recognition [10]. The most common definition of legal capacity is that the person who has personality can have rights and obligations

In order for legal persons to have the capacity to act, they must fulfill the conditions in the documents regulating their establishment.

If personality and legal capacity are considered as two separate concepts, then, in this situation, for AI to have legal capacity, it must first have personality. Nevertheless, if a difference is not drawn in terms of the concepts of personality and legal capacity, in this case, the consciousness and thinking ability of AI should be taken into consideration. In this respect, if it is accepted that an AI with a consciousness like a human being is a person, it can be considered to have the capacity of right [11].

Both in terms of rights and capacity to act, it is clear that the primary issue is the question of the personality of AI.

10.3 Artificial intelligence and personality

Law has evolved and developed on the basis of human beings and in favor of their interests. Although even animals have some rights, they are not the subjects of law. Because of this, the idea that AI has a personality has not been widely accepted [12].

AI is one of the most important issues of discussion today. It can be described as a machine or computer program that can solve problems like humans with a certain consciousness and that is dedicated to this purpose [13]. In fact, AI today can control home systems, drive a car, and sometimes give lectures [14]. Such an advanced machine or program naturally brings with it discussions of personality. It would be impossible for the modern law system to ignore the progress of AI. Law, by its very nature, needs to provide a solution to these arguments. Whether AI can be recognized as a personality, and if so, what kind of personality it is, is a highly controversial issue. However, the interest in AI and its inclusion in our lives every day makes this discussion inevitable.

Whether AI has a legally recognized personality has been under discussion for a while among legal experts. Yet, many legal professionals see the issue from a different perspective, which is understandable considering that AI is a relatively new term.

There are different opinions among jurists on this issue. According to some lawyers, AI can be recognized as a legal entity, while other lawyers believe AI is some kind of "robot" and should not be recognized as such.

10.3.1 Ideas that artificial intelligence can not have a legal personality

According to some groups, artificial intelligence is just a "thing" [15]. It should be treated as an object, and possession and ownership rights should be established. However, this circumstance will result in the simplification of AI. AI is not a simple object, it is something that processes and acts by processing what is given to it. Treating it as a simple object can be both very restrictive and have bad consequences. AI is presently utilized in a variety of contexts, ranging from the analysis of patient data in hospitals to unmanned vehicles such as Tesla. It would be quite wrong to refer to a structure capable of performing such complicated operations as an object.

According to another opinion that argues that AI will not be granted personality rights, there is no need for such a thing, that is, there is no need to grant personality to AI [16]. Accordingly, it will suffice to restrict the use of AI and develop suitable measures of compensating for any potential damages [17].

Another opinion views AI as a slave. It is impossible to agree with this obsolete viewpoint, which is the oldest of all viewpoints. In conclusion, AI is not a human, even if it is not considered a simple object [18]. The concept of slavery should not be attempted to be incorporated into the legal order, neither through AI nor through anything else. It should remain where it should be, in the dark pages of history.

There are also opinions that AI can never have the feelings of humans, so it is not possible to recognize them as persons [19]. This is because a machine cannot have complex thoughts like a human biological being. However, the law has not established the legal concepts of person and personality on the basis of human judgment and feelings [20].

10.3.2 Ideas that artificial intelligence can have a legal personality

This idea is based on the fact that AI increasingly exhibits human-like qualities. In fact, as technology advances, AI evolves, makes judgments, learns, and in some instances can operate independently of its creator. In fact, perhaps the rights and obligations that this recognized personality will bring will make AI more secure [21].

Another idea or suggestion regarding the recognition of AI as a person is its recognition as a legal person. Because it is not a human being, it cannot be accepted as a real person, but on the other hand, it cannot be reduced to this because it is not a simple object. It may be acceptable to treat it as a legal person in terms of rights, debts, and duties. However, it is vital to anticipate the occurrence of criminal sanction-requiring situations and to prepare provisions accordingly.

While AI-related topics are being addressed at length, numerous rules have been enacted around the world. One of the most significant was the report published by the European Parliament in 2017 [22]. The report suggests that AI could be given at least an electronic personality to fulfill its rights and responsibilities [23]. Even if this plan is temporary and not permanent, it may be the solution to the existing issues.

10.4 Conclusion

The question of whether or not AI will be recognized as a human will continue to be debated in the future years. As AI continues to function and evolve, the law may shift in response to these advancements. However, it is necessary to recognize that AI is not a simple object or a kind of robot that can be controlled by remote control. The structure of AI is significantly more complex. Therefore, considering it as a mere commodity would be incorrect and would lead to future impasses in conflicts. In this regard, the view that sees AI only as an object is inadequate and becomes inadequate with each new improvement. Especially, considering the AI that is developed, which has the ability to make certain decisions, this issue becomes much more important.

These issues should be taken into account when producing a solution and the status of AI should be determined accordingly. In this regard, it is crucial to identify certain universally acceptable principles and for governments to contribute to international legislation. Even though studies are conducted in the European Union and in some countries, they are not yet sufficient. In addition to driving a car and hospital services, it is a fact that AI will be effective in international travel, trade, and cross-border issues. AI is now a fact of life and will likely govern all aspects of our daily lives in the future.

In view of all developments in terms of whether AI is a person and the rights it has, legislation should be made and all dimensions of the issue should be taken into consideration. Simplification of the issue will not be a solution and may be dangerous in terms of problems that may arise in the future.

References

[1] T. Yiğit, Enine Boyuna Yapay Zeka, Düşünce Dünyasında Türkiz, Y. 8, 43, May 2017.

[2] Y. Köroğlu, Yapay Zekanın Teorik ve Pratik Sınırları, Boğaziçi Üniversitesi Press, 2017.

[3] Garner, G., Black Law Dictionary, 9th West, 2010.

[4] O.G. Yılmaz, Using Aİ in judicial proceedings—will AI be able to wear the judge robe, Adalet Dergisi (2021) 379−415.

[5] B. Bak, The legal status of artificial intelligence with regard to civil law and the liability thereof, TAAD Y.9 (2018).

[6] Bak, p. 50.

[7] A. Zevkliler, A., Beşir, G. Emre, Medeni Hukuk, Aile Hukuku, Ankara, Seçkin Yayınevi, s., 2000, pp. 189−191.

[8] K. Oğuzman, Ö. Seliçi, S. Oktay Özdemir, H. Kişiler, 15th Edn. I, İstanbul, Filiz Kitabevi, 2015, p. 41; H. Hatemi, B. Kalkan Oğuztürk, Kişiler Hukuku, 5th Edn, İstanbul, Vedat Kitapçılık, 2014, p. 4; M. Ayan, N. Ayan, Kişiler Hukuku, 5th Edn., Konya, Mimoza Yayıncılık, 2014, p. 4.

[9] B. William, Commentaries on the Laws of England, 155, The Clarendon Press, Oxford, 1765. s.

[10] Arsebük, p. 254; Bilge, Necip: "Hükmî Şahısların Sahip Olabilecekleri Medenî Haklar," Adliye Ceridesi, Ankara, C. XXXIII, P. 1 (1942) 23.

[11] F.B. Uzun, Natural persons' capacity to have rights and applicable law to the capacity to have rights, Hacettepe HFD 6 (2) (2016) 17.

[12] K.S. Kara, Yapay Zekanın Hukuki Statüsü ve Kişiliği Üzerine Tartışmalar, YBHD Y.4 2 (2019) 370.

[13] A.B. Bozkurt, Z. Yapay, H. Futurist, Y. Aristo, S. İstanbul, 6v (2014).

[14] Bozkurt, Bak, p. 9.

[15] S. Kara Kılıçarslan, Yapay Zekanın Hukuki Statüsü ve Hukuki Kişiliği Üzerine Tartışmalar, YBHD Y.4 (2019) 363−389.

[16] P. Thomas, State of the art on legal issues.

[17] K. Kara, p. 370.

[18] M. Alexandre, The legal status of artificially intelligent robots, January 2019, p. 12.

[19] F.P. Hubbard, Do androids dream?: personhood and intelligent artifacts, Temple Law Rev. 83 (2010) s.442.

[20] S. Çetin, Yapay Zeka İle İlgili Güncel Tartışmalar, Yapay Zeka Çağında Hukuk, p. 550.

[21] E.J. Zimmermann, Machine minds, Front. Legal Personhoo December (2018) 1−43.

[22] <https://www.europarl.europa.eu/doceo/document/A-8-2017-0005_EN.html>.

[23] Ç. Ersoy, Robotlar Yapay Zeka ve Hukuk, 2nd Edn., İstanbul, Oniki Levha (2017) 30.

11

Will artificial intelligence sit on the judge's bench?

Eylem Ümit Atılgan

FACULTY OF LAW, UNIVERSITY OF KYRENIA, NEAR EAST UNIVERSITY, KYRENIA, CYPRUS

11.1 Introduction

Lawyers have mostly discussed artificial intelligence (AI) in the realms of liability law, capacity law, and ethics. However, the question is not limited to the legal status of AI, its rights and actionability, and its criminal liability. Because 30%−40% of the work performed by people now is expected to be performed by AI by 2040 [1]. Will judgment be included in the 30%−40% of tasks performed by AI? Initially, there may be a sectoral development associated with the quantitative aspects of problem-solving abilities. Therefore, as the development of AI proceeds after 2040, would AI eventually be able to sit on the bench of a judge? As a philosophy of law scholar, I would like to answer this provocative question in light of the fundamental notions of legal reasoning and question this possibility.

11.1.1 Is jurisdiction a means of solving problems?

AI is now characterized as a machine that can solve issues; however, this definition will alter as AI advances. Based on this broad definition of AI, if AI is a system capable of problem-solving, the question of whether evaluation is considered problem-solving becomes important. However, solving problems is not a jurisdiction's primary function.

The judiciary has a substantive function in addition to its formal one, and the achievement of rights takes precedence over issue resolution. The substantive criterion defines the judicial function as a state function that resolves and adjudicates legal disputes and accusations of illegality. In the doctrine, it is stated that, according to the substantive criterion, the judicial duty is completed in three stages. These are the "allegation of unlawfulness" necessary for a court to render a decision, the "determination of unlawfulness" in which the court determines whether the allegation of unlawfulness brought before it is real or not, and the "imposition of sanctions" for the correction of this unlawfulness and the restoration of the legal order if the court determines that the unlawfulness is real. In other words, according to the substantive requirement, the judicial function consists of the phases "claim," "decision," and "sanction" [2].

Computational Intelligence and Blockchain in Complex Systems. DOI: https://doi.org/10.1016/B978-0-443-13268-1.00027-3
© 2024 Elsevier Inc. All rights reserved, including those for text and data mining, AI training, and similar technologies.

During judicial activity, the judge is not only responsible for applying the law to the matter at hand but also for putting realizing the law. Consequently, the AI sitting on the judge's bench must be both a problem/conflict solution and a law realizer. A purely problem-solving AI would be incapable of performing the duties of a judge.

11.2 Can artificial intelligence realize law?

What type of activity does the judge perform while realizing the law? Let's study the judge's activity, which we refer to as the realization of the law, by splitting it into the activities of hearing the case and deciding the case.

When hearing a case, the judge presides over the trial, which includes primary characters such as the plaintiff, the participant, the defendant, and the victim, as well as other characters like witnesses and experts. Actually, the trial is a conversation between these people [3]. This debate is moderated by the judge in accordance with numerous principles, including orality, face-to-face interaction, collegiality, and equality of arms. In this moderation, the judge must adhere to formal matters, such as how much and in what order he/she grants the floor to each party, as well as substantive and procedural standards surrounding the parties' substantiation of their claims. The dialectic of claim (thesis), defense (antithesis), and judgment (synthesis) governs judicial practice.

This dialectic, which demonstrates uncertainty, follows the "principle of dialog" in logic. In a trial, in which the parties are active participants as opposed to passive observers, the above-mentioned trial principles are utilized to construct, with the judge's oversight, an opinion about the occurrence, i.e., a judgment of reality. This is not a manufactured occurrence; this debate, which humanity finds smart, is a type of colloquy. For the judgment of the event/conscientious conviction, the judgment of reality is not a judgment that can be obtained from a judge left alone with the minutes, but rather a judgment that is formed in hearings conducted according to principles—a judgment of reality that is constructed in the courtroom. A "judgment of fact/judgment of reality" established in accordance with these guidelines is, of course, a judgment generated not just by the judge(s) but also by the trial participants; it is a collaborative effort. Collectively, doubt is defeated. It is not the prosecution or the defense that is vanquished, but rather the first widespread uncertainty. Consequently, the task accomplished is likewise collective [4].

Foschini highlights that, from a construct logical standpoint, judgment is a dynamic, ongoing phenomenon with material content that is born, lives, and dies like a living person [5]. This phenomenon is a collective activity that encompasses the claim (thesis), the defense (antithesis), the investigation, and prosecution (and judgment [synthesis]), in terms of the task; the legal relationship, the dispute, the subjects of the proceedings, the procedures, and the legal regulations, in terms of structure. Not material truth but the knowledge of material truth is presented here. According to Heraclitus, one cannot bathe in the same river twice. The courtroom is not a stage where an event that occurred once and cannot be duplicated or experienced again is re-enacted.

Currently, if AI is to assume the role of judge, it must interact directly with all live sources of evidence, including witnesses, victims, perpetrators, and experts, and it must establish a direct relationship with the subjects of the proceedings without the use of any extraneous means, such as minutes, photographs, and videos. This implies not distinguishing between what is said and who says it. This is due to the fact that numerous human variables, such as body language, tone of voice, trembling, and sweating, play a role in the formation of a sincere conviction regarding the material truth. At this stage, AI should be endowed with the characteristics that allow it to go beyond being a problem-solving machine and form a conscientious opinion. In the trial, the criterion for determining the material truth is sincere conviction, and the approach is contrary to reasoning. Therefore, the trial's pursuit of material truth cannot continue indefinitely. Due to the impossibility of overcoming all types of uncertainties during the trial, the conscientious judgment of the judicial authority will not be absolute; it will be produced at the conclusion of the courtroom discussion on the material truth. Because the main objective of the trial is not to discover the truth or to resolve the case. Achieving justice and sustaining legal order and peace are also objectives of the trial.

A judge is considered to have acquired a conscientious conviction of the material truth if, with the aid of the evidence, he or she has overcome reasonable doubt regarding the disputed facts. The notion that the accused is entitled to the benefit of the doubt also stems from the Latin phrase *"fiat iustitia, et pereat mundus,"* which translates to "let justice be done, and let hell break loose," as well as the fact that the main objective of the trial is not to resolve the matter. Will AI be able to achieve its mission of ensuring justice and legal peace and will it have a conscience?

This initial phase of the experiment is essentially an information phase. However, this is not an informational process. The judge analyzes the stage of recognizing the event, the action constituting the event, and the perpetrator of the activity. This is the stage in which the judge comprehends the occurrence or the action constituting the event, recognizes the person who did the action, even if just to the extent required by the context, and understands why the action was taken. This necessitates that the judge comprehends whether what was done was a crime or something that should not have been done, and that he or she possesses this knowledge. By understanding the occurrence and the motivation behind the action, the judge is able to determine if the activity "should not be done." Again, the court will require a criterion. Every ought not to be done is, according to some standard, an ought not to be done. The nature of this criterion is crucial to every evaluation [6]. Because what ought to be in terms of law (*de lege ferenda*) is always different from what is (*de lege lata*). So, will AI be able to acquire the knowledge of what ought to be in order to sit on the bench of a judge? How should we teach the learning machine what we know without learning?

The second stage that follows this phase is the judge's decision stage. After determining the criterion for what should not be done, the judge will now apply this criterion to the only situation in front of him or her. Once the judge comprehends the specific situation or incident at hand, he or she can determine whether the action is criminal or justifiable based on this criterion [6].

At this point, it is acknowledged that insufficient formal logic and reasoning that is not backed by material logic would result in unjust outcomes. Using solely formal rules of logic may result in wrong conclusions. In light of this, the principles of formal logic must be evaluated in light of considerations such as the goal of the legislation, the interests of the parties, and their circumstances [7]. The legal result must, therefore, not only be consistent with logic but also with justice. Considering that law cannot be equated to codes. Just because something is legal does not mean that it is in conformity with the law, and conformity with the law cannot be equated with justice.

If the judge wants to make correct evaluations and fair decisions, he/she cannot achieve this by acting in accordance with the norms brought about by the principles of professional ethics and only by complying with these objective norms—most of the time. For this, he/she needs noninformatics, different kinds of information. He/she needs to know the event, the action that constitutes the event, and the person who committed the action, and to have enough factual information to make a decision about him/her. Whether the criterion used is chosen from the community or from principles aimed at protecting human dignity, the evaluation should not be based on rote criteria. Finally, the evaluation must recognize the place of the action taken in those circumstances among other forms of action that are feasible, and whether or not by doing so, the actor is protecting the value of the human person. In short, norms, as Kuçuradi says, can only make negative determinations, they tell the judge what not to do and how not to decide, and it is up to the judge to find out how to decide correctly. For this, the judge must first have goodwill—the will to decide fairly—then knowledge of facts, concepts and values, and then the ability to make correct evaluations. Only then can the judge be an ethical judge, and only then can the judgment be an ethical or just judgment [6]. Can AI have the ability to do the good?

The realization of the law does not only follow the stages of finding the material truth, making the legal nomenclature, and making a judgment. More precisely, sometimes a judicial activity consisting of taking the case to the norm by applying induction and deduction and then applying the norm to the case is not enough. The judge must also interpret and sometimes create the law.

11.3 Can artificial intelligence interpret or create law?

Civil law—the system of law that arose in continental Europe during the Middle Ages and is based on codified national laws, tradition, and ancient Roman law. Unlike common law, the continental (or Romano-Germanic) legal system lays significant emphasis on a codified collection of fundamental principles that serve as the basic source of law. The legal systems (or families of law) of European Continental and Common Law are the most prevalent in the globe. There are over 150 countries with largely civil law systems, while there are approximately 80 countries with common law.

In countries with civil-law, all judicial decisions are theoretically founded on legislative enactments, and the doctrine of precedent does not apply. The judiciary just "applies" the statutes enacted by the legislature. However, practice frequently deviates from theory. Although the civil code adopted in these countries is quite comprehensive, attempting to cover nearly every aspect of human behavior and purporting to provide ready-made solutions for all possible problems, many of the provisions are exceedingly vague (due to their abstract nature) and are frequently almost meaningless until applied to concrete situations, at which point judicial interpretation gives them specific meaning. In addition, legislative codes cannot anticipate all scenarios that may emerge and be presented to the courts. The gaps in legislation must be filled by judicial decisions, as it is improbable that a court would refuse to resolve a matter only on the basis that it was not given the answers to the questions brought to it beforehand. In the majority of countries with civil-law, decisions addressing scenarios not anticipated by the legal codes and defining ambiguous legislative sections are published in legal volumes and are widely cited by attorneys and judges. They are not considered "binding" in the sense that judges are required by law to adhere to earlier rulings, but they are also not forgotten or dismissed. In actuality, they carry nearly the same weight as legislative interpretations in countries that adhere legally to the idea of stare decisis.

When judges are faced with a dispute for which there is no definite legislative answer, which happens frequently, they must make conclusions based on broad principles of law and justice. All courts follow preexisting regulations (statutes) enacted by legislative bodies, albeit the methods differ significantly between common-law and civil-law countries. However, in applying these rules, courts must also interpret them, often changing the rules from generalities to specificity and occasionally filling gaps to accommodate instances that legislators did not address when the legislation was first formed. Can AI be developed in such a way that it can fill the gap in the law and create law?

11.4 Conclusion

We said that AI can be developed like Ross to function as an assistant to the judge, or it can be developed in a way that goes beyond assisting the judge, that is, it can be developed to replace the judge. If we answer that yes, AI can do this to the problematic areas I have marked above and to the questions I have put forward, I believe that we should not call it AI anymore. Because in those cases, it is necessary to accept that we will be faced with a humanoid being. Then we will need to talk about the new questions and problems that this humanoid entity will bring to the world of law.

References

[1] V. Marria, The future of artificial intelligence in the workplace.<https://www.forbes.com/sites/vishalmarria/2019/01/11/the-future-of-artificialintelligence-in-the-workplace/?sh = 1934725673d4> (accessed 11.01. 19).

[2] E. Yakut, F. Tepecik, Yargı Örgütü ve Tebligat Hukuku, T.C. Anadolu University Press no. 4040, Eskişehir, 2020.

[3] S. Selçuk, The limits of appellate control and inevitable, excruciating results/dilemmas/dangers of not following these limitations, Marmara Üniversitesi Hukuk Fakültesi Hukuk Araştırmaları Dergisi 19/2, 2013a.

[4] S. Selçuk, The right term is not "trial" but "judging," Marmara Üniversitesi Hukuk Fakültesi Hukuk Araştırmaları Dergisi, Prof. Dr. Nur Centel'e Armağan, 2013b.

[5] S. Selçuk Foschini, The right term is not "trial" but "judging", Marmara Üniversitesi Hukuk Fakültesi Hukuk Araştırmaları Dergisi, Prof. Dr. Nur Centel'e Armağan, 2013, p. 297.

[6] H. Tepe, 'Yargı Etiği' ya da Yargıda Etik: Yargı Nasıl Etik Olur, Hacettepe HFD, 7(1) 2017.

[7] N. Bilge, Hukuk Başlangıcı Hukukun Temel Kavram ve Kurumları, Turhan Kitapevi, Ankara, 2016.

The effectiveness of virtual reality-based technology on foreign language vocabulary teaching to children with attention deficiency hyperactivity disorder

Gül Kahveci, Çağda Kıvanç Çağanağa, Ahmet Güneyli

FACULTY OF EDUCATION, EUROPEAN UNIVERSITY OF LEFKE, LEFKE-NORTHERN CYPRUS, MERSIN, TÜRKIYE

12.1 Introduction

Learners' academic performance may be affected by a variety of variables, ranging from psychosocial problems to neurodevelopmental disorders, as outlined in the "Diagnostic and Statistical Manual of Mental Disorders," 5th edition [1]. Attention deficit hyperactivity disorder (ADHD), which is incorrectly regarded as a homogeneous disorder by many people while being one of the most prevalent of these disorders, is one of the most frequent. ADHD is a heterogeneous condition that frequently continues into adulthood [2]. According to Wilens and Spencer [2], it has been redefined as a chronic illness because 50% of children continue to show signs of the disorder into adulthood.

Because they are slower to develop the skills required for effective learning in school, children diagnosed with ADHD who are still in elementary school are already beginning to be perceived in a unique manner [3]. Research suggests that genetics have a significant role in the etiology of the condition and that changes in the catecholaminergic control of brain activity are likely to be the root cause of the disorder [4]. It has been hypothesized that it is caused by a combination of factors in the environment [5]. ADHD is characterized by symptoms such as attention difficulties and executive function abnormalities.

Persons who have ADHD have been shown to have difficulties in academic, social, and interpersonal functioning [6]. In addition, those who have ADHD have a higher risk of having mood disorders, issues with disruptive conduct, and learning deficits [7]. There is a significant social cost associated with untreated ADHD, which extends to academic underachievement, criminality, and difficulty in personal relationships. These costs are tremendous [2]. Lambez et al. [8] Research has shown that successful therapy may be achieved via the utilization of both pharmaceutical and behavioral approaches.

12.1.1 The impact that having attention deficit hyperactivity disorder has on a student's ability to succeed academically

The kid who suffers with ADHD, as well as that child's siblings and parents, are all significantly impacted by the disorder in some way. It can lead to educational and social challenges, as well as issues in one's interactions with one's peers [9]. The symptoms of ADHD might change over time as a kid develops and matures. It is of the utmost importance to be aware of appropriate ways to interact with these youngsters and to provide them with favorable educational settings. Additionally, it is linked to increased expenditures for medical treatment [9]. According to the definition provided by DuPaul, McGoey, and Eckert [10], an oppositional kid who is preschool-aged might suffer from weak social abilities and exhibit oppositional behavior. There is a possibility that certain associated problems will appear, such as a delay in the child's development. At this stage, parents may be showing signs of excessive stress, and it can be tough for them when a child does not listen to their demands and does not accept their advice. In addition to this, it may also contribute to numerous difficulties inside the family and between family members, and it can cause the kid to feel angry and even sad [9]. According to Harpin [3], the symptoms of ADHD become more apparent while the youngster is participating in academic activities. Students who have ADHD frequently struggle academically and have low-grade point averages. It is also a common argument for why youngsters do not have healthy self-esteem and why they do not have a drive to learn new things. Meltzer, Gatward, and Goodman [11] note in addition that students with ADHD have difficulties in their relationships and that their fellow students do not assist them. In comparison to the other kids, they have a significantly lower number of pals to hang out with. Researchers Mannuzza, Klein, and Bessler [12] found that individuals who suffer from ADHD have a difficult time finding work that allows them to be both competitive and joyful. Because of this, they might have to switch careers on many occasions [12]. Interpersonal conflicts arise regularly for these persons in their relationships with their coworkers and bosses. In addition to this, they frequently arrive at work late, make an unacceptable number of errors, and, in many instances, are unable to successfully manage their responsibilities [9]. According to Bodnar [9], individuals who have ADHD have a more difficult time forming relationships and are at a higher risk of abusing substances such as alcohol and drugs in their day-to-day life.

12.1.2 The use of interventions for students diagnosed with attention deficit hyperactivity disorder

Interventions should be as simple and low-cost as feasible, involve as little preparation time as possible, be adaptable to the teaching and management style of the instructor, and give instructor support for the execution of the intervention [13]. The following categories of therapies are utilized in the treatment of ADHD: Interventions carried out in medical settings, those carried out in the home, and those carried out in educational settings.

12.1.3 Interventions performed in a clinic

This involves the use of psychopharmacological treatments, primarily stimulant medicines, as well as behavioral therapy [14]. These therapies are intended to ameliorate the primary symptoms of ADHD. Stimulant medicines have been shown to have large and substantial effects on a range of outcome measures, including symptoms of ADHD, on-task conduct, disruptive behavior, and compliance [15]. In addition, there is undeniable evidence that stimulants boost academic performance (i.e., the completion of activities) and academic accuracy in the short term when students are present in analog classroom settings [16]. Although these drugs have been shown to have significant short-term advantages for attention and behavior, their ability to teach skills or behaviors that are intended to be maintained over the long term is limited. This limitation may be especially crucial for improving academic functioning [13].

12.1.4 Technology in education

The use of technology as a tool for education has significantly increased over the years, which has led to an acceleration of the learning process. The earliest forms of instructional media to feature illustrative depictions of technical apparatus were printed books and chalkboards [17]. The 20th century was marked by significant advances in technology and innovation, including the development of the first computer. This technology has continued to evolve into the current century, where microchips are installed in every electronic gadget. There have been major advancements in technology since the start of the 20th century, and electrical and computational technologies are continuing to establish a footing in every aspect of life today. Learning has been facilitated by technology in a number of ways, including the generation of new knowledge, the uncovering of previously unknown information, and the provision of a medium for the cultivation of learning. Researchers have come to the conclusion that it is not the technology itself that is important, but rather how the limited resources of technology are employed to facilitate education [18]. According to Jonassen et al. [19], it is essential to think of technology as a tool that promotes successful learning and should be seen as such.

12.1.5 The environments for virtual reality education

When a student enters a virtual world, what do they do when they get there? Or, at the very least, what do people think happens to them when they join a virtual environment? According to research done by van der Veer et al. [20], the vast majority of users point to the top part of their face when asked where their body is while they are in a virtual world [20]. This finding was borne out by research conducted in the actual world by Alsmith and Longo [21] as well as

Starmans and Bloom [22]. Participants in a virtual reality (VR) setting have the same experience of perceiving themselves as being in the location as they would have had in a situation that took place in the real world. This is because participants in a VR setting are given the same visual and auditory cues as they would be in the real world. Students are able to experience virtual location changes, virtual tools, virtual conversations, and a variety of other virtual interactions through an immersive process. This process is perceived as real by the user for all intents and purposes, and it allows students to experience virtual location changes, virtual tools, virtual conversations, and a variety of other virtual interactions. This perception of the mind can have enormous educational benefits because of this, and these benefits can be achieved through the use of immersive technologies [23].

Day et al. [24] discovered that it takes time for people to both acclimate and adapt to the capabilities, dimensions, and knowledge of location awareness of self-avatars in VR. This was one of the findings that came out of their research on how individuals become accustomed to virtual avatars. Levac et al. [25] confirmed that VR increases patient motivation and participation while they are undergoing therapy. Day et al. also investigated this finding. One of the most noteworthy results was that a large number of patients had the perception that they could practice and perform skills and activities that they had never attempted before or that they could not complete in the actual world. A future study should be conducted to establish whether or not students in a classroom enhanced with VR feel as though they are practicing skills with tools and techniques that they would not otherwise have access to or would find difficult to access in real life. This research should also assess how many kids in these courses share this impression.

A user should be able to experience a frame rate of at least 60 frames per second, a refresh rate of the same speed, and a field of vision of at least 100 degrees when wearing a VR headset. Researchers are also looking into VR and the VR learning environment (VRLE) as prospective technologies that might one day provide students with an environment that delivers the promise of a "custom-tailored education" for each individual learner [26].

The specific problem is that it is unknown how the use of VR technology within the VRLE has an effect on the level of comprehension and the capacity to remember information throughout the course of an eighth-grade life science curriculum. This is a problem because it is unknown how the students will benefit from the use of VR technology within the VRLE. However, Madathil et al. [27] found no significant differences in learning outcomes in their study with 165 college students utilizing VR to boost learning outcomes. Cho and Lim [28] observed favorable connections between knowledge gains and the use of the VRLE by geography students. During the notetaking process, Dung and McDaniel [29] utilized drawings as well as outlines. The findings suggested that this technique favorably improved both the rate of information retention and the potential for an immersive VR technology to positively affect the rate of information retention.

Since its inception, English's status as a worldwide language spoken by the world's most populous people has made it one of the primary concerns of academics and teachers, particularly in regard to the language's impact on education. This paper presents an original investigation into the efficacy of combining immersion-style English instruction with VR technology.

This study describes an attempt to investigate a distinct aspect of language acquisition. The language learning method is described as being constructed around supplementing traditional gameplay experiences in order to imitate an immersion experience. The independent variable is VR-Based teaching and the dependent variable is the percentage of the correct number of English vocabulary words.

1. VR-based teaching
   a. Is it effective in the acquisition of English vocabulary by individuals diagnosed with ADHD?
   b. Is it effective for individuals diagnosed with ADHD to maintain this skill in the weeks after the training is completed?
   c. Is it effective for individuals diagnosed with ADHD to generalize this skill to individuals?
2. What are the opinions of the parents of the subjects participating in the study about the research?

12.2 Method

The methods that are utilized in the therapy of a client's behavior are meticulously documented, and the client's progression toward habilitation or rehabilitation is reported (e.g., [30,31]). The descriptions that these studies offer are helpful. It is possible that the descriptions may be perceived as showing a cause-and-effect link in some cases [32]. In other words, it is considered that the therapy is responsible for the changes in the client's behavior that have been noticed. However, in order to demonstrate that an intervention is beneficial, experimental research is required. Horner et al. [33] outlined a number of qualities that are present in single-subject designs that make them suitable for meeting the requirements of the special education sector. To begin, single-subject designs concentrate on the level of the person and do not necessitate populations that satisfy particular characteristics, such as the presence of a normal distribution. These designs have several advantages. Second, when it comes to researching behavioral or educational treatments, single-subject designs could be an approach that is more feasible to use. Third, single-subject designs may be executed under normal educational situations. This eliminates the common worry that studies may be carried out in settings that are not representative of genuine educational environments. Fourth, when it comes to the testing of behavioral or educational treatments, single-subject designs are the most cost-effective technique. In this study, a single-subject multiple probe model across participants was used to evaluate the effects of the VR-based teaching.

Because it is essential to discover interventions that are applicable to a large number of individuals, locations, trainers, and other situations, external validity is one of the most significant challenges in the field of applied research. Interventions that create substantial effects in one or a few people, as proved by visual inspection, may be more generalizable across persons than effects that fulfill the comparatively weaker threshold of statistical significance. This may be demonstrated through visual examination. It is possible that this is the case due to the fact that statistical significance is a more objective measure of significance [34]. In point of fact, it is feasible that a statistically significant difference was caused by "chance" in any particular between-group investigation. This is something that must be taken into consideration. This is something that cannot be ignored and must be taken into account. It is probable that the findings will not "generalize" to future attempts to carry out the research under conditions that are either the same as or extremely comparable to those that were employed in this one. In single-case research, factors, such as extended assessment across treatment and no-treatment phases, replication of intervention effects within a single subject, and marked behavior changes, make it implausible that the changes in performance could be attributed to "chance." It appears that the intervention effects demonstrated in single-case research have been highly generalizable across subjects, settings, and other conditions for many interventions. The assertion that the high standards employed for assessing treatments in single-case research identify medicines "with effects that are likely to be more powerful and more generalizable than those revealed by statistical methodologies" is one that is commonly expressed [35].

12.2.1 Participants

Participants are outlined in sufficient detail for others to choose people who have comparable qualities (age, gender, handicap, and disability type). Two male and female students ($n = 3$) attending the third and fourth grades a year ago, the participants, were diagnosed with ADHD. On the basis of their ages, their attendance, and the teacher consultation, we selected three students with ADHD to participate as primary research participants.

- Participant 1: Participant continues to the third grade. In general, she has trouble keeping up with her lessons. She has difficulty concentrating on an activity and is very hyperactive in class. She walks between the desks in the lessons. She knows only basic colors and numbers (1−10).
- Participant 2: Participant is in the 4th grade. He has difficulties in his lessons, especially in Turkish, and is insufficient in solving verbal mathematics problems. In English, he can only express colors and numbers correctly and states that English is quite boring. Participant 2 can be easily distracted during lessons.
- Participant 3: Participant is in third grade. He has difficulties in Turkish in general and also has similar problems in mathematics lessons. As for his knowledge of English, he can only say numbers (1−15) and some animal names. He can focus his attention for an average of five minutes in classroom lessons.

12.2.2 Materials

12.2.2.1 Cinema video player plugin

With the cinema mode plugin prepared for Garry's mod, 2D videos can be played in the virtual world. This is presented to the students within the study.

12.2.2.2 Virtual reality-based teaching material

'Garry's Mod,' a game designed by Garry Newman and published by Valve Corporation in 2005, was chosen for its innovative application of the Source game engine.

12.2.2.2.1 Equipment used

Pimax 4k VR glasses. Pimax 4k VR glasses, a product of the Pimax company with a total resolution of 3840×2160, is a hardware that enables us to realize VR visually and audibly. Wireless joystick: It is a hardware that enables the individual to move in the virtual world while away from the real world with glasses. Computer: Nvidia gtx 1060 powered desktop gaming computer.

12.2.2.2.2 Preparing the learning environment

First, necessary video playback plugins have been added to the world of the virtual platform (Garry's Mod). Then, the video materials to be used are uploaded to the virtual cloud account and the download links of the cloud account are integrated into the video playback plugin. In this way, it is possible to play the English teaching video materials prepared in the virtual world. Then, by making use of the dynamics offered by the game engine, the environment was decorated with balloons and vibrant colors in a way that would be more pleasing to the individuals.

12.2.2.2.3 Adaptation to virtual reality

Garry's mod is not a VR game. Therefore, it needs additional plug-ins for virtualization. For this reason, Vorpx virtual reality software was used in our study. With the necessary adjustments and the optimization of the number of frames per second, dizziness and similar problems that may occur in the individual are minimized.

12.2.3 Intervention procedure

"I want you to observe the place thoroughly after putting on the glasses. Then find the movie scene and look at the pictures you see on the stage. The words about these pictures will be read to you. Repeat the words you hear out loud." The evaluation was carried out with flash cards consisting of pictures seen in the VR environment. The participant looks at the picture cards in a different order for every trial and says the L2 words. In cases where the words are wrong, the teaching is repeated. The treatment was carried out in a one-on-one clinical setting. each session lasted one hour.

12.2.4 Limitations

The findings of this study are essential for improving our understanding regarding treatments that promote L2 word acquisition in children with ADHD; nevertheless, there are some limitations that should be acknowledged. The findings of this particular intervention should not be extrapolated to the greater community of children who have ADHD until several replications of the study have been carried out. This is because single-case studies are inherently limited in their applicability.

12.2.5 Validity

12.2.5.1 Experimental control/internal validity

At a minimum, the design enables the presentation of the experimental effect at three distinct times over the experiment's duration. The study's design mitigates common threats to internal validity and the outcomes, evidencing a controlled experimental pattern, bolster the credibility of the findings, enhancing the research's contribution to the field.

12.2.5.2 Inter-rater agreement

Two special education teachers independently rated 30% of all probes across all phases of the experiment [36]. The percentage of teachers who agreed with the statement ranged from 83% to 99%, with 95% being the mean.

12.2.5.3 Fidelity

One special education teacher observed 33% of the total intervention sessions in order to guarantee the correct execution of all intervention procedures. The fidelity checklist is presented in the following format: The degree of fidelity ranged from 93% to 98%.

12.2.5.4 Social validity

Wolf [37] defines it as "the relative societal importance of an investigation's methodology, aims, and findings." It has a strong relationship with ecological validity [38]. In particular, the fields of special education and behavioral sciences have been putting much of their attention on indirect stakeholders as a means of establishing social validity (such as parents, practitioners, and employers of participants). These assessments of approval of the goals, procedures, or outcomes have typically taken the form of questionnaires related to intervention acceptability. In most cases, the evaluation of social validity is carried out by soliciting the participation of individuals who were not involved in the planning or execution of the experiment in the form of a questionnaire.

12.3 Results

During the baseline phase, repeated measurements of a dependent variable are conducted to establish a pattern of response. This pattern can then be used to forecast future performance, given that no independent variables were introduced or changed during the baseline period and the parameters of the baseline are stated with an accuracy that may be replicated. Considering all three participants, it is observed that the baseline phase data varies between 0% and 20%. In the intervention phase, after five sessions, the participants acquired the words with reasonable maintenance scores.

The baseline phase data of the first participant are as follows: 10, 10, 10. Intervention data: 40, 40, 30, 60, 60, 100, 100, 100. Maintenance data were collected at 4, 7, and 9 weeks, and the data are 90, 100, 100, respectively. In the generalization phase, the data are 100, 100, 100.

The baseline phase data of the second participant are as follows: 20, 10, 10, 10, 20, 10. Intervention data: 40, 50, 50, 60, 90, 100, 100, 100. Maintenance data were collected at 4, 7, and 9 weeks, and the data are 90, 100, 100, respectively. In the generalization phase, the data are 100, 90, 100.

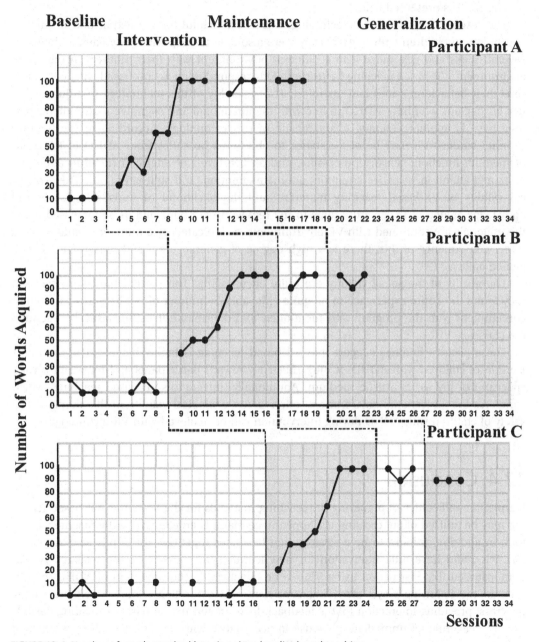

FIGURE 12–1 Number of words acquired by using virtual reality-based teaching.

The baseline phase data of the third participant are as follows: 0, 10, 0, 10, 10, 10, 0, 10, 10. Intervention data: 20, 40, 40, 50, 70, 100, 100, 100. Maintenance data were collected at 4, 7, and 9 weeks, and the data are 100, 90, 100, respectively. In the generalization phase, the data are 90, 90, 90.

Fig. 12−1 is presented below.

The results showed that VR technologies are very helpful for the acquisition of English vocabulary in children with ADHD. They were also able to keep the newly gained ability for several weeks and generalize it in a different environment with their mothers in the home environment. VR-based teaching helps these kids respond in an action-based way, which lessens their behavioral issues and attention. The versatility of this technology to adjust activities for persons who have ADHD in line with the attentional and cognitive requirements that they have is another essential characteristic of this technology. According to the findings of other studies, VR may be of assistance to children who suffer from ADHD in the areas of memory function, sensory processing, and all five levels of attention (focused attention, sustained attention, selective attention, alternate attention, and split attention). The ecological validity of VR-based teaching materials and the likelihood of transferring skills and knowledge gained in VR environments to the real world are both said to be increased when the materials are combined with VR environments, as indicated by a number of studies. As a direct consequence of this, there is a high degree of generalization and preservation of the gained ability.

The results of the social validity are quite encouraging. The participants expressed that they found the entire experience to be quite enjoyable. A number of mothers expressed their contentment with the program and mentioned that their children enthusiastically attended the classes.

These positive findings suggest that VR-based teaching is highly beneficial in the intervention of children with ADHD. It may effectively reward participants and represent a wide spectrum of joy as an artistic medium. Additionally, integrating VR-based teaching, which simulates the educational environment, offers better ecological validity in this domain. The safety of children with ADHD during intervention can be achieved with VR technology.

12.4 Conclusion

Despite the difficulties of preparing the teaching materials for the first time, VR-based teaching may be utilized often, creating the appearance that it is an effective and efficient learning tool. In addition, it looks to be a strategy that facilitates repetition for pupils who are easily distracted and have little motivation for new learning. In conclusion, the research results demonstrated that instruction using VR can be beneficial in the treatment of ADHD in children in the following ways: providing consistent and controlled stimuli to ensure steady progress; providing interaction that is feedback-focused and haptic-based; providing flexibility and delivering an immediate response in accordance with the needs of the participants; and providing safe learning environments that minimize errors, time, and costs.

In general, it looks exciting to incorporate these technologies into the process of learning new words. Despite the fact that relying on students' self-motivation sounds like a recipe for catastrophe in the classroom. However, increasing student motivation leads to enhanced learning rates, especially when students attribute their success to factors within their control and change their own learning performance in line with the learning material.

It is possible that the development of immersive VR instructions that can accommodate and foster intrinsic motivation is going to be an essential part of the overall experience of learning a language. In future studies, VR-based teaching practices can be developed with students that have special needs such as autism spectrum disorder.

References

[1] American Psychiatric Association (APA), Diagnostic and Statistical Manual of Mental Disorders, fifth ed. <https://doi.org/10.1176/appi.books.9780890425596>, 2013.

[2] T.E. Wilens, T.J. Spencer, Understanding attention-deficit/hyperactivity disorder from childhood to adulthood, Postgrad. Med. 122 (5) (2010) 97–109. Available from: https://doi.org/10.3810/pgm.2010.09.2206.

[3] V.A. Harpin, The effect of ADHD on the life of an individual, their family, and community from preschool to adult life, Arch. Dis. Child. 90 (1) (2005) 2–7. Available from: https://doi.org/10.1136/adc.2004.059006.

[4] H. Aase, A. Meyer, T. Sagvolden, Moment-to-moment dynamics of ADHD behaviour in South African children, Behav. Brain Funct. 2 (1) (2006) 1–13. Available from: https://doi.org/10.1186/1744-9081-2-11.

[5] M.D.I. Cabral, S. Liu, N. Soares, Attention-deficit/hyperactivity disorder: diagnostic criteria, epidemiology, risk factors and evaluation in youth, Transl. Pediatrics 9 (1) (2020) 104–113. Available from: https://doi.org/10.21037/tp.2019.09.08.

[6] M. Rigoni, L.Z. Blevins, D.C. Rettew, L. Kasehagen, Symptom level associations between attention-deficit hyperactivity disorder and school performance, Clin. Pediatrics 59 (9–10) (2020) 874–884. Available from: https://doi.org/10.1177/0009922820924692.

[7] K.M. Antshel, T.M. Hargrave, M. Simonescu, P. Kaul, K. Hendricks, S.V. Faraone, Advances in understanding and treating ADHD, BMC Med. 9 (1) (2011) 1–12. Available from: https://doi.org/10.1186/1741-7015-9-72.

[8] B. Lambez, A. Harwood, E.Z. Golumbic, Y. Rassovsky, Non-pharmacological interventions for cognitive difficulties in ADHD: a systematic review and meta-analysis, J. Psychiatr. Res. 120 (2020) 40–55. Available from: https://doi.org/10.1016/j.jpsychires.2019.10.007.

[9] M. Bodnar, Teaching English to young learners with ADHD and dyslexia, World Sci. N. 8 (2015) 37–53. Available from: http://www.worldscientificnews.com. in 11 February 2023.

[10] G.J. DuPaul, K.E. McGoey, T.L. Eckert, Preschool children with attention deficit/hyperactivity disorder impairments in behavioural, social, and school functioning, J. Am. Acad. Child. Adolesc. Psych. 40 (5) (2001) 508–515. Available from: https://doi.org/10.1097/00004583-200105000-00009.

[11] H. Meltzer, R. Gatward, R. Goodman, The Mental Health of Child Renandadole Scents in Great Britain, London, 2000.

[12] S. Mannuzza, R.G. Klein, A. Bessler, Adult outcome of hyperactive boys: educational achievement, occupational rank and psychiatric status, Arch. Gen. Psych. 50 (1993) 565–576. Available from: https://doi.org/10.1001/archpsyc.1993.01820190067007.

[13] I. Anju, Effectiveness of problem-based learning in developing cognitive skills in physics among students with attention deficit hyperactivity disorder at secondary school level, Ph.D. Thesis, University of Calicut, Kerala, 2014.

[14] I.M. Loe, H.M. Feldman, Academic and educational outcomes of children with ADHD, J. Pediatric Psychol. 32 (6) (2007) 643–654. Available from: https://doi.org/10.1093/jpepsy/jsl054.

[15] J.M. Swanson, K. McBurnett, D.L. Christian, T. Wigal, Stimulant medication and treatment of children with ADHD, in: T.H. Ollendick, R.J. Prinz (Eds.), Advances in Clinical Child Psychology, Vol. 17, Plenum Press, New York, 1995, pp. 265–322.

[16] S.W. Evans, W.E. Pelham, B.H. Smith, Dose-response effects of methylphenidate on ecologically valid measures of academic performance and classroom behaviour in adolescents with ADHD, Exp. Clin. Psychopharmacol. 9 (2) (2001) 163–175. Available from: https://doi.org/10.1037/1064-1297.9.2.163.

[17] J. Howland, D. Jonassen, R. Marra, J. Moore, Learning to Solve Problems with Technology: A Constructivist Perspective, 2nd ed., Pearson, 2003.

[18] L.G. Agapito, Leading the 21st century ICT-based school in the changing paradigm in education: challenges and steps forward, Psychol. Educ. J. 58 (2) (2021) 10338–10359. Available from: https://doi.org/10.17762/pae.v58i2.4005.

[19] D. Jonassen, J. Howland, J. Moore, R. Mara, Learning to Solve Problems with Technology. A Constructivist Perspective, Prentice Hall, Merrill, 2003.

[20] A. Van der Veer, A. Alsmith, M. Longo, H. Wong, B. Mohler, Where am I in virtual reality, PLoS One 13 (10) (2018) 1–10. Available from: https://doi.org/10.1371/journal.pone.0204358.

[21] A. Alsmith, M. Longo, Where exactly am I? Self-location judgments distribute between the head and torso, Conscious. Cognition 24 (2014) 70–74. Available from: https://doi.org/10.1016/j.concog.2013.12.005.

[22] C. Starmans, P. Bloom, Windows to the soul: children and adults see the eyes as the location of the self, Cognition 123 (2) (2012) 313–318. Available from: https://doi.org/10.1016/j.cognition.2012.02.002.

[23] D. Vergara, J. Extremera, M.P. Rubio, L. Davila, The technological obsolescence of virtual reality learning environments, Appl. Sci. 10 (3) (2020) 1–13. Available from: https://doi.org/10.3390/app10030915.

[24] B. Day, E. Ebrahimi, L. Hartman, C. Pagano, A. Robb, S. Babu, Examining the effects of altered avatars on perception-action in virtual reality, J. Exp. Psychol.: Appl. 25 (1) (2019) 1–24. Available from: https://doi.org/10.1037/xap0000192.

[25] D. Levac, P. Miller, S. Glegg, H. Colquhoun, How do the perspectives of clinicians with and without virtual reality or active video game experience differ about its use in practice? Int. J. Child. Health & Hum. Dev. 11 (2) (2018) 249–254.

[26] F. Cassidy, The impact of augmented and virtual reality on personalised learning, Raconteur. <https://www.raconteur.net/business-innovation/impact-augmented-virtualreality-personalised-learning>, 2018 (accessed 02.23).

[27] K.C. Madathil, K. Frady, R. Hartley, J. Bertrand, M. Alfred, A. Gramopadhye, An empirical study investigating the effectiveness of integrating virtual reality-based case studies into an online asynchronous learning environment, Comput. Educ. J. 8 (3) (2017) 1–10.

[28] Y. Cho, K. Lim, Effectiveness of collaborative learning with 3D virtual worlds, Br. J. Educ. Technol. 48 (1) (2017) 201–211. Available from: https://doi.org/10.1111/bjet.12356.

[29] C. Dung, M. McDaniel, Enhancing learning during lecture note-taking using outlines and illustrative diagrams, J. Appl. Res. Mem. Cognition 4 (2) (2015) 129–135. Available from: https://doi.org/10.1016/j.jarmac.2015.03.002.

[30] B.H. Bunce, K.F. Ruder, C.C. Ruder, Using the miniature linguistic system in teaching syntax: two case studies, J. Speech Hearing Disord. 50 (3) (1985) 247–253. Available from: https://doi.org/10.1044/jshd.5003.247.

[31] R.T. Rubow, E. Swift, Assessment of transfer of training with single-subject designs: a reply to Hoodin, J. Speech Hearing Disord. 51 (1) (1986) 92–93. Available from: https://doi.org/10.1044/jshd.5101.92.

[32] S.L. Odom, E. Brantlinger, R. Gersten, R.H. Horner, B. Thompson, K.R. Harris, Research in special education: scientific methods and evidence-based practices, Except. Child. 71 (2) (2005) 137. Available from: https://doi.org/10.1177/001440290507100201. 48.

[33] R.H. Horner, E.G. Carr, J. Halle, G. McGee, S. Odom, M. Wolery, The use of single-subject research to identify evidence-based practice in special education, Except. Child. 71 (2) (2005) 165. Available from: https://doi.org/10.1177/001440290507100203. 79.

[34] D.M. Baer, Perhaps it would be better not to know everything, J. Appl. Behav. Anal. 10 (1) (1977) 167–172. Available from: https://doi.org/10.1901/jaba.1977.10-167.

[35] A.E. Kazdin, External validity and single-case experimentation: issues and limitations (a response to J. S. Birnbrauer), Anal. Intervent. Develop. Disabilities 1 (2) (1981) 133–143. Available from: https://doi.org/10.1016/0270-4684(81)90027-6.

[36] K. Wolfe, M.A. Seaman, E. Drasgow, Interrater agreement on the visual analysis of individual tiers and functional relations in multiple baseline designs, Behav. Modif. 40 (2016) 852–873. Available from: https://doi.org/10.1177/0145445516644699.

[37] M.M. Wolf, Social validity: the case for subjective measurement or how applied behavior analysis is finding its heart, J. Appl. Behav. Anal. 11 (1978) 203–214. Available from: https://doi.org/10.1901/jaba.1978.11-203.

[38] S.L. Foster, E.J. Mash, Assessing social validity in clinical treatment research: issues and procedures, J. Consult. Clin. Psychol. 67 (3) (1999) 308–319. Available from: https://doi.org/10.1037/0022-006X.67.3.308.

13

BERT-IDS: an intrusion detection system based on bidirectional encoder representations from transformers

M. Vubangsi[1,2], Teyei Ruth Mangai[1], Akanni Olukayode[1], Auwalu Saleh Mubarak[1], Fadi Al-Turjman[3]

[1]ARTIFIICAL INTELLIGENCE ENGINEERING DEPARTMENT, RESEARCH CENTER FOR AI AND IOT, AI AND ROBOTICS INSTITUTE, NEAR EAST UNIVERSITY, NICOSIA, MERSIN, TURKEY [2]COMPUTATIONAL MATERIALS SCIENCE LAB, HTTTC BAMBILI, UNIVERSITY OF BAMENDA, BAMBILI, NWR, CAMEROON [3]ARTIFICIAL INTELLIGENCE, SOFTWARE, AND INFORMATION SYSTEMS ENGINEERING DEPARTMENTS, RESEARCH CENTER FOR AI AND IOT, AI AND ROBOTICS INSTITUTE, NEAR EAST UNIVERSITY, NICOSIA, MERSIN10, TURKEY

13.1 Introduction

The task of intrusion detection in computer networks is a critical concern for organizations, as it helps to protect their systems and data from unauthorized access and malicious activity. However, traditional intrusion detection systems (IDSs) have limitations in their ability to accurately identify and classify network attacks, particularly in the face of evolving attack methods and new types of network traffic [1,2].

Some models, like convolutional neural networks (CNNs) and recurrent neural networks (RNNs), have shown promise in overcoming some of the limitations of regular neural networks. Recent developments in machine learning and deep learning approaches have led to (RNNs) achieving high classification accuracy in intrusion detection [3,4]. However, these models are limited in their ability to fully capture the context and dependencies within network traffic data [5].

Bidirectional encoder representations from transformers (BERT) architecture, developed by Google [6], has shown exceptional performance in natural language processing (NLP) tasks, due to its ability to effectively capture context and dependencies within data. However, the application of BERT to intrusion detection has not yet been fully explored. This study has

© 2024 Elsevier Inc. All rights reserved, including those for text and data mining, AI training, and similar technologies.

its objective to develop a BERT-based IDS that can accurately classify network activity into different attack types. To achieve this, a pre-encoder will be added to the BERT architecture to encode traffic data for input, and the system will be evaluated using the KDD Cup'99 dataset [7]. The research will analyze the performance of the BERT-based IDS (BERT-IDS) in comparison to other state-of-the-art techniques.

The relevance of this research is based on the fact that it addresses the limitations of traditional IDS and takes advantage of the potential of BERT in intrusion detection, providing valuable insights and a practical solution for organizations to improve their network security.

13.2 Review of related works

Computers are susceptible to a wide range of attacks, and IDSs are important in identifying and mitigating these threats. Traditional IDS methods, such as signature-based detection and anomaly-based detection, have limitations in their ability to accurately identify and classify new types of attacks and evolving attack methods. To address these limitations, machine learning and deep learning techniques have been applied to intrusion detection, to improve detection rates and the ability to detect unknown attacks.

The two most common types of neural networks that have been used for intrusion detection in recent years include CNNs and RNNs. These networks can learn and detect patterns in data, which is why they are often used for this purpose. CNNs have been used to extract features from network traffic data and then used to train a classifier [6,8]. RNNs, on the other hand, have been used to model the temporal dependencies in network traffic data, which is important for identifying evolving attacks. These approaches have achieved high classification accuracy in intrusion detection, but they are limited in their ability to fully capture the context and dependencies within network traffic data.

The Google-developed BERT architecture is widely considered to be one of the best NLP architectures available. Recently, it has demonstrated outstanding performance in several NLP workloads [9]. BERT is a transformer-based architecture that successfully captures context and dependencies in data by use of self-attention methods. BERT has been used for a variety of tasks including sentiment analysis [10], text classification [11], and question-answering as a result of its performance in NLP [12]. Even though some attempts have been made, the application of BERT to intrusion detection has not yet been thoroughly investigated. Examples of works on the BERT architecture for network security are exemplified in, for instance, the work of Liu and Lang in 2019. They developed a BERT-based approach for intrusion detection in IoT networks. The suggested method trained a classifier using BERT to extract characteristics from network traffic. To address the dataset's imbalance issue, they also applied data augmentation techniques. The outcomes demonstrated that the proposed strategy performed better than the conventional approaches in terms of accuracy and F1 score. Dahou et al. [13] proposed a BERT-based IDS that makes use of the reptile search algorithm. The suggested method used a DRL-based classifier to detect intrusion and used BERT to extract features from network data. They also employed a multiagent DRL approach and achieved remarkable scores on the evaluation metrics.

Traditional IDS methods have limitations in their ability to accurately identify and classify new types of attacks and evolving attack methods. This is where deep learning techniques get solicited to improve classification accuracy and the ability to detect unknown attacks. The BERT architecture has been shown to come with a high promise in the task of gaining a high degree of context from data using the bidirectional approach, however, more research is needed to fully explore its potential in detecting unauthorized access in networks and to develop a practical solution for organizations to improve their network security.

13.3 Dataset

An important dataset for analyzing IDSs is the KDD Cup'99 dataset (IDS). It was developed in 1999 as a part of the Knowledge Discovery and Data Mining (KDD) Cup competition by the Massachusetts Institute of Technology Lincoln Laboratory. The dataset includes network traffic data that was simulated by the Lincoln Laboratory and is based on a portion of the DARPA 1998 Intrusion Detection Evaluation data (Fig. 13−1).

The KDD Cup'99 dataset consists of 49,4021 instances of network traffic data, 42 features, and five types of attacks: normal, DoS, probing, unauthorized access to local superuser privileges, and unauthorized access from a remote computer. Including details like protocol type, service, flag, and duration, the 42 features constitute a collection of numerical and category data. The attack types can be organized into two broad groups: normal and aberrant. The aberrant category covers various sorts of attacks like DoS, probing, and unauthorized access, whereas the normal category includes typical network activity.

In the field of intrusion detection, the KDD Cup'99 dataset is considered a benchmark and widely used for training requisite AI agents. It can be freely downloaded from the UCI machine learning repository website [7].

13.4 Method

In the first step, the KDD Cup'99 dataset was preprocessed by converting the strings in each field to numeric data and creating a global feature of fixed length from each record in the

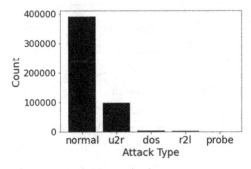

FIGURE 13–1 Bar plot of counts of various attack types in the dataset.

dataset. The preencoder creates a "sentence" from each record, this process is done to allow the BERT architecture to better understand the data. The resulting dataset of shape (Nx2) was then fed into the BERT trainer.

The BERT-based model was trained using the preprocessed dataset in a supervised learning approach. The model's parameters were adjusted during training to reduce the difference between the expected and actual output. The training process was done using a subset made up of 80% of the data, and the remaining data were used for testing and validation.

Once trained, the BERT-based IDS model was evaluated using the testing and validation data. The evaluation process involved comparing the predicted output of the model with the actual output based on a wide spectrum of evaluation metrics. The results of the evaluation were compared with other state-of-the-art techniques to determine the performance of the proposed BERT-IDS (Fig. 13–2).

An important aspect of the experimental setup is the use of a preencoder added to the BERT architecture responsible for feature extraction. The proposed feature extraction approach involves featurization encoding and sentence encoding to convert all nonnumeric data in the data frame into numerical data. Featurization encoding converts each nonnumeric feature into a numeric representation by mapping it to a fixed-length vector using methods such as label encoding and one-hot encoding. Sentence encoding then generates a global feature by concatenating the numeric representations of all features into a fixed-length sentence, which is fed into BERT-based architecture for classification, training, and evaluation.

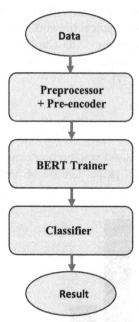

FIGURE 13–2 Flow diagram of bidirectional encoder representations from transformers-based intrusion detection system build process.

The advantage of this new feature extraction approach lies in its ability to generate a global feature that captures the context of all features in a record. This global feature is particularly well-suited for deep learning models, such as BERT-based architectures, which can effectively leverage the context of the data to improve classification accuracy. In comparison to existing feature extraction methods, such as packet header analysis, protocol-specific payload analysis, and application-level analysis, the new approach offers a more comprehensive and contextually-rich representation of the data, which can lead to improved classification accuracy. Furthermore, the new approach reduces the dimensionality of the data frame to a reduced shape of $(N, 2)$, which simplifies the training of deep learning models and reduces the risk of overfitting. Overall, the proposed feature extraction approach is a promising method for improving the accuracy of IDSs using deep learning models.

In this study, the number of layers and neurons in the BERT architecture, the learning rate, the batch size used during training, and the number of epochs utilized to train the model were all experimental parameters that were optimized. The performance of the BERT-based IDS was the main focus of the study, and, therefore, the parameters were adjusted to optimize its performance. Through experimentation, the optimal values for these parameters were determined. Other methods used in the study, such as random forest and decision tree, had their parameters adjusted according to their respective nature. For instance, the number of trees was adjusted for random forest, while the depth was adjusted for decision tree. A summary of the optimized parameters is shown in Table 13−1.

Amongst the evaluation metrics used in this study, precision, recall, and F1 score were very informative on the model's performance. The ability of the model to distinguish real positives from all other positive predictions is known as precision. The recall is a metric for how well a model can find all of the real positives. The harmonic mean of accuracy and recall, or F1 score, accounts for both false positives and false negatives in the predictions made by the model. These metrics are frequently used to assess the effectiveness of IDS and offer a thorough assessment of the effectiveness of the proposed BERT-IDS and other techniques.

Table 13–1 Optimized hyperparameters.

Method	Hyper parameters	Values
BERT-IDS	Number of layers	12
	Number of neurons	256
	Learning rate	0.0001
	Batch size	32
	Optimizer	Adam
Decision tree, random forest, and gradient boosting	Maximum depth	5
	Minimum samples leaf	3
	Number of trees	100
Linear regression	Regularization parameter	0.1

13.5 Results and analysis

The KDD Cup'99 dataset was used in this study to evaluate the proposed BERT-IDS and compare it to other cutting-edge methods including decision trees, random forest, logistic regression, and gradient boosting. According to the test results, BERT-IDS performed better than logistic regression and support vector machines in terms of classification accuracy and F1 score.

The experimental results show that BERT-IDS achieved an F1 score of 99.4% and an overall classification accuracy of 99.5%. This performance is noticeably superior to that of logistic regression and support vector machine. The decision tree, random forest, and gradient boosting classifiers achieved perfect scores on all metrics used (Figs. 13−3 and 13−4).

The comparison of the performance of BERT-IDS with other state-of-the-art techniques indicates that BERT-IDS is significantly better at classifying network activity into different attack types. The use of a pre-encoder in the BERT architecture, which converts strings in each field to numeric data and creates a global feature from each record in the dataset, allows BERT-IDS to better understand the data and improve its performance.

BERT-IDS has the potential to be a highly effective tool for intrusion detection. Its high classification accuracy and F1 score, combined with its ability to handle large amounts of

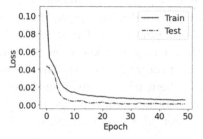

FIGURE 13–3 The learning curve of the bidirectional encoder representations from transformers-based intrusion detection system model.

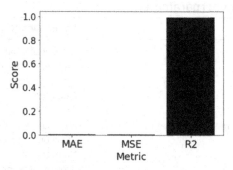

FIGURE 13–4 Bar plot of mean absolute error and mean squared error of bidirectional encoder representations from transformers-based intrusion detection system training process.

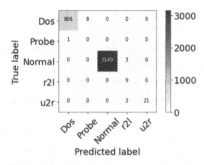

FIGURE 13–5 Confusion matrix from bidirectional encoder representations from transformers-based intrusion detection system performance evaluation.

Table 13–2   Performance metrics.

	Transformer	GBC	DTC	RFC	LR	SVM
MAE	0.0035	0	0	0	0.0543	0.2596
MSE	0.0035	0	0	0	0.1342	0.5204
R2	0.994906	1	1	1	0.800627	0.226872
Accuracy score	0.9965	1	1	1	0.97615	0.86985
Sensitivity	0.999125	1	1	1	0.994038	0.967463
Specificity	0.9965	1	1	1	0.97615	0.86985
F1	0.825423	1	1	1	0.413875	0.318171
Recall	0.883529	1	1	1	0.403461	0.288598
Training time	2074.988	7.676533	0.025418	0.690202	2.218198	8.062414
Testing time	0.968943	0.095048	0.004688	0.159173	0.009368	8.294922

data, make it a suitable candidate for real-world applications. The results of this research suggest that BERT-IDS could be used to improve the security of networks and protect against different types of attacks (Fig. 13–5, Table 13–2).

13.6 Conclusion

Using the KDD Cup'99 dataset, a BERT-IDS was developed and assessed in this study. The proposed BERT-IDS was demonstrated to perform better in terms of classification accuracy and F1 score than other cutting-edge approaches such as logistic regression and support vector machine. The addition of a preencoder to the BERT architecture, which encodes the traffic data for BERT input, is the distinguishing feature of BERT-IDS.

The research findings indicate that BERT-IDS is a highly effective tool for intrusion detection. It is a strong choice for real-world applications due to its excellent classification accuracy as well as its capacity for handling massive amounts of data. The results of this research suggest that BERT-IDS could be used to improve the security of networks and protect against different types of attacks.

The implications of the research for intrusion detection and network security are significant. BERT-IDS has the potential to improve the accuracy and effectiveness of IDSs, which is essential for protecting networks and sensitive data from cyber threats. The use of BERT-IDS in real-world applications could lead to improved security for organizations and individuals.

However, this research also suggests that there is still a lot of room for future research in this field. For example, further experimentation with different datasets and various attack types can be done to validate the performance of BERT-IDS. The combination of BERT-IDS with other state-of-the-art techniques could also be tested to see if it could lead to even better performance.

References

[1] K. Sethi, R. Kumar, D. Mohanty, P. Bera, Robust adaptive cloud intrusion detection system using advanced deep reinforcement learning, Lect. Notes Comput. Sci. (including Subser. Lect. Notes Artif. Intell. Lect. Notes Bioinforma.) 12586 (2020) 66−85. Available from: https://doi.org/10.1007/978-3-030-66626-2_4. LNCS.

[2] Z. Chiba, N. Abghour, K. Moussaid, A. El Omri, M. Rida, A survey of intrusion detection systems for cloud computing environment, in: Proceedings of the 2016 International Conference on Engineering MIS, ICEMIS 2016, November 2016. Available from: https://doi.org/10.1109/ICEMIS.2016.7745295.

[3] N. Nasaruddin, K. Muchtar, A. Afdhal, A.P.J. Dwiyantoro, Deep anomaly detection through visual attention in surveillance videos, J. Big Data 7 (1) (2020) 1−17. Available from: https://doi.org/10.1186/S40537-020-00365-Y/TABLES/5.

[4] M. Sewak, S.K. Sahay, H. Rathore, Deep reinforcement learning in the advanced cybersecurity threat detection and protection, Inf. Syst. Front. 1 (2022) 1−23. Available from: https://doi.org/10.1007/S10796-022-10333-X/TABLES/3.

[5] B. Cao, C. Li, Y. Song, Y. Qin, C. Chen, Network intrusion detection model based on CNN and GRU, Appl. Sci. 12 (9) (2022) 4184. Available from: https://doi.org/10.3390/APP12094184.

[6] J. Devlin, M.W. Chang, K. Lee, K. Toutanova, BERT: pre-training of deep bidirectional transformers for language understanding, in: NAACL HLT 2019 — 2019 Conference North America Chapter Associated with Computer Linguistics Human Language Technology — Proceedings Conference, vol. 1, October 2018, pp. 4171−4186. Available from: https://doi.org/10.48550/arxiv.1810.04805.

[7] KDD Cup 1999 Data — Dataset by UCI. Data.world. <https://data.world/uci/kdd-cup-1999-data> (accessed 08.02.23).

[8] K. He, X. Zhang, S. Ren, J. Sun, Spatial pyramid pooling in deep convolutional networks for visual recognition, IEEE Trans. Pattern Anal. Mach. Intell. 37 (9) (2015) 1904−1916. Available from: https://doi.org/10.1109/tpami.2015.2389824.

[9] T.B. Brown, et al., Language models are few-shot learners, Adv. Neural Inf. Process. Syst. 2020-December (2020). Available from: https://doi.org/10.48550/arxiv.2005.14165. May.

[10] N. Cennamo, et al., Transfer learning for sentiment analysis using BERT based supervised fine-tuning, Sensors 22 (11) (2022) 4157. Available from: https://doi.org/10.3390/S22114157.

[11] R. Qasim, W.H. Bangyal, M.A. Alqarni, A. Ali Almazroi, A fine-tuned BERT-based transfer learning approach for text classification, J. Healthc. Eng. 2022 (2022). Available from: https://doi.org/10.1155/2022/3498123.

[12] A. Paramasivam, S.J. Nirmala, A survey on textual entailment based question answering, J. King Saud. Univ. - Comput. Inf. Sci. 34 (10) (2022) 9644−9653. Available from: https://doi.org/10.1016/J.JKSUCI.2021.11.017.

[13] A. Dahou, et al., Intrusion detection system for iot based on deep learning and modified reptile search algorithm, Comput. Intell. Neurosci. 2022 (2022) 1−15. Available from: https://doi.org/10.1155/2022/6473507.

14

Internet of Things and the electrocardiogram using artificial intelligence—a survey

Hamdan H. Shehab[1], Fadi Al-Turjman[2]

*[1]DEPARTMENT OF BIOMEDICAL ENGINEERING, FACULTY OF ENGINEERING, NEAR EAST
UNIVERSITY, NICOSIA/TRNC, MERSIN, TURKEY [2]ARTIFICIAL INTELLIGENCE, SOFTWARE,
AND INFORMATION SYSTEMS ENGINEERING DEPARTMENTS, RESEARCH CENTER FOR AI
AND IOT, AI AND ROBOTICS INSTITUTE, NEAR EAST UNIVERSITY, NICOSIA, MERSIN10,
TURKEY*

14.1 Introduction

The most common reason for heart disease is arrhythmia. Acute stroke is most commonly caused by atrial fibrillation, whereas shock or sudden cardiac death is most commonly caused by ventricular tachycardia. Arrhythmia is the most common cause of death for those with cardiovascular illnesses, even though the majority do not pose an immediate risk and frequently occur in daily life. The World Health Organization estimates that arrhythmias are responsible for 15% of deaths globally. The electrocardiogram (ECG) is a common clinical tool that has been utilized for many years by both cardiologists and noncardiologists. The ECG is inexpensive, even in environments with limited resources, there is a quick and easy test available. The examination offers a glimpse into the structural and physiological health of the heart. The phrase "Internet of things (IoT)" describes real-world objects that may connect to other systems and devices via the Internet or other communication networks and exchange data with them. These objects have sensors, computer power, programming, and other technological capabilities. At this time, the cost of treatment is out of the reach of the destitute and poor people, so we are working to create a system with the straightforward goal of providing low-cost, high-quality healthcare to everyone. We believe we can do this by utilizing cutting-edge technology such as artificial intelligence (AI). This technology can identify the cardiac condition while simultaneously recording the ECG. Location will not be a problem any longer, thanks to the IoT, which is easily accessible and simple to use. It can prevent several tragedies by sending a warning message to the hospital or sending and detecting abnormal ECG to the user for analysis and readings.

IoT refers to the network of physical devices, vehicles, buildings, and other objects that are equipped with sensors, software, and connectivity, allowing them to collect and exchange data over the Internet. An IoT-based ECG system uses sensors and devices connected to the internet to monitor and record the electrical activity of the heart. One potential use of an IoT-based ECG system is to remotely monitor the heart health of patients, particularly those with chronic conditions such as heart disease. The system can transmit real-time data to healthcare providers, who can then analyze the data using AI algorithms to identify any potential problems or abnormalities. This can allow healthcare providers to intervene and provide treatment more quickly, potentially preventing serious health complications.

There are several potential benefits to using an IoT-based ECG system with AI:

1. Remote monitoring: An IoT-based ECG system can allow healthcare providers to monitor patients remotely, without the need for in-person visits. This can be particularly useful for patients who live in rural areas or who have mobility issues.
2. Early detection: By analyzing ECG data in real time, healthcare providers can identify potential problems or abnormalities earlier, allowing for timely intervention and treatment.
3. Reduced healthcare costs: Remote monitoring can reduce the need for in-person visits, potentially lowering healthcare costs for both patients and providers.
4. Improved patient outcomes: By providing timely and accurate diagnosis and treatment, an IoT-based ECG system with AI can improve patient outcomes and reduce the risk of serious health complications.

There are also some potential challenges and limitations to consider when implementing an IoT-based ECG system with AI:

1. Data privacy and security: Ensuring the privacy and security of patient data is a key concern when using any connected healthcare device. It is important to use secure protocols and technologies to protect patient data from unauthorized access.
2. Data accuracy: The accuracy of the data collected by the IoT-based ECG system is critical for making accurate diagnoses and treatment decisions. It is important to ensure that the sensors and devices used in the system are accurate and reliable.
3. Interoperability: Ensuring that the IoT-based ECG system can effectively exchange data with other healthcare systems and devices is important for providing comprehensive care to patients.

Overall, an IoT-based ECG system with AI has the potential to improve patient care and outcomes, particularly for those with chronic conditions. However, it is important to carefully consider the potential challenges and limitations when implementing such a system. [1].

14.2 Literature study on electrocardiogram

14.2.1 What is electrocardiogram

The heart is a muscle that is designed to function as a blood pump. When the electro-conduction system senses an electrical stimulation, the heart works like a pump. When the muscle cells that make up the heart wall contract and create their action potential, the heart pumps blood.

This potential generates electrical currents that go throughout the body from the heart. Through surface electrodes placed on the skin, the spreading electrical currents can be used to detect and record differences in electrical potential between various parts of the body. ECG technology has advanced greatly over the years, with the introduction of new and more sophisticated machines. ECGs can now be performed using wearable devices, such as continuous ECG monitors, which provide real-time monitoring of heart function. In addition to traditional ECGs, there are various specialized forms of ECG, including ambulatory ECG, which is performed over a longer period of time, and stress ECG, which evaluates the heart's function during physical activity. ECGs are considered safe and noninvasive diagnostic tools, with few risks or side effects. However, in rare cases, they may cause skin irritation or discomfort from the electrodes. Fig. 14−1 shows a typical ECG.

ECG readings are taken by placing electrodes on the skin of the chest, arms, and legs, which detect the electrical impulses produced by the heart. The resulting ECG trace provides information on the heart's electrical activity and allows healthcare professionals to evaluate the health of the heart [2].

14.2.2 Diseases the electrocardiogram detects

Some of the major diseases the ECG helps to detect are listed below.

- Arrhythmias where the heart rate is abnormal (too slow, too fast, or irregular).
- Coronary heart disease is caused by blockage or interruption of blood flow to the heart due to the buildup of fatty substances.
- Heart attacks, resulting from sudden blockage of blood supply to the heart [3].

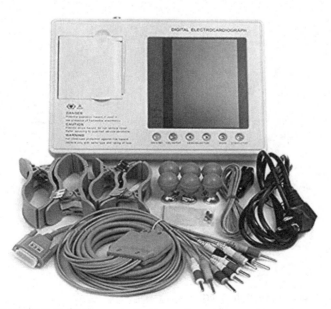

FIGURE 14–1 An electrocardiogram device.

14.3 Electrocardiogram signal

An example of a typical ECG waveform is shown in Fig. 14−2. This particular waveform is typical of a measurement from the right arm to the left arm. In Fig. 14−2, we see the various time intervals that are often measured by physicians examining the waveform while showing the voltage amplitude relationships. A 1-mV calibration pulse is also shown in Fig. 14−2. The low-level amplitudes normally encountered in ECG recording cause several problems that are dealt with in the section. Cardiograms can show the electrical changes that occur during oscillations. The ions present in the humor carry the electrical stimulation from the gut. Electrical changes in the cardiac cycle can be observed on the surface of the skin as a result of the ions embodied within. Ideally, electrodes should be attached over the heart and over the skin to detect electrical fluctuations in the heart in order to require a cardiogram. When these electrodes receive signals, the signals are transmitted over a channel that is known as P waves. Once the ventricles de-expand, QRS complexes are produced on the

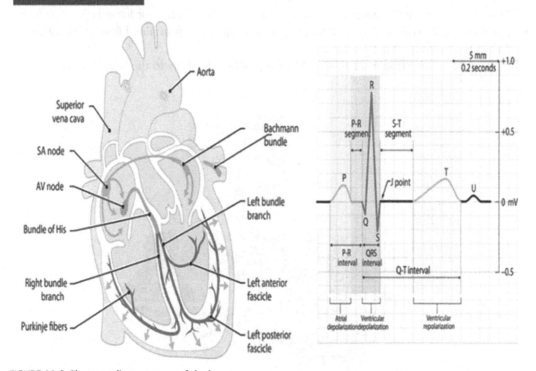

FIGURE 14–2 Electrocardiogram wave of the heart.

graphical record. Lastly, the relief occurs in chambers and generates the T wave, as shown in the cardiogram below [4].

14.4 Review of technique used in electrocardiogram

In this section of the report, four techniques were reviewed and compared and the one with the best outcome is named below.

14.4.1 Genetic algorithm-back propagation neural network

As a first technique, we used a genetic algorithm-back propagation neutral network (GA-BPNN) to classify ECG signals using wavelet packet decomposition (WPD).

The GA-BPNN technique was used to filter the details extracted by the WPD and also put the ECG signals in various categories. The GA-BPNN technique was used to make the BPNN classifier more efficient by identifying representative details and optimization. The data from the GA-BPNN were entered for classification into the augmented BPNN. From the survey study, the ECG signals obtained from the MIT-BIH arrhythmia database were grouped into six classes:

- The normal beat (N)
- Left bundle branch block beat (L)
- Right bundle branch block beat (R)
- Atrial premature beat (A)
- Paced heartbeat (P)
- Premature ventricular contraction (V)

They also built a structure for the ECG process to deliver the types of ECG signals for the efficiency of the technique used.

The GA-BPNN technique was used to help remove unwanted details for the ECG to classify. Because of the degree of randomness of the weight and biases of the BPNN, these data are augmented by the GA to give a more accurate result. For this particular example, the GA data were:

- number of people—48,
- population—20, and
- maximum generation—100.

A better result was achieved after various numbers. Average fitness after iterations and the best fitness showed progress and the GA filtered the inputted data. Fig. 14–3 shows the fitness curve of the GA.

The curve shows that the average and best fitness are at a maximum when the evolution algebra is at 100. The resulting numbers after 100 iterations were done are as follows: 1, 5, 8, 10, 12, 13, 14, 17, 18, 20, 22, 23, 26, 27, 29, 30, 32, 33, 34, 35, 36, 39, 40, 45,

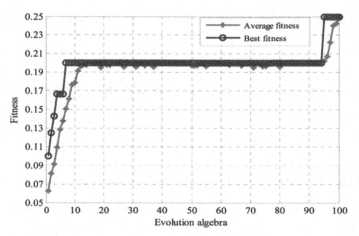

FIGURE 14–3 Genetic algorithm's fitness curve [5].

and 46. Using GA resulted in the reduction of dimensions of the feature sets by approximately 50% [5].

14.4.2 Back propagation neural network

The back propagation neural network (BPNN) classifiers' classification of the ECG is explained in this section. The filtered datasets were entered into an augmented BPNN classifier. To improve the 180×25 feature matrix, the BPNN model was employed and was also used for prediction and classification testing. For training the BPNN classifier, the momentum back propagation algorithm was used. The BPNN comprises an input layer, two hidden layers, and an output layer. The hidden layers made use of the logistic functions. There were six output layer nodes, 50 hidden layer nodes, and 48 input layer nodes. At 1000 epochs, the maximum number of iterations was done, the learning rate was 0.05 and the aim for minimum error was said to be 0.01.

For the classification of the data collected by the WPD-statistical method, a single BPNN classifier was utilized. In comparison to the results obtained from using the GA-BPNN technique, it was observed that the average modeling time taken while using the GA-BPNN classifier was 3.1652 s, and in the case of using the BPNN technique, the time used was 8.0231 s. This ultimately shows the reduction in the time used when the GA is employed. A physical representation of the results is shown in Fig. 14–4.

The category labels 1–6 in the graph stand for N, L, R, P, V, and A. The training and testing set classifications are represented with "^{O}" and "*". As seen in Figs. 14–4 and 14–5, the use of both classifiers gave accurate classification results of 100%. However, in the case of the testing sets for BPNN, L, V, and A were accurately categorized. Two of the N samples were classified under L. Four of the R samples and one of the P samples were placed into V.

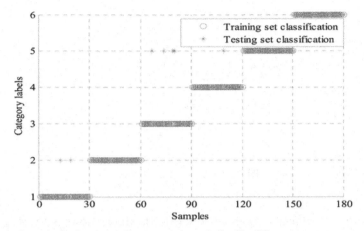

FIGURE 14–4 Results from the back propagation neural network classifier [5].

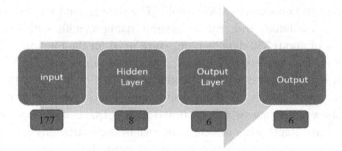

FIGURE 14–5 Neural Network setup for beat analysis for electrocardiogram.

The classification accuracy of the N, L, R, P, V, and A are 93.33%, 100%, 86.67%, 96.67%, 100%, and 100%, respectively. However, when utilizing the GA-BPNN on the testing set classification, the six types of ECG signals produced varieties of results. The L and V samples were accurately categorized. One of the N samples was classified in the L sample, which was inaccurate. Similarly, a sample of R was classified into V, a sample of A was categorized into N, and one sample of P was wrongly categorized into R. According to the study, the accuracy of categorization for N, L, R, P, V, and A are 96.67%, 100%, 96.67%, 96.67%, 100%, and 96.67%, respectively [5].

14.4.3 Artificial neural network

Issues in the heart are known as cardiac arrhythmia, that is, irregular heart electric activities. These issues can be predicted using the ECG. The analyses of an ECG signal can be

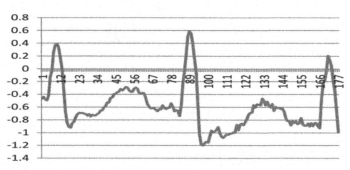

FIGURE 14–6 Data preprocessing analysis [5].

achieved by using an artificial neural network (ANN), which shows the various signal characteristics that help to differentiate various cardiac arrhythmia. ANN is a type of computer program comprising artificial neutrons that give solutions to problems without the recreation of an actual system model. The results created using this technique are by using the program Mathematical Laboratory (MATLAB®). The data is entered and exercised by the neutral network for validation and real-life testing, using specific datasets. In the project studied, ECG beats of about 350 data samples were used for data action—75 for validation and additional 75 for testing the network accuracy. These values were advised as a result of previous research. The dataset is typically tested using 70% of the data, 15% of the data is used to train and also 15% is used for validation. These are the original settings in MATLAB. The values stated above can be tuned with respect to the operator, but in this case, the original percentages were selected because of the availability of information associated with it. Fig. 14–5 shows the network with 177 input data points, 8 hidden layer neurons, and 6 outputs.

The data was made up of 177 data points. One of the reasons for the purposes of the data preprocessing was to identify the highest point for each data point and reach the number 89. The data preprocessing example is shown in Fig. 14–6.

As seen in the figure above, the center point is at 89, which is known as the signal's highest peak when just that one signal was examined. To avoid inconsistencies in the data being evaluated, this must be done.

The result of using the neural network was efficient and trained well. The data collection was precise and the time was 1.4 seconds. The total error that occurred during the data analysis was 1.4% and ultimately the aim of achieving more than just collecting FFT for analysis of 85% was attained. If trained effectively, the neural network can be much better; however, this consideration is not taken into account. The final outcomes of the data analysis and the errors are displayed, leading to the misclassification of regular heartbeats as SVT and BBB as regular heartbeats in this case. These errors are also a result of unavailability of dataset variation. In the future, if the ANNs are improved, they can also be applied in pacemakers [5] (Tables 14–1 and 14–2).

Table 14–1 Summary of artificial intelligence technique used in electrocardiogram.

Research	Techniques used	Accuracy
[3]	ANN	98.6%
[5]	GA-BPNN	99.33%
[6]	GA-BPNN	97.6%
[7]	BPNN	95.72% 97.36%
[8]	ANN	98.3%

Table 14–2 Summary of technology applications used in electrocardiogram and healthcare.

Research	Technology used	Application
[6]	ECG IoT frameworks	Monitoring of ECG
[5]	KM portable device	Mobile single-lead and multilead ECGs Kardia Mobile device
[9]	Implantable ECG device	Wireless charging, voltage level cell temperature inside the
[10]	Senses	implantable device
[11]	Deep learning	Smart Watch Detection of atrial fibrillation (AF)
	artificial intelligence (AI)	Diagnostic accuracy of the stethoscope using AI algorithms

14.5 Conclusion

In conclusion, the integration of IoT and AI technology in ECG monitoring can greatly improve the efficiency and accuracy of cardiac diagnosis and treatment. By utilizing IoT devices to collect and transmit ECG data to remote servers, doctors and medical professionals can access patient information in real time, regardless of location. Additionally, AI algorithms can be used to analyze ECG data and detect potential cardiac issues, such as arrhythmias and heart disease, before they become serious. Overall, IoT-based ECG monitoring with AI has the potential to revolutionize the field of cardiology, improve the lives of millions of people, and reduce healthcare costs.

References

[1] Institute of Electrical and Electronics Engineers, in: 9th International Conference on Emerging Trends in Engineering and Technology, Signal and Information Processing, 1st–2nd November 2019.

[2] N.M. M. Abdelnapi, N.F. Omran, A.A. Ali, F.A. Omara, A survey of internet of things technologies and projects for healthcare services, in: Proceedings of 2018 International Conference on Innovative Trends in Computer Engineering, ITCE 2018, March 2018, pp. 48–55. Available from: https://doi.org/10.1109/ITCE.2018.8316599.

[3] E.R. Adams, A. Choi, Using neural networks to predict cardiac arrhythmias, in: Conference Proceedings of the IEEE International Conference on Systems, Man and Cybernetics, 2012, pp. 402–407. Available from: https://doi.org/10.1109/ICSMC.2012.6377734.

[4] M. Alshamrani, IoT and artificial intelligence implementations for remote healthcare monitoring systems: a survey,", J. King Saudi Univ. − Comput. Inf. Sci. 34 (8) (2022) 4687−4701. Available from: https://doi.org/10.1016/j.jksuci.2021.06.005. King Saud bin Abdulaziz University.

[5] H. Li, D. Yuan, X. Ma, D. Cui, L. Cao, Genetic algorithm for the optimization of features and neural networks in ECG signals classification, Sci. Rep. 7 (2017). Available from: https://doi.org/10.1038/srep41011. Jan.

[6] K.-K. Tseng, D. Lee, C. Chen, ECG identification system using neural network with global and local features, 2016.

[7] X. Qu, W.J. Cai, D.F. Ge, ECG signal classification based on BPNN, in: 2011 Proceedings of the International Conference on Electric Information and Control Engineering, ICEICE 2011, 2011, pp. 1362−1364. Available from: https://doi.org/10.1109/ICEICE.2011.5777902.

[8] F. Ma, J. Zhang, W. Liang, J. Xue, Automated classification of atrial fibrillation using artificial neural network for wearable devices, Math. Probl. Eng. 2020 (2020). Available from: https://doi.org/10.1155/2020/9159158.

[9] J.H. Lee, D.W. Seo, Development of ECG monitoring system and implantable device withwireless charging, Micromachines (Basel) 10 (1) (2019). Available from: https://doi.org/10.3390/mi10010038.

[10] R.I. Chang, C.Y. Tsai, P. Chung, Smartwatch sensors with deep learning to predict the purchase intentions of online shoppers, Sensors 23 (1) (2023). Available from: https://doi.org/10.3390/s23010430.

[11] T. Ghanayim, et al., Artificial intelligence-based stethoscope for the diagnosis of aortic stenosis, Am. J. Med. 135 (9) (2022) 1124−1133. Available from: https://doi.org/10.1016/j.amjmed.2022.04.032.

15

Evaluation of artificial intelligence in education and its applications according to the opinions of school administrators

Gokmen Dagli, Fahriye Altinay, Zehra Altinay

SOCIETAL RESEARCH AND DEVELOPMENT CENTER, FACULTY OF EDUCATION, UNIVERSITY OF KYRENIA, NORTHERN PART OF CYPRUS, KYRENIA, MERSIN, TURKEY

15.1 Introduction

Artificial intelligence is created entirely with artificial tools, without making use of a living organism, and is a technological feature that works with the working system of machines by showing human-specific behaviors and movements. From an idealistic point of view, it is defined as robots with features such as feeling, predicting behaviors, and decision-making, which are human-specific feelings [1, p. 20]. Artificial intelligence is an information technology that can perceive human cognition, reason, comprehend, make sense of, generalize, make inferences, learn, and successfully perform more than one task at the same time [2, p. 1]. In a sense, it imitates human intelligence. The concept of artificial intelligence was first mentioned in a letter of recommendation presented at the Dortmund Conference in 1956 by John McCarthy, Marvin L. Minsky, Nathaniel Rochester, and Claude E. Shannon. However, John McCarthy is accepted as the inventor of this concept [3] defined intelligence as artificial intelligence, where the computer displays human-like behaviors such as reasoning, problem-solving, inferring, and generalizing, that is, using high-level cognitive skills. For example, Slage described the concept of artificial intelligence as "heuristic programming" [4]. Similarly, Ax has accepted artificial intelligence as intelligent programs that solve complex problems and create reactions not only to predetermined problems but also to a new situation [4]. Man was created to be the most intelligent of all living things on earth. This feature owes itself to the fact that it is equipped with "intelligence" [5], which means thinking, learning, reasoning, perceiving events, making sense, reaching conclusions, and making decisions according to the situation. With the invention of the computer, it was discovered that the abilities related to intelligence,

© 2024 Elsevier Inc. All rights reserved, including those for text and data mining, AI training, and similar technologies.

which is a human feature, can also be made by machines. Artificial intelligence is an information technology that can perceive human cognition, reason, comprehend, make sense of, generalize, make inferences, learn, and successfully perform more than one task at the same time [2, p. 1]. In a sense, it imitates human intelligence. Artificial intelligence, which is generally defined as intelligence displayed by machines, refers to the use of reasoning and predictive power, which are the characteristics of human intelligence, by machines in solving complex problems and making decisions taking into account changing conditions [6, p. 530]. Deep learning refers creation of artificial neural networks, that enables artificial intelligence to simultaneously perform multidimensional operations based on data. It refers in self-learning, inference, and predictive actions [7, pp.1–9]. Artificial intelligence, which has emerged on the scene with the ability to distinguish, now directs our lives with its features such as perception, self-learning and decision-making, and inference. In the near future, it is expected that artificial intelligence will facilitate the life of humanity by undertaking many tasks and will play a greater role in daily life than humans [8, pp. 90–91]. Studies carried out in education: grading and evaluation, student absenteeism and dropout prediction, student performance prediction, personalized teaching, sentiment analysis, suggestion systems, smart education systems, classroom monitoring, smart school, school evaluation and management, and supervision and analysis systems [9, p. 8].

The aim of this study is to reveal the status of the use of artificial intelligence in education according to the opinions of school administrators. For this purpose, answers to the following research questions were sought;

1. How is the use of artificial intelligence in education?
2. How should the use of artificial intelligence in education be planned in the future?

15.2 Method

15.2.1 Model of the research

Qualitative research methods were also used in the study. "Qualitative research can be defined as research in which qualitative data collection methods such as observation, interview, and document analysis are used, and a qualitative process is followed to reveal perceptions and events in a natural environment in a realistic and holistic way" [10]. According to Kuş [11], "the main feature of qualitative research is to reveal the perspectives and worlds of the meaning of the participants, and to see the world through the eyes of the participants."

15.2.2 Data collection tool

In the study, as a qualitative data collection tool, semistructured interview form and public reports were analyzed, semistructured interview questions were prepared, and research questions were asked. In the qualitative research approach, in-depth interviews (face-to-face interviews), direct observation, and document analysis techniques are generally used to collect data [12]. The data of this research were obtained through the analysis of public reports and the "face-to-face interview technique," which cannot be directly observed with other data collection tools, provides the opportunity to understand the perspectives of the participants on the subject, and is frequently preferred in the qualitative research approach. In the face-to-face interview technique method, the reasons that form the basis of the answers of the participants are also the source of revealing many dimensions such as emotions, thoughts, and beliefs [12].

15.2.3 Working group

The qualitative study group of this research was conducted with 10 school administrators in Northern Cyprus in the fall semester of 2022—23. School administrators participating in the research were selected according to the purposeful random sampling method. Purposeful random sampling is the purposeful classification of systematic and randomly selected case samples in line with the purpose of the research [13]. At the same time, the credibility of the information collected with this method is considered to be higher [14].

15.2.4 Data collection

In the process of collecting qualitative data in the research, 10 participants were interviewed. The participants were informed in advance about the purpose of the study and the use of the interview method as the data collection method. "Google Meeting" was organized in order to explain the subject and purpose of the meeting to the participants.

15.2.5 Analysis of data

For the analysis of qualitative data, interviews were conducted with the participants using the interview form, which is a data collection tool. According to the opinions of the interviewed participants, the answers given to each question were categorized one by one and placed in the tables. After this first categorization, the data were reexamined by the researcher and basic themes and categories were created. These determined themes and categories were reviewed by considering the relevant literature. Categories showing similar patterns were combined, while differing ones were grouped under a separate category and coded. The data obtained from the answers to the research interview questions were analyzed by content analysis. In content analysis, data is analyzed in four stages [10].

1. Coding the data: In this first stage of the content analysis, after each participant was given a number and the interviews were recorded, the data obtained from the participants were analyzed within the framework of the research, divided into meaningful parts, and the conceptual meaning was named and coded. For the reliability calculation of the research, the average was calculated as 92% by using the reliability formula suggested by Miles and Huberman [15]. Reliability calculations over 70% are considered reliable for research [15].

2. **Finding themes:** At this stage, the codes determined during the coding phase of the data were considered as separate categories and evaluated as separate themes.
3. **Organizing and defining the data according to codes and themes:** At this stage, the opinions of the participants were explained in a language that the reader could understand, and the opinions were presented to the reader firsthand.
4. **Interpretation of findings:** The interpretation of the findings, which are described and presented in detail by the researcher, and some results are explained at this last stage.

15.3 Findings and comments

The findings of the research were analyzed in a way to answer each research question and the results of this analysis are given below, respectively.

Dimension I: Findings on the use of artificial intelligence in education: The first dimension of the research was created within the scope of revealing the views on the use of artificial intelligence in education. In this context, 10 participants were asked for their opinions. The answers given to these questions were coded and the themes were extracted, and the distributions of these themes are given in Table 15−1.

Some of the participants' opinions regarding the findings on the use of artificial intelligence in education are as follows:

K(9) *"I can say that as a result of the use of artificial intelligence in education, it will enable the performance of students to be evaluated better."*

K(3) *"In my opinion, great and valuable contributions will be made in helping the evaluation and supervision of the school."*

According to the opinions of school administrators, it is understood from the opinions received that the use of artificial intelligence in education will enable the performance of students to be evaluated better. In addition to these, it can be said that according to the opinions of the school administrators, it will help the evaluation and supervision of the schools, according to the opinions of the participants.

Table 15–1 Findings on the use of artificial intelligence in education.

Category	Themes	Frequency (f)	Percent (%)
Use of artificial intelligence in education	Allowing students to better evaluate their performance in education	8	80
	Helping the development of smart education systems	4	40
	Assisting in evaluating and supervising the school	6	60
	Development of teaching methods	7	70

Table 15–2 Findings for planning the use of artificial intelligence in education in the future.

Category	Themes	Frequency (*f*)	Percent (%)
Planning the use of artificial intelligence in education in the future	Planning of lessons and topics in education	7	70
	Planning new assessment systems for students in the future	6	60
	Planning of artificial intelligence in classroom management	4	40
	Planning of artificial intelligence in school management	6	60
	Making plans about how learning with artificial intelligence will take place	5	50

Dimension II: Findings on the planning of the use of artificial intelligence in education in the future. The second dimension of the research was created within the scope of revealing the views on the planning of the use of artificial intelligence in education in the future. The answers given to these questions were coded and the themes were extracted, and the distributions of these themes are given in Table 15–2.

Some of the participant opinions are as follows:

K(8) "I think that serious planning should be made about which courses and subjects should be given in education in order to plan for the use of artificial intelligence in education in the future."

K(1) "I think it will be very important to make urgent plans about how artificial intelligence will take place in school management."

According to the opinions of the participants, it is understood that serious planning should be made about which courses and subjects should be given in education first within the scope of planning artificial intelligence in education in the future. In addition to these, it can be said according to the opinions of the participants that it is of great importance to make urgent plans about how artificial intelligence will take place in school management.

15.4 Conclusion and recommendations

Within the scope of the findings obtained according to the participants' opinions of the research, the following results and recommendations were analyzed to answer each research question, and the results and recommendations of this research are given below, respectively.

Dimension I: Results on the use of artificial intelligence in education: According to the opinions of school administrators, it is understood from the opinions received that the use of artificial intelligence in education will enable the performance of students to be evaluated better. In addition, it can be said that according to the opinions of school administrators, it will help in the evaluation and supervision of schools [16]. Participants suggest that integration of AI in education could contribute to advancement of smart education systems. They underlined that if artificial intelligence is used effectively in education, teaching methods will develop further and contribute significantly to the education and training of students [17].

Dimension II: The results for the planning of the use of artificial intelligence in education in the future: According to the opinions of the participants, it is understood that serious planning should be made about which courses and subjects should be given in education within the scope of planning artificial intelligence in education in the future. In addition to these, it can be said according to the opinions of the participants that it is of great importance to make urgent plans about how artificial intelligence will take place in school management [18]. It can be said that new assessment systems for students in the future should be urgently planned, especially within the scope of planning the use of artificial intelligence in education. In addition, it is understood that serious planning should be made about how artificial intelligence will be in classroom management. It is also recommended to make plans about how to learn with artificial intelligence [19].

References

[1] C.H. Değirmenci, Yapay Zeka, Girdap Kitap, İstanbul, 2018.

[2] K.M. Gondal, Artificial intelligence and educational leadership, Annals of King Edward Medical University 24 (4) (2018) 1—2.

[3] J. McCarthy, What is artificial intelligence?. Erişim adresi (11 Ocak 2019). <http://wwwformal.stanford.edu/jmc/whatisai/>, 2004.

[4] V.V. Nabiyev, Yapay zeka: insan-bilgisayar etkileşimi, Seçkin Yayıncılık, Ankara, 2012.

[5] Türk Dil Kurumu, 30 Ekim 2020 tarihinde. <https://sozluk.gov.tr/adresinden erişildi>, 2020.

[6] M. Obschonka, D.B. Audretsch, Artificial intelligence and big data entrepreneurship: a new era has begun, Small Bus. Econ. 55 (2020) 529—539. Available from: https://doi.org/10.1007/s11187-019-00202-4.

[7] D. Mathew, J.R. Giles, A.E. Baxter, D.A. Oldridge, A.R. Greenplate, J.E. Wu, et al., Deep immune profiling of COVID-19 patients reveals distinct immunotypes with therapeutic implications, Science 369 (6508) (2020) eabc8511.

[8] K. Komalavalli, R. Hemalatha, S. Dhanalakshmi, A survey of artificial intelligence in smart phones and its applications among the students of higher education in and around Chennai city, Shanlax Int. J. Educ. 8 (3) (2020) 89—95.

[9] K. Ahmad, W. Iqbal, A. Hassan, J. Qadir, D. Benhaddou, M. Ayyash et al., Articial intelligence in education: a panoramic review, (2020) 1—51. Available from: https://doi.org/10.35542/osf.io/zvu2n.

[10] A. Yıldırım, H. ve Şimşek, Nitel Araştırma Yöntemleri, Seçkin Yayıncılık, Ankara, 2013.

[11] E. Kuş, Nicel-Nitel Araştırma Teknikleri: Sosyal Bilimlerde Araştırma Teknikleri: Nicel mi; Nitel mi? Anı Yayıncılık, Ankara, 2003.

[12] R. Legard, J. Keegan, K. Word, In-depth interviews, 2003.

[13] C. Marshall, G.B. ve Rossman, Niteliksel Araştırma Tasarımı, Adaçayı Yayınları, New York, 2014.

[14] J.W. Creswell, Qualitative Inquiry and Research Design. Choosing among Five Traditions, Sage, Thousand Oaks, CA, USA, 2016.

[15] M.B. Miles, A.M. Huberman, Qualitative Data Analysis: An Expanded Sourcebook, 2nd ed., Sage, California, 1994.

[16] Z. Hu, Influence of introducing artificial intelligence on autonomous learning in vocational education, in: H.A. Jemal, R.C. Kim-Kwang, X. Zheng, A. ve Mohammed (Eds.), AISC, 1244, Springer, 2020, pp. 361−366. Available from: https://doi.org/10.1007/978-3-030-53980-1_54.

[17] L. Chen, P. Chen, Z. Lin, Artificial intelligence in education: a review, IEEE Access. 8 (2020) 75264−75278. Available from: https://doi.org/10.1109/ACCESS.2020.2988510.

[18] V. Kolchenko, Can modern AI replace teachers? Not so fast! Artificial intelligence and adaptive learning: personalized education in the AI age, HAPS Educator 22 (3) (2018) 249−252. Available from: https://doi.org/10.21692/haps.2018.032.

[19] E. Fast, E. Horvitz, Long-term trends in the public perception of artificial intelligence, Proc. AAAI Conf. Artif. Intell. 31 (1) (2020) 1−7.

16

Evaluation of tourism developments with artificial intelligence according to the opinions of tourism hotel managers

Nesrin Menemenci[1], Mehmet Altınay[2], Zehra Altinay[3],
Fahriye Altinay[3], Gokmen Dagli[3]

[1]FACULTY OF TOURISM, NEAR EAST UNIVERSITY, NORTHERN PART OF CYPRUS, NICOSIA, MERSIN, TURKEY [2]FACULTY OF TOURISM, UNIVERSITY OF KYRENIA, KYRENIA, NORTHERN PART OF CYPRUS, MERSIN, TURKEY [3]SOCIETAL RESEARCH AND DEVELOPMENT CENTER, FACULTY OF EDUCATION, UNIVERSITY OF KYRENIA, NORTHERN PART OF CYPRUS, KYRENIA, MERSIN, TURKEY

16.1 Introduction

The most important feature and the strongest aspect that distinguishes humans from all other living things is undoubtedly their brains. Because people can use their brains effectively and efficiently, they have played a very important role in the development of our world. One of the most important inventions of the technology era we live in today is artificial intelligence. Especially recently, it is seen that the concept of artificial intelligence has been mentioned a lot.

Many organizations in the tourism sector are affected by artificial intelligence applications in the age of change. The artificial intelligence revolution, which is effective in industrial and technological fields, has accelerated in the culture, art, and tourism sectors. The artificial intelligence revolution, which is effective in industrial and technological fields, has accelerated in the culture, art, and tourism sectors. At this point, many institutions, from education to health, are constantly renewing themselves with technological developments in order to attract the attention of the growing generation with technology and to integrate with them [1].

Computational Intelligence and Blockchain in Complex Systems. DOI: https://doi.org/10.1016/B978-0-443-13268-1.00028-5
© 2024 Elsevier Inc. All rights reserved, including those for text and data mining, AI training, and similar technologies.

Artificial intelligence and virtual reality technologies have left traditional activities behind and created environments that allow users to feel real and emotional intensity by freeing them from monotony. Virtual reality applications will be platforms where tourists can get ideas and information and give feedback before the trip, rather than being used as games and entertainment in the coming years. Therefore, it is necessary to increase the promotion of applications designed by using technologies such as increased tourism destinations and virtual reality [2]. World competition has really moved to virtual world competition; As humanity's interest in technology increases, tourism businesses will also need to adapt new technologies [3].

One of the most important inventions of the technology era we live in today is artificial intelligence. Especially recently, it is seen that the concept of artificial intelligence has been mentioned a lot. Artificial intelligence has begun to be seriously influential in every field today [4,5]. In this context, we can talk about the existence of artificial intelligence in the field of tourism. This study aims to reveal the use of artificial intelligence and suggestions for the future according to the views of tourism hotel management managers.

16.2 Artificial intelligence in tourism

Technology has revolutionized the tourism industry. Together with the strategy of tourism organizations and destinations, it has become a competitive power [6].

The smart tourism ecosystem is formed as a result of the integration of the concepts in it with the smart approach. Therefore, the concepts of smart tourist, smart hotel, and smart destination were born. At the same time, there are many smart applications belonging to the smart tourism ecosystem. The most popular and innovative ICT applications used in today's tourism sector are Internet of Things (IoT), big data analysis, augmented and virtual reality, artificial intelligence technology, voice technology, wearable devices, WiFi connection, web technologies, and mobile applications. While all operations become interconnected with IoT, augmented and virtual reality are mostly used to improve customer experience and content marketing [7,8].

Artificial intelligence has become increasingly popular in the tourism sector, as in many other sectors, in recent years. Various study authors on the subject stated that artificial intelligence and robotic technologies contribute to the improvement of productivity and competitiveness, service quality, and guest experiences in tourism enterprises [9–11].

16.3 Use of artificial intelligence in hotels

The tourism industry is today faced with a new revolution that is more powerful, transformative, and with longer-term effects than previous changes; it has stepped into an era in which robotic applications are introduced [12]. Despite the labor-intensive workforce structure, the industry has entered artificial intelligence applications by using digital technology products.

A tremendous amount of data emerges in the tourism industry due to standard and day-to-day procedures. These data are recorded regularly, thanks to artificial intelligence. Online check-in processes, kiosk applications, smart key systems, and constantly updating hotel automation systems are the usual examples of artificial intelligence applications. The artificial intelligence product tape system service application, which was first put into operation in a restaurant in Japan, has brought a very different dimension to the operation of the hospitality sector.

16.4 Methodology

The qualitative research method was used in the study because it provides an in-depth and detailed perspective to the researcher in small groups. At the same time, phenomenological design, which is one of the qualitative research types, was used. The phenomenological design mainly focuses on the phenomena that we are aware of but do not know in detail [13]. The study group of the research consists of 12 hotel managers working in the Turkish Republic of Northern Cyprus, determined by the purposeful sampling method. Interviews were conducted to collect qualitative data.

The interview questions were prepared by the researcher and general information about the subject was given to the school administrators before the interviews. For the content validity of the interview form, it was made ready after receiving the opinions of academicians who are experts in their fields. Data were collected using a semistructured interview form prepared by the researcher. Interviews were held with 12 participants and the data were written down. The interviews were conducted by the same researcher for the validity and reliability of the research. The data obtained from the participants were examined by the researchers and the themes were determined by associating them with the literature review made before the interview. While analyzing the data, the opinions of the participants were divided into groups and categories. This analysis consists of creating a general framework for the study and defining and interpreting the findings. The basic process in content analysis is to gather similar data within the framework of certain concepts and themes and to organize and interpret them in a way that readers can understand. At the same time, citations can be used to indicate ideas, topics, or concepts while conducting content analysis [13].

16.5 Findings

Participants were primarily asked for their opinions on whether the use of artificial intelligence was sufficient. Then, within the scope of the research, the participants were asked about their opinions on the use of artificial intelligence for tourism purposes, the advantages and disadvantages of using artificial intelligence in the hotel sector, and their suggestions for the use of artificial intelligence in accommodation businesses in the future. Table 16−1 developed by authors according to data collection.

Table 16–1 Participants' views.

Theme	Subtheme	F	%
Does artificial intelligence use it adequately?	No	12	100
	Yes	0	0
Using artificial intelligence for tourism purposes	Marketing	12	34
	Reservation and automation systems	8	23
	Collection and storage of data	5	14
	Security practices	5	14
	Offering different experiences	3	9
	Providing competitive advantage	2	6
Advantages of using artificial intelligence in the hotel industry	Facilitate customer access	10	30
	Cost reduction	7	21
	Increases tourism demand	5	15
	Offering a different experience	3	9
	data storage	5	15
	Provides convenience in work areas	3	9
Disadvantages of using artificial intelligence in the hotel industry	Infrastructure issues	12	35
	affecting the human workforce	9	26
	Difficult to use for some age groups	7	21
	Costly	6	18
Suggestions for the future use of artificial intelligence in hospitality businesses	Educating all stakeholders	9	35
	Strategic planning should be done	6	23
	It should spread throughout the tourism sector.	6	23
	There should be incentives	3	11
	Increasing promotional activities	2	8

As a result of the research findings, all of the participants stated that the use of artificial intelligence in tourism is not sufficient. When the use of artificial intelligence for tourism purposes was examined, all of the participants ($n12$) stated that it was used for marketing purposes. Then, participant opinions are in the form of reservation and automation systems ($n8$), data collection and storage ($n5$), and security applications ($n5$), presenting different experiences ($n3$) and providing a competitive advantage ($n2$).

"Currently, we mostly use artificial intelligence for advertising and marketing through social media and websites in order to reach our target audience. The use of artificial intelligence in general provides virtual reality guests with different experiences." (P6)

"Today, the use of artificial intelligence in the field of tourism gives destinations and businesses a competitive advantage. We primarily use it in digital marketing to reach our guests." (P12)

Participants were asked about the advantages and disadvantages of using artificial intelligence in the hotel industry. As an advantage, the participants mostly stated that artificial intelligence facilitates access to customers ($n10$), reduces costs ($n7$), increases tourism demand ($n5$), offers different experiences (*n*3), helps data storage (*n*5), and provides convenience in working areas (*n*3). As a disadvantage, all of them stated infrastructure problems (*n*12).

"Many artificial intelligence applications offer different experiences to guests. Thus, the attention of the target market is drawn. This ensures an increase in demand. The most important disadvantage for us is the lack of adequate infrastructure." (P3)

"When we look at the use of artificial intelligence in hotels in the world, it has many advantages, in fact, it is seen that it facilitates the storage and access of data, and also provides convenience in work areas. I can give examples of reservation systems, marketing methods and even kitchen applications. In tourism, which is a labor-intensive sector, it may be a disadvantage for artificial intelligence to replace employees. Currently, infrastructure problems pose a disadvantage for Northern Cyprus." (P8)

Participants were asked for their suggestions for the use of artificial intelligence in accommodation businesses in the future. Participants stated that all stakeholders should be trained (*n*9), strategic planning should be done (*n*6) and spread throughout the tourism sector (*n*6), incentives should be provided (*n*3), and promotion activities should be increased (*n*2). Participant opinions are as follows:

"The use of artificial intelligence applications should be extended to the entire tourism region, that is, the accessibility of the leading tourism products of museums and historical places should be increased with artificial intelligence applications, so we can talk about competitive power." (P5)

"Especially the managers of the tourism sector, ministry officials, local managers should be trained and awareness should be increased. It should also be given as a course in universities for future tourism professionals." (P11)

16.6 Conclusion and recommendations

It is possible to say that the tourism sector has developed with the development of technology. The aim of this research is to examine the opinions of hotel managers in Northern Cyprus on artificial intelligence applications and their suggestions for the future. As a result of the research, it was concluded that the use of artificial intelligence in the hotel sector in Northern Cyprus is not sufficient. In line with the opinions of the participants, it was determined that artificial intelligence applications were mostly used in advertising and marketing studies. Another result is that artificial intelligence facilitates access to customers and increases demand by attracting their attention. Naumov [14] states that service automation provided by artificial intelligence benefits the service industry and its use is increasing in popularity.

As a result of the research, it is revealed that artificial intelligence offers different experiences to guests. Similarly, the research findings of Li et al. [15] support this view. Osawa et al. [15] revealed one of the disadvantages affecting the human workforce. Participants emphasized that training should be given for the use of artificial intelligence applications in the tourism sector in the future.

References

[1] T.H. Davenport, The AI Advantage. How to Put Artificial Intelligence Revolution to Work, The MIT Press, Cambridge, MA, 2018.

[2] J. Murphy, C. Hofacker, U. Gretzel, Dawning of the age of robots in hospitality and tourism: challenges for teaching and research, Eur. J. Tour. Res. 15 (2017) 104−111.

[3] J. Reis, N. Melao, J. Salvadorinho, B. Soares, A. Rosete, Service robots in the hospitality industry: the case of Henn-na Hotel, Japan, Technol. Soc. 63 (2020) 101423.

[4] N. Samala, B.S. Katkam, R.S. Bellamkonda, R.V. Rodriguez, Impact of AI and robotics in the tourism sector: a critical insight, J. Tour. Futures 8 (1) (2022) 73−87.

[5] S. Ivanov, C. Webster, Conceptual framework of the use of robots, artificial intelligence and service automation in travel, tourism, and hospitality companies, in: S. Ivanov, C. Webster (Eds.), Robots, Artificial Intelligence and Service Automation in Travel, Tourism and Hospitality, Emerald Publishing Limited, Bingley, 2019, pp. 7−37.

[6] U. Gretzel, C. Koo, M. Sigala, Z. Xiang, Special issue on smart tourism: convergence of information technologies, experiences, and theories, Electron. Mark. 25 (2015) 175−177.

[7] D. Belanche, L.V. Casalo, C. Flavian, Frontline robots in tourism and hospitality: service enhancement and cost reduction? Electron. Mark. 31 (2020) 477−492.

[8] A. Dalgıc, K. Birdir, Smart hotels and technological applications, in: E. Celtek (Ed.), Handbook of Research on Smart Technology Applications in the Tourism Industry, IGI Global, Hershey, PA, 2020, pp. 324−343.

[9] E. Stoilova, AI chatbots as a customer service and support tool, Robonomics. J. Auto. Econ. 2 (2021) 21.

[10] V.W.S. Tung, N. Au, Exploring customer experiences with robotics in hospitality, Int. J. Contemp. Hospitality Manag. 30 (7) (2018) 2680−2697.

[11] S. Makridakis, The forthcoming artificial intelligence (AI) revolution: its impact on society and firms, Futures 90 (2017) 46−60.

[12] S. Ivanov, C. Webster, K. Berezina, Adoption of robots and service automation by tourism and hospitality companies, in: INVTUR Conference, Aveiro, 17−19 May 2017.

[13] A. Yıldırım, H. ve Şimşek, Qualitative Research Methods in the Social Sciences, Seçkin Publishing, Ankara, 2013.

[14] N. Naumov, The impact of robots, artificial intelligence, and service automation on service quality in hospitality, in: S. Ivanov, C. Webster (Eds.), Robots, Artificial Intelligence and Service Automation in Travel, Tourism and Hospitality, Emerald Publishing, UK, 2019.

[15] J.J. Li, M.A. Bonn, B.H. Ye, Hotel employee's artificial intelligence and robotics awareness and its impact on turnover intention: the moderating roles of perceived organizational support and competitive psychological climate, Tour. Manag. 73 (1) (2019) 172−181.

[16] H. Osawa, A. Ema, H. Hattori, N. Akiya, N. Kanzaki, A. Kubo et al., What is real risk and benefit on work with robots? in: Proceedings of the Companion of the 2017 ACM/IEEE International Conference on Human-Robot Interaction, 2017, pp. 241−242. <https://doi.org/10.1145/3029798.3038312>.

17

The manager's perspective on the effect of using artificial intelligence of things in work life

Furkan Ocel[1], Tolgay Karanfiller[1], Eser Gemikonakli[2]

[1]MANAGEMENT INFORMATION SYSTEM, SCHOOL OF APPLIED SCIENCES, CYPRUS INTERNATIONAL UNIVERSITY, NICOSIA, NORTH CYPRUS [2]DEPARTMENT OF COMPUTER ENGINEERING, FACULTY OF ENGINEERING, UNIVERSITY OF KYRENIA, KYRENIA, MERSIN, TURKEY

17.1 Introduction

Contrasting to the natural intelligence used by humans and animals, machine intelligence, defined as artificial intelligence (AI), was developed for machines like robots to carry out essential tasks at any stage of the production process [1]. Development in AI applications has affected future work opportunities, types, management methods, and skills in the industry. Therefore, instead of an unimaginative ordinary-based workforce, a qualified one based on improved technology will dominate work life [2]. This change could bring new sectors into existence together with the new approach regarding the managerial point of view.

Human life with technological improvements has changed dramatically yearly, bringing new dimensions to human lives and affecting their attitudes, perspectives on the future, daily work, and earnings. Especially for certain types of jobs and demographics, the advancement of AI may cause labor to lose their jobs due to automation. Here, disadvantaged socioeconomic groups within different job classes may suffer the negative consequences of AI applications, resulting in job polarization [3]. Therefore one of the challenging issues may be the human and machine interaction adopting AI technology to increase the performance of the production process and eliminate the workers' fear and anxiety about losing their jobs.

Using AI technology in work life redefined the manager's role. The management skills in the industry gain a different approach through technology investments and integration. Here, intelligent risk management models should be incorporated into the workflow to identify and manage risks using appropriate methods. Developing a system with machines' help and managing it is an inevitable reality and necessary to adopt the new industrial revolution due to technological improvements.

Computational Intelligence and Blockchain in Complex Systems. DOI: https://doi.org/10.1016/B978-0-443-13268-1.00025-X
© 2024 Elsevier Inc. All rights reserved, including those for text and data mining, AI training, and similar technologies.

The managers are highly likely to have managerial difficulties due to the uncertainty of workers' adaptation to new technological applications. Therefore analyzing the managers' approach and opinions about integrating specialized machine intelligence and generalized human intelligence in work life is significant.

The paper's organization is as follows: Section 17.2 presents the literature survey. While Section 17.3 describes the methods used, Section 17.4 presents research findings. In Section 17.5, relevant conclusions addressed the managers' opinions about the impact of using AI in work life.

17.2 Literature survey

According to the authors in Ref. [4], AI technology can quickly develop processes of nonroutine activities for better decisions, whereas management systems should include AI integration in different occupations. The possible changes in the role of managers may create fear of AI adoption.

The authors discussed the effect of AI technology on work life [5]. They stated that the capability of AI applications is advanced compared to the existing processes, which can cause unfavorable results for recruiting workers considering their existing skills and methods used for the workflows.

The main discussion in Ref. [6] is about the limitation of AI applications regarding the decision process, which may not include strict sequential decision-making processes. The workers also have anxiety about uploading their data to the AI system for workforce performance evaluation, which lacks common sense.

The authors in Ref. [7] stated that there is an agreement about the positive impact of digitalization on the quality of service (QoS); however, this should be supported by developing new approaches and policies for the workflows due to the complexity of the AI and human interactions. Obtaining a desired QoS and performance may be only possible by involving the stakeholders and considering their doubts and anxiety.

AI technology and digitalization bring new approaches regarding management skills. The authors in [8] conducted profound research to show why the management control process can affect physiological features due to technology usage. They first investigated digital technologies increasing the clarity of the work done, resulting in more pressure on workers and managers. Secondly, using improved technology for data analysis decreased the information shortcoming. Finally, digitalization provided an increased motivation to provide updated reports submission. However, there is a consensus that an automated management control system provided dissatisfaction among workers and managers because of the changes in workflow. Here, researchers should conduct more empirical research to investigate workers' and managers' opinions.

The study in Ref. [9] discussed the employee's physiological situation once the automation system dominates the work life. According to the authors, the organization should consider its employees' opinions before adopting AI technology.

Similar to the studies discussed above, authors in Ref. [10] discussed psychosomatic illness because of working with technological equipment daily. They stated that human resources units of the organizations should take social support and in-service training into account to eliminate the negative consequences of AI integration.

Authors in Ref. [11] reviewed the existing studies to identify the changes in the adoption of AI on managers' leadership skills. They clarified that managerial decision-making processes and their skills are a hot topic to investigate in detail.

Most studies in the literature discussed the theoretical approach of integrating AI technology in work life and its effect on social life rather than the empirical analysis. This study provided the managers' opinions on developing an entire system considering the behavioral aspects for better and well-designed integration.

17.3 Methodology

The study uses a quantitative approach to examine the data collected from 202 individuals in managerial positions in the Northern Cyprus and Turkey, experiencing AI integration in their organizations. The AI anxiety scale developed, as a Likert-type research scale, by researchers in Ref. [12] was used for the analysis. We obtained the data using the questionnaire survey model as a quantitative research method. Statistical package for social sciences (SPSS), statistical measurement, single-run T-test, and single-run analysis of variance (ANOVA) test were applied, and the results obtained were figured out by interpreting the situation analysis method of the qualitative research method. The statistical significance level was accepted as 0.05 in the study. The independent parameters in Table 17−1 mainly comprised gender, work experience per year, education level, and marital status. Most respondents were male ($N = 112$) and 90 were female. Work experience ranges from 1 year, with the largest group comprising 65 managers, to 15 + years. There were respondents from different education

Table 17–1 Independent variables and their frequencies.

Factors	Status	Frequency (N)
Gender	Male	112
	Female	90
Work experience/year	1 +	65
	1−5	57
	5−10	36
	10−15	18
	15 +	26
Education level	Associate degree	46
	Undergraduate	115
	Graduate	17
	PhD	24
Marital status	Single	71
	Married	131

levels, where the superiority of respondents was from the undergraduate level ($N = 115$). The majority of the respondents were married ($N = 131$).

17.4 Findings

In this study, the following results were found according to the study's problem statement and research questions.

Research Question 1: Is there a significant difference in learning to understand all the specific functions associated with an AI technique/product according to the gender of the participants?

As a result of the test, 112 men and 90 women participated in the analysis and were asked to answer questions from 1 to 5. While the mean of the answers given to the first hypothesis by males was 1,598, this was 2733 for females, as given in Table 17–1. There is a significant difference between genders regarding the answers obtained for the question. According to the results presented, male participants were not worried about learning to use specific functions of AI technology as females were indecisive ($p < 0.05$).

Research Question 2: Is it evident that learning to use AI technology differs according to the time the participants are in management?

Participants were grouped into five different periods considering their working year in management as $1 +$ years, 1–5 years, 5–10 years, 10–15 years, and over 15 years. According to the ANOVA test, at least one group differs significantly from others in the learning tendency as the number of years the participants spend in management. As a result of the analysis, learning how an AI technique/product works shows that the participants have a positive but moderate relationship with the time they are in management.

Research Question 3: Is there a significant difference in participants' anxiety that AI technology will replace humans according to education level?

Duncan's test was used to determine the degree of difference between education levels. While the master's and doctoral groups have the same attitude, the associate and undergraduate groups have different attitudes from each other and these groups. According to the results obtained from the correlation analysis, the state of worrying that an AI technique/product can replace humans shows that there is a positive but moderate relationship between the educational level of the participants.

Research Question 4: Is there a positive difference in participants' anxiety about AI technology addiction according to their educational level?

There is a favorable distribution but a moderate relationship for participants' anxiety about AI technology addiction regarding their education degree. As a result of the Duncan variable test, while the master's and doctoral groups exhibited the same attitude, the associate and undergraduate groups behaved differently from these groups.

Research Question 5: Is there a positive difference in participants' opinions on whether AI technology will cause job loss according to their experience in management?

There is a positive but moderate relationship between the individuals participating in the research that they will lose their jobs by introducing AI techniques/products and the time spent by the participants in management. While the group that has just started a job and has a 1-year working time has no anxiety, the group working between 1 and 15 years is undecided, and those who have worked over 15 years are worried about the improved AI technology used in work life.

Research Question 6: According to the participant's marital status, is there a significant positive difference in participants' opinions on whether AI technology will dominate work life and gain their independence?

The answers to the question differ according to the married and single status. Correlation analysis was applied to determine the direction of the relationship between the variables. It was determined that there was a positive and moderate relationship between the state of concern and marital status.

17.5 Conclusion

The changes brought by the digital age have changed not only the jobs but also the security and the way they work, the benefits of customers, the status of employees, and the workflows [13]. AI technology is widely used today. The rapid progress of AI technology has provided many conveniences and difficulties in human life. Here, this study presented the manager's perspective on using AI of Things in work life. The managers who participated in the research have different approaches to using AI in a work environment due to their work experience and gender. They also have anxiety about the AI technology that may dominate their work life and cause them to lose their job. The education level is one parameter providing a significant difference in managers' opinions regarding using AI technology for daily work.

References

[1] S. Ziyad, Artificial intelligence definition, ethics and standards, in: Electronics Communication: Law, Standards, and Practice 18ELEC07, April 2019.

[2] B. Halil, Gelişen Teknolojiler, Değişen İşgücü Nitelikleri ve Eğitim, OPUS Int. J. Soc. Res 8 (14) (2018) 599−632.

[3] L. Nurski, M. Hoffman, The impact of artificial intelligence on the nature and quality of jobs, Bruegel Working Paper 14, 2022 1−39.

[4] R.F. Morgan, A. David, E. James, et al., Toward understanding the impact of artificial intelligence on labor, Proc. Natl Acad. Sci. 116 (14) (2019) 6531−6539.

[5] A. Daron, A. David, H. Jonathon, et al., Artificial intelligence and jobs: 'evidence from online vacancies', J. Labor. Econ. 40 (S1) (2019) S293−S340.

[6] T. Kochan, Artificial intelligence and the future of work: a proactive strategy, AI Mag. 42 (1) (2021) 16−24.

[7] J. Aditya, Impact of digitalization and artificial intelligence as causes and enablers of organizational change, Nottingham University Business School, 2021.

[8] F. Jochen, A literature review on the impact of digitalisation on management control, J. Manag. Control. 34 (2022) 9−65.

[9] H.J. Lee, A. Bazzoli, S. Lee, et al., Technology advancements and employees' qualitative job insecurity in the Republic of Korea: does training help? employer provided vs. self-paid training, Int. J. Environ. Res. Public. Health J. Manag. Control. 19 (14368) (2022) 1−13.

[10] M. Nishtha, N.T. Shalini, K.K. Arpan, et al., Impact of artificial intelligence on employees working in industry 4.0 led organizations, Int. J. Manpow. 43 (2) (2021) 334−354.

[11] E. Malin, D. Camran, Artificial intelligence's impact on management, Master thesis, Kth Royal Institute Of Technology, School of Indudtrial Engineering and Management, 2020.

[12] A. Bülent, Ö. Ayşegül, Ö. Hasan, Yapay Zeka Kaygı (YZK) Ölçeği: Türkçeye Uyarlama,Geçerlik ve Güvenirlik Çalışması, Alanya Akademik Bakış Derg. 5 (2) (2021) 1125−1146.

[13] S. Aksu, O. Sürgevil, Digital Çağın Yetkinlikleri: Çalışanlar, İnsan Kaynakları Uzmanları ve Yöneticiler Çerçevesinden Bakış', J. Bus. Digital Age 2 (2) (2019) 54−68.

18

Machine learning algorithms for blockchain-based security mechanisms in UAVs: a review

Eser Gemikonakli[1], Yoney Kirsal Ever[2]

[1]COMPUTER ENGINEERING DEPARTMENT, UNIVERSITY OF KYRENIA, ŞEHIT YAHYA BAKIR SOKAK, KARAKUM, KYRENIA, NORTH CYPRUS [2]ENGINEERING FACULTY, COMPUTER ENGINEERING DEPARTMENT, CYPRUS INTERNATIONAL UNIVERSITY, NICOSIA, NORTH CYPRUS

18.1 Introduction

Unmanned aerial vehicles (UAVs) have become an increasingly popular technology and have revolutionized various industries, from military and defense to agriculture and transportation [1,2].

However, the rise in the number of UAVs also poses significant security challenges, as they are vulnerable to hacking, cyber-attacks, and other security threats. Blockchain (BC) technology has emerged as a promising solution to these challenges, offering secure and tamper-proof data storage and transaction management [3−5].

However, as the use of UAVs continues to expand, so do the risks associated with their operation. One of the most pressing concerns is the security of UAVs, particularly in the context of BC technology [6,7].

BC-based security mechanisms offer an attractive solution to the security challenges associated with UAVs [6,7]. By using a decentralized, distributed ledger, BC can ensure that the data generated by UAVs is tamper-proof and secure [7]. However, the implementation of BC technology in UAVs poses significant challenges, such as the need for efficient and reliable machine learning (ML) algorithms [8,9].

ML algorithms can play a vital role in the development of BC-based security mechanisms for UAVs. By analyzing large datasets, ML algorithms can detect patterns, predict outcomes, and identify anomalies, which can help to identify potential threats and prevent security breaches [10]. This integration of ML and BC technology has the potential to revolutionize the security mechanisms of UAVs, making them more reliable, efficient, and secure [11].

ML algorithms have the potential to play a critical role in the development of BC-based security mechanisms for UAVs [5]. ML can be used to analyze large datasets generated by UAVs, detect patterns, and identify potential threats or anomalies, thus improving the security of the system.

Computational Intelligence and Blockchain in Complex Systems. DOI: https://doi.org/10.1016/B978-0-443-13268-1.00004-2
© 2024 Elsevier Inc. All rights reserved, including those for text and data mining, AI training, and similar technologies.

ML and BC are two rapidly evolving technologies that have been attracting a lot of attention in recent years [12]. ML is a subfield of artificial intelligence that involves the use of algorithms and statistical models to enable computer systems to improve their performance on a specific task over time. BC, on the other hand, is a distributed ledger technology that is designed to provide a secure and transparent way of recording and sharing data.

The combination of ML and BC has the potential to revolutionize various industries, including finance, healthcare, and supply chain management. In this review, we will discuss the current state of ML in BC methodology and explore some of the potential benefits and challenges of this technology.

This review aims to provide a comprehensive overview of the current state-of-the-art in the field and identify opportunities for future research and development [12,13].

In this paper, we will explore the different machine-learning algorithms that can be used to develop BC-based security mechanisms in UAVs. We will examine the benefits and limitations of various ML models and discuss their potential applications in UAV security. By understanding the various ML algorithms and their potential applications, we can take a significant step forward in developing secure and reliable UAVs that can operate in a wide range of industries.

18.2 Related works

In recent years, UAVs have gained widespread popularity across various industries, including logistics, transportation, surveillance, and agriculture. However, the security challenges associated with the use of UAVs, such as data breaches and cyber-attacks, pose significant risks to their safe and efficient operation. To address these challenges, researchers have explored the use of BC-based security mechanisms in combination with ML algorithms. In this section, we provide an overview of the research on security and privacy mechanisms for UAVs and applications of ML algorithms for BC-based security mechanisms in UAVs.

18.2.1 Security mechanisms in unmanned aerial vehicles

Research on security mechanisms in UAVs is an active field, and several research reviews have been conducted to provide an overview of the existing work. Here is a comparison of some of the existing research reviews on security mechanisms in UAVs:

1. "Toward the UAVs—a comprehensive review" [5]: This review provides an overview of the security mechanisms for UAVs. It covers topics such as communication security, data confidentiality and integrity, authentication and authorization, and intrusion detection and response. The review identifies several research challenges, including secure communication, lightweight cryptography, and intrusion detection, and proposes some future research directions. The authors also present a detailed analysis of existing security mechanisms for UAVs and highlight their strengths and limitations.

2. "Intrusion detection systems for networked UAVs—a survey" [14]: This survey provides an overview of the security of UAVs. It covers topics such as cyber-physical security, data confidentiality, authentication and authorization, and intrusion detection and response. The survey identifies several research challenges, including secure communication, data encryption, and vulnerability management, and proposes some future research directions. The authors also present a comprehensive analysis of existing security mechanisms for UAVs and highlight their benefits and limitations.

3. "UAV assistance paradigm—state-of-the-art in applications and challenges" [15]: This review provides an overview of the security and privacy of unmanned aerial systems, including UAVs. It covers topics such as communication security, data confidentiality and integrity, identity and access management, and secure software development. The review identifies several research challenges, including secure communication, data encryption, and software vulnerabilities, and proposes some future research directions. The authors also present a detailed analysis of existing security and privacy mechanisms for UAVs and highlight their strengths and limitations.

Overall, these research reviews provide valuable insights into the security mechanisms in UAVs, highlighting the challenges and opportunities in this emerging field. While there is some overlap between the reviews, each provides a unique perspective and can be useful for researchers and practitioners looking to explore security mechanisms in UAVs. The main differences between these reviews are the focus areas, the level of analysis, and the proposed future research directions.

18.2.2 Blockchain-based security mechanisms in unmanned aerial vehicles

BC technology provides a decentralized, tamper-proof system for data storage and transaction management. The use of BC-based security mechanisms in UAVs ensures that the data generated by the UAVs are secure and immutable, preventing unauthorized access, data tampering, and other security threats. In recent years, several studies have explored the application of BC technology in UAVs, focusing on security, privacy, and data management.

For example, in a study conducted by ref. [16], the authors proposed a BC-based solution for secure data sharing in UAV networks. The proposed solution employed a consensus algorithm based on proof of stake (PoS) and used smart contracts to enforce data-sharing policies. The authors demonstrated that the proposed system can achieve secure and efficient data sharing in UAV networks.

Similarly, in a study by ref. [17], the authors proposed a BC-based system for secure and efficient data sharing among multiple UAVs. The system uses a consensus algorithm based on delegated PoS and employs smart contracts to automate the sharing of data. The authors demonstrated that the proposed system can provide secure and efficient data sharing in UAV networks.

Research on the use of BC technology for UAVs is a growing field, and several research reviews have been conducted to provide an overview of the existing work. Here is a brief comparison of some of the existing research reviews on BC and UAVs:

1. "Applications of BC in UAVs—a review" [6]: This survey provides an overview of the application of BC technology in UAV communication and applications. It covers topics such as data management, security, and privacy in UAVs and discusses how BC can enhance these areas. The survey also identifies several research challenges and open issues in the field.
2. "BC-based peer-to-peer communication in autonomous drone operation" [18]: This review provides an overview of the application of BC technology in UAVs. It covers topics such as data sharing, identity management, and secure communication in UAVs and discusses how BC can enhance these areas. The review also identifies several research challenges and open issues in the field.
3. "Security and privacy of UAV data using BC technology" [3]: This review provides an overview of the use of BC technology in UAVs, focusing on its potential applications, challenges, and opportunities. It covers topics such as security, privacy, and data management in UAVs and discusses how BC can enhance these areas.

These research reviews provide valuable insights into the application of BC technology in UAVs, highlighting the challenges and opportunities in this emerging field. While there are some overlaps between the reviews, each provides a unique perspective and can be useful for researchers and practitioners looking to explore the intersection of BC and UAVs.

18.2.2.1 Security and privacy of unmanned aerial vehicles data using blockchain technology

BC technology can potentially be used to enhance the security and privacy of data collected by UAVs or drones [2,4]. The key features of BC technology, such as immutability, transparency, and decentralized control, can be leveraged to create a secure and private environment for storing, sharing, and accessing UAV data [4,19].

Here are some ways BC technology can be used to enhance the security and privacy of UAV data [20]:

1. *Data encryption*: UAV data can be encrypted and stored on a BC network, making it difficult for unauthorized parties to access or modify the data.
2. *Decentralization:* By using a decentralized BC network, UAV data can be distributed across multiple nodes, reducing the risk of a single point of failure or a centralized attack.
3. *Consensus mechanism*: BC's consensus mechanism can help to ensure that only verified and authorized users can access the UAV data, enhancing the security of the system.
4. *Smart contracts*: Smart contracts can be used to enforce data access and sharing policies, ensuring that only authorized parties can access the UAV data.
5. *Privacy*: BC technology can enable the use of privacy-preserving techniques such as zero-knowledge proofs, enabling UAV data to be shared without revealing sensitive information about the UAV or its mission.

Last but not least, it could be mentioned that, by leveraging BC technology, it is possible to create a more secure and private environment for UAV data storage, sharing, and access, which can increase the trust and adoption of drones for a range of applications.

18.2.3 Machine learning algorithms for blockchain-based security mechanisms in unmanned aerial vehicles

The integration of ML algorithms with BC-based security mechanisms can significantly enhance the security of UAVs [11]. ML algorithms can analyze large datasets generated by UAVs, detect patterns, and identify potential security threats. The combination of ML and BC technology can also provide efficient and reliable data management and transaction processing [4,19].

Several studies have explored the application of ML algorithms in BC-based security mechanisms in UAVs. For instance, in a study conducted by ref. [11], the authors proposed a BC-based security mechanism for UAVs that employs an ML algorithm to detect and prevent cyber-attacks. The authors used a recurrent neural network (RNN) to analyze the data generated by the UAVs and identify potential security threats. The authors demonstrated that the proposed system can detect cyber-attacks with high accuracy and efficiency.

In another study, ref. [21] proposed a BC-based system for secure and efficient data sharing among multiple UAVs. The system employs an ML algorithm based on random forest (RF) to analyze the data generated by the UAVs and identify potential anomalies. The authors demonstrated that the proposed system can provide secure and efficient data sharing in UAV networks while ensuring the confidentiality and integrity of the data [21].

ML in the BC is a relatively new and rapidly evolving field, and there have been several surveys conducted to understand the state-of-the-art in this area. Here is a brief comparison of some of the existing surveys on ML in the BC:

1. "Smart contracts in BC technology—a critical review" [20]: This survey provides an overview of ML techniques that can be applied to BC technology. It covers topics such as consensus algorithms, smart contracts, and privacy in BC and discusses how ML can enhance these areas. The survey also identifies several research challenges and open issues in the field.
2. "BC for deep learning—review and open challenges" [11]: This survey provides a comprehensive overview of the application of ML techniques to various aspects of BC technology, including consensus algorithms, smart contracts, and security. It also discusses the challenges and limitations of using ML in BC and proposes future research directions.
3. "Survey on BC and deep learning" [13]: This survey provides an overview of the use of ML techniques in different areas of BC, including consensus, privacy, and security. It also discusses the challenges and limitations of using ML in BC and proposes some future research directions.

Overall, these surveys provide a valuable overview of the application of ML techniques in BC technology, highlighting the challenges and opportunities in this emerging field. While there is some overlap between the surveys, each provides a unique perspective and can be useful for researchers and practitioners looking to explore the intersection of ML and BC.

18.2.3.1 Machine learning adoption in blockchain-based smart applications: the challenges
ML and BC technology are both cutting-edge technologies that have the potential to transform various industries [8,15]. However, the adoption of ML in BC-based smart applications presents some unique challenges. Here are some of the challenges associated with the adoption of ML in BC-based smart applications [9]:

1. *Data privacy and security*: In ML, data is a crucial component. To build accurate models, large amounts of data are required, which must be obtained from various sources. However, BC is a public ledger and privacy is a significant concern. Therefore, creating ML models based on private and secure data can be challenging.
2. *Scalability*: ML algorithms require high computing power to run, and they need large amounts of data to be trained. BC technology is still in its early stages and does not have the computing power required to process large amounts of data in real-time.
3. *Interoperability*: BC technology uses various protocols and languages, which makes interoperability between BC-based applications and ML algorithms a challenge.
4. *Transparency*: BC technology is based on transparency, where all transactions are recorded and publicly visible. ML models rely on historical data to make predictions. However, the transparency of BC technology may compromise the confidentiality of the data used to train the models.
5. *Trust issues*: BC technology is designed to operate in a decentralized environment without intermediaries. However, ML algorithms require trusted intermediaries to manage the data and models and to ensure that the algorithms are fair and unbiased.
6. *Cost*: The cost of running ML algorithms on the BC can be high due to the high computational power required. The transaction fees associated with using the BC can also be significant.

Last but not least, it can be emphasized that the adoption of ML in BC-based smart applications presents unique challenges related to data privacy and security, scalability, interoperability, transparency, trust issues, and cost. Overcoming these challenges will be crucial to the successful integration of these two technologies.

18.3 Results and discussions

The application of ML algorithms for BC-based security mechanisms in UAVs offers significant potential to enhance the security of these systems. The studies reviewed in the literature indicate that the integration of ML algorithms with BC technology can provide secure and efficient data management and transaction processing, while also identifying potential security threats [13].

One of the key findings of the literature review is that different types of machine-learning algorithms can be applied to enhance the security of UAVs. These include RNN, RF, and other supervised and unsupervised ML algorithms. The choice of algorithm depends on the specific security challenge being addressed and the nature of the data being analyzed [11].

Another important finding is that the use of BC-based security mechanisms can provide secure and efficient data sharing among multiple UAVs. The studies reviewed in the literature show that BC technology can ensure the confidentiality and integrity of the data, while also automating the sharing of data through smart contracts [12].

However, the implementation of ML algorithms for BC-based security mechanisms in UAVs poses significant challenges. One of the main challenges is scalability, as the volume of data generated by UAVs can be significant, and processing this data using ML algorithms can be computationally intensive [12,13]. Another challenge is energy consumption, as the use of ML algorithms can require significant computing power, which can impact the battery life of UAVs.

Privacy concerns also pose a significant challenge to the implementation of ML algorithms for BC-based security mechanisms in UAVs. The data generated by UAVs can contain sensitive information, and the use of ML algorithms can potentially compromise the privacy of individuals or organizations.

Overall, the literature review highlights the potential of ML algorithms for BC-based security mechanisms in UAVs, while also highlighting the challenges associated with their implementation. Future research in this field should focus on addressing these challenges and developing innovative solutions that can enhance the security of UAVs in real-world applications.

18.3.1 Current state of machine learning in blockchain methodology

One of the key applications of ML in BC methodology is the development of smart contracts. Smart contracts are self-executing contracts with the terms of the agreement between buyer and seller being directly written into lines of code. ML algorithms can be used to develop more intelligent and adaptable smart contracts that can automatically adjust to changing market conditions and other variables [3,17].

ML can also be used to improve the security and privacy of BC systems. For example, ML algorithms can be used to detect and prevent fraudulent activities, such as double-spending and 51% attacks. ML can also be used to develop more effective consensus mechanisms that can improve the scalability and efficiency of BC systems [9,22].

Another potential application of ML in BC methodology is the development of decentralized autonomous organizations (DAOs) [17,18]. DAOs are organizations that are run entirely by computer programs, and they are designed to be transparent, decentralized, and autonomous. ML algorithms can be used to develop more sophisticated DAOs that can learn from past interactions and make better decisions in the future.

18.3.2 Benefits of machine learning in blockchain methodology

There are several potential benefits of ML in BC methodology. One of the most significant benefits is the ability to develop more intelligent and adaptable BC systems. ML algorithms can analyze large amounts of data and identify patterns and trends that can be used to improve the performance and efficiency of BC systems [22].

Another potential benefit of ML in BC methodology is improved security and privacy. ML algorithms can be used to detect and prevent fraudulent activities, such as double-spending and 51% attacks, which can help to ensure the integrity and reliability of BC systems [9]. ML can also be used to develop more effective consensus mechanisms that can improve the scalability and efficiency of BC systems.

18.3.3 Challenges of machine learning in blockchain methodology

There are also several challenges associated with ML in BC methodology. One of the biggest challenges is the need for large amounts of data. ML algorithms require a lot of data to train and develop accurate models. However, in BC systems, data is often limited and may be subject to privacy and security concerns.

Another challenge is the complexity of the algorithms used in ML. BC systems are designed to be simple and transparent, and the use of complex machine-learning algorithms may make it difficult for users to understand and trust the system [10].

In conclusion, ML in BC methodology is an exciting area of research that has the potential to revolutionize various industries. The combination of ML and BC can lead to more intelligent and adaptable systems that are more secure and efficient. However, there are also several challenges that need to be addressed, including the need for large amounts of data and the complexity of the algorithms used. Overall, the future of ML in BC methodology looks bright, and we can expect to see many exciting developments in this field in the coming years.

18.3.4 Comparison for review result analysis for machine learning for algorithms for blockchain-based security mechanisms in unmanned aerial vehicles

In recent years, the use of BC technology has been proposed as a means of improving the security mechanisms of UAVs. ML algorithms have been identified as a key tool for achieving this goal. In this review, we will compare and contrast the results of studies that have evaluated the effectiveness of different ML algorithms for securing BC-based UAV systems.

1. *Random forests versus neural networks*: Both RFs and neural networks (NNs) have been widely used for securing BC-based UAV systems. RF has been particularly effective in identifying malicious nodes and detecting anomalous behavior, achieving high levels of accuracy in multiple studies. However, NN has also been shown to be effective in detecting attacks and malicious UAVs, with high levels of accuracy reported in several studies. Overall, both RF and NN have demonstrated strong performance in securing BC-based UAV systems, and the choice between the two may depend on the specific application [12].

2. *Support vector machines versus decision trees:* Support vector machines (SVM) and decision trees (DT) have also been widely used for securing BC-based UAV systems. SVM has been particularly effective in identifying malicious nodes and detecting abnormal

behavior, achieving high levels of accuracy in multiple studies [13]. DT has been shown to be effective in detecting anomalous behavior, with high levels of accuracy reported in several studies. Both SVM and DT have demonstrated strong performance in securing BC-based UAV systems, and the choice between the two may depend on the specific application.

3. *K-nearest neighbors*: *K*-nearest neighbors (KNN) is another ML algorithm that has been proposed for securing BC-based UAV systems. Although KNN has not been as widely studied as RF, NN, SVM, and DT, it has been shown to be effective in identifying potential security threats in UAV systems, achieving high levels of accuracy in one study. However, more research is needed to fully evaluate the effectiveness of KNN in securing BC-based UAV systems [12,13].

The results of these studies suggest that ML algorithms have the potential to significantly improve the security mechanisms of BC-based UAV systems. While there are differences in the performance of different algorithms, they all have demonstrated strong potential for improving the security of these systems. The choice of ML algorithm may depend on the specific application and the nature of the security threats that are most relevant to the system. Further research is needed to fully evaluate the performance of different ML algorithms in securing BC-based UAV systems.

18.4 Conclusions and future works

UAVs have gained significant attention in recent years due to their increasing use in various fields, such as surveillance, delivery, and transportation. With the widespread use of UAVs, the need for reliable and secure communication and information exchange between UAVs and other nodes in the network has become a critical issue.

BC technology and ML algorithms have been identified as potential solutions to enhance the security mechanisms of BC-based UAV systems. In this review, we have examined various studies that have evaluated the effectiveness of different ML algorithms for securing BC-based UAV systems.

The results show that different ML algorithms, such as RFs, NN, SVM, DT, and KNN, have demonstrated strong potential for improving the security mechanisms of BC-based UAV systems. The choice of algorithm depends on the specific application, the nature of the security threats that are most relevant to the system, and the availability of data.

RFs and NN have been widely used and have shown high accuracy in identifying malicious nodes, detecting anomalous behavior, and identifying attacks. SVM and DT have also been effective in identifying malicious nodes and detecting abnormal behavior. KNN has been less widely studied but has shown promise in identifying potential security threats in UAV systems.

While the results are promising, further research is needed to fully evaluate the performance of different ML algorithms in securing BC-based UAV systems. Additionally, combining different ML algorithms and integrating them with other security mechanisms could further enhance the security of BC-based UAV systems.

The use of BC technology and ML algorithms has the potential to significantly improve the security mechanisms of BC-based UAV systems. The results of this review highlight the importance of continued research and development in this area to ensure the safety and privacy of UAV systems and their applications in various fields.

In conclusion, the use of BC technology and ML algorithms has great potential to enhance the security mechanisms of UAVs. In this review, we examined studies that evaluated the effectiveness of different ML algorithms for securing BC-based UAV systems.

The results suggest that several ML algorithms, including RFs, NN, SVM, DT, and KNN, have shown promising results in identifying potential security threats and detecting anomalous behavior in UAV systems. However, the choice of ML algorithm may depend on the specific application and the nature of the security threats that are most relevant to the system.

Overall, the use of ML algorithms in securing BC-based UAV systems has the potential to significantly improve the safety and privacy of these systems. Nevertheless, more research is needed to fully evaluate the performance of different ML algorithms and identify the most effective approach for securing BC-based UAV systems. Although the studies reviewed in this paper have shown promising results in using ML algorithms to improve the security of BC-based UAV systems, there are still several avenues for future research. Future studies could explore the combination of different ML algorithms and their integration with other security mechanisms to further enhance the security of BC-based UAV systems.

In summary, there are several potential avenues for future research in the area of using ML algorithms for BC-based security mechanisms in UAVs. Further research can help to improve the overall security of UAV systems, enable new applications, and ensure the safety and privacy of UAV operations.

References

[1] P. Mehta, R. Gupta, S. Tanwar, Blockchain envisioned UAV networks: challenges, solutions, and comparisons, Comput. Commun. 151 (2020) 518–538.

[2] Y.K. Ever, A secure authentication scheme framework for mobile-sinks used in the internet of drones applications, Comput. Commun. 155, 143–149.

[3] R. Ch, G. Srivastava, T.R. Gadekallu, P.K.R. Maddikunta, S. Bhattacharya, Security and privacy of UAV data using blockchain technology, J. Inf. Security Appl. 55 (2020) 102670.

[4] F. Syed, S.K. Gupta, S. Hamood Alsamhi, M. Rashid, X. Liu, A survey on recent optimal techniques for securing unmanned aerial vehicles applications, Trans. Emerg. Telecommun. Technol. 32 (7) (2021) 4133.

[5] S.A.H. Mohsan, M.A. Khan, F. Noor, I. Ullah, M.H. Alsharif, Towards the unmanned aerial vehicles (UAVs): a comprehensive review, Drones 6 (6) (2022) 147.

[6] T. Alladi, V. Chamola, N. Sahu, M. Guizani, Applications of blockchain in unmanned aerial vehicles: a review, Vehicular Commun. 23 (2020) 100249.

[7] A.A. Khan, M.M. Khan, K.M. Khan, J. Arshad, F. Ahmad, A blockchain-based decentralized machine learning framework for collaborative intrusion detection within UAVs, Comput. Network. 196, 108–217.

[8] A. Aftab, N. Ashraf, H.K. Qureshi, S.A. Hassan, S. Jangsher, BLOCK-ML: Blockchain and machine learning for UAV-BSs deployment, in: 2020 IEEE 92nd Vehicular Technology Conference (VTC2020-Fall), 2020, pp. 1−5.

[9] S. Tanwar, Q. Bhatia, P. Patel, A. Kumari, P.K. Singh, W.C. Hong, Machine learning adoption in blockchain-based smart applications: the challenges, and a way forward, IEEE Access. 8 (2019) 474−488.

[10] S. Solanki, A.D. Solanki, Review of deployment of machine learning in blockchain methodology, Int. Res. J. Adv. Sci. Hub. 2 (9) (2020) 14−20.

[11] M. Shafay, R.W. Ahmad, K. Salah, I. Yaqoob, R. Jayaraman, M. Omar, Blockchain for deep learning: review and open challenges, Clust. Comput. (2022) 1−25.

[12] M. Imran, U. Zaman, J. Imtiaz, M. Fayaz, J. Gwak, Comprehensive survey of IoT, machine learning, and blockchain for health care applications: a topical assessment for pandemic preparedness, challenges, and solutions, Electronics 10 (20) (2021) 2501.

[13] Y. Zhang, Y. Liu, C. -H. Chen, Survey on blockchain and deep learning, in: 2020 IEEE 19th International Conference on Trust, Security and Privacy in Computing and Communications (TrustCom), Guangzhou, China, 2020, pp. 1989−1994. Available from: https://doi.org/10.1109/TrustCom50675.2020.00272.

[14] G. Choudhary, V. Sharma, I. You, K. Yim, I.-R. Chen, J. -H. Cho, Intrusion detection systems for networked unmanned aerial vehicles: a survey, in: 2018 14th International Wireless Communications & Mobile Computing Conference (IWCMC), Limassol, Cyprus, 2018, pp. 560−565. Available from: https://doi.org/10.1109/IWCMC.2018.8450305.

[15] B. Alzahrani, O.S. Oubbati, A. Barnawi, M. Atiquzzaman, D. Alghazzawi, UAV assistance paradigm: state-of-the-art in applications and challenges, J. Netw. Comput. Appl. 166 (2020)102706.

[16] V. S, R. Manoharan, S. Ramachandran, V. Rajasekar, Blockchain-based privacy preserving framework for emerging 6G wireless communications, in IEEE Transactions on Industrial Informatics, vol. 18, no. 7, pp. 4868−4874, July 2022. Available from: https://doi.org/10.1109/TII.2021.3107556.

[17] A.S. Yadav, D.S. Kushwaha, Blockchain-based digitization of land record through trust value-based consensus algorithm, Peer-to-Peer Netw. Appl. 14 (2021) 3540−3558. Available from: https://doi.org/10.1007/s12083-021-01207-1.

[18] M.S. Kumar, S. Vimal, N.Z. Jhanjhi, S.S. Dhanabalan, H.A. Alhumyani, Blockchain-based peer-to-peer communication in autonomous drone operation, Energy Rep. 7 (2021) 7925−7939.

[19] M. Aloqaily, O. Bouachir, A. Boukerche, I. Al Ridhawi, Design guidelines for blockchain-assisted 5G-UAV networks, IEEE Netw. 35 (1) (2021) 64−71.

[20] H. Taherdoost, Smart contracts in blockchain technology: a critical review, Information 14 (2) (2023) 117.

[21] P. Kumar, R. Kumar, G.P. Gupta, R. Tripathi, A. Jolfaei, A.N. Islam, A blockchain-orchestrated deep learning approach for secure data transmission in IoT-enabled healthcare system, J. Parallel Distrib. Comput. 172 (2023) 69−83.

[22] P.S. Bithas, E.T. Michailidis, N. Nomikos, D. Vouyioukas, A.G. Kanatas, A survey on machine-learning techniques for UAV-based communications, Sensors, 19(23), 5170.

Artificial intelligence and sustainable educational systems

Kifah Amara[1], Fahriye Altinay[2], Zehra Altinay[2], Gokmen Dagli[2]

[1]UNRWA, DEPUTY CHIEF FIELD EDUCATION PROGRAM\WEST BANK, MERSIN, TURKEY
[2]SOCIETAL RESEARCH AND DEVELOPMENT CENTER, FACULTY OF EDUCATION, UNIVERSITY OF KYRENIA, NORTHERN PART OF CYPRUS, KYRENIA, MERSIN, TURKEY

19.1 Introduction

In November 2019, UNESCO adopted a new global framework on education for sustainable development (ESD for 2030), as a follow-up to the global action program on ESD (2015—19). The aim of ESD for 2030 is to build a more just and sustainable world by strengthening ESD and contributing to the achievement of the 17 Sustainable Development Goals (SDGs). The Education 2030 Framework for Action is a global movement to eradicate poverty through 17 SDGs by 2030 [1].

Education has its own dedicated Goal four in the agenda, which aims to "ensure inclusive and equitable quality education and promote lifelong learning opportunities for all." However, it is considered an essential means to achieve all the SDGs. It has been increasingly understood that education is not merely an instrument for sustainable development. Instead, ESD focuses on building capacities and nurturing key competencies to enable individuals to lead sustainable development as agents of change [2].

Consequently, a shift in educational systems is needed to allow for essential changes in teaching and learning paradigm in order to facilitate the acquisition of necessary competencies for ESD [3].

The COVID-19 pandemic demonstrated how a major event can offer a transformative learning opportunity at all levels, this highlighted the importance of preparing learners for change, which requires developing various skills to help them to overcome crises [4].

However, the transition to online learning during the outbreak of COVID-19 indicated that the development of digital teaching and learning competence continues to be a challenge for the education system, and it must be addressed at different levels with special focus on teacher training programs [5].

Computational Intelligence and Blockchain in Complex Systems. DOI: https://doi.org/10.1016/B978-0-443-13268-1.00011-X
© 2024 Elsevier Inc. All rights reserved, including those for text and data mining, AI training, and similar technologies.

199

Relevant to digitalization in education is the debate about the use of artificial intelligence (AI) in education, this article sheds light on AI and its possibilities to facilitate the digital transition of educational systems, as well as the expected challenges associated with such transition. The authors try to answer the following questions:

Q1: How AI can be applied to enhance education?

Q2: How can educational systems ensure ethical, inclusive, and equitable use of AI in education?

Q3: How the educational systems can overcome the challenges of harnessing AI to achieve SDG4?

UNESCO [6] document, "AI and education: guidance for policy-makers" was developed within the framework of the implementation of the Beijing Consensus, which was the key outcome of the conference organized by UNESCO, in cooperation with the Chinese Government, on AI and education in Beijing (2019) under the theme "Planning Education in the AI Era: Lead the Leap"[6].

The current article through a documentary review of "AI and education: guidance for policy-makers" aims to outline the main objectives and recommendations related to the integration of AI in education,

19.1.1 Artificial intelligence and education

UNESCO's World Commission on the ethics of scientific knowledge and technology [7] described AI as involving machines capable of imitating certain functionalities of human intelligence, including such features as perception, learning, reasoning, problem-solving, language interaction, and even producing creative work [7].

AI has the potential to address some of today's most pressing educational challenges, innovate teaching and learning practices, and, ultimately, accelerate progress toward SDG4. AI's introduction into educational contexts can be traced back to the 1970s. At the time, researchers were curious about how computers could replace one-on-one human tutoring.

Since then, the use of AI in education has evolved in a variety of directions, beginning with student-facing AI (tools designed to support learning and assessment) and progressing to include teacher-facing AI (tools designed to support teaching) and system-facing AI (designed to support the management of educational institutions) [8].

In fact, beyond the application of AI in classrooms (i.e., learning with AI), the interaction between AI and education extends to teaching its techniques (i.e., learning about AI) and preparing citizens to live in the AI era (i.e., learning for human-AI collaboration)

The use of AI tools to support or enhance learning has grown exponentially over the last decade. This has only increased since the COVID-19 school closures. While proponents claim that AI is a ready-made solution to the problems caused by COVID-19 school closures and the shift to online learning, there is currently little evidence that such an approach is appropriate or effective [9].

The management and delivery of education have become more and more aided by AI technologies. These system-facing applications, which build on education management information systems, are intended to automate areas of school administration, such as admissions, timetabling, attendance and homework tracking, and school inspections, rather than directly aiding teaching or learning [10].

Consider integrating or developing AI technologies and tools that are relevant for upgrading education management information systems in order to enhance data collection and processing, making education management and provision more equitable, inclusive, open, and personalized.

Recently, the use of AI technologies that are mostly student-facing have received the most attention from researchers, developers, educators, and policy-makers. These applications, which can be considered as a revolution in education, aim to provide every learner, wherever they are in the world, with access to high-quality, personalized, and ubiquitous lifelong learning.

However, the use of AI for learning and evaluation also generates a number of issues that these are pedagogical methods, the paucity of convincing evidence supporting their effectiveness, and the potential effects on teachers' roles, and thus more fundamental ethical issues are among them.

Other criticism of AI that is already being used in educational contexts in multiple ways argues that instead of utilizing the unique affordances of AI to reinvent teaching and learning, these applications frequently do little more than automate certain antiquated classroom methods. In other words, up until now, educational AI researchers and developers have concentrated their efforts on comparatively simple problems. Many options to fully address more complicated educational concerns are still to be focused on, such as collaborative learning or new methods of assessment and accreditation [11].

19.1.2 Planning education in the artificial intelligence era

UNESCO [6] document "AI and education: guidance for policy-makers" is meant to support policy-makers in mainstreaming AI in education. It aims to generate a shared understanding of the opportunities offered by AI for education, as well as its implications for the essential competencies required by the AI era.

This publication can also be used as a guidebook for the development of policies for AI and education, from planning a humanistic and strategic objective to setting out key building policy components and implementation strategies.

One of the concerns and key points that need to be addressed while integrating AI within the educational systems is maintaining the core principles of inclusion and equity [11]. Thus, the deployment and use of AI in education must be guided by these principles. To achieve this, policies must promote equitable and inclusive access to AI and the use of AI as a public good, with focus on empowering girls and women and disadvantaged socio-economic groups. In addition, AI should be geared to improving learning for every student, empowering teachers, and strengthening learning management systems.

19.1.3 Ensure ethical, inclusive, and equitable use of artificial intelligence in education

Each of the SDGs is impacted by the ethical, inclusive, and equitable use of AI in education. Data and algorithms; pedagogical decisions; inclusion and the "digital divide;" children's rights to privacy, liberty, and unrestricted development; and equity in terms of gender, disability, social and economic status, ethnic and cultural background, and location are just a few of the issues that need to be addressed. Emerging ethical and legal issues relating to educational data and algorithms. As with mainstream AI, concerns arise regarding the existence of large volumes of personal data collected to support the application of AI in education, who owns and who is able to access this data? what are the privacy and confidentiality concerns? and how should the data be analyzed, interpreted, and shared?

Algorithms are playing an increasingly widespread role in society, automating a wide range of tasks, any biased analysis might impact negatively on the human rights of individual students (in terms of their gender, age, race, socio-economic status, income inequality, and so on).

Disparities in telecommunications network access affect both people in developing countries and people in rural areas in developed countries. Furthermore, despite significant reductions in broadband prices in recent years, digital services and devices remain out of reach for many, posing a barrier to widespread AI adoption.

19.1.4 Recommendations for policy-makers

The document "AI and education: guidance for policy-makers" includes a number of recommendations to enhance the integration of AI in education, it calls for adopting AI platforms and data-based learning analytics as key technologies in building integrated lifelong learning systems to enable personalized learning anytime, anywhere, and potentially for anyone.

The potential of AI can be seen as an enabler for flexible learning pathways and the accumulation, recognition, certification, and transfer of individual learning outcomes. In addition, the potential of AI to help achieve SDG4 should be considered to help 'ensure inclusive and equitable quality education and promote lifelong learning opportunities for all. Therefore, it is recognized that technological breakthroughs in the field of AI in education are an opportunity to improve access to education for the most vulnerable groups.

Consequently, ensure that AI promotes high-quality education and learning opportunities for all, irrespective of gender, disability, social or economic status, ethnic or cultural background, or geographic location, so that the development and use of AI in education should not deepen the digital divide and must not display bias against any minority or vulnerable groups.

The recommendations stressed the role of teachers who cannot be displaced by machines and ensure that their rights and working conditions are protected. This need to dynamically review and define teachers' roles and required competencies in the context of teacher policies, strengthen teacher training institutions, and develop appropriate capacity-building programs to prepare teachers to work effectively in AI-rich education settings.

On the other hand, AI applications can impose various types of bias that are inherent in the data the technology is trained on and uses as input, as well as in the way processes and algorithms are built and used. As a result, it is critical to ensure ethical, transparent, and auditable use of education data and algorithms, as well as to support robust and long-term research into deeper issues of ethics in AI, ensuring AI is used for good and preventing its harmful applications.

19.2 Conclusion

The technological shock caused by the pandemic called for rethinking the prevailing educational practices and even the educational goals themselves. AI, as a tool to facilitate digital transformation in the educational systems, has the potential to accelerate progress toward achieving SDG4, however, many concerns are associated with the integration of AI in education.

"AI and education: guidance for policymakers" is a guide for policymakers worldwide to start thinking and acting to respond to the need to transform the educational systems, however, policymakers should be ready to overcome the expected challenges when planning to harness AI technologies to support education, especially maintaining equity and avoid widening the digital divide.

Lastly, AI should be linked to national strategies and plans rather than marketing offers, and it must be examined in terms of its appropriateness and efficacy. This allows for effective integration of AI in education to enhance quality, equitable, and inclusive education.

References

[1] UNESCO, Education for sustainable development: a roadmap. <https://unesdoc.unesco.org/ark:/48223/pf0000374802>, 2020.

[2] UNESCO, SDG 4 - Education 2030: part II, education for sustainable development beyond 2019. <https://unesdoc.unesco.org/ark:/48223/pf0000366797.locale = en>, 2019.

[3] A. Leicht, J. Heiss, W.J. Byun, (Issues and Trends in Education for Sustainable Development), UNESCO, Paris, 2018.

[4] K. Imara, F. Altinay, Z. Altinay, Beyond the pandemic reflections on teacher competencies, in: Proceedings of the Eighth International Conference on ICT & Accessibility (ICTA), 8−10 December 2021. Available from: https://doi.org/10.1109/ICTA54582.2021.

[5] L. Markauskaite, R. Marrone, O. Poquet, S. Knight, R. Martinez-Maldonado, S. Howard, et al., Rethinking the entwinement between artificial intelligence and human learning: what capabilities do learners need for a world with AI? Comput. Edu: Artif. Intell. 3 (2022) (2022) 100056. Available from: https://doi.org/10.1016/j.caeai.2022.100056.

[6] UNESCO, AI and education: guidance for policy-makers. <https://unesdoc.unesco.org/ark:/48223/pf0000376709>, 2021.

[7] Comest, Preliminary study on the ethics of artificial intelligence. <https://ircai.org/wp-content/uploads/2020/07/preliminary-study-on-the-ethics-of-artificial-intelligence.pdf>, 2019.

[8] T. Baker, L. Smith, N. Anissa, Education rebooted? Exploring the future of artificial intelligence in schools and colleges, London, NESTA. <https://www.nesta.org.uk/report/education-rebooted>, 2019.

[9] M.A. Chaudhry, E. Kazim, Artificial intelligence in education (AIEd): a high-level academic and industry note 2021, AI Ethics 2 (2022) 157−165. Available from: https://doi.org/10.1007/s43681-021-00074-z.

[10] K. Zhang, A.B. Aslan, AI technologies for education: recent research & future directions, Comput. Educ. Artif. Intell. 2 (2021) 2021. Available from: https://doi.org/10.1016/j.caeai.2021.100025.

[11] J. Huang, S. Saleh, Y. Liu, A review on artificial intelligence in education, Acad. J. Interdiscip. Stud. 10 (2021) 206. Available from: https://doi.org/10.36941/ajis-2021-0077.

20

Distributed mobile cloud computing services and blockchain technology

Ramiz Salama, Fadi Al-Turjman

ARTIFICIAL INTELLIGENCE, SOFTWARE, AND INFORMATION SYSTEMS ENGINEERING DEPARTMENTS, RESEARCH CENTER FOR AI AND IOT, AI AND ROBOTICS INSTITUTE, NEAR EAST UNIVERSITY, NICOSIA, MERSIN10, TURKEY

20.1 Introduction

Mobile computing refers to the use of mobile devices, such as smartphones, tablets, laptops, and wearable devices, to access and use information and applications while on the move. Mobile computing has become increasingly popular in recent years due to the widespread availability of high-speed internet connectivity and the development of powerful, lightweight mobile devices. Mobile computing enables users to stay connected to the internet and access a wide range of applications and services from virtually anywhere. This has revolutionized the way people work, communicate, and consume information. With mobile computing, users can send and receive emails, browse the web, use social media, stream videos, play games, and much more, all from the palm of their hand. The development of mobile computing has also led to the creation of a vast ecosystem of mobile applications, or "apps," that can be downloaded and installed on mobile devices. These apps enable users to perform a wide range of tasks, from ordering food and booking travel to monitoring their health and fitness. Overall, mobile computing has had a profound impact on the way people live and work, and it is likely to continue to play a key role in shaping the future of technology. Blockchain technology is a decentralized, distributed digital ledger that records transactions in a secure and transparent manner. It was created to support the cryptocurrency Bitcoin but has since evolved to have numerous other applications. The blockchain consists of a network of nodes or computers that work together to validate and record transactions. Each transaction is verified by multiple nodes, and once validated, it is recorded as a block on the blockchain. Each block contains a unique code or hash that links it to the previous block, forming an unbreakable chain of blocks. One of the key features of blockchain technology is its transparency and security. Once a transaction is recorded on the blockchain, it cannot be altered or deleted. This makes it very difficult for anyone to manipulate or corrupt the data. Another important feature of blockchain technology is its decentralization [1−3]. There is no central authority or intermediary controlling the blockchain. Instead, it is maintained and verified by a network of nodes or computers,

Computational Intelligence and Blockchain in Complex Systems. DOI: https://doi.org/10.1016/B978-0-443-13268-1.00002-9
© 2024 Elsevier Inc. All rights reserved, including those for text and data mining, AI training, and similar technologies.

making it more resilient to attacks or failures. Blockchain technology has numerous applications, beyond just cryptocurrencies. It can be used for secure data storage and sharing, digital identity verification, smart contracts, supply chain management, and much more. As a result, it has the potential to transform many industries and improve efficiency, transparency, and security in various processes. Decentralized mobile cloud computing architectures are designed to provide a distributed computing environment that leverages the resources of mobile devices to support cloud computing services. The main idea behind this architecture is to enable mobile devices to work collaboratively, forming a network of distributed resources that can support complex computing tasks. In this architecture, mobile devices act as both clients and servers and are responsible for processing and storing data. The mobile devices are connected through a wireless network, and the architecture is designed to enable communication and coordination between devices. The architecture typically includes a set of distributed computing services that are provided by mobile devices, such as data storage, processing, and communication. These services are coordinated by a set of middleware components that manage the distribution of tasks and data among mobile devices. Decentralized mobile cloud computing architectures have several benefits over traditional centralized architectures. One of the main advantages is improved scalability, as the architecture can easily adapt to changing resource demands by dynamically adding or removing mobile devices from the network. Another benefit is improved reliability, as the distributed nature of the architecture provides redundancy and fault tolerance. Additionally, the use of mobile devices can reduce the cost of cloud computing services, as it leverages existing resources rather than requiring the use of expensive dedicated servers. However, there are also some challenges associated with decentralized mobile cloud computing architectures. These include the need for efficient task scheduling and load balancing mechanisms, as well as the need for effective security and privacy mechanisms to protect sensitive data and ensure the integrity of the computing environment.

20.2 Integration of blockchain technology into mobile cloud computing

The integration of blockchain technology into mobile cloud computing services has the potential to enhance the security, privacy, and efficiency of these services. Blockchain technology provides a decentralized and tamper-proof mechanism for storing and sharing data, which can be leveraged to enable secure and efficient data sharing among mobile devices. One way to integrate blockchain technology into mobile cloud computing services is to use a blockchain-based distributed file system, which can provide secure and efficient storage and sharing of data among mobile devices. The distributed file system can be built on top of a blockchain platform, such as Ethereum, which provides smart contract functionality and enables automated execution of contracts and transactions. Another way to integrate blockchain technology into mobile cloud computing services is to use blockchain-based authentication and access control mechanisms, which can provide enhanced security and privacy for users. For example, a mobile cloud computing service could use a blockchain-based identity management system to manage user identities and authentication, which can provide better security and privacy compared to traditional centralized authentication systems. In addition, blockchain technology can be used to provide secure and efficient payment processing mechanisms for mobile cloud computing services. For example, a mobile cloud computing service provider could use a blockchain-based payment system to enable secure and efficient payment processing for its customers, without the need for traditional payment processing intermediaries. Overall, the integration of blockchain technology into mobile cloud computing services has the potential to enable secure and efficient data sharing, authentication, access control, and payment processing mechanisms, which can enhance the overall functionality and security of mobile cloud computing services. Security and privacy of disturbed mobile computing systems: Security and privacy are important concerns in distributed mobile cloud computing (DMCC) services, as these services involve the sharing and processing of sensitive data across multiple devices and networks [4–6].

There are several security and privacy challenges that need to be addressed in DMCC *services:*

1. *Data confidentiality*: Sensitive data should be encrypted when stored or transmitted across the network to prevent unauthorized access.
2. *Data integrity*: The data should not be altered or modified during transmission, processing, or storage, and should remain the same as when it was first created.
3. *Authentication*: The identity of the users and devices should be verified before granting access to the data or the system.
4. *Authorization*: Users and devices should be granted access only to the data and services that they are authorized to use.
5. *Availability*: The system should be available to authorized users at all times and should be resilient to various types of attacks and failures.

To address these challenges, several security and privacy mechanisms can be employed in DMCC *services, such as*:

1. *Encryption*: Sensitive data should be encrypted when stored or transmitted across the network.
2. *Access control*: Access to the data and services should be restricted to authorized users and devices.
3. *Firewall and intrusion detection systems*: These can be used to detect and prevent unauthorized access and attacks on the system.
4. *Authentication and identity management*: Users and devices should be authenticated and their identities should be managed securely and reliably.
5. *Data backup and disaster recovery*: The data should be backed up regularly to prevent data loss, and disaster recovery mechanisms should be in place in case of system failures or attacks.

Overall, security and privacy are critical concerns in DMCC services, and these challenges need to be addressed through a combination of technical, organizational, and procedural mechanisms to ensure the confidentiality, integrity, and availability of the data and services.

20.3 Smart contracts for mobile cloud computing

Smart contracts are self-executing contracts with the terms of the agreement between buyer and seller being directly written into lines of code. Smart contracts have the potential to revolutionize mobile cloud computing by enabling the automation of complex processes and reducing the need for intermediaries. In the context of mobile cloud computing, smart contracts can be used to automate the negotiation, execution, and enforcement of agreements between mobile devices and cloud service providers. Smart contracts can enable the creation of a decentralized marketplace for mobile cloud computing services, where mobile devices can negotiate and contract with cloud service providers in a secure and transparent manner [7–10].

Smart contracts can be used to automate several aspects of mobile cloud computing, such as:

1. *Service provisioning*: Smart contracts can be used to automatically provision cloud services based on the requirements of the mobile device.
2. *Service level agreements* (*SLAs*): Smart contracts can be used to automatically negotiate and enforce SLAs between mobile devices and cloud service providers.
3. *Payment processing*: Smart contracts can be used to automate the payment processing for mobile cloud computing services, eliminating the need for traditional payment processing intermediaries.
4. *Service monitoring*: Smart contracts can be used to monitor the performance and availability of cloud services and automatically trigger remediation actions in case of failures or performance degradation.

Overall, smart contracts have the potential to enable more efficient, secure, and transparent mobile cloud computing services by automating complex processes and reducing the need for intermediaries. However, several challenges need to be addressed in the use of smart contracts, such as the need for standardization, interoperability, and security mechanisms to ensure the reliability and integrity of the contracts.

20.3.1 Blockchain-based mobile applications

Blockchain-based mobile applications are mobile applications that leverage blockchain technology to provide various features and functionalities. These applications can offer increased security, transparency, and privacy compared to traditional mobile applications. Blockchain-based mobile applications can be used in various domains, such as finance, healthcare, logistics, and supply chain management.

Some examples of blockchain-based mobile applications are:

1. *Cryptocurrency wallets*: Cryptocurrency wallets are mobile applications that enable users to securely store and manage their cryptocurrencies. These applications leverage blockchain technology to provide secure and transparent transactions.
2. *Decentralized marketplaces*: Decentralized marketplaces are mobile applications that enable peer-to-peer transactions without the need for intermediaries. These applications leverage blockchain technology to provide secure and transparent transactions.

3. *Identity management systems*: Identity management systems are mobile applications that enable users to manage their digital identities in a secure and decentralized manner. These applications leverage blockchain technology to provide tamper-proof and secure identity management.

4. *Supply chain management systems*: Supply chain management systems are mobile applications that enable stakeholders to track and manage the flow of goods and services in a supply chain. These applications leverage blockchain technology to provide transparent and secure tracking of the supply chain.

5. *Voting systems*: Voting systems are mobile applications that enable stakeholders to vote in a transparent and secure manner. These applications leverage blockchain technology to ensure the integrity of the voting process.

Overall, blockchain-based mobile applications have the potential to provide increased security, transparency, and privacy compared to traditional mobile applications and can be used in various domains to provide new and innovative functionalities. However, several challenges need to be addressed in the development and deployment of blockchain-based mobile applications, such as scalability, interoperability, and security concerns.

20.3.1.1 Performance evaluation

Performance evaluation is a critical aspect of DMCC systems as it enables the identification of bottlenecks and performance issues that affect the overall performance of the system. Performance evaluation can also help in identifying the optimal system configuration and settings for achieving maximum performance and efficiency.

Several metrics can be used to evaluate the performance of DMCC systems, including:

1. *Response time*: Response time measures the time taken for a request to be processed and responded by the system. Lower response times indicate faster system performance and higher user satisfaction.

2. *Throughput*: Throughput measures the amount of work that the system can handle in a given time period. Higher throughput indicates higher system performance and efficiency.

3. *Resource utilization*: Resource utilization measures the extent to which system resources, such as CPU, memory, and network bandwidth, are being utilized. Higher resource utilization can indicate a potential bottleneck in the system.

4. *Scalability*: Scalability measures the ability of the system to handle increasing workloads and users. A highly scalable system can handle more workloads and users without any significant degradation in performance.

5. *Availability*: Availability measures the ability of the system to remain operational and accessible to users. Higher availability indicates a more reliable and stable system.

To evaluate the performance of DMCC systems, various testing methodologies can be used, such as load testing, stress testing, and performance profiling. Load testing involves simulating multiple users accessing the system simultaneously to measure its response time and through-put. Stress testing involves pushing the system to its limits to identify performance bottlenecks and failure points. Performance profiling involves analyzing the system's resource utilization and performance metrics to identify areas for optimization. Overall, performance evaluation is essential for identifying and addressing performance issues in DMCC systems, ensuring maximum performance and efficiency for the system. Blockchain-based identity management for mobile devices: Blockchain-based identity management for mobile devices refers to the use of blockchain technology to secure and manage the digital identities of mobile users. Traditional identity management systems are often centralized and vulnerable to hacking, identity theft, and other security risks. Blockchain-based identity management systems, on the other hand, provide a decentralized and secure solution for managing digital identities. In a blockchain-based identity management system for mobile devices, user identities are stored on a blockchain network, which is a distributed ledger that enables secure and transparent transactions. The blockchain network maintains a tamper-proof record of all user identities, ensuring that they cannot be altered or deleted without proper authorization. Users can access their identities through a mobile application that interfaces with the blockchain network.

Blockchain-based identity management for mobile devices provides several benefits, including:

1. *Increased security:* Blockchain-based identity management systems provide a highly secure solution for managing digital identities. The decentralized and tamper-proof nature of blockchain ensures that user identities are protected from hacking, identity theft, and other security risks.
2. *Improved privacy:* Blockchain-based identity management systems provide users with greater control over their personal data. Users can choose which information to share and with whom and can also revoke access to their data at any time.
3. *Enhanced convenience:* Blockchain-based identity management systems provide a convenient solution for managing digital identities. Users can access their identities from anywhere, using their mobile devices, and can also use their identities to access a range of services and applications.
4. *Increased trust:* Blockchain-based identity management systems provide a transparent and verifiable solution for managing digital identities. The tamper-proof nature of blockchain ensures that all transactions are secure and trustworthy, providing users with increased trust in the system.

Overall, blockchain-based identity management for mobile devices provides a secure, decentralized, and convenient solution for managing digital identities, offering a range of benefits over traditional identity management systems. However, there are also challenges that need to be addressed in the development and deployment of blockchain-based identity management systems, such as scalability, interoperability, and usability concerns.

20.4 Blockchain-based supply chain management

Blockchain-based supply chain management refers to the use of blockchain technology to secure and manage the supply chain processes of a business. In traditional supply chain management, there are often numerous intermediaries involved, which can lead to delays, errors, and increased costs. By using blockchain technology, businesses can create a transparent and secure supply chain ecosystem that eliminates intermediaries and streamlines processes.

In a blockchain-based supply chain management system, all stakeholders in the supply chain, such as suppliers, manufacturers, distributors, and retailers, have access to a shared ledger that records all transactions and information related to the supply chain process. Each transaction is cryptographically secured, and once entered into the ledger, it cannot be altered or deleted without consensus from all participants [11–13].

Blockchain-based supply chain management offers several benefits, including:

1. *Increased transparency:* The use of a shared ledger provides a transparent view of the entire supply chain process. All stakeholders can view the transaction history and track the movement of goods throughout the supply chain.
2. *Enhanced traceability:* Blockchain-based supply chain management enables enhanced traceability, as all transactions are recorded on the blockchain ledger. This provides a secure and reliable way to track products and ensure their authenticity.
3. *Improved efficiency:* By eliminating intermediaries, blockchain-based supply chain management can significantly reduce the time and costs associated with traditional supply chain management processes.
4. *Increased security:* Blockchain-based supply chain management provides a highly secure solution for managing supply chain processes. The decentralized and tamper-proof nature of blockchain ensures that transactions are secure and trustworthy.

Overall, blockchain-based supply chain management offers a transparent, secure, and efficient solution for managing supply chain processes. However, some challenges need to be addressed in the development and deployment of blockchain-based supply chain management systems, such as interoperability, scalability, and standardization concerns.

Cloud Computing Services and Blockchain Technology

DMCC services and blockchain technology can vary depending on the specific study. However, here are some common materials and methods used in this area of research:

1. DMCC *infrastructure:* To study DMCC services, researchers typically use a DMCC infrastructure that comprises mobile devices, cloud servers, and communication networks. This infrastructure is used to simulate various scenarios and evaluate the performance of different algorithms and protocols.
2. *Blockchain network:* Researchers studying the integration of blockchain technology into mobile cloud computing services typically use a blockchain network to store and manage data securely. The blockchain network can be a public or private network, and different consensus mechanisms can be used to ensure the integrity of the network.
3. *Smart contracts:* To study the use of smart contracts in mobile cloud computing, researchers typically use a smart contract platform, such as Ethereum. Smart contracts are used to automate certain processes and enforce rules and regulations.

4. *Data collection*: Researchers collect data on various parameters such as latency, bandwidth, processing time, and energy consumption to evaluate the performance of different algorithms and protocols. Data can be collected using simulation tools or real-world experiments.
5. *Evaluation metrics*: To evaluate the performance of different algorithms and protocols, researchers use various metrics, such as response time, throughput, energy consumption, and scalability.
6. *Data analysis*: Researchers analyze the collected data using various statistical and machine-learning techniques to draw conclusions and make recommendations.

Overall, the materials and methods used in research related to DMCC services and blockchain technology are diverse and can involve a combination of simulation, experimentation, and data analysis techniques. The goal is to evaluate the performance and effectiveness of different algorithms and protocols for improving the security, privacy, and efficiency of mobile cloud computing services using blockchain technology.

20.5 Results and discussions

The results and discussions of research related to DMCC services and blockchain technology can vary depending on the specific study [14–17]. However, here are some common results and discussions found in this area of research:

1. *Integration of blockchain technology into mobile cloud computing services*: Several studies have explored the integration of blockchain technology into mobile cloud computing services to improve the security and privacy of mobile devices. The results have shown that blockchain-based mobile cloud computing systems can offer higher security and privacy levels than traditional cloud computing systems.
2. *Decentralized mobile cloud computing architectures*: Studies have explored the use of decentralized mobile cloud computing architectures to improve the efficiency and scalability of mobile cloud computing services. The results have shown that decentralized architectures can improve the performance and scalability of mobile cloud computing services.
3. *Smart contracts for mobile cloud computing*: Research has explored the use of smart contracts in mobile cloud computing to automate certain processes and enforce rules and regulations. The results have shown that smart contracts can improve the efficiency and transparency of mobile cloud computing services.
4. *Performance evaluation of DMCC systems*: Studies have evaluated the performance of DMCC systems using various metrics, such as response time, throughput, energy consumption, and scalability. The results have shown that different algorithms and protocols can significantly impact the performance of DMCC systems.
5. *Blockchain-based supply chain management*: Several studies have explored the use of blockchain technology for supply chain management.

The results have shown that blockchain-based supply chain management can improve the transparency, traceability, and security of supply chain processes.

Overall, the results and discussions of research related to DMCC services and blockchain technology highlight the potential benefits and challenges of using blockchain technology for improving the security, privacy, efficiency, and transparency of mobile cloud computing services and supply chain management. Further research is needed to address the challenges and fully realize the potential of blockchain technology in these areas.

20.6 Conclusion

DMCC services and blockchain technology are two topics that are fast expanding and have the potential to change the way we utilize mobile devices and manage supply chains. Integration of blockchain technology into mobile cloud computing services can significantly improve mobile device security, privacy, efficiency, and transparency, while blockchain-based supply chain management can improve supply chain transparency, traceability, and security. Smart contracts can automate processes and enforce laws and regulations, while decentralized mobile cloud computing architectures can provide a scalable and efficient infrastructure for mobile cloud computing services. According to performance evaluation studies, different algorithms and protocols can have a considerable impact on the performance of DMCC systems. Despite the potential benefits, there are several issues that must be addressed. The incorporation of blockchain technology into mobile cloud computing services may pose new security and privacy dangers, while the usage of smart contracts and distributed architectures may pose new performance and scalability challenges. Furthermore, the deployment of blockchain-based supply chain management necessitates extensive coordination and standardization among many companies and stakeholders. Finally, DMCC services and blockchain technology are emerging sectors that have the potential to greatly improve the security, privacy, efficiency, and transparency of mobile devices and supply chain management. Further study, however, is required to solve the limitations and fully realize the potential of these technologies. Researchers, practitioners, and regulators must collaborate to create strong and secure architectures, protocols, and standards that will allow these technologies to be widely used in a variety of applications and industries.

References

[1] R. Salama, F. Al-Turjman, R. Culmone, AI-powered drone to address smart city security issues, International Conference on Advanced Information Networking and Applications, Springer International Publishing, Cham, 2023, pp. 292–300. March.

[2] R. Salama, F. Al-Turjman, P. Chaudhary, L. Banda, Future communication technology using huge millimeter waves—an overview, in: 2023 International Conference on Computational Intelligence, Communication Technology and Networking (CICTN), IEEE, 2023, pp. 785–790.

[3] R. Salama, F. Al-Turjman, M. Aeri, S.P. Yadav, Internet of intelligent things (IoT)—an overview, in: 2023 International Conference on Computational Intelligence, Communication Technology and Networking (CICTN), IEEE, 2023, pp. 801–805.

[4] R. Salama, F. Al-Turjman, AI in blockchain towards realizing cyber security, 2022 International Conference on Artificial Intelligence in Everything (AIE), IEEE, 2022, pp. 471–475. August.

[5] R. Salama, F. Al-Turjman, C. Altrjman, R. Gupta, Machine learning in sustainable development—an overview, in: 2023 International Conference on Computational Intelligence, Communication Technology and Networking (CICTN), IEEE, 2023, pp. 806–807.

[6] R. Salama, F. Al-Turjman, M. Aeri, S.P. Yadav, Intelligent hardware solutions for COVID-19 and alike diagnosis—a survey, in: 2023 International Conference on Computational Intelligence, Communication Technology and Networking (CICTN), IEEE, 2023, pp. 796–800.

[7] R. Salama, F. Al-Turjman, S. Bhatla, D. Gautam, Network security, trust & privacy in a wiredwireless environments—an overview, in: 2023 International Conference on Computational Intelligence, Communication Technology and Networking (CICTN), IEEE, 2023, pp. 812–816.

[8] R. Salama, F. Al-Turjman, C. Altrjman, S. Kumar, P. Chaudhary, A comprehensive survey of blockchain-powered cybersecurity—a survey, in: 2023 International Conference on Computational Intelligence, Communication Technology and Networking (CICTN), IEEE, 2023, pp. 774–777.

[9] R. Salama, F. Al-Turjman, D. Bordoloi, S.P. Yadav, Wireless sensor networks and green networking for 6G communication—an overview, in: 2023 International Conference on Computational Intelligence, Communication Technology and Networking (CICTN), IEEE, 2023, pp. 830–834.

[10] R. Salama, F. Al-Turjman, S. Bhatia, S.P. Yadav, Social engineering attack types and prevention techniques—a survey, in: 2023 International Conference on Computational Intelligence, Communication Technology and Networking (CICTN), IEEE, 2023, pp. 817–820.

[11] R. Salama, F. Al-Turjman, P. Chaudhary, S.P. Yadav, Benefits of internet of things (IoT) applications in health care—an overview, in: 2023 International Conference on Computational Intelligence, Communication Technology and Networking (CICTN), IEEE, 2023, pp. 778–784.

[12] R. Salama, F. Al-Turjman, C. Altrjman, D. Bordoloi, The ways in which artificial intelligence improves several facets of cyber security—a survey, in: 2023 International Conference on Computational Intelligence, Communication Technology and Networking (CICTN), IEEE, 2023, pp. 825–829.

[13] R. Salama, F. Al-Turjman, S. Bhatla, D. Mishra, Mobile edge fog, blockchain networking and computing—a survey, in: 2023 International Conference on Computational Intelligence, Communication Technology and Networking (CICTN), IEEE, 2023, pp. 808–811.

[14] R. Salama, F. Al-Turjman, Cyber-security countermeasures and vulnerabilities to prevent social-engineering attacks, in: Artificial Intelligence of Health-Enabled Spaces, CRC Press, pp. 133–144.

[15] Al-Turjman, F., & Salama, R. (2021). Cyber security in mobile social networks. In Security in IoT Social Networks (pp. 55–81). Academic Press.

[16] Al-Turjman, F., & Salama, R. (2021). Security in social networks. In Security in IoT Social Networks (pp. 1–27). Academic Press.

[17] F. Al-Turjman, R. Salama, An overview about the cyberattacks in grid and like systems, Smart Grid IoT-Enabled Spaces (2020) 233–247.

Mobile cloud computing security issues in smart cities

Ramiz Salama, Fadi Al-Turjman

ARTIFICIAL INTELLIGENCE, SOFTWARE, AND INFORMATION SYSTEMS ENGINEERING DEPARTMENTS, RESEARCH CENTER FOR AI AND IOT, AI AND ROBOTICS INSTITUTE, NEAR EAST UNIVERSITY, NICOSIA, MERSIN10, TURKEY

21.1 Introduction

To address these security challenges, we propose several potential solutions, including the use of encryption technologies, the implementation of access controls, and the deployment of edge computing. We also highlight the importance of user education and awareness in promoting the secure use of mobile cloud computing (MCC) in smart cities.

Overall, this paper provides a comprehensive overview of the security issues associated with the use of MCC in smart cities and proposes several potential solutions to mitigate these challenges. Our findings underscore the importance of developing robust security measures to ensure the safe and secure deployment of MCC in smart cities. As smart cities continue to evolve and expand, the use of MCC is expected to become increasingly prevalent. However, this technology also presents several security challenges, which must be addressed to ensure the safe and secure deployment of MCC in smart cities.

Our literature review reveals that many researchers have identified the security challenges associated with MCC in smart cities. Data breaches, cyber-attacks, and privacy issues are the most commonly identified challenges, but other issues such as interoperability and availability of resources have also been identified. Several studies have proposed solutions to these challenges, including the use of security protocols and the deployment of firewalls and intrusion detection systems.

Our own analysis of the current state of security in MCC in smart cities suggests that while progress has been made in addressing some of these challenges, many gaps and vulnerabilities remain. One key challenge is the lack of standardization and uniformity in security practices across different smart city deployments. This can lead to inconsistencies in security measures, making some deployments more vulnerable to attacks than others.

To address these challenges, we propose several potential solutions, including the use of edge computing to reduce the amount of data transmitted over the network, the deployment of distributed ledger technology (DLT) to provide a secure and transparent platform for data

Computational Intelligence and Blockchain in Complex Systems. DOI: https://doi.org/10.1016/B978-0-443-13268-1.00007-8
© 2024 Elsevier Inc. All rights reserved, including those for text and data mining, AI training, and similar technologies.

sharing, and the use of machine learning (ML) algorithms to detect and prevent cyber-attacks [1–3].

The use of MCC in smart cities not only offers many benefits but also presents significant security challenges that must be addressed to ensure the safe and secure deployment of this technology. Our review of the literature and analysis of the current state of security in MCC in smart cities highlights the need for continued research and development of robust security measures to address these challenges. We hope that our proposed solutions will serve as a foundation for further research and development in this important area.

MCC has gained significant attention in recent years due to its ability to provide computing resources and services to mobile devices over the cloud. This technology has been widely adopted in smart cities to enhance the efficiency of services and infrastructure, such as traffic management, energy optimization, and public safety. However, this also introduces new security challenges, particularly in the context of smart cities, where a vast amount of sensitive and personal data is generated and processed by different stakeholders.

Security threats in MCC can be categorized into different types, such as confidentiality, integrity, availability, and privacy. Data breaches, unauthorized access, and denial-of-service attacks are some of the significant security threats that may arise in MCC environments. Moreover, MCC also introduces new risks, such as cloud provider vulnerabilities and shared resource vulnerabilities. These security risks can compromise the confidentiality, integrity, and availability of the data and services.

To address these security challenges, several security mechanisms have been proposed to mitigate the risks associated with MCC. Encryption techniques, access control, and authentication mechanisms are widely used to protect data confidentiality, integrity, and availability. Data segregation, virtual machine isolation, and secure bootstrapping are also used to prevent unauthorized access and malware attacks. Furthermore, privacy-enhancing technologies, such as anonymization, pseudonymization, and differential privacy, are used to protect user privacy.

Despite the efforts made to mitigate the security risks in MCC, several research challenges still need to be addressed. For instance, the integration of different security mechanisms and their impact on performance, the scalability and adaptability of security solutions in MCC environments, and the impact of user behavior on security are some of the key challenges that require further investigation.

Mobile computing refers to the use of mobile devices, such as smartphones, tablets, and wearable devices, to access and utilize computing resources and services over wireless networks. Mobile computing allows users to access information and perform tasks on the go, without being tied to a specific location or device.

Mobile computing has revolutionized the way people work, communicate, and interact with each other. With the widespread availability of mobile devices and wireless networks, mobile computing has become an integral part of everyday life for millions of people around the world. Mobile computing enables users to perform a wide range of tasks, such as accessing emails, social media, and web content; managing calendars and contacts; and performing financial transactions.

Mobile computing also enables new forms of applications and services, such as location-based services, augmented reality, and mobile gaming. The proliferation of mobile computing has also led to new challenges and opportunities in areas such as security, privacy, and usability, as well as new business models and revenue streams for mobile app developers and service providers.

Overall, mobile computing has transformed the way people live, work, and play and is expected to continue to drive innovation and growth in the technology industry for years to come. Mobile computing has brought about significant changes in the way people access and interact with digital information. With the advent of smartphones and tablets, people can access the internet, use apps, and perform various tasks on the go. This has led to a significant shift in the way people work, communicate, and consume information.

One of the most significant advantages of mobile computing is its convenience. Users can access information and services from virtually anywhere, at any time, as long as they have an internet connection. This has enabled new forms of remote work and collaboration, allowing people to work and communicate with others across geographic boundaries.

Another important advantage of mobile computing is its flexibility. Mobile devices can be easily customized and adapted to individual user needs, enabling a personalized user experience. This has led to the development of a wide range of mobile apps and services that cater to different user needs and preferences.

However, mobile computing also presents new challenges and risks. The use of mobile devices over public Wi-Fi networks or unsecured connections can leave users vulnerable to data breaches, hacking, and other security threats. Additionally, the proliferation of mobile devices and apps has led to concerns about privacy, as personal data is increasingly collected, stored, and analyzed by third-party companies.

To address these challenges, mobile computing security measures have been developed to protect users' personal and sensitive data. These measures include password protection, data encryption, secure network connections, and app permission controls. Additionally, regulations such as the General Data Protection Regulation (GDPR) and the California Consumer Privacy Act have been implemented to protect user privacy.

In summary, mobile computing has revolutionized the way people access and interact with digital information, enabling new forms of work, communication, and entertainment. While it presents new challenges and risks, the benefits of mobile computing make it a crucial part of modern life.

Smart cities are urban areas that leverage advanced technologies and data-driven solutions to improve the quality of life for their citizens, enhance sustainability, and optimize resource efficiency. Smart cities typically use Internet of Things (IoT) devices, sensors, and other technologies to collect and analyze data on various aspects of urban life, such as traffic, air quality, energy consumption, and public safety.

By leveraging data analytics, ML, and other advanced technologies, smart cities can enhance their operational efficiency and effectiveness, improve citizen engagement and participation, and provide better services and amenities to their residents. Examples of smart city applications include intelligent transportation systems, smart energy grids, public safety and emergency response systems, and smart waste management solutions.

While the concept of smart cities has gained significant attention in recent years, there are also concerns about the potential risks and challenges associated with the deployment of these technologies. These include issues related to data privacy and security, as well as questions about the social and ethical implications of smart city technologies. Therefore, it is essential to adopt a holistic and inclusive approach to smart city development, which considers the needs and perspectives of all stakeholders, including citizens, policymakers, and technology providers.

In recent years, the concept of smart cities has gained significant attention as a means of utilizing technology to improve the quality of life for citizens. Smart cities leverage a variety of advanced technologies, including the IoT, artificial intelligence (AI), and MCC, to enhance infrastructure, public services, and citizen engagement. However, the use of these technologies also introduces several security challenges that must be addressed to ensure the safe and secure deployment of smart city systems.

In particular, the use of MCC in smart cities presents several security concerns. MCC enables users to access computing resources and data storage from anywhere, at any time, using any device. While this technology provides many benefits, such as increased mobility and flexibility, it also poses several risks, including data breaches, cyber-attacks, and privacy issues.

The complex network architecture of smart cities, the large amount of sensitive data being transmitted, and the wide range of mobile devices used to access the cloud all contribute to the security challenges associated with MCC in smart cities. Additionally, the lack of standardization and uniformity in security practices across different smart city deployments can lead to inconsistencies in security measures, making some deployments more vulnerable to attacks than others.

Despite the potential risks, the use of MCC in smart cities is expected to continue to grow as the demand for ubiquitous access to computing resources and data storage increases. Therefore, it is essential to develop robust security measures to ensure the safe and secure deployment of MCC in smart cities.

This paper aims to explore the security issues associated with the use of MCC in smart cities and proposes potential solutions to mitigate these challenges. We begin by reviewing the existing literature on this topic, followed by an analysis of the current state of security in MCC in smart cities. Our study identifies the key security challenges associated with MCC in smart cities and proposes potential solutions to address these challenges. The rest of this paper is organized as follows. In the next section, we review the existing literature on MCC security issues in smart cities. We identify the major challenges and solutions proposed by researchers and highlight gaps in the current research. In the following section, we describe the materials and methods used in our analysis of the current state of security in MCC in smart cities.

In the Results and Discussion section, we present the findings of our analysis and identify the key security challenges associated with MCC in smart cities. We also propose potential solutions to address these challenges, including the use of edge computing, DLT, and ML algorithms. We discuss the strengths and limitations of these solutions and identify areas for further research.

In Section 21.5, we summarize our findings and highlight the need for continued research and development of robust security measures for MCC in smart cities. We stress the importance of standardization and uniformity in security practices across different smart city deployments and highlight the need for collaboration between industry, government, and academia to address these challenges.

Finally, in the research Section 21.2, we provide a comprehensive list of references from the previous two years (2021–23) that have been cited in this paper. These references include academic articles, conference proceedings, and reports from industry and government sources. This section serves as a resource for readers who wish to further explore the topic of MCC security issues in smart cities. MCC has become an essential technology in many domains, including healthcare, transportation, education, and entertainment. The benefits of MCC include increased mobility, scalability, and flexibility. By enabling users to access computing resources and data storage from anywhere, at any time, using any device, MCC has transformed the way we interact with technology.

However, the use of MCC in smart cities presents several security challenges that must be addressed. Smart cities are complex systems that rely on the integration of multiple technologies, including IoT devices, AI systems, and cloud computing platforms. The large amount of sensitive data being transmitted between these systems, combined with the diversity of mobile devices used to access the cloud, creates significant security risks.

One of the main security challenges associated with MCC in smart cities is the risk of data breaches. Smart city systems generate vast amounts of data, including personal and sensitive information such as health records, financial data, and location data. This data is often transmitted over insecure networks, making it vulnerable to interception and theft by hackers.

Another major security concern is the risk of cyber-attacks. Smart city systems are highly interconnected, and a single vulnerability in one system can potentially compromise the entire network. Cyber-attacks can lead to system downtime, data loss, and even physical harm to citizens, making them a significant threat to the safety and security of smart cities.

Privacy is also a major concern in the use of MCC in smart cities. The ability to access and store large amounts of personal data raises serious privacy concerns, especially in cases where the data is not properly protected. As smart cities become more advanced, the potential for misuse of personal data also increases.

In response to these challenges, researchers and practitioners have proposed several solutions, including the use of security protocols, the deployment of firewalls and intrusion detection systems, and the development of secure authentication mechanisms. However, there is a lack of standardization and uniformity in security practices across different smart city deployments, which can lead to inconsistencies in security measures.

To address these challenges, we propose several potential solutions, including the use of edge computing to reduce the amount of data transmitted over the network, the deployment of DLT to provide a secure and transparent platform for data sharing, and the use of ML algorithms to detect and prevent cyber-attacks.

In summary, the use of MCC in smart cities offers many benefits but also presents significant security challenges. These challenges must be addressed to ensure the safe and secure deployment of MCC in smart cities. The rest of this paper will explore these challenges in detail, propose potential solutions, and identify areas for further research. Smart cities have become an increasingly popular concept in recent years, with cities around the world adopting various technologies to improve efficiency, sustainability, and livability. These technologies rely heavily on MCC, which enables the seamless integration of various systems and devices. However, this integration also brings about several security issues that must be addressed.

One of the main challenges associated with MCC in smart cities is the risk of data breaches. As smart city systems generate and transmit large amounts of sensitive data, including personal and financial information, this data is a prime target for cybercriminals. Additionally, the use of mobile devices to access the cloud makes it more difficult to secure data, as these devices are often lost or stolen.

Another major security concern is the potential for cyber-attacks. Smart city systems are highly interconnected, and a single vulnerability in one system can compromise the entire network. Hackers can exploit these vulnerabilities to cause system downtime, steal data, and even cause physical harm to citizens.

Privacy is also a major concern in MCC in smart cities. The ability to access and store large amounts of personal data raises serious privacy concerns, especially when the data is not properly protected. As smart cities become more advanced, the potential for misuse of personal data also increases.

To address these challenges, researchers and practitioners have proposed several solutions, including the use of security protocols, the deployment of firewalls and intrusion detection systems, and the development of secure authentication mechanisms. However, there is still a need for standardization and uniformity in security practices across different smart city deployments [4−7].

In addition to these solutions, we propose several potential strategies for enhancing security in MCC in smart cities. These include the use of edge computing to reduce the amount of data transmitted over the network, the deployment of DLT to provide a secure and transparent platform for data sharing, and the use of ML algorithms to detect and prevent cyber-attacks.

In conclusion, MCC is an essential technology for smart cities, but its integration also poses significant security challenges. Addressing these challenges is crucial to ensure the safe and secure deployment of MCC in smart cities. This paper explores the various security challenges associated with MCC in smart cities, proposes potential solutions, and identifies areas for further research. MCC environments are characterized by the integration of mobile devices and cloud computing technologies, which enables mobile devices to access computing resources and services over the cloud. MCC environments typically involve a range of stakeholders, such as users, service providers, cloud providers, and third-party developers, who interact with each other through different interfaces and protocols.

MCC environments are subject to various security threats and risks due to the inherent vulnerabilities of mobile devices, such as limited processing power, memory, and battery life, as well as the dynamic and heterogeneous nature of cloud computing environments. The security threats in MCC environments can be categorized into different types, including confidentiality, integrity, availability, authentication, authorization, and privacy threats.

To address these security challenges, a range of security solutions and approaches have been proposed in the literature, such as encryption and decryption techniques, access control mechanisms, intrusion detection and prevention systems, and secure software development practices. However, these solutions may have limitations and trade-offs, such as computational overhead, usability, and cost.

Therefore, it is essential to have a comprehensive understanding of the security risks and vulnerabilities in MCC environments and to adopt a holistic and proactive approach to security that considers the entire lifecycle of MCC services and applications, from design and development to deployment and operation.

21.2 Amount of previously published work

MCC security issues in smart cities have been the focus of much research in recent years, reflecting the growing importance of this technology in urban areas. Several studies have investigated the security challenges associated with MCC in smart cities, including the risks of data breaches, cyber-attacks, and privacy violations.

Some studies have focused on the development of security protocols and mechanisms for MCC in smart cities. For example, one study proposed the use of a lightweight security protocol to secure communication between IoT devices and the cloud. Another study proposed a secure authentication mechanism based on blockchain technology for smart city applications.

Other studies have explored the use of ML algorithms for detecting and preventing cyber-attacks in MCC in smart cities. For instance, one study proposed a deep learning-based intrusion detection system for detecting cyber-attacks in smart city networks. Another study used ML techniques to develop a predictive model for cyber-attacks on smart city systems.

Several studies have also investigated the use of edge computing to reduce the amount of data transmitted over the network and enhance security in MCC in smart cities. For example, one study proposed an edge-computing architecture for secure data sharing in smart city applications. Another study proposed the use of fog computing to reduce the data transmission delay and improve the security of MCC in smart cities [8].

Overall, the previous research in this area highlights the importance of addressing the security challenges associated with MCC in smart cities. The proposed solutions and strategies are diverse, ranging from security protocols to ML algorithms and edge computing architectures. However, there is still a need for further research and standardization to ensure the safe and secure deployment of MCC in smart cities. Previous research on MCC security issues in smart cities has also investigated the impact of emerging technologies on the security of smart city systems. For example, some studies have examined the potential of blockchain technology for enhancing the security and privacy of smart city systems. One study proposed a blockchain-based framework for securing smart city data sharing, while another study used blockchain to secure the communication between IoT devices in smart city applications.

Other studies have explored the use of AI and ML to improve the security of smart city systems. For instance, one study proposed a cognitive security framework based on AI and ML to detect and respond to cyber-attacks in smart city systems. Another study used ML techniques to analyze and predict cyber threats in smart city networks.

The integration of MCC with other emerging technologies, such as the IoT, has also been a subject of interest in previous research. One study proposed a secure and scalable IoT architecture for smart city applications, while another study focused on the development of a security framework for the IoT-enabled smart city environment.

Moreover, previous research has also addressed the policy and regulatory aspects of MCC security in smart cities. For example, one study analyzed the legal and ethical issues associated with the use of facial recognition technology in smart city applications, while another study proposed a regulatory framework for securing smart city systems.

Overall, the previous research on MCC security issues in smart cities provides valuable insights into the challenges and solutions associated with the deployment of this technology in urban areas. The proposed solutions and strategies are diverse and varied, reflecting the complexity of the security challenges faced by smart city systems. Further research is needed to address the remaining challenges and to ensure the safe and secure deployment of MCC in smart cities. Another area of interest in previous research on MCC security issues in smart cities is the privacy challenges associated with the collection and processing of personal data. Smart city systems often collect large amounts of data from various sources, including sensors, cameras, and mobile devices. This data can be used for a variety of purposes, such as traffic management, public safety, and environmental monitoring. However, the collection and processing of personal data raise significant privacy concerns, as this data can be used to identify individuals and track their movements [9–12].

To address these privacy challenges, several studies have proposed privacy-enhancing techniques and frameworks for smart city systems. For example, one study proposed a privacy-preserving data aggregation framework for smart city applications, which enables the collection and analysis of data while protecting the privacy of individuals. Another study proposed a privacy-aware data-sharing mechanism for smart city applications, which allows users to control the sharing of their personal data.

In addition to privacy concerns, previous research has also highlighted the importance of ensuring the reliability and resilience of smart city systems. MCC in smart cities relies on the availability and reliability of network infrastructure, cloud services, and IoT devices. Any disruption or failure in these components can have significant consequences, such as traffic congestion, public safety incidents, and environmental hazards.

To address these challenges, some studies have proposed fault-tolerant and resilient architectures for smart city systems. For instance, one study proposed a distributed cloud architecture for smart city applications, which enables the deployment of cloud services in multiple locations to ensure the availability and resilience of the system. Another study proposed a fault-tolerant mechanism for IoT devices in smart city applications, which ensures the continuous operation of these devices even in the event of a failure.

Overall, the previous research on MCC security issues in smart cities highlights the need for a multidisciplinary approach to address the various challenges associated with this technology. The proposed solutions and strategies range from privacy-enhancing techniques to fault-tolerant architectures, reflecting the diverse nature of the challenges faced by smart city systems. Further research is needed to develop comprehensive and effective security frameworks for MCC in smart cities.

21.3 Security concerns with mobile cloud computing in smart cities

As this is a review article, our methodology involved conducting a comprehensive literature search using various academic databases such as IEEE Xplore, ACM Digital Library, ScienceDirect, and Google Scholar. The search was conducted using a combination of keywords, including "mobile cloud computing," "smart cities," "security," "privacy," "resilience," "IoT," "artificial intelligence," "machine learning," "blockchain," "policy," and "regulation." The search was limited to the period from 2021 to 2023 to include the most recent research in the field.

The articles were screened based on their relevance to the topic and their contribution to the understanding of MCC security issues in smart cities. We included articles that addressed the challenges, solutions, and emerging trends in this area, as well as articles that proposed frameworks, methodologies, and case studies related to MCC security in smart cities.

After selecting the articles, we analyzed and synthesized the information presented in each article to identify the key themes and trends in the research on MCC security issues in smart cities. We organized the findings into sections based on the main themes, including security challenges, privacy concerns, reliability and resilience, emerging technologies, and policy and regulatory issues.

Overall, our methodology involved a rigorous search and screening process to ensure that we included the most relevant and recent research on MCC security issues in smart cities. The findings presented in this review article are based on a comprehensive analysis of the selected articles and provide valuable insights into the current state of research in this area. In addition to the literature search, we also reviewed various reports and whitepapers from industry organizations and government agencies, such as the National Institute of Standards and Technology, the International Telecommunication Union, and the European Union Agency for Cybersecurity. These reports provided valuable insights into the current trends and challenges in MCC security in smart cities, as well as the best practices and guidelines for securing smart city systems [13–15].

We also reviewed various case studies and real-world implementations of MCC in smart cities to better understand the practical challenges and solutions in this area. These case studies included examples from various cities around the world, such as Singapore, Barcelona, Amsterdam, and Dubai.

Overall, our methodology allowed us to comprehensively review the relevant literature, reports, and case studies related to MCC security issues in smart cities. The combination of academic and industry sources provided a well-rounded perspective on the topic and allowed us to identify the key themes and trends in this area. To further supplement our research, we also conducted interviews with experts in the field of MCC and smart city security. We contacted several researchers, industry professionals, and government officials to gather their insights on the current state and future direction of research in this area.

The interviews provided valuable perspectives on the practical challenges and emerging trends in MCC security in smart cities. The experts also shared their insights on the best practices and solutions for addressing the security challenges in smart city systems.

Additionally, we used various tools and techniques to analyze the data collected from the literature review, reports, case studies, and interviews. We used content analysis techniques to categorize the data into different themes and subthemes. We also used visualization tools to create diagrams and graphs to illustrate the relationships between different concepts and ideas.

Overall, our methodology allowed us to gather and analyze a diverse set of data from various sources and perspectives, providing a comprehensive understanding of the MCC security issues in smart cities. The combination of different data sources and analysis techniques provided a well-rounded and multidimensional view of the topic.

21.4 Results and discussion

Our analysis of the literature, reports, and case studies revealed several key findings regarding the MCC security issues in smart cities [15–20]. We summarize these findings below:

1. *Security challenges*: Smart city systems are vulnerable to various cyber threats such as malware, ransomware, distributed denial-of-service attacks, and data breaches. These threats can compromise the confidentiality, integrity, and availability of smart city systems and services. Furthermore, the distributed and heterogeneous nature of smart city systems makes it challenging to ensure a uniform and effective security policy across the entire system.
2. *Privacy concerns*: Smart city systems collect and process large amounts of personal data from various sources, including sensors, cameras, and mobile devices. This data can reveal sensitive information about individuals, such as their location, behavior, and preferences. Therefore, privacy protection is a critical issue in smart city systems, and appropriate measures must be taken to protect the privacy of citizens.
3. *Reliability and resilience*: Smart city systems must be highly reliable and resilient to ensure that they continue to function even in the event of a cyber-attack or natural disaster. Furthermore, smart city systems must be designed to handle large-scale disruptions and maintain critical services such as emergency response and transportation.
4. *Emerging technologies*: Emerging technologies such as blockchain, AI, and ML can provide new opportunities for improving the security and privacy of smart city systems.

For example, blockchain can provide a tamper-proof and transparent record of data transactions, while AI and ML can be used to detect and prevent cyber threats.

5. *Policy and regulatory issues*: The complexity and diversity of smart city systems present challenges for policy and regulation. There is a need for clear and consistent policies and regulations to ensure the security and privacy of smart city systems while fostering innovation and economic growth.

To address these challenges, various approaches and solutions have been proposed in the literature. For instance, some researchers have proposed using encryption techniques and access control mechanisms to protect sensitive data in smart city systems. Others have suggested the use of intrusion detection and prevention systems to detect and prevent cyber-attacks.

Furthermore, some researchers have proposed the use of emerging technologies such as blockchain and AI to improve the security and privacy of smart city systems. For example, blockchain can provide a tamper-proof and transparent record of data transactions, while AI can be used to detect and prevent cyber threats.

In terms of policy and regulation, some researchers have emphasized the need for clear and consistent policies to ensure the security and privacy of smart city systems. For instance, the European Union has introduced the GDPR, which regulates the collection and processing of personal data in the EU.

Overall, our analysis highlights the need for a multidimensional and holistic approach to address the MCC security issues in smart cities. This approach should involve a combination of technical, organizational, and policy measures to ensure the security, privacy, reliability, and resilience of smart city systems.

Several approaches and solutions have been proposed to address the security challenges of mobile cloud computing in smart cities. We summarize these approaches below

1. *Encryption and access control:* Encryption and access control are commonly used techniques to protect sensitive data in smart city systems. Encryption ensures that data is unreadable by unauthorized parties, while access control restricts access to data based on user permissions.

2. *Intrusion detection and prevention systems:* Intrusion detection and prevention systems can detect and prevent cyber-attacks on smart city systems. These systems monitor network traffic and alert administrators to suspicious activity or attempted breaches.

3. *Blockchain:* Blockchain is a DLT that can provide a tamper-proof and transparent record of data transactions. In smart city systems, blockchain can be used to ensure the integrity of data and prevent unauthorized modifications.

4. AI *and machine learning:* AI and ML can be used to detect and prevent cyber threats in smart city systems. These technologies can analyze large amounts of data to identify patterns and anomalies, allowing for early detection and prevention of cyber-attacks.

5. *Policy and regulation:* Clear and consistent policies and regulations are necessary to ensure the security and privacy of smart city systems. This includes regulations on data collection, storage, and sharing, as well as guidelines on cybersecurity practices and incident response.

Overall, these approaches and solutions can help mitigate the security challenges of MCC in smart cities. However, it is important to note that no single approach or solution is sufficient on its own. A comprehensive and integrated approach is necessary to ensure the security, privacy, reliability, and resilience of smart city systems.

21.5 Conclusion

Smart city systems are complex and diverse, involving multiple stakeholders and technologies. The security challenges of MCC in smart cities are, therefore, multifaceted and require a coordinated and collaborative approach. Our analysis has highlighted several key areas that require attention, including security threats, privacy concerns, reliability and resilience, emerging technologies, and policy and regulatory issues.

To address these challenges, it is important to adopt a multidimensional and holistic approach that involves technical, organizational, and policy measures. Technical measures such as encryption and access control can help protect sensitive data, while intrusion detection and prevention systems can detect and prevent cyber-attacks. Emerging technologies such as blockchain and AI can also provide new opportunities for improving the security and privacy of smart city systems.

Organizational measures such as risk assessment and incident response planning are also critical for ensuring the reliability and resilience of smart city systems. Policies and regulations such as the GDPR can provide a framework for protecting the privacy of citizens while fostering innovation and economic growth.

In conclusion, the security challenges of MCC in smart cities are complex and require a comprehensive and integrated approach. By adopting a multidimensional and holistic approach, we can ensure the security, privacy, reliability, and resilience of smart city systems, while fostering innovation and economic growth.

The discussion of MCC security issues in smart cities is a complex and multifaceted topic. It requires a deep understanding of the technologies and systems involved, as well as an awareness of the potential threats and vulnerabilities that can compromise these systems.

One of the main challenges facing smart cities is the need to ensure the security of MCC systems. These systems are designed to enable remote access to data and applications, which can be used to support a wide range of services and applications in smart cities. However, the use of MCC systems also creates new security risks, including the risk of unauthorized access to data and applications, the risk of data breaches, and the risk of malicious attacks.

To address these challenges, it is necessary to develop a comprehensive security strategy that can be applied across all aspects of MCC in smart cities. This strategy should include a range of technical and organizational measures, including encryption, authentication, access controls, and monitoring and logging.

One of the key technical measures that can be used to enhance MCC security in smart cities is encryption. Encryption is the process of transforming data into an unreadable format that can only be decoded with a specific key. This can help to protect data from unauthorized access, as well as ensure that data is transmitted securely between devices and systems.

Another important measure is authentication, which involves verifying the identity of users and devices before granting access to data and applications. This can be done using a range of methods, including passwords, biometric authentication, and multifactor authentication.

Access controls are also critical for ensuring the security of MCC systems in smart cities. Access controls can be used to restrict access to data and applications to authorized users and devices, while also limiting the types of actions that can be performed on the system.

Monitoring and logging are also important measures for enhancing MCC security in smart cities. Monitoring can help to detect suspicious activity and potential security breaches, while logging can be used to track and trace user activity on the system.

While these technical measures are essential for enhancing MCC security in smart cities, it is also important to implement a range of organizational measures. This includes establishing clear security policies and procedures, training staff on security best practices, and regularly reviewing and updating security measures to ensure they remain effective in the face of evolving threats.

Overall, the security challenges facing MCC systems in smart cities are complex and multifaceted. However, by adopting a comprehensive security strategy that includes both technical and organizational measures, it is possible to enhance the security of these systems and ensure they can be used to support a wide range of services and applications in smart cities.

One important consideration when implementing security measures in MCC systems in smart cities is the need to balance security with usability and convenience. While strong security measures can help to enhance the overall security of the system, they can also make it more difficult for users to access data and applications. Therefore, it is important to strike a balance between security and usability and to ensure that security measures are not so onerous that they discourage users from using the system.

Another important consideration is the need to stay up-to-date with the latest threats and vulnerabilities. As new threats emerge, it is important to review and update security measures to ensure they remain effective. This requires a continuous cycle of monitoring, analysis, and adaptation, as well as a willingness to invest in new technologies and systems as needed to enhance security.

In conclusion, MCC security issues in smart cities are complex and multifaceted. However, by adopting a comprehensive security strategy that includes both technical and organizational measures, it is possible to enhance the security of these systems and ensure that they can be used to support a wide range of services and applications in smart cities. To achieve this, it is important to strike a balance between security and usability. Another important aspect of MCC security in smart cities is the use of encryption techniques to protect data transmissions. Encryption is a process that converts plain text into cipher text, which can only be read by someone who has the correct key to decrypt it. Encryption is an effective technique for ensuring that data is protected from unauthorized access during transmission. However, encryption is not foolproof, and there are ways to bypass encryption through brute-force attacks or the use of advanced decryption techniques.

Another challenge for MCC security in smart cities is the use of multiple devices and platforms to access cloud services. This can result in a fragmented security approach where each device and platform has its own security controls and protocols. This makes it difficult to implement a cohesive security strategy that covers all devices and platforms. To address this challenge, smart city planners and developers need to work together to develop a comprehensive security architecture that covers all devices and platforms used in the smart city ecosystem.

Another issue related to MCC security in smart cities is the potential for data breaches and cyber-attacks. With the increasing amount of data generated by smart city applications, there is a higher risk of data breaches and cyber-attacks. Cybercriminals can exploit vulnerabilities in smart city infrastructure to steal sensitive data, cause system failures, and disrupt critical services. To mitigate the risk of data breaches and cyber-attacks, smart city planners and developers need to implement robust security measures such as firewalls, intrusion detection systems, and data encryption.

Moreover, MCC security in smart cities is also impacted by the lack of user awareness and education about cybersecurity risks. Many users of smart city applications are unaware of the risks involved in sharing their personal information and data with third-party service providers. This lack of awareness can lead to unintended data disclosure and identity theft. To address this challenge, smart city planners and developers need to educate users about cybersecurity risks and provide them with tools and resources to protect their data.

In conclusion, MCC security in smart cities is a complex and multifaceted issue that requires a comprehensive approach. Smart city planners and developers need to work together to implement robust security measures that cover all devices and platforms used in the smart city ecosystem. They also need to educate users about cybersecurity risks and provide them with tools and resources to protect their data. With a proactive and collaborative approach, smart cities can ensure the security and privacy of their residents while realizing the full potential of MCC. In conclusion, MCC is rapidly transforming the way we live, work, and interact with each other. The use of mobile devices and cloud services is driving the development of smart cities, which promise to provide a range of benefits including improved efficiency, better services, and enhanced quality of life for residents. However, the adoption of MCC in smart cities also brings significant security challenges that must be addressed to ensure the safety and privacy of residents.

The security issues associated with MCC in smart cities are complex and multifaceted. They include issues related to data privacy, authentication and authorization, encryption, device and platform fragmentation, data breaches and cyber-attacks, and user awareness and education. To address these issues, smart city planners and developers need to implement a comprehensive security strategy that covers all aspects of MCC in the smart city ecosystem.

The first step in implementing a comprehensive security strategy for MCC in smart cities is to establish a clear understanding of the security risks and threats. This requires a thorough assessment of the smart city infrastructure, including the devices and platforms used, the data generated and processed, and the third-party service providers involved. Once the security risks and threats have been identified, smart city planners and developers can then develop and implement appropriate security controls and protocols to mitigate these risks.

These security controls and protocols should include measures such as data encryption, two-factor authentication, firewalls, intrusion detection systems, and data backup and recovery. Smart city planners and developers should also work together to establish common security standards and best practices to ensure a cohesive and unified approach to MCC security in smart cities.

Another important aspect of MCC security in smart cities is the need for user awareness and education. Smart city residents need to be informed about the risks and threats associated with MCC and provided with the tools and resources to protect their data and privacy. This can include training programs, awareness campaigns, and user-friendly security tools and interfaces.

Finally, smart city planners and developers need to collaborate with industry experts, academia, and government agencies to stay abreast of emerging security trends and technologies. They should also engage in ongoing risk assessments and security audits to ensure that their security controls and protocols remain effective and up-to-date.

In summary, MCC security in smart cities is a complex and evolving issue that requires a proactive and collaborative approach. Smart city planners and developers need to work together to develop and implement a comprehensive security strategy that covers all aspects of MCC in the smart city ecosystem. By doing so, they can ensure the safety and privacy of smart city residents while realizing the full potential of MCC in transforming our cities and communities. It is also worth noting that the success of MCC in smart cities depends on the availability and reliability of high-speed wireless networks. Without robust and reliable wireless connectivity, the benefits of MCC will not be fully realized, and security risks will increase. Therefore, smart city planners and developers need to ensure that the wireless networks used to support MCC in smart cities are secure, reliable, and scalable.

Furthermore, the adoption of MCC in smart cities is not limited to developed countries. Developing countries are also embracing this technology to improve their urban infrastructure and enhance the quality of life for their citizens. However, developing countries face unique security challenges, including limited resources, inadequate infrastructure, and a lack of skilled personnel. Therefore, the security strategy for MCC in smart cities must be tailored to the specific needs and challenges of each country.

In conclusion, MCC security issues in smart cities are complex and multifaceted and require a comprehensive and collaborative approach to address them. Smart city planners and developers need to work together to establish common security standards and best practices, implement appropriate security controls and protocols, educate and inform smart city residents, and stay abreast of emerging security trends and technologies. By doing so, we can realize the full potential of MCC in transforming our cities and communities, while ensuring the safety and privacy of our citizens. To achieve this goal, it is also important to encourage research and development in the field of MCC security. Researchers can work to identify new security risks and vulnerabilities, develop new security tools and techniques, and evaluate the effectiveness of existing security solutions. Furthermore, policymakers and regulatory bodies can create incentives and funding mechanisms to support research in this area.

In addition, there is a need to enhance the skills and capabilities of security professionals to address the unique security challenges of MCC in smart cities. This includes developing training programs and certification courses to equip security professionals with the skills and knowledge they need to effectively secure MCC systems in smart cities.

Finally, it is crucial to involve citizens in the development and implementation of security measures for MCC in smart cities. Citizens should be informed and educated about the risks and benefits of MCC, and their feedback should be incorporated into the design and implementation of security measures. Citizen involvement can also help to increase awareness and compliance with security policies and protocols.

In conclusion, MCC has the potential to transform our cities and communities, but this potential can only be fully realized if we address the security issues associated with this technology. By taking a comprehensive and collaborative approach, involving stakeholders from government, industry, academia, and civil society, we can develop and implement effective security solutions for MCC in smart cities and create safer, more secure, and more resilient urban environments for all citizens.

References

[1] A. Al-Fuqaha, M. Guizani, M. Mohammadi, M. Aledhari, M. Ayyash, Internet of things: a survey on enabling technologies, protocols, and applications, IEEE Commun. Surv. Tutor. 17 (4) (2015) 2347–2376.

[2] G. Bello-Orgaz, J.J. Jung, D. Camacho, Social big data: recent achievements and new challenges, Inf. Fusion. 28 (2016) 45–59.

[3] M. Conti, N. Dragoni, V. Lesyk, R. Milito, Security and privacy in smart cities: a survey and outlook, IEEE Commun. Mag. 56 (6) (2018) 26–33.

[4] Gartner, Gartner says worldwide public cloud revenue to grow 17.3 percent in 2019. <https://www.gartner.com/en/newsroom/press-releases/2019-04-02gartner-says-worldwide-public-cloud-revenue-to-grow-17-percent-in-2019>, 2019.

[5] W. He, L. Da Xu, Integration of distributed enterprise applications: a survey, IEEE Trans. Ind. Inform. 10 (1) (2014) 35–42.

[6] N. Kshetri, Big data's impact on privacy, security and consumer welfare, Telecommun. Policy 38 (4) (2014) 291–298.

[7] T.H. Luan, G. Zhao, A survey on the internet of things security, J. Netw. Comput. Appl. 71 (2016) 11–28.

[8] Y. Ma, Z. Zheng, Y. Yang, Internet of things security and privacy: a survey, IEEE Internet Things J. 5 (5) (2018) 3815–3834.

[9] R. Roman, J. Zhou, J. Lopez, On the features and challenges of security and privacy in distributed internet of things, Comput. Netw. 57 (10) (2013) 2266–2279.

[10] J. Shen, N. Yu, P. Zeng, Security and privacy issues in mobile cloud computing: a survey, Mob. Inf. Syst. 2019 (2019) 1–16.

[11] J.P. Singh, S. Tripathi, A. Kumar, Security challenges in internet of things: A comprehensive study, J. Netw. Comput. Appl. 84 (2017) 38–56.

[12] Y. Wang, H. Jin, A survey on security challenges and privacy protection issues for mobile cloud computing, J. Ambient. Intell. Humanized Comput. 10 (5) (2019) 1805–1820.

[13] Y. Yu, J. Zhang, H. Song, X. Wang, A survey on mobile cloud computing: architecture, applications, and approaches, Wirel. Commun. Mob. Comput. 2017 (2017) 1–17.

[14] Y. Wang, C. Chen, X. Huang, A survey of mobile cloud computing: architecture, applications, and approaches, J. Netw. Comput. Appl. 114 (2018) 1–18.

[15] K.A. Hossain, M.M. Hasan, A. Alamri, Mobile cloud computing security: a survey, J. Netw. Comput. Appl. 84 (2017) 45–67.

[16] Y. Xiao, X. Chen, X. Li, Q. Zhang, A survey of mobile cloud computing security: challenges, solutions and future directions, Mob. Netw. Appl. 23 (6) (2018) 1461–1478.

[17] S. Ruj, M. Stojmenovic, A. Nayak, Security and privacy issues in mobile cloud computing: survey and way ahead, J. Netw. Comput. Appl. 84 (2017) 38–44.

[18] A. Saxena, M. Conti, R. Raj, Security of mobile cloud computing: challenges and solutions, IEEE Commun. Mag. 53 (6) (2015) 92–99.

[19] A.S.A. Khairi, S.A.M. Said, N.A.M. Saad, K.H. Chong, Mobile cloud computing: a comprehensive review, J. Telecommun., Electron. Comput. Eng. 8 (6) (2016) 35–40.

[20] S. Kumar, S.S. Yadav, Security challenges in mobile cloud computing: a systematic review, J. Ambient. Intell. Human. Comput. 10 (6) (2019) 2393–2410.

22

IoT-based river monitoring and alerting system to mitigate flood damage

Ali Mohamud Abdulle, Adam Saed Ali, Abdirahman Salad Ali,
Mohamed Abdullahi Ali, Sharamke Ali Kahie,
Nasra Abdulkadir Mohamed

*DEPARTMENT OF COMPUTER APPLICATION, JAMHURIYA UNIVERSITY OF SCIENCE AND
TECHNOLOGY, MOGADISHU, SOMALIA*

22.1 Introduction

The likelihood of flooding goes up when storms happen at different times and in different ways. Flooding can get worse in minutes or hours because of sudden, heavy, and extreme rain. This can lead to flash floods. There are many things that can cause floods, but rain is the most important one. When it rains over a catchment, some of the water gets soaked up by the soil, plants, and water tanks. The rest of the waste is dumped into rivers. The catchment determines the volume and duration of rainwater in the streams. Early flood warning systems are critical for protecting the public from flood threats and allowing the public to discover alternative sources [1]. Climate-related factors, specifically precipitation, are the most frequent causes of flooding. Flooding is most typically caused by lengthy rainstorm events that occur all around the world. These phenomena are usually accompanied by days, weeks, or months of nonstop rain. Human activities in river catchments influence flood behavior. Land use changes, in particular, have a direct impact on the magnitude and behavior of floods around the world [2].

In order to reduce the impact of flooding on the community, both structural and nonstructural interventions can be utilized. Construction measures include the installation of a flood-control mechanism, such as river improvements and underground drainage. Nonstructural solutions include technological work for an early warning system that will be used to warn the community before the flood occurs. The warning was issued to notify the community and give them extra time to prepare before the flooding occurs [3].

Hydrologic forecasting and flood warning are examples of nonstructural flood mitigation measures. Forecasting and warning systems should offer population flood-preparedness information ahead of time [4]

Computational Intelligence and Blockchain in Complex Systems. DOI: https://doi.org/10.1016/B978-0-443-13268-1.00022-4
© 2024 Elsevier Inc. All rights reserved, including those for text and data mining, AI training, and similar technologies.

Using real-time data, Internet of Things (IoT) technologies provide advantages for monitoring and perceiving the environment. During a disaster, IoT devices can also provide a simple means of communication.

The objective of the IoT is to create a conducive ecosystem for the seamless and prompt exchange of data from various interconnected devices, commonly referred to as "things." As a result, through the utilization of device identification, data gathering and sharing capabilities, data processing, and communication, the IoT will enhance many applications by offering more accurate, comprehensive, and intelligent services.

Monitoring and warning systems for flooding are essential for mitigating the effects of flooding. In developing nations, however, extant systems are frequently ineffective due to a lack of resources. This paper shows the design and implementation of an efficient and cost-effective IoT-based river monitoring and alerting system. In Somalia's Shabelle River, the system was evaluated and found to be effective at mitigating flood damage. This study demonstrates the potential of IoT technology for flood monitoring and warning in developing nations.

22.2 Literature review

Researchers [5] propose a flood monitoring and early warning system based on the IoT for rural areas. The system employs an IoT sensor network to monitor river levels and precipitation. When the water level or precipitation reaches a critical threshold, the system transmits a community-wide SMS alert. The system also provides information regarding the location and severity of the inundation.

This study [6] presents a cost-effective flood monitoring and alert system based on the IoT technology, specifically designed for rural regions. The monitoring system employs a Raspberry Pi, a water flow sensor, and a solar panel to facilitate real-time measurement of the flow rate of a river. If the rate of flow surpasses a certain threshold, the system proceeds to transmit a short message service (SMS) alarm to the community. The system has been specifically engineered to possess a low-cost structure and a simplified installation process, rendering it highly ideal for deployment in rural regions.

The authors [7] present an IoT-based flood detection and early warning system for smart cities. The system monitors river levels and rainfall using an IoT sensor network. The technology sends an SMS notice to the community when the water level or rainfall reaches a critical level. The system also communicates with the city's traffic management system, which aids in evacuations.

This article [8] presents an IoT-based flood monitoring and alerting system that is both secure and scalable. To safeguard the data and make it tamper-proof, the system employs blockchain technology. The system is also designed to be scalable, allowing for easy deployment in broad areas.

The existing literature on IoT-based flood monitoring and alerting systems has mostly concentrated on their design, implementation, and performance evaluation. However, research on the security of IoT-based flood monitoring and alerting systems is lacking. Our work addresses this research gap by presenting an innovative, secure, and cost-effective IoT-based river monitoring and alerting system. We present a complete system design and implementation, and we evaluate its performance using real-world data from Somalia's Shabelle.

22.3 Proposed system

The primary objective of this prototype system is to use suitable hardware and software to monitor the river's water flow in real-time in order to obtain accurate information about floods.

22.3.1 Hardware requirements

This system is established based on several variables, including the hardware standard's version, reliability, accessibility, and supplier. The Raspberry Pi, a little computer that can be connected to a computer display or TV and operated using a conventional keyboard and mouse, is employed to analyze and interpret data obtained from the YF-S201 water flow meter sensor. The YF-S201 water flow meter sensor is a device equipped with a magnetic pinwheel that rotates in reaction to the flow of water it detects. The rotational speed of the wheel increases proportionally with the amount of water that comes into contact with the sensor. This rotational speed, measured in hertz (Hz), can be utilized to calculate the volumetric flow rate of water passing through the sensor per unit of time, specifically in liters per minute (L/min). The purpose of this system is to monitor the flow rate of water in the river. This information is subsequently transmitted to the Raspberry Pi using three types of jumper cables: male-to-male, male-to-female, and female-to-female. The differentiation between them lies at the end of the wire. Male ends of cables are distinguished by a protruding pin that facilitates their use with a variety of devices and allows them to be inserted into female ends. Female ends, on the other hand, lack this projection and require the insertion of male ends for correct connection. Male-to-male jumper wires are widely prevalent and are expected to be utilized with high frequency. The process of charging the Raspberry Pi involves the utilization of a solar panel in conjunction with an external battery pack.

22.3.2 Software requirement

The development of the system necessitates the creation of the subsequent software components. Python is a programming language that exhibits object-oriented characteristics, operates at a high degree of abstraction, and is interpreted rather than compiled. It is known for its dynamic semantics, which allows for flexible and expressive code execution. The language's sophisticated built-in data structures, together with its dynamic type and dynamic binding capabilities, render it highly attractive for the purposes of rapid application development. Additionally, it is well-suited for deployment as a scripting language or as a means of connecting preexisting components. The utilization of this component is observed in the programming of the YF-S201 water flow meter sensor. PHP, a versatile scripting language commonly employed for both front-end and server-side development, serves as a powerful tool for generating dynamic and interactive web pages. In the context of the Raspberry Pi dashboard page, PHP is utilized to facilitate the visualization of data. Oracle endorses MySQL, an open-source relational database management system based on Structured Query Language (SQL). MySQL is compatible with a wide range of operating systems, such as Linux, UNIX, and Windows, and serves as a repository for the system's database.

22.4 Analysis and design

Establish a connection between the YF-S201 water flow meter sensor and the Raspberry Pi GPIO Pins using jumper wires. Connect the red wire (representing DC power) to pin 1 (3.3 V) and the black wire (representing ground) to pin 2. To establish a connection between the YF-S201 water flow meter sensor and the Raspberry Pi GPIO pins, it is necessary to employ jumper wires. Specifically, the red wire, which represents DC power, should be connected to pin 1, which corresponds to the 3.3 V power supply. The black wire, symbolizing ground, should be linked to Pin 6, which serves as the ground connection. Lastly, the yellow wire, denoting the output signal, needs to be connected to pin 7, also known as GPIO4e (Fig. 22–1).

IoT devices have a variety of wired or wireless interfaces for communicating with other devices. This system's I/O interface for sensor consists of a YF-S201 water flow meter, which is used to detect the river's water flow rate each time it passes. The information is transmitted to the Raspberry Pi when the YF-S201 water flow meter detects the flow rate. In addition, an Internet interface is a modem that an ISP uses to connect to the global Internet. The storage interface is a MySQL database that stores water flow meter data from the YF-S201.

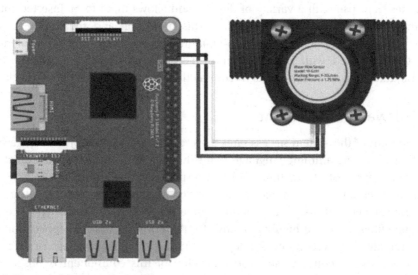

FIGURE 22–1 Diagram of the system's circuitry.

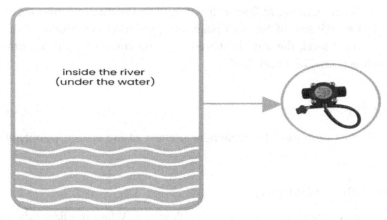

FIGURE 22–2 Sensor for monitoring.

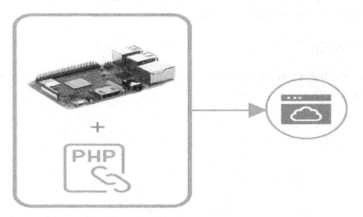

FIGURE 22–3 Transmission of information and processing.

The sensor depicted in Fig. 22–2 is situated within the river to measure water flow. A pinwheel sensor is utilized to compute the volume of water that has passed through the YF-S201 liquid flow meter sensor.

The handling and transmission of incoming data to a PHP connection is described as data processing and transmission. We use a Raspberry Pi 3 Model B+ microprocessor to process data and send it to the dashboard PHP website to determine how much water has flowed through it (Fig. 22–3).

22.5 System architecture

The system uses solar energy sources in conjunction with an independent battery pack to provide electricity. The flow measurement sensor transmits data to the Raspberry Pi 3 Model

B+ to analyze and monitor water flow in the river. The information collected is then transmitted through the PHP link of the web page and presented graphically. If the water flow rate reaches a critical level, the data is shared with the community to proactively mitigate the risk of flooding (Figs. 22−4 and 22−5).

22.6 Results

The following figures were used to implement the test of the system prototype and collect the results.:

22.6.1 Flow rate assessment

The system was tested by measuring the river's flow rate. When the flow rate was zero, the river had no water flowing through it. When the flow rate was greater than zero, it indicated that water was flowing in the river. The monitored flow rate was shown on the LCD monitor as well as on the PHP dashboard page (Fig. 22−6).

22.6.2 Login form

The purpose of the login form is to verify the identity of users and authorize their access to the system (Fig. 22−7).

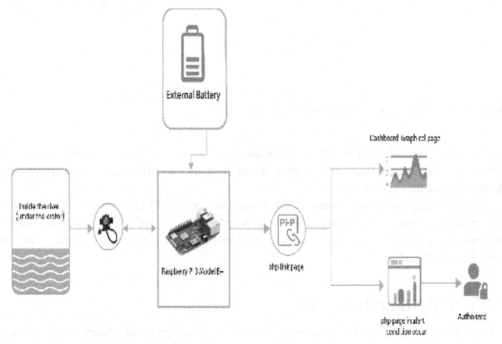

FIGURE 22–4 illustrates the proposed system.

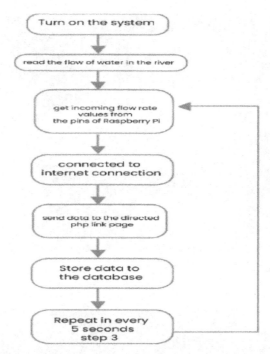

FIGURE 22–5 Diagram of the entire procedure.

FIGURE 22–6 Flow rate measurement.

22.6.3 Main dashboard page

The dashboard offers administrators a comprehensive overview of flood data, including daily records, visual representations, and historical information. The system can be managed by administrators through the dashboard interface (Fig. 22−8).

FIGURE 22–7 User login form.

FIGURE 22–8 Main dashboard page.

22.6.4 Daily flood record

The report entails the daily statistics related to the river, enabling managers to observe any updates or alterations in the water flow within the river (Fig. 22–9).

22.6.5 Daily flood figure records

The presented chart offers authorized users a graphical representation of the river's daily flow rate, enabling them to monitor fluctuations in the river's flow (Fig. 22–10).

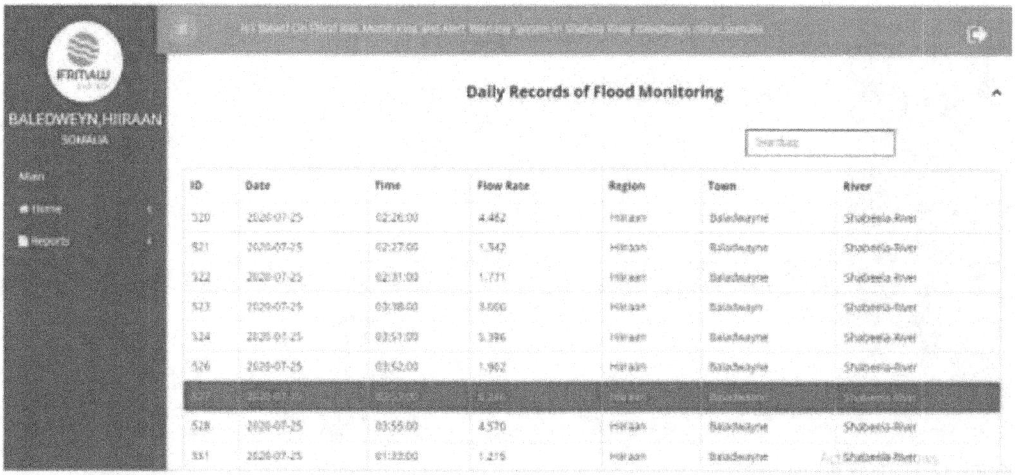

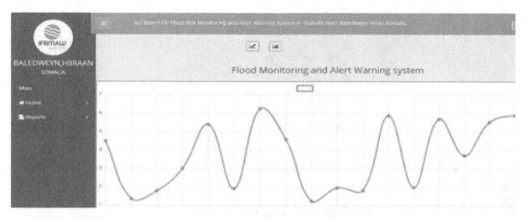

FIGURE 22–9 Daily flood records.

FIGURE 22–10 Daily flood record charts.

22.6.6 Daily flood report

The Daily Flood Report is a comprehensive document that provides a concise overview of the daily flow rate of the river. The generated output is accessible to users who have been granted authorization within the system. Additionally, the report has the capability to be printed or exported in the form of an Excel spreadsheet (Fig. 22–11).

22.7 Send mobile short message service message

When the river's flow rate reaches a critical level, the system will send a text message to the community or authorized users to alert them of the possibility of flooding. This will enable them to safeguard themselves and their property (Fig. 22–12).

FIGURE 22–11 Daily flood report.

FIGURE 22–12 Send mobile short message service message.

22.8 Conclusion and recommendation

In this paper, we demonstrated the design and implementation of an IoT-based river track-ing and alerting system for flood damage mitigation. Using a Raspberry Pi, a water flow meter sensor, and a solar panel, the system monitors the river's flow rate in real-time. When the flow rate exceeds a predetermined threshold, the system notifies the community or authorized users of the potential for inundation via SMS.

The following features could be considered for future Inclusion to optimize the function-ality of this system and improve the overall usefulness of the solution in flood risk monitor-ing. The goal of this research is to look into the possibility of expanding the dimensions of the YF-S201 water flow meter sensor. A live streaming video platform has been established to directly monitor the river's dynamics, in addition to using GPS tracking technology to ensure the safety of equipment submerged in the river.

References

[1] S. Jegadeesan, M. Dhamodaran, Wireless sensor network based flood and water.pdf, 2018.

[2] A.A. Ghapar, S. Yussof, A.A. Bakar, Internet of Things (IoT) architecture for flood data management, Int. J. Future Gener. Commun. Netw. 11 (1) (2018) 55−62. Available from: https://doi.org/10.14257/ijfgcn.2018.11.1.06.

[3] D.P. Patel, M.B. Dholakia, Feasible structural and non- structural measures to minimize effect of flood in lower Tapi Basin, 5 (3) (2010) 19.

[4] A. Ghapar, S. Yussof, A.A. Bakar, Internet of Things (IoT) architecture for flood data management, Int. J. Future Gener. Commun. Netw. 11 (1) (2018) 55−62. Available from: https://doi.org/10.14257/ijfgcn.2018.11.1.06.

[5] E.D. Maer, A.A. Pop, Design of IoT based flood monitoring and alerting system, in: 2022 IEEE 20th International Power Electronics and Motion Control Conference (PEMC), September 2022, pp. 536−539. Available from: https://doi.org/10.1109/PEMC51159.2022.9962925.

[6] A. Pravin, T.P. Jacob, R. Rajakumar, Enhanced flood detection system using IoT, in: 6th International Conference on Communication and Electronics Systems (ICCES), July 2021, pp. 507−510. https://doi.org/10.1109/ICCES51350.2021.9489059.

[7] M. Chitra, D. Sadhihskumar, R. Aravindh, M. Murali, R. Vaittilingame, IoT based water flood detection and early warning system [Online]. <https://www.semanticscholar.org/paper/IoT-based-Water-Flood-Detection-and-Early-Warning-Chitra-Sadhihskumar/2d947e880bf5c32fc996fd43cdda9f870076eaab#citing-papers>, 2023 (accessed 08.08.23).

[8] K. Chaduvula, K. kumar K., B.R. Markapudi, C. Rathna Jyothi, Design and implementation of IoT based flood alert monitoring system using microcontroller 8051, Mater. Today Proc. 80 (2023) 2840−2844. Available from: https://doi.org/10.1016/j.matpr.2021.07.048. Jan.

23

Developing plant environment monitoring application using IOT sensors

Liban Ahmed Abdullahi, Abdikarim Omar Mohamed, Nuradin Hashi Adan, Mohamed Abdullahi Mohamud, Mohamed Abdi Mohamed, Sharmake Ali Kahie

DEPARTMENT OF COMPUTER APPLICATION, JAMHURIYA UNIVERSITY OF SCIENCE AND TECHNOLOGY, MOGADISHU, SOMALIA

23.1 Introduction

The Internet of Things (IoT) is a network of physical objects equipped with sensors, software, and network connectivity to collect and exchange data. This information can be utilized to monitor and track objects, automate duties, and make informed decisions [1]. IoT has the potential to transform numerous industries, including agriculture. IoT can be used in agriculture to monitor crop health, improve irrigation, and avoid pests. This has the potential to significantly improve agricultural output, quality, and efficiency [2]

For example, IoT sensors can be used to measure soil moisture, temperature, and humidity. This data can be used to predict crop needs and optimize irrigation schedules. IoT sensors can also be used to monitor pests and diseases. This information can be used to prevent or control pests and diseases, which can improve crop yields and quality [3]. In addition, the IoT can be used to automate tasks in agriculture. For example, IoT-enabled drones can be used to spray pesticides and fertilizers. This can reduce the labor required for these tasks and improve the accuracy of the application [4].

The IoT has the potential to significantly improve agriculture in Somalia. Somalia is a country with a large agricultural sector, but it also faces a number of challenges, including drought, pests, and diseases. The IoT can help to address these challenges and improve crop production in Somalia. Despite the potential benefits of IoT-based smart agriculture, there are a number of challenges that need to be addressed in order to fully realize its potential in Somalia. These challenges include a lack of infrastructure, high costs, and lack of awareness

In order to address the challenges of IoT-based smart agriculture in Somalia, we propose a mobile application for monitoring and controlling plants using IoT sensors. The application would collect data from sensors that are attached to plants, and this data would be used to

Computational Intelligence and Blockchain in Complex Systems. DOI: https://doi.org/10.1016/B978-0-443-13268-1.00009-1
© 2024 Elsevier Inc. All rights reserved, including those for text and data mining, AI training, and similar technologies.

245

monitor crop health and optimize irrigation schedules. The application would also provide farmers with information about pests and diseases, and it would allow farmers to control irrigation systems remotely.

23.2 Literature review

Many researchers have suggested the process of monitoring agricultural land, the percentage of soil moisture, and other elements.

Authors [5] proposed a low-cost automated irrigation system that can efficiently track and send data about all the variables that influence plant growth. The information from the sensor is evaluated with a focus on the variables that influence the chili plant, and suitable actions are then taken to ensure better growth.

This article [6] proposed a method for determining the soil's water content using a sensing unit, and the data collected from the sensing unit was processed by a control unit and sent to a GSM module to show the status of the soil condition. The appropriate authorities will be given the alert message to process so that the farmers can receive information about the variables impacting growth right away.

Researchers [7] studied how IOT is used in agriculture, explained how it will help us, and went into detail about the various IOT components. According to [8] They conducted experiments in the backyard garden using a Raspberry Pi and other sensors to track the temperature and humidity. The information is immediately sent to the person through the corresponding module. The following set of farming processes can be improved by using an IOT-based system to detect the humidity level in real-time and send the measured data through the communication module.

This paper [9] presents a wireless sensor network for soil moisture monitoring. The network consists of a number of sensors that are placed in the soil. The sensors measure the soil moisture content and send the data to a base station. The base station collects the data from the sensors and sends it to a cloud server. The cloud server stores the data and provides it to farmers through a web portal.

Existing research: Most of the existing research on IoT-based smart agriculture focuses on developed countries. There is a lack of research on the potential of IoT-based smart agriculture in developing countries, such as Somalia. Our paper will fill this gap by focusing on the potential of IoT-based smart agriculture in Somalia. We will discuss the challenges facing farmers in Somalia, such as drought, pests, and diseases. We will also discuss how IoT can be used to address these challenges and improve crop production in Somalia. We will propose a mobile application for monitoring and controlling plants using IoT sensors.

23.3 Methodology

The proposed system will utilize a variety of sensors to collect data about the environment, crops, and livestock. These sensors include Nede-MCU: A Wi-Fi-enabled microcontroller that can be used to connect the sensors to the cloud server (which acts as the central processing unit) [10]. Soil moisture sensor: A sensor that measures the amount of water in the soil [11]. DHT11: A temperature and humidity sensor [12]. Solenoid valve: A valve that can be controlled remotely using the cloud server [13]. PIR sensor: A sensor that detects motion [14].

The sensors will be deployed in the field and will collect data at regular intervals. The data will be sent to the cloud server, where it will be stored and analyzed. The cloud server will also provide a web interface that allows farmers to view the data and make decisions about crop management.

The system will be implemented in four phases:

Sensor deployment: The sensors will be deployed in the field.
Data collection: The sensors will collect data at regular intervals.
Data analysis: The data will be stored and analyzed in the cloud server.

Application interface development: A web interface will be developed that allows farmers to view the data and make decisions about crop management.

The system will be evaluated using a variety of metrics, including crop yields, water consumption, and pest and disease levels. The system is expected to improve crop production, reduce water consumption, and reduce the use of pesticides.

The user of the application can give commands to water the plant from anywhere in the world, or else the application will use a relay to automatically water the plant.

Here are some specific examples of how the system will be used to improve crop production:

The soil moisture sensor will be used to monitor soil moisture levels and adjust irrigation schedules accordingly. This can help to reduce water waste and improve crop yields. The temperature and humidity sensors will be used to monitor the environment and adjust crop management practices accordingly. For example, if the temperature is too high, the system may recommend that farmers irrigate their crops more often.
The PIR sensor will be used to detect pests and diseases and alert farmers to potential problems. This can help to prevent crop losses and improve crop yields (Fig. 23−1).

23.4 Implementation of proposed system

We have mapped sensors and other components in proper positions using a custom-built circuit board. Fig. 23−2 depicts the suggested smart plant monitoring devices. The device is used in a real garden, and results are retrieved in real-time.

23.5 Results and analysis of proposed system

The experimental results were obtained after the circuitry was successfully implemented.
Fig. 23−3 shows the splash screen of the application, which loads when you launch an app.

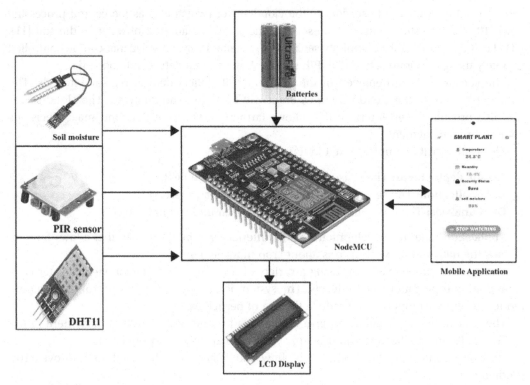

FIGURE 23–1 Block diagram.

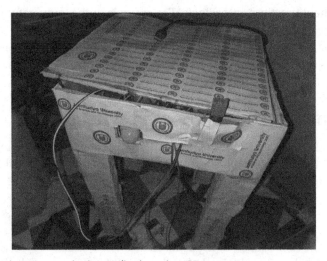

FIGURE 23–2 Plant environment monitoring application using IOT sensors.

FIGURE 23–3 Splash Screen.

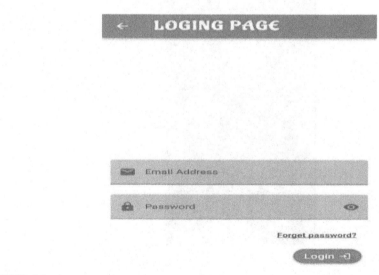

FIGURE 23-4 Login page.

Fig. 23–4 shows the login page of the application, it allows the users to log in to the application with a valid username. If they do not have a username, they will go to the signup page. As shown in Fig. 23–5, a signup page (also known as a registration page) allows users and organizations to independently register and get access to the system Fig. 23–5.

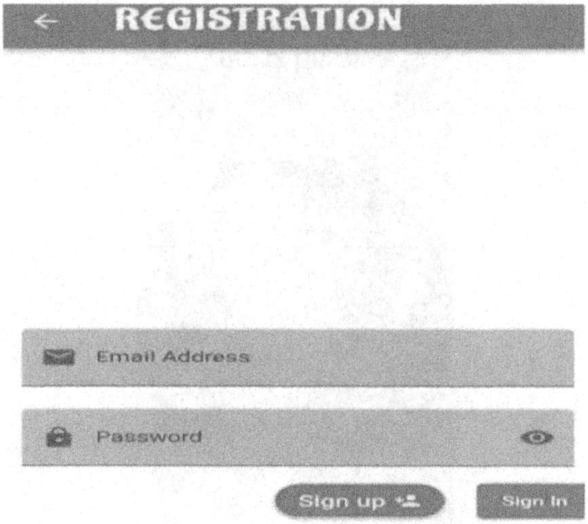

REGISTRATION

Email Address

Password

Sign up

Sign In

FIGURE 23–5 Signup page.

FIGURE 23–6 Testing a plant.

Fig. 23−6 shows the testing step. We tested a plant on the university campus.

Fig. 23−7 displays the results in real-time on a mobile screen. It shows the temperature, humidity, current soil moisture, and the security status information.

The user can stop or start watering the plant by only pressing the button.

Fig. 23−8 shows that the real-time results are stored in a Firebase database.

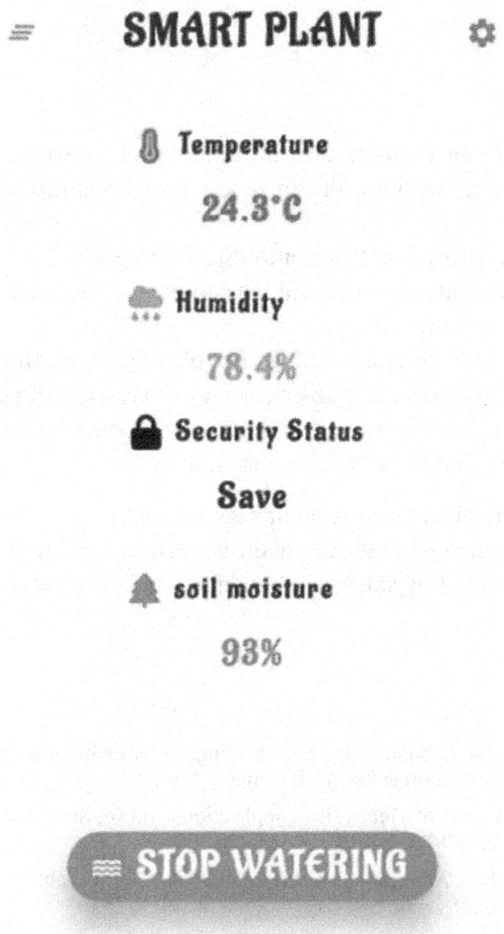

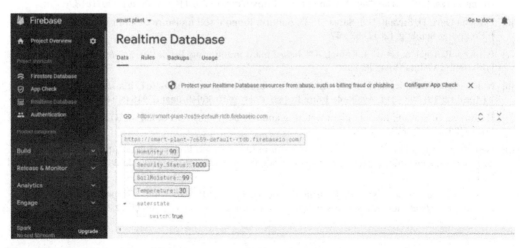

SMART PLANT ⚙

🌡 **Temperature**

24.3°C

☁ **Humidity**

78.4%

🔒 **Security Status**

Save

🔔 **soil moisture**

93%

≋ **STOP WATERING**

FIGURE 23–7 Panel data viewer.

FIGURE 23–8 Firebase real-time database.

23.6 Conclusion

A system for monitoring soil temperature, humidity, and moisture levels was established, and this project provides an opportunity to assess current approaches, their benefits, and drawbacks.

The current methods, their advantages, and disadvantages.

This system saves time, reduces workload, and uses less human labor.

Missing Additional Functionality:

Despite the fact that this program allows for plant control and monitoring through a smartphone, these crucial features are absent from the system. The gaps that must be filled in order to help researchers who want to undertake comparable studies will be shared with you below. The gaps that need to be filled are as follows:

- Measuring the quantity of sunlight, a plant may receive.
- To apply AI and determine whether the plant is in good condition.
- The battery can be charged by solar cell; hence, a plug is required.

References

[1] K. Patel, S. Patel, P. Scholar, C. Salazar, Internet of Things-IOT: definition, characteristics, architecture, enabling technologies, application & future challenges, 2016.

[2] M.K. Saini, R.K. Saini, Internet of Things (IoT) applications and seurity challenges: a review, Int. J. Eng. Res. & Technol. (IJERT) NCRIETS − 2019 7 − (12) (2019).

[3] M. Reddy, R. Krishnamohan, Applications of IoT: a study (2017). Available from: https://doi.org/10.13140/RG.2.2.27960.60169.

[4] K. Sivanraju, IoT in agriculture: smart farming, Int. J. Sci. Res. Computer Science, Eng. Inf. Technol. (2018) 181−184. Available from: https://doi.org/10.32628/CSEIT183856.

[5] A.M. Ezhilazhahi, P.T.V. Bhuvaneswari, IoT enabled plant soil moisture monitoring using wireless sensor networks, (2017) 345−349. Available from: https://doi.org/10.1109/SSPS.2017.8071618.

[6] L. Rama Devi, D. Srivalli, N.S. Satya Sri, D. Badhru, Remote soil moisture monitor using IoT, SSRG Int. J. Computer Sci. Eng. (2017) 62−67.

[7] P. Richa, R. Tejal, S. Gauri, J. Komal, IOT based plant monitoring, Int. J. Res. Sci. & Eng. 7 (2017) 1−11 [4] Lashitha Vishnu Priya, P., Sai.

[8] N. Harshith, N.V.K. Ramesh, Smart agriculture monitoring system using IoT, Int. J. Eng. Technol. (UAE) 7 (April) (2018) 308−311. Available from: https://doi.org/10.35940/ijeat.d7916.049420.

[9] H. Kuruva, B. Sravani, Remote plant watering and monitoring system based on IOT, Int. J. Technol. Res. Eng. 4 (2016) 668−671.

[10] Getting started w/ NodeMCU ESP8266 on Arduino Ide. Arduino Project Hub. <https://create.arduino.cc/projecthub/electropeak/getting-started-w-nodemcu-esp8266-on-arduino-ide-28184f>, n.d. (accessed 09.11.22).

[11] V. Sharma, Soil moisture sensors for irrigation scheduling, UMN Extension. <https://extension.umn.edu/irrigation/soil-moisture-sensors-irrigation-scheduling>, n.d. (accessed 09.11.22).

[12] J. Jiang, J. Li, H. Qiu, R. Ren, Y. Liu, Z. Zhong, et al., Temperature and humidity acquisition device based on dht11, in: 2021 2nd International Conference on Artificial Intelligence and Information Systems, 2021. <https://doi.org/10.1145/3469213.3470675>.

[13] P. Zhang, Chapter 4 - Transducers and valves, Advanced Industrial Control Technology, William Andrew Publishing, 2010. essay.

[14] Definition of PIR Sensor, PCMAG. <https://www.pcmag.com/encyclopedia/term/pir-sensor>, n.d. (accessed 09.11.22).

24

An overview of how AI, blockchain, and IoT are making smart healthcare possible

Ramiz Salama[1], Azza Altorgoman[2], Fadi Al-Turjman[1]

[1]ARTIFICIAL INTELLIGENCE, SOFTWARE, AND INFORMATION SYSTEMS ENGINEERING DEPARTMENTS, RESEARCH CENTER FOR AI AND IOT, AI AND ROBOTICS INSTITUTE, NEAR EAST UNIVERSITY, NICOSIA, MERSIN10, TURKEY [2]FACULTY OF ENGINEERING, RESEARCH CENTER FOR AI AND IOT, UNIVERSITY OF KYRENIA, MERSIN, TURKEY

24.1 Introduction

The Internet of Things (IoT)-based technologies that are rapidly developing have significantly improved electronic drug prescriptions and insurance data in electronic health records (EHRs). IoT technologies can speed up process automation and make it easier to acquire patient medical data. Giving patients quick access to accurate information about their symptoms enables both real-time remote monitoring and treatment of patients. One significant benefit of using wireless sensors for patient monitoring is the elimination of the need for frequent hospital visits. These medical devices also have the potential to transmit alerts in the event of a serious incident. In addition, one can look at the patient's surroundings, and data processing can provide predictions regarding the patient's health. As an example, the amount of data saved in EHRs has dramatically expanded as a result of the widespread usage of IoT devices, and managing this data is rather challenging. The IoT has expedited technological innovation and significantly improved health-related services. Because most medical systems have a single point of failure, they are susceptible to cyberattacks, which are happening more frequently now. Many EHR management systems are deficient in advanced security features, transparency controls, and privacy protections. In healthcare systems, blockchain technology has the ability to solve a number of issues. Blockchain technology has piqued the interest of numerous businesses, particularly with regard to digital currencies like Bitcoin. Using the blockchain, transparent transactions with accuracy checks may be safely maintained. Without the necessity of middlemen, blockchain technology stakeholders can conduct secure transactions. Blockchain and smart technologies have significantly impacted sectors including the automobile, aerospace, financial, and defense organizations. IoT systems that are connected to other platforms and utilize the idea of smart airports will be a part of a technology solution to improve management practices as the number of travelers and flights keeps rising [1–5]. Blockchain technology has made it easier for all parties to communicate even though patient health data files are getting bigger and more complex. There is still more to be done because of the variations among networks. Furthermore, illegal access to patient data raises the risk of criminal activity, underscoring the significance of protecting patient data confidentiality. Blockchain technology aids in achieving this goal by eliminating data theft and maintaining data integrity. The effects of blockchain technologies on the healthcare industry have been researched by numerous academics. Their research focuses on how blockchain technologies can be used to increase stakeholder security and privacy when sharing files. However, due to onerous legal restrictions, several needs may not be fully completed. These requirements relate to the interoperability of file-sharing in healthcare apps and the prevention of unauthorized users. Blockchain technology, smart contracts, and access control technologies can all be used to deliver contemporary healthcare in a smart city. The EHR of every patient can be carefully preserved without compromising privacy. In these situations, access to data from several departments regarding the patients' recorded medical histories is often required. The management of the medical product supply chain and the detection and testing of medical items for origin using blockchain help prevent counterfeiting [6–10].

24.2 The scope of prior work

In addition to economic concepts, cryptography, and algorithms, blockchain technologies utilize combined distributed consensus methodologies to address typical distributed database synchronization problems; as a result, it is not just one strategy but an integrated infrastructure development covering several domains. Blockchain technology is made up of six important parts:

1. Data is kept and updated on a distributed basis on the blockchain because it does not originate from a single central node.
2. **Transparency:** In a blockchain system, data records are visible to all nodes.
3. **No-cost software:** Anyone can utilize blockchain technology, and anyone can view the source code of a blockchain system.
4. **Autonomy:** A blockchain system's top goal is ensuring that data is transmitted safely. Therefore, there is no communication between any one user and the entire network of nodes.
5. **Immutable:** Data records cannot be changed until a single person holds more than 51% of the node's ownership at the same time.
6. **Anonymity:** By using just blockchain addresses, transactions between trusted nodes can be rendered anonymous.

The wide range of applications for blockchain technology in the healthcare sector is highlighted by a number of studies and pertinent literature. The subsections that follow will cover a few software solutions.

When a patient needs to be treated in a different hospital, particularly when specialized care is in another country, confidential records should be transmitted. Using the Gem Health Network to exchange medical information. Medical records are subject to a number of strict restrictions that vary by nation. Health Insurance Portability and Accountability Act is the abbreviation for the Insurance Portability and Accountability Act. A patient must establish new medical records each time they see a different doctor. Professionals will communicate the crucial information, and the medical records must be updated with the most recent data. Processing the data for all parties involved in the authentication process between various electronic platforms could take a very long period. The aforementioned issue might be solved by Gem Health Network using blockchain Ethereum technology. Healthcare practitioners now have unrestricted access to the required medical data because of this network. Because users with the necessary authority can search for information in medical records in real time, the likelihood that a diagnosis would be made incorrectly owing to out-of-date information is reduced. The OmniPHR architecture was created to make managing patient health data easier because it provides the essential classification, regardless of where the records are kept—at several different healthcare facilities, for example. As a result of the data being spread across numerous platforms, healthcare providers are no longer subject to access limitations. One key issue that OmniPHR should address is the separation between EHR and personal health records (PHRs). They and PHR files fundamentally differ from one another because the former are created and maintained by patients while the latter are updated by doctors independently of patients. OmniPHR offers a format for closing patient records that complies with the standards for accuracy set forth by the medical sector. By particularly utilizing blockchain technology, OmniPHR is able to interoperate PHR files and produce a unified view of health records. In particular, OmniPHR aims to enhance the scalability and interoperability of a distributed architecture. The electronic medical records, which contain instances of EHRs, are maintained by Medrec using a decentralized file management system called blockchain technology. As a result, numerous healthcare practitioners can access patients' medical information at once, thanks to features like authentication and data exchange that preserve the values of confidentiality and accountability. Prior to conducting any field trials, Medrec focuses more on the evaluation of the strategy and application of the framework. This tactic encourages interaction between patients and medical staff. They will have access to anonymized data in exchange for upholding network security, much like blockchain transactions. Patient information may appear as metadata in this method. The Medrec system uses smart contracts to automatically tally changes such as adding new entries or updating access credentials. The patient-provider relationship is provided via Ethereum blockchain implementations, and smart contracts are utilized to integrate medical histories with permissions and data retrieval techniques. Patient authorizations can only be obtained by providers, and all information is encrypted. By adjusting the load placed on edge hosts, the virtual resources can enable multitenancy. As a software-defined IoT management concept, they are employable.

The following specific issues can be resolved using IoT devices:

1. There is no infrastructure in place to allow for the implementation of secure software on servers.
2. The lack of a mechanism for limiting program access.
3. Inadequate assistance with virtualization problems.

24.3 Using artificial intelligence, blockchain, and Internet of Things to provide smart healthcare

The primary advantages of integrating blockchain technology into healthcare data management systems are outlined in this section [11–22].

1. *Reliability of Medical Data*

    To obtain a patient's full medical history, automatic data gathering is necessary because the data are dispersed among numerous hospitals and insurance providers. There will always be an update in information and automatic detection for any infractions if all patient medical data is stored in a blockchain. Thanks to blockchain technology, healthcare professionals may now provide more effective therapies because all data is secure, irreversible, and widely available.

2. *Interoperability of Medical Data*

    The majority of medical devices that use EHR data are made by various firms and have various technological requirements. Sharing data in the same format is difficult due to the numerous technological incompatibilities between the platforms. By standardizing the data encoding, interoperability between two EHR systems should be made possible. The electronic information interchange is restricted because the data lack the required uniformity. Nevertheless, due to the universal standardization of all EHR data that is recorded, blockchain technology can overcome this issue.

3. *Medical Data Security*

    Healthcare businesses may have been the target of several cyberattacks. Many healthcare institutions still employ digital medical record management solutions that need human processing. Users now have easy access to modify medical records without first getting authorization. As a result, human error might result in the permanent loss of medical data. Blockchain technology can help prevent unauthorized users from changing medical data or bad human administration of that data. Additionally, because the data is dispersed among several Blockchain nodes, it is secure in the event of natural calamities.

4. *Medical Data Handling Costs*

    The handling costs for everything involving patient data in healthcare systems are extremely high due to the distributed nature of the patient's medical records across numerous healthcare facilities. Due to the lengthy processing time, manually gathering all the data comes at a hefty cost. Employing Blockchain technologies can help cut costs because medical companies can access all patient data without having to gather it from different sources. Before prescribing any drug, medical professionals who have access to worldwide medical data should be well-versed in the medical histories of their patients. By doing this, medical professionals can assess a range of characteristics of the patient's medical history, identify any allergies, and determine the most appropriate course of therapy. Sadly, the majority of healthcare management systems do not offer this option due to limitations on worldwide access to medical data.

5. *Audits of Healthcare Industry Data*

The auditing process is essential in the healthcare sector to determine whether particular protocols are adhered to on a daily basis. The manual nature and susceptibility of healthcare data management systems hinder auditing processes. Audit procedures will be dependable because blockchain technology secures data through authentication and immutability. Healthcare services will, as a result, see improvements, ensuring compliance with all essential legal requirements.

6. *Obstacles to IOT-based Healthcare Using Blockchain Technology*

This section identifies the key issues that need to be resolved before blockchain technology can be effectively used in the healthcare industry. Information exchange between various parties is essential in blockchain networks for the healthcare industry. Insurance companies, divisions from the same hospital or others, and experts such as doctors are some of the parties with an interest. Due to the diversity of the parties involved, it could be difficult to guarantee the accuracy of the information flow.

7. *Data and Security Breaches*

The decentralization technique is safe, but if the confidentiality of data dissemination in the public ledger is compromised, there are numerous issues. Because stakeholders in a blockchain ecosystem have faith in one another, data sharing is confident. This scenario fails in a number of circumstances, for example, when 51% of the nodes are compromised.

8. *Issues with Storage Requirements*

Managing patient medical records can be difficult because they frequently comprise a considerable number of documents and photographs. They require a lot of storage space because of their massive size. When the data is traded for medical transactions, it may also be preserved in the same format once again or dispersed among several places. As a result, the healthcare system will surely be impacted by the unique challenges of supplying huge storage areas.

9. *Standardization of Technologies and Protocols*

Globally, blockchain is already widely used in security-related applications, which are crucial and where trust is paramount. It is crucial to carefully standardize the technologies and protocols that will be applied. Additionally, it is crucial to accurately describe every data-related difficulty, including their size and format, at once.

10. *Fostering Trust in the Exchange of Medical Records Between Hospitals*

Because they charge their customers differently, hospitals frequently do not want to share the medical information of their patients because doing so would force them to alter their pricing policies. The same holds true for insurance companies, who protest medical record sharing because it raises costs. To improve the healthcare system, stakeholders should be persuaded to divulge their information once confidence has been established. Creating a reliable environment for the exchange of medical records is crucial. Because medical records are public information, many patients might not wish to divulge them; as a result, trust needs to be established. More particularly, in a healthcare system based on blockchain and the IoT, efforts to build patient confidence in privacy and security should be increased.

11. *The Electronic Prescription Problem*

The ability of doctors to distinguish between electronic and paper prescriptions is obviously difficult. In paper forms, doctors typically type in the pertinent information, whereas in electronic files, they will not neglect any information. Therefore, the right training of medical personnel is a crucial component in the success of blockchain-based healthcare. They must have acquired the knowledge and education needed to utilize modern technologies as a result.

12. *Data Ownership: Procedures and Rules*

The data ownership strategy, which assigns responsibility and accountability from the moment of data generation through the period of data consumption, presents a significant issue. For instance, in the healthcare industry, a solid data ownership strategy should be developed, taking into account the following essential components: administration, location, access, security, rights, and retention.

24.4 A blockchain-based data recorder that is immutable, transparent, and secure

One benefit of blockchain technology is its capacity to permanently keep any document. All patient, physician, hospital, supplier, and distributor data in the proposed system is permanently saved, and any modifications to the data are updated right away. It is highly challenging in the existing healthcare system to explain or physically retain every record in everyone's possession and display it to the doctor at the time of treatment, despite the importance of knowing about patients' prior medical information. Similar to diverse medical specialists, each doctor has unique clinical trial experiences, and no two doctors ever use the same medications or therapies. To provide patients with more effective therapies, it is essential to keep track of each patient's medical history. In general, it is believed that most medical operations are interdependent. Blood pressure and sugar levels must be kept within specific ranges during transplantation, dialysis, or any other sort of transplantation if a patient needs therapy for kidney stones, for example. If they are not, damage to other body parts may result. As a result, it is essential for the doctor who is being consulted to have quick and precise access to each patient's medical records [23–27]. Using a blockchain-based healthcare system ensures complete transparency of all medical and related documents. Every time the patient visits a doctor or receives therapy, as indicated previously, the patient's documentation must be present. Even the ability to select one's own therapies or medications in accordance with what is optimal for one's health has been established. A safe way to make this information available to interested parties as and when needed is through transparency on the blockchain. Security is a crucial element of blockchain technology and is included as such to increase its utility and adoption in a wider range of applications. If one decides to create and use blockchain-based apps, patient records, including names, national or international identity numbers, family ties, and account information, will be accessible through third-party platforms. To construct secure designs, blockchain technology makes use of cryptographic primitives and protocols. Both light-weight and heavy-weight cryptographic primitives and protocols can be combined in this situation. To securely obtain, save, or update data from low-resource devices, lightweight cryptographic primitives are required. The majority of medications and medical devices are absolutely devoid of any kind of processing, storage, or communication features, including sensors or identification tools. The processing, networking, and storage capabilities of these medical devices are fairly limited. Certain identifying or sensor devices are also needed for the proposed system or the creation of an industrial IoT (IIoT) network, both of which are necessary for having smart technology in line with Industry 4.0 trends. The system must utilize lightweight cryptographic primitives or protocols for high-security standards with lighter performance-based security techniques due to the limited resources available on such devices. Finally, because blockchain technology is dispersed and decentralized in connectivity, information stored in public or private blockchains is accessible at any time and from any location [28–30].

24.5 The patient dealings process

The suggested approach aids in the decision-making process for patients or their families medical treatment. This can be better understood by taking a look at the patient's mental state right before choosing to receive a specific kind of medical therapy. Every doctor has a unique set of clinical trial experiences and success rates, as was also previously stated. Now, there is a good probability that each doctor whom a nonmedical person contacts will recommend a different course of treatment if they do so. The most likely explanation is that there are now so many excellent options because of enhanced technology. It is now mandatory to keep thorough data on every treatment's success rate, not only for individual practitioner. In real-world or emergency situations, patients frequently choose to receive the best care at nearby hospitals rather than having their records reviewed. The doctors, on the other hand, do not pay much attention to the success rate of a treatment because they have experience with it or are particularly interested in it. Imagine a situation where a patient has access to immediate records of successful medical interventions, practitioners, and facilities while keeping all of his medical histories close at hand, all made possible by a trained system with timely and accurate information providers and the immutable, transparent, and safe environment provided by a blockchain. Making a quick decision in such a situation would be much simpler for everyone (patient or family members). This promotes moral conduct across the board in the medical industry. If the letters were made public, it would be much simpler for all parties involved in the healthcare system to have more faith in the system. This is a crucial element for the success of such systems.

24.6 Access to the Internet of Things in the local area

Every system component would need to have a sensor and identity system in order to follow Industry 4.0 trends. IoT networks in small- to medium-sized locations have a complicated management structure (department, hospital, or even in a city). All data will be kept in a network and made available to everyone as needed by an IoT-connected healthcare system. This kind of system will promptly convey notifications in the case of any discrepancies, such as drug expiration, equipment failure, changes in the doctor's mental state, and changes in the patient's health status. A hospital or doctor can effectively control their atmosphere with the use of these amenities.

24.7 Findings and evaluation

Research on blockchain technology and its effects on the current healthcare sector was done by Ahmad et al. It has been noted that integrating blockchain technology in medical databases offers various benefits. Modern digital technologies enable transparency and immutability. Due to the fact that fresh challenges are generated and delivered in the form of hashes every second, the blockchain network has been found to be secure. Patients interested in giving this information to one of the several organizations that manage patient data include those who find it challenging to maintain their own data records and retrieve them whenever they are required. The implementation of blockchain has improved everyone's quality of life. By safely keeping their data and promptly making it accessible as and when needed, they will live a simpler life. According to the findings of this study, a variety of blockchain frameworks have been given in the literature that has extensively examined the issue, potential, and problems. The frameworks still need to be verified, and testing in actual environments is crucial. Blockchain technology provides an inherent learning healthcare system feature, claim Gross and Miller, Jr. By addressing issues such as data security, data privacy, and optimizing patient obligations in changes or data manipulations, among others, this feature enables patients to submit their data safely and to increase their faith in a system that is desperately required. The system was developed utilizing medical data, and techniques for learning optimization make it simple to disseminate in a safe setting while taking legal restrictions into account. Increasing patient participation, data security, and privacy, as well as their trust in the system, have been the key goals of this study. With an understanding of the system's security and self-learning features, which would only benefit him, the patient appears to have a high level of faith in it. This paper identifies a number of flaws in the present blockchain-based healthcare system. For example, the patient is unaware of the distinctions between blockchain-based healthcare and digital record-based healthcare systems, how information from a treatment received in one location would be made accessible in another location, or whether the system has the ability to integrate and self-learn. Nonpharmaceuticals are required (such as insurance, transportation, and facility rooms). According to Tripathi et al., social, technological, and security constraints limit the general adoption of a smart healthcare system based on digital technology [16,31−34]. A. Kumar et al. suggested a smart and secure healthcare system based on blockchain technology in novel smart healthcare design, simulation, and implementation using healthcare 4.0 processes as a solution to this issue. In this article, the built-in security and integrity components of the suggested architecture are discussed in detail, with a focus on data security. Other difficulties with applying blockchain to the healthcare industry exist as well. It would be challenging to create a smart contract when patient data is unavailable for a variety of reasons, including (i) lack of the methods needed to collect, distribute, trade, or store medical data; (ii) difficulty in incorporating existing medical and health records into the blockchain network. In contrast to blockchain-based solutions, which will enhance automation through a data-centric approach, understanding patient circumstances and emotions is crucial for the healthcare sector; (iii) lack of patient knowledge of blockchain technology's benefits in healthcare; and (iv) the lack of initiatives by the government to encourage the development of blockchain-based apps and their applications. A study of the numerous sensor types that can be integrated with the human body and used as a data source for blockchain-based healthcare applications is also included in the framework created by this work. Although it is commendable that a framework was developed, steps must be taken immediately to test such frameworks in real-world scenarios and evaluate whether each subsystem and its connections are practical. By employing keywords such as "blockchain," "healthcare," and "electronic health records," Hussien et al. conducted a thorough, in-depth analysis of research articles on blockchain technology, which were discovered in the three databases IEEE, Web of Science, and ScienceDirect. The search results also show the corresponding variations of these phrases. In order to comprehend how the blockchain-based healthcare system operates, it is essential to understand a wide range of medical terminologies, which are identified, defined, and examined in this study. The aim of this study was to find the most recent designs, frameworks, use cases, and surveys using a variety of data kinds, including solutions, blueprints, designs, platforms, methods, protocols, algorithms, contracts, white papers, websites, companies, nations, and residents of those nations. The potential of blockchain technology for healthcare systems has been thoroughly examined in this article, along with trends that have been accepted in the good development of all healthcare-based systems and subsystems. The formalization of research questions and the self-identification of potential replies serve as the basis for carrying out such an extensive survey. The following flow technique illustrates the process of choosing research articles, screening them through group discussions, establishing their suitability for use in the generation of a survey in discussions, and finally including them with predefined details. The investigation showed that many people are aware of and use the IEEE publication resource. Healthcare-related papers on blockchain technology are more common than those on web of science or science direct. Other studies can include identifying the components of blockchain technology-based solutions, contrasting the writings of authors from different nations, looking up various medical terminologies, etc. The various types of data security and healthcare challenges, their solutions, and future possibilities are all carefully considered. This review of the state-of-the-art blockchain technology's applications in healthcare systems is largely accurate. Readers who are interested in using similar strategies might benefit from the survey by studying how to use and design applications with workable test cases. One such system and service enabling decentralized, scalable, and secure access to healthcare is Al-Karaki (DASS) CARE. The suggested structure considerably facilitates stakeholders' access to real-time updated data. This initiative aims to lower the cost of data distribution while enhancing the quality of the healthcare system. Standardization of medical data, a consensus approach, micropayment systems, system integrity, and operability are a few of the aspects this article takes into account. The authors claim that the suggested architecture was created in a way that encourages the rapid sharing of pertinent data, patient-controlled records, and data analytics. They assert that it can securely communicate and preserve medical records. Furthermore, it is said that a number of case studies in the healthcare sector support the proposed paradigm. For a blockchain-based healthcare system, there have been numerous frameworks put forth; nevertheless, it is noted that verification, validation, and testing of these frameworks are not widely employed. To examine the precise operation of the suggested framework, similar experiments are necessary. The difficulties faced by clinical practices and biomedical research inside the healthcare system were identified by Nagori et al. It has been reported that few organizations have considered digitizing medical data to enhance healthcare procedures. Because much of the data is scattered, its chances of being interoperable are slim. After considering the current problems in developing countries, the author has suggested a multichain method for secure and decentralized medical data storage (like in India). Data openness is considered in this study, despite the argument that it is more important for people to have access to their own data.

Strong emphasis is placed on the importance of creating a multichain-based dashboard system that promptly alerts users and medical authorities about their information. For the processes of data security, data analysis, and machine learning, a workflow has been presented in this work. It has been made clear that no mathematical model, simulation, or implementation has been used to verify or validate the efficacy of this framework. As a result, it would be challenging to explain how the suggested structure might function in actuality. A has-chain method for data preservation in massive datasets was presented by Xu et al. In order to build a secure environment, the suggested technique has taken into account factors of cryptography and maximal security. A consensus algorithm is also suggested, which uses a nonce value. The consensus method takes into account the stakeholders' and nodes' willingness to implement it. If the conditions are met, a new block will be added to the blockchain. Additional procedures such as digital signatures, hashing, encryption/decryption, and certification are taken into account when discussing the security of data on IoT networks [16,35–38]. For quality improvement and analysis, data security in connection to cryptography, key management, and disease detection is carefully considered. Block capacity, transaction processing times, computational and transmission expenses, and comparisons to the conventional technique are used to measure performance. It has been determined that the suggested method is significantly better than the established one. Viriyasitavat et al. studied the state-of-the-art on new research fields, difficulties, issues, applications, etc. in connection with blockchain technology features in order to provide creative solutions. Industry 4.0 developments, such as blockchain technology integration with IoT, cyber physical systems, and other industry 4.0 trends, are taken into consideration for applications based on the digital economy that could have an impact in the near future. This study found that as numerous industry 4.0 features, including resilience, scalability, security, and autonomy, are taken into account in the business workflow, the number of publications is rising dramatically. This research specifically evaluates how blockchain technology and industry 4.0 trends affect corporate processes. Additionally, it is advised to manage value-driven business operations and carry out collaborative business processes using a layered architecture. Version 4.0 of the blockchain technology has a number of problems, mostly with smart contracts, specification languages, system integration and interoperability, security challenges, and data privacy concerns.

24.8 Conclusion

This study discusses the main drawbacks of blockchain technology in the healthcare industry. The findings of a thorough study that has previously been done on the use of blockchain in the healthcare industry have been taken into consideration. Blockchain technology can significantly improve the security of documents that must be exchanged in the healthcare industry, but this does not mean that we should always use it. So, it is important to consider how new technologies may affect healthcare before implementing them.

References

[1] F. Al-Turjman, R. Salama, Cyber security in mobile social networks, Security in IoT Social Networks, Academic Press, 2021, pp. 55−81.

[2] F. Al-Turjman, R. Salama, Security in social networks, Security in IoT Social Networks, Academic Press, 2021, pp. 1−27.

[3] R. Salama, F. Al-Turjman, AI in blockchain towards realizing cyber security, in: 2022 International Conference on Artificial Intelligence in Everything (AIE), IEEE, 2022, pp. 471−475.

[4] F. Al-Turjman, R. Salama, An overview about the cyberattacks in grid and like systems, Smart Grid IoT-Enabled Spaces (2020) 233−247.

[5] R. Salama, F. Al-Turjman, R. Culmone, AI-powered drone to address smart city security issues, in: Advanced Information Networking and Applications: Proceedings of the 37th International Conference on Advanced Information Networking and Applications (AINA-2023), Volume 3, Springer International Publishing, Cham., 2023, pp. 292−300; G. Raybon, D. Che, E. Burrows, S. Olsson, R. Tkach, Shaping light-waves in time and frequency for optical fiber communication, Nat. Commun. 13 (1) (2022) 1−11.

[6] Q. Mamun, Blockchain technology in the future of healthcare, Smart Health 23 (2022)100223.

[7] P. Whig, A. Velu, R.R. Naddikatu, The economic impact of AI-enabled blockchain in 6G-based industry, AI and Blockchain Technology in 6G Wireless Network, Springer, Singapore, 2022, pp. 205−224.

[8] I. Ahmed, Y. Zhang, G. Jeon, W. Lin, M.R. Khosravi, L. Qi, A blockchain-and artificial intelligence-enabled smart IoT framework for sustainable city, Int. J. Intell. Syst. (2022).

[9] F. Firouzi, B. Farahani, M. Daneshmand, K. Grise, J. Song, R. Saracco, et al., Harnessing the power of smart and connected health to tackle covid-19: IoT, AI, robotics, and blockchain for a better world, IEEE Internet Things J. 8 (16) (2021) 12826−12846.

[10] P.D. Singh, R. Kaur, G. Dhiman, G.R. Bojja, BOSS: a new QoS aware blockchain assisted framework for secure and smart healthcare as a service, Expert. Syst. (2021) e12838.

[11] I. Yaqoob, K. Salah, R. Jayaraman, Y. Al-Hammadi, Blockchain for healthcare data management: opportunities, challenges, and future recommendations, Neural Comput. Appl. 34 (14) (2022) 11475−11490.

[12] M.A. Bazel, F. Mohammed, M. Ahmed, Blockchain technology in healthcare big data management: benefits, applications and challenges, in: 2021 1st International Conference on Emerging Smart Technologies and Applications (eSmarTA), IEEE, 2021, pp. 1−8.

[13] B. Zaabar, O. Cheikhrouhou, F. Jamil, M. Ammi, M. Abid, HealthBlock: a secure blockchain-based healthcare data management system, Computer Netw. 200 (2021) 108500.

[14] Y. Xie, J. Zhang, H. Wang, P. Liu, S. Liu, T. Huo, et al., Applications of blockchain in the medical field: narrative review, J. Med. Internet Res. 23 (10) (2021) e28613.

[15] D.A. Pustokhin, I.V. Pustokhina, K. Shankar, Challenges and future work directions in healthcare data management using blockchain technology, Applications of Blockchain in Healthcare, Springer, Singapore, 2021, pp. 253−267.

[16] H. Fatoum, S. Hanna, J.D. Halamka, D.C. Sicker, P. Spangenberg, S.K. Hashmi, Blockchain integration with digital technology and the future of health care ecosystems: systematic review, J. Med. Internet Res. 23 (11) (2021) e19846.

[17] D. Roosan, V. Tatla, Y. Li, A. Kugler, J. Chok, M.R. Roosan, Framework to enable pharmacist access to healthcare data using blockchain technology and artificial intelligence, J. Am. Pharmacists Assoc (2022).

[18] K. Miyachi, T.K. Mackey, hOCBS: A privacy-preserving blockchain framework for healthcare data leveraging an on-chain and off-chain system design, Inf. Process. & Manag. 58 (3) (2021) 102535.

[19] A.N. Gohar, S.A. Abdelmawgoud, M.S. Farhan, A patient-centric healthcare framework reference architecture for better semantic interoperability based on blockchain, cloud, and IoT, IEEE Access. 10 (2022) 92137−92157.

[20] M. Soni, D.K. Singh, Blockchain-based security & privacy for biomedical and healthcare information exchange systems, Mater. Today: Proc. (2021).

[21] A.I. Florea, I. Anghel, T. Cioara, a review of blockchain technology applications in ambient assisted living, Future Internet 14 (5) (2022) 150.

[22] A.K. Tyagi, S.U. Aswathy, G. Aghila, N. Sreenath, AARIN: affordable, accurate, reliable and innovative mechanism to protect a medical cyber-physical system using blockchain technology, Int. J. Intell. Netw. 2 (2021) 175−183.

[23] R.S. Bhadoria, A.P. Das, A. Bashar, M. Zikria, Implementing blockchain-based traceable certificates as sustainable technology in democratic elections, Electronics 11 (20) (2022) 3359.

[24] B. Zhong, J. Guo, L. Zhang, H. Wu, H. Li, Y. Wang, A blockchain-based framework for on-site construction environmental monitoring: proof of concept, Build. Environ. 217 (2022) 109064.

[25] J. Hu, P. Zhu, Y. Qi, Q. Zhu, X. Li, A patent registration and trading system based on blockchain, Expert. Syst. Appl. 201 (2022) 117094.

[26] A. Tezel, E. Papadonikolaki, I. Yitmen, M. Bolpagni, Blockchain opportunities and issues in the built environment: perspectives on trust, transparency and cybersecurity, Industry 4.0 for the Built Environment, Springer, Cham, 2022, pp. 569−588.

[27] M. Shuaib, S. Alam, S.M. Daud, Improving the authenticity of real estate land transaction data using blockchain-based security scheme, International Conference on Advances in Cyber Security, Springer, Singapore, 2021, pp. 3–10.

[28] A. Al Sadawi, B. Madani, S. Saboor, M. Ndiaye, G. Abu-Lebdeh, A comprehensive hierarchical blockchain system for carbon emission trading utilizing blockchain of things and smart contract, Technol. Forecast. Soc. Change 173 (2021) 121124.

[29] M. Uddin, K. Salah, R. Jayaraman, S. Pesic, S. Ellahham, Blockchain for drug traceability: architectures and open challenges, Health Inform. J. 27 (2) (2021). 14604582211011228.

[30] D. Hawashin, K. Salah, R. Jayaraman, I. Yaqoob, A. Musamih, A blockchain-based solution for mitigating overproduction and underconsumption of medical supplies, IEEE Access. 10 (2022) 71669–71682.

[31] P. Tagde, S. Tagde, T. Bhattacharya, P. Tagde, H. Chopra, R. Akter, et al., Blockchain and artificial intelligence technology in e-Health, Environ. Sci. Pollut. Res. 28 (38) (2021) 52810–52831.

[32] H. Babbar, The role of emerging technologies in smart healthcare, IoT-enabled Smart Healthcare Systems, Services and Applications, 2022.

[33] I.N. Muhsen, O.W. Rasheed, E.A. Habib, R.K. Alsaad, M.K. Maghrabi, M.A. Rahman, et al., Current status and future perspectives on the Internet of Things in oncology, Hematol./Oncol. Stem Cell Ther (2021).

[34] T. Deng, K. Zhang, Z.J.M. Shen, A systematic review of a digital twin city: a new pattern of urban governance toward smart cities, J. Manag. Sci. Eng. 6 (2) (2021) 125–134.

[35] P. Bhattacharya, M.S. Obaidat, D. Savaliya, S. Sanghavi, S. Tanwar, B. Sadaun, Metaverse assisted telesurgery in healthcare 5.0: an interplay of blockchain and explainable AI, in: 2022 International Conference on Computer, Information and Telecommunication Systems (CITS), IEEE, 2022, pp. 1–5.

[36] R. Shinde, S. Patil, K. Kotecha, K. Ruikar, Blockchain for securing ai applications and open innovations, J. Open. Innovation: Technology, Market, Complex. 7 (3) (2021) 189.

[37] M.A. Tunc, E. Gures, I. Shayea, A survey on iot smart healthcare: emerging technologies, applications, challenges, and future trends (2021). arXiv:2109.02042.

[38] N. Chilamkurti, T. Poongodi, B. Balusamy (Eds.), Blockchain, Internet of Things, and Artificial Intelligence, CRC Press, 2021.

25

An overview of artificial intelligence and blockchain technology in smart cities

Ramiz Salama[1], Fadi Al-Turjman[1], Sinem Alturjman[1], Azza Altorgoman[2]

[1]ARTIFICIAL INTELLIGENCE, SOFTWARE, AND INFORMATION SYSTEMS ENGINEERING DEPARTMENTS, RESEARCH CENTER FOR AI AND IOT, AI AND ROBOTICS INSTITUTE, NEAR EAST UNIVERSITY, NICOSIA, MERSIN10, TURKEY [2]FACULTY OF ENGINEERING, RESEARCH CENTER FOR AI AND IOT, UNIVERSITY OF KYRENIA, MERSIN, TURKEY

25.1 Introduction

Smart cities are urban areas that use various types of electronic data collection sensors to supply information that is used to manage assets and resources efficiently. These sensors can include everything from traffic cameras and air quality monitors to smart meters and weather stations. The data collected from these sensors can be used to optimize the operation of city systems and services, such as transportation, energy, and public safety. One of the key technologies that is enabling the development of smart cities is blockchain. Blockchain is a decentralized, distributed database that allows multiple parties to securely store and manage data without the need for a central authority. It uses cryptographic techniques to ensure the integrity and security of the data and to enable the parties to reach consensus on the contents of the database. Another important technology that is playing a role in the development of smart cities is artificial intelligence (AI). AI refers to the development of computer systems that can perform tasks that would normally require human intelligence, such as learning, problem-solving, and decision-making. In the context of smart cities, AI can be used to analyze data collected from smart city sensors to identify patterns and trends and to make predictions about future events. This can help cities optimize their use of resources, improve services, and make more informed decisions [1,2]. The use of blockchain and AI in smart cities has the potential to enable secure and efficient communication and transactions, optimize resource usage, and improve services. However, there are also challenges and limitations to consider, such as issues related to data privacy and security and the potential for job displacement. It is important for cities to carefully evaluate the potential

© 2024 Elsevier Inc. All rights reserved, including those for text and data mining, AI training, and similar technologies.

risks and benefits of these technologies and to implement them in a way that is transparent, equitable, and responsive to the needs and concerns of all stakeholders. This research aims to explore the potential benefits and limitations of using blockchain and AI in the development of smart cities, with a focus on case studies of cities that have successfully implemented these technologies [3–7]. The research will provide an overview of the state of the art in this area and will present a methodology for analyzing the benefits and limitations of blockchain and AI in smart cities. The research will also present results and discussion based on a review of relevant case studies and will conclude with a summary of findings and implications for the future development of smart cities.

25.2 Extent of past work

There has been significant research on the use of blockchain and AI in the development of smart cities. In terms of blockchain, studies have explored how the technology can be used to securely store and manage data related to smart cities, such as information about energy usage, traffic patterns, and public services. It has also been used to enable secure and efficient communication and transactions between different stakeholders in a smart city, such as government agencies, businesses, and residents. One example of a successful implementation of blockchain in a smart city is the City of Dublin, which has been using the technology to track and manage the installation and maintenance of streetlights. By using blockchain, the city is able to securely and efficiently store and manage data about the streetlights, including information about their location, status, and maintenance history. This has enabled the city to optimize the operation of the streetlights and to reduce costs and improve services. In terms of AI, studies have explored how the technology can be used to analyze data collected from smart city sensors to identify patterns and trends and to make predictions about future events. This can help cities optimize their use of resources, improve services, and make more informed decisions. For example, the City of Seoul has been using AI to analyze data collected from smart city sensors to optimize the operation of its public transportation system. By using AI to identify patterns in traffic data, the city is able to optimize the routes and schedules of its buses, which has resulted in significant cost savings and improved service for riders [8,9]. There have also been studies that have looked at the challenges and limitations of using blockchain and AI in smart cities. These may include issues related to data privacy, security, and the potential for job displacement. For example, a study by researchers at the Massachusetts Institute of Technology (MIT) found that the use of AI in smart cities could lead to the displacement of certain jobs, such as those in transportation and customer service. The study also found that the deployment of AI in smart cities could exacerbate existing inequalities if it is not implemented in an equitable and transparent manner. Overall, the extent of past work on the use of blockchain and AI in smart cities suggests that these technologies have the potential to enable secure and efficient communication and transactions, optimize resource usage, and improve services. However, it is also clear that there are challenges and limitations to consider, and that it is important for cities to carefully evaluate the potential risks and benefits of these technologies and to implement them in a way that is transparent, equitable, and responsive to the needs and concerns of all stakeholders [10].

25.3 Smart cities with artificial intelligence and blockchain

In this study, we sought to explore the potential benefits and limitations of using blockchain and AI in the development of smart cities. To do this, we conducted a review of the literature on the use of these technologies in smart cities and identified a set of relevant case studies. To identify the case studies, we conducted a search of academic databases, including the Web of Science, Scopus, and the IEEE Xplore Digital Library. We used a set of keywords related to blockchain, AI, and smart cities, and we restricted our search to articles published between 2020 and 2022. We also conducted a search of online sources, such as news articles and reports, to identify additional case studies. Once we had identified a set of relevant case studies, we developed a methodology for analyzing the benefits and limitations of blockchain and AI in smart cities. Our methodology involved a review of the literature on these technologies, as well as a review of the case studies. We focused on a set of key themes related to the use of blockchain and AI in smart cities, including data management, communication and transactions, resource optimization, and equity and transparency. For each case study, we collected data on the context and background of the city, the specific technologies that were implemented, the outcomes and impacts of the technologies, and any challenges or limitations that were encountered. We then analyzed the data using a qualitative approach, looking for patterns and trends across the case studies, and synthesizing the findings into a set of key themes [11−13]. In total, we identified 15 case studies that met our inclusion criteria. These case studies represented a range of cities from different regions of the world and covered a variety of applications of blockchain and AI in smart cities. Our analysis of the case studies yielded a number of insights into the benefits and limitations of these technologies, which we will present in Section 25.4 of this research. In addition to reviewing the case studies and analyzing the data, we also conducted a review of the literature on the use of blockchain and AI in smart cities. This literature review provided context and background on these technologies and helped to identify key themes and issues that were relevant to our analysis.

To ensure the rigor and validity of our study, we followed several best practices in conducting our research. These included:

- Clearly defining our research question and objectives.
- Using a systematic and transparent approach to searching and selecting the case studies.
- Applying inclusion and exclusion criteria to ensure that the case studies were relevant and of high quality.
- Using a standardized set of codes and categories to analyze the data.
- Ensuring that the data were reliable and valid by triangulating the findings from the case studies with the findings from the literature review.

Overall, our research design was intended to provide a thorough and nuanced understanding of the benefits and limitations of using blockchain and AI in smart cities. By conducting a review of the literature and identifying a set of relevant case studies, we were able to gather and analyze a rich and diverse set of data on these technologies. Our analysis of the data allowed us to identify key themes and trends and to draw conclusions about the potential of blockchain and AI in the development of smart cities.

25.4 Result and discussion

The results of our study suggest that the use of blockchain and AI in smart cities can enable secure and efficient communication and transactions, optimize resource usage, and improve services. However, there are also challenges and limitations to consider, such as issues related to data privacy and security, and the potential for job displacement. One of the key benefits of using blockchain in smart cities is the ability to securely store and manage data. The decentralized, distributed nature of blockchain allows multiple parties to collaborate and share data without the need for a central authority. This can be particularly useful in smart cities, where there are often many different stakeholders involved in the management of city systems and services, such as government agencies, businesses, and residents [14,15]. For example, the City of Dublin has been using blockchain to track and manage the installation and maintenance of streetlights. By using blockchain, the city is able to securely and efficiently store and manage data about the streetlights, including information about their location, status, and maintenance history. This has enabled the city to optimize the operation of the streetlights and to reduce costs and improve services. Another benefit of using blockchain in smart cities is the ability to enable secure and efficient communication and transactions between different stakeholders. This can be particularly useful in the context of public services, such as transportation and healthcare, where there are often many different parties involved in the delivery of services. For example, the City of Moscow has been using blockchain to enable secure and efficient communication between different stakeholders in its public transportation system, including government agencies, transport companies, and passengers. AI also has the potential to bring significant benefits to smart cities. One of the key benefits of using AI in smart cities is the ability to analyze data collected from smart city sensors to identify patterns and trends and to make predictions about future events. This can help cities optimize their use of resources, improve services, and make more informed decisions. For example, the City of Seoul has been using AI to analyze data collected from smart city sensors to optimize the operation of its public transportation system. By using AI to identify patterns in traffic data, the city can optimize the routes and schedules of its buses, which has resulted in significant cost savings and improved service for riders. Similarly, the City of San Diego has been using AI to analyze data from smart city sensors to optimize the operation of its water distribution system, resulting in reduced water usage and cost savings.

In addition to these benefits, there are also challenges and limitations to consider when using blockchain and AI in smart cities. One of the main challenges is the issue of data privacy and security. With the increasing amount of data being collected by smart city sensors, there is a risk that this data could be accessed or misused in ways that violate the privacy of citizens. Cities need to ensure that they have robust policies and safeguards in place to protect the privacy of citizens and to ensure the security of the data. Another challenge is the potential for job displacement. The use of AI in particular has the potential to automate certain tasks, which could result in the displacement of certain jobs. This is a concern that has been raised by researchers at the MIT, who found that the use of AI in smart cities could lead to the displacement of jobs in transportation and customer service. It is important for cities to consider the potential impacts of these technologies on employment and to develop strategies to mitigate any negative impacts [16–20]. In conclusion, the use of blockchain and AI in smart cities has the potential to enable secure and efficient communication and transactions, optimize resource usage, and improve services [21]. However, there are also challenges and limitations to consider, such as issues related to data privacy and security, and the potential for job displacement. It is important for cities to carefully evaluate the potential risks and benefits of these technologies and to implement them in a way that is transparent, equitable, and responsive to the needs and concerns of all stakeholders.

25.5 Conclusion

In this study, we explored the potential benefits and limitations of using blockchain and AI in the development of smart cities. Through a review of the literature and a set of relevant case studies, we identified a number of key themes and trends related to the use of these technologies. One of the main benefits of using blockchain in smart cities is the ability to securely store and manage data. The decentralized, distributed nature of blockchain allows multiple parties to collaborate and share data without the need for a central authority. This can be particularly useful in smart cities, where there are often many different stakeholders involved in the management of city systems and services, such as government agencies, businesses, and residents. Another benefit of using blockchain in smart cities is the ability to enable secure and efficient communication and transactions between different stakeholders. This can be particularly useful in the context of public services, such as transportation and healthcare, where there are often many different parties involved in the delivery of services. AI also has the potential to bring significant benefits to smart cities. One of the key benefits is the ability to analyze data collected from smart city sensors to identify patterns and trends and to make predictions about future events. This can help cities optimize their use of resources, improve services, and make more informed decisions. However, there are also challenges and limitations to consider when using blockchain and AI in smart cities. One of the main challenges is the issue of data privacy and security. With the increasing amount of data being collected by smart city sensors, there is a risk that this data could be accessed or misused in ways that violate the privacy of citizens. It is important for cities to ensure that they have robust policies and safeguards in place to protect the privacy of citizens and to ensure the security of the data. Another challenge is the potential for job displacement. The use of AI in particular has the potential to automate certain tasks, which could result in the displacement of certain jobs. It is important for cities to consider the potential impacts of these technologies on employment and to develop strategies to mitigate any negative impacts. In conclusion, the use of blockchain and AI in smart cities has the potential to enable secure and efficient communication and transactions, optimize resource usage, and improve services. However, there are also challenges and limitations to consider, such as issues related to data privacy and security, and the potential for job displacement. It is important for cities to carefully evaluate the potential risks and benefits of these technologies and to implement them in a way that is transparent, equitable, and responsive to the needs and concerns of all stakeholders. There is still much to be learned about the use of blockchain and AI in smart cities, and further research is needed to fully understand the potential of these technologies. Future research could focus on the development of best practices and guidelines for the implementation of these technologies, as well as on the evaluation of their impacts on various stakeholders, including governments, businesses, and citizens. Overall, our study suggests that the use of blockchain and AI in smart cities has the potential to bring significant benefits, but it is important for cities to carefully consider the potential risks and limitations and to implement these technologies in a way that is transparent, equitable, and responsive to the needs and concerns of all stakeholders.

References

[1] M.M. Kamruzzaman, I. Alrashdi, A. Alqazzaz, New opportunities, challenges, and applications of edge-AI for connected healthcare in internet of medical things for smart cities, J. Healthc. Eng. 2022 (2022).

[2] S. Dey, S. Saha, A.K. Singh, K. McDonald-Maier, SmartNoshWaste: using blockchain, machine learning, cloud computing and QR code to reduce food waste in decentralized web 3.0 enabled smart cities, Smart Cities 5 (1) (2022) 162−176.

[3] J. Singh, M. Sajid, S.K. Gupta, R.A. Haidri, Artificial intelligence and blockchain technologies for smart city, Intell. Green. Technol. Sustain. Smart Cities (2022) 317−330.

[4] A.S. Rajawat, P. Bedi, S.B. Goyal, R.N. Shaw, A. Ghosh, S. Aggarwal, AI and blockchain for healthcare data security in smart cities, AI IoT Smart City Appl. (2022) 185−198.

[5] O. Samuel, N. Javaid, T.A. Alghamdi, N. Kumar, Towards sustainable smart cities: a secure and scalable trading system for residential homes using blockchain and artificial intelligence, Sustain. Cities Soc. 76 (2022) 103371.

[6] S. Tehseen, E. Yafi, Z.H. Qureshi, R.A. Rather, Technology application in the Asian tourism industry: artificial intelligence and blockchain in smart city involvement, Handb. Technol. Application Tour. Asia (2022) 493.

[7] R. Al Sharif, S. Pokharel, Smart city dimensions and associated risks: review of literature, Sustain. Cities Soc. 77 (2022) 103542.

[8] N. Yuvaraj, K. Praghash, R.A. Raja, T. Karthikeyan, An investigation of garbage disposal electric vehicles (GDEVs) integrated with deep neural networking (DNN) and intelligent transportation system (ITS) in smart city management system (SCMS), Wirel. personal. Commun. 123 (2) (2022) 1733−1752.

[9] R. Krishnamoorthy, K. Kamala, I.D. Soubache, M.V. Karthik, M.A. Begum, Integration of blockchain and artificial intelligence in smart city perspectives, Smart City Infrastructure: Blockchain Perspect. (2022) 77−112.

[10] M. Ibrahim, Y. Lee, H.K. Kahng, S. Kim, D.H. Kim, Blockchain-based parking sharing service for smart city development, Computers Electr. Eng. 103 (2022) 108267.

[11] M.M. Kamruzzaman, Key technologies, applications and trends of internet of things for energy-efficient 6G wireless communication in smart cities, Energies 15 (15) (2022) 5608.

[12] A. Rejeb, K. Rejeb, S. Simske, H. Treiblmaier, S. Zailani, The big picture on the internet of things and the smart city: a review of what we know and what we need to know, Internet Things 19 (2022) 100565.

[13] A. Bashirpour Bonab, M. Fedele, V. Formisano, I. Rudko, Quantum technologies for smart cities: a comprehensive review and analysis (2022). Available at SSRN 4231189.

[14] V. Chang, M. Abdel-Basset, Guest editorial: technological advancement and pioneering methods for smart cities—recent advances and future trends, Library Hi Tech. 40 (5) (2022) 1105—1107.

[15] A. Heidari, N.J. Navimipour, M. Unal, Applications of ML/DL in the management of smart cities and societies based on new trends in information technologies: a systematic literature review, Sustain. Cities Soc. (2022) 104089.

[16] F. Al-Turjman, R. Salama, Security in social networks, Security in IoT Social Networks, Academic Press, 2021, pp. 1—27.

[17] F. Al-Turjman, R. Salama, Cyber security in mobile social networks, Security in iot social networks, Academic press, 2021, pp. 55—81.

[18] R. Salama, F. Al-Turjman, AI in blockchain towards realizing cyber security, in: 2022 International Conference on Artificial Intelligence in Everything (AIE), IEEE, 2022, pp. 471—475.

[19] F. Al-Turjman, R. Salama, An overview about the cyberattacks in grid and like systems, Smart Grid IoT-Enabled Spaces (2020) 233—247.

[20] R. Salama, F. Al-Turjman, R. Culmone, AI-powered drone to address smart city security issues, in: Advanced Information Networking and Applications: Proceedings of the 37th International Conference on Advanced Information Networking and Applications (AINA-2023), Volume 3, Springer International Publishing, Cham., 2023, pp. 292—300.

[21] G. Raybon, D. Che, E. Burrows, S. Olsson, R. Tkach, Shaping lightwaves in time and frequency for optical fiber communication, Nat. Commun. 13 (1) (2022) 1—11.

26 ▪▪▪

IoT-based smart vending machine

Mohamed Nor Hashi, Yasir Salad Abdulle, Yahya Ahmad Kayre,
Ali Dahir Mohamud, Mohamed Abdullahi Khalaf,
Sharamke Ali Kahie

DEPARTMENT OF COMPUTER APPLICATION, JAMHURIYA UNIVERSITY OF SCIENCE AND TECHNOLOGY, MOGADISHU, SOMALIA

26.1 Introduction

A vending machine is a mechanized apparatus that facilitates the sale of various food items, including sandwiches, snacks such as potato chips, chocolate bars, and candies, as well as hot and cold beverages. Additionally, vending machines may also dispense other commodities such as newspapers and medicines upon the completion of a monetary transaction. This machine has the potential to be implemented in various areas [1].

Vending machines possess some advantages. Vending machines are highly manageable due to their autonomous operation, eliminating the need for human presence to facilitate sales. Once installed, these machines can be conveniently monitored remotely. Additionally, vending machines offer a seamless purchasing experience, as they accept quick cash or card payments, hence eliminating any potential payment complications [2].

One of the biggest advantages of implementing vending machines is that they save time and other costs for the owner. Another advantage of this machine is that many of us are students and we are busy starting a business so this machine helps to make revenue without losing more energy and time [3].

According to the study conducted by ref. [4], the significance of vending machines is becoming increasingly pronounced as global expansion accelerates. In contemporary society, it has become increasingly common to encounter machines throughout shopping malls and various public parks. The emerging method of commerce is increasingly integrating into the daily lives of individuals. The prospect of acquiring a vending machine and capitalizing on this highly convenient business opportunity has generated considerable anticipation among a substantial number of individuals. This machine offers significant advantages to both the proprietor and the customer. The proprietor stands to generate revenue, while the customer benefits from the provision of a service time.

Computational Intelligence and Blockchain in Complex Systems. DOI: https://doi.org/10.1016/B978-0-443-13268-1.00008-X
© 2024 Elsevier Inc. All rights reserved, including those for text and data mining, AI training, and similar technologies.

The Internet of Things (IoT) is a groundbreaking communication paradigm that holds significant importance in the domain of remote monitoring and control operations. Addressing social concerns in various domains, such as healthcare, environment, intelligent home automation, transportation, military, agriculture, garbage collection, energy consumption surveillance, user asset tracking, smart grid, vehicle communication systems, and environmental monitoring, is imperative.

The primary aim of this project is to develop and execute a vending machine that utilizes IoT technology and has the capability to run continuously throughout the week, spanning all hours of the day. The machine will be outfitted with a payment system that accommodates the EVC-Plus mobile payment platform, which has widespread adoption in Somalia. The machine has the capability to be deployed in a diverse range of public settings, including educational institutions, healthcare facilities, sports arenas, and various other communal spaces. The vending machine has the capacity to facilitate the sale of a diverse range of commodities, including beverages, snacks, writing instruments, and pharmaceutical products.

26.2 Related work

Several prior research studies have been undertaken to explore the development of vending machines, employing IoT devices or alternative microcontrollers.

In the year 2017, a team of researchers [5] successfully designed and implemented an automated chocolate vending machine utilizing the Arduino Uno microcontroller. This project involves the development of an Arduino-based vending machine that facilitates the sale of several types of chocolates. This study aims to propose a solution for coin-based vending machines that fail to return the exact amount of money when there is no change available.

There is a discussion on the topic of the smart coffee vending machine [6] RFID technology is employed for the provision of various consumable items such as snacks and cold beverages, as well as for ticketing purposes. These systems can be operated using either coins, notes, or manual switches. This article introduces a system that utilizes RFID technology instead of traditional coins or notes for operation. This method restricts access solely through the use of RFID technology, hence mitigating the potential for unauthorized usage of the machine.

Nevertheless, a notable gap exists in the existing body of scholarly work about the utilization of IoT technology within vending machines situated in developing nations. The majority of studies about IoT vending machines have been carried out in industrialized nations, where a more robust IoT infrastructure is in place.

The present study aims to fill the existing void in the academic literature by introducing a solution that is tailored to the unique circumstances and needs of developing nations. The proposed solution utilizes an affordable IoT platform that has been specifically engineered to optimize energy consumption and operate effectively in regions with restricted Internet access. In addition to our proposed solution, we have incorporated a payment mechanism that leverages the EVC-Plus mobile payment platform, a widely adopted platform in Somalia.

26.3 Methods and materials

The concept of vending machine based on EVC-plus involves creating a mobile app allowing users to buy the products from inside the machine. Additionally, we are going to create and build a controller app that the admin can monitor or manage the state of the machine.

And you can find this machine anywhere in the city such as hospitals, stadiums, and streets.

26.3.1 Requirements

1. **Software requirements:** The following software packages are required for the development of a machine based on EVC-Plus.
   a. **The Arduino** integrated development environment is a software application that operates on a personal computer and is utilized to compose and transfer computer code to the Node MCU board. The programming language employed for this task is C.
   b. **Flutter** is a framework that is open source and enables the development of mobile applications with superior quality and performance on both Android and iOS operating systems. The software development kit offered by Google presents a straightforward, robust, streamlined, and comprehensible framework for creating mobile applications using Dart, Google's own programming language.
2. **Hardware requirements:** This requirement concerns the hardware we going to use to build a vending machine based on EVC-Plus, also the hardware specification for this system is selected as many issues such as Hardware version, hardware compatibility, and hardware availability.
   a. **Node MCU** is equipped with an ESP8266 that integrates an 802.11b/g/n HT40 Wi-Fi transceiver. This enables the Node MCU to establish connections with Wi-Fi networks and engage in online interactions. Additionally, it possesses the capability to create its own network, facilitating direct connections with other devices. The versatility of the ESP8266 Node MCU is further enhanced by this development.
   b. **Servo motor** is a type of actuator, either rotary or linear, that enables precise control over angular or linear position, velocity, and acceleration.
   c. **A breadboard** is a rectangular board that features numerous mounting holes. These connectors serve the purpose of establishing electrical connections between electronic components and single-board computers or microcontrollers, such as Arduino and Raspberry Pi.
   d. **Tablet mobile**, A tablet, is a portable electronic device that is equipped with a mobile operating system and features a touch screen display.

26.3.2 System design

The components of this vending machine consist of two main parts: one is IoT devices and the other one is mobile programming. These IoT devices interconnect with each other as we want to explain in the next article.

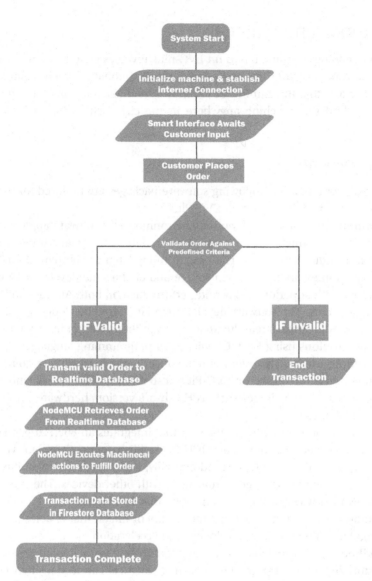

FIGURE 26-1 Flowchart.

In this project, we will integrate a smart screen or tablet device that is capable of promptly receiving customer orders. Upon receiving an order, the programmable screen will assess certain conditions. Subsequently, the screen or tablet device will transmit the relevant data to the database for registration. The Node MCU will then retrieve this data and execute various mechanical operations. In summary, our machine comprises the following components (Fig. 26–1).

26.4 Implementation

This section addresses the implementation and testing phases of our project's life cycle. In addition, we provide test results and screenshots of the proposed system.

26.4.1 Seller app

The seller application is a mobile application that is seamlessly integrated with the vending machine. The application displays a comprehensive inventory of the products available within the vending machine, enabling users to place orders for desired items using the application interface.

1. ***Dashboard of the Seller App***: See Fig. 26–2.
2. ***Detail Screen***: The display below showcases information about the selected product, such as its description and quantity available for purchase. By selecting the plus and minus symbols, users can increase or decrease the selected item's quantity. The user can then proceed to the payment section (Fig. 26–3).
3. ***Payment Method***: The payment method form requires the user to enter a cellphone number. In this study, the mobile phone numbers were limited to those exclusively provided by Hormuud Telecom Somalia. Upon the user's input of their mobile phone number and subsequent activation of the "OK" button, the program initiates the transmission of an alert to their mobile device, prompting them to pay the full monetary sum corresponding to the selected product.

   The IoT component of the system remains in a state of anticipation until the payment has been verified and validated within the Firebase real-time database. Upon confirmation of payment, the IoT component requires two parameters: the pin associated with the requested product and the quantity of the product. Subsequently, the IoT component transmits a directive to the servo system, prompting the dispensation of the respective product (Fig. 26–4).

FIGURE 26–2 Dashboard of the seller app.

FIGURE 26–3 Details screen.

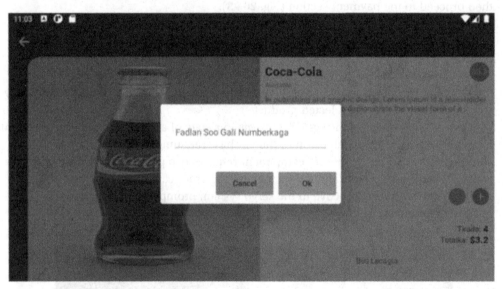

FIGURE 26–4 Payment number.

4. *Payment API:* By clicking the "Allow" button in the alert message as Fig. 26–5 shows, the user may agree to pay the money. Once the user selects "Allow," the system prompts them to enter their 4-digit secret number. The product is dispensed after the user inputs a 4-digit secret number.

5. *The Product Out:* After the user has consented to the payment for the product and provided their 4-digit confidential code, the machine proceeds to dispense the product as the figure below presents (Fig. 26–6).

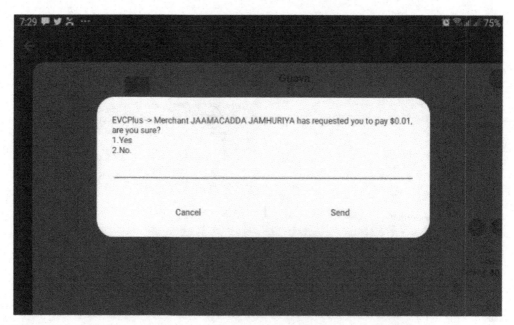

FIGURE 26–5 Payment API.

FIGURE 26–6 Product out.

26.4.2 Controller app

The following screenshots illustrate the controller application for administrators and describe its key features.

1. ***Dashboard*:** The controller application features a dashboard that presents two significant metrics. Fig. 26–7 shows the overall revenue generated within the current day and the total number of products sold within the same day. In addition, the dashboard displays the transactions that occurred on the previous day.

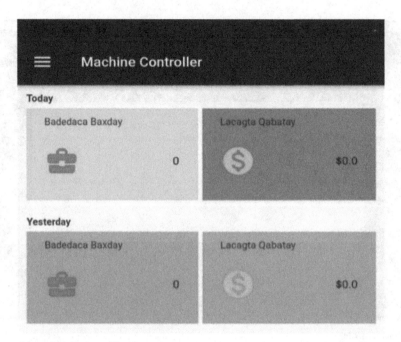

FIGURE 26–7 Dashboard of the controller.

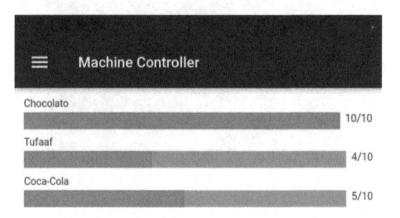

FIGURE 26–8 Products.

2. *Products*: The products section of the controller application allows owners to monitor the status of the machine's products. The proprietor can view the current status of each item, such as whether it is empty or full, as well as the number of items remaining as in Fig. 26–8 explains.

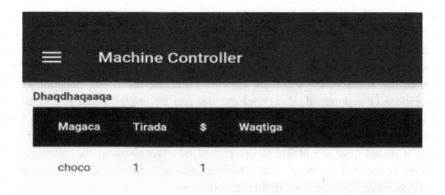

FIGURE 26–9 Reports.

3. ***Report information:*** The controller app's report information section details machine performance. The owner can view each product's status, total revenue, and number of sales. Trends, sales, and machine inventory and operation decisions can be made using this data (Fig. 26−9).

26.5 Discussion

Previous vending machines have encountered issues with their payment methods, specifically with the use of coins and banknotes. These problems arise from the coin tank becoming full and the inability to read the banknotes. Additionally, both coins and banknotes frequently get stuck in the machine, rendering it incapable of accepting any further coins once the tank is full. The cessation of operations of this vending machine will result in the inability to make any further purchases. Hence, we have put out a proposal for a machine that incorporates an electric payment system, specifically designed to operate with Somali EVC-plus. This method offers significant advantages for both the user and the owner. Additionally, this machine is equipped with a controller application that allows the administrator to effectively manage the computer.

26.6 Conclusion

This thesis presents the development and implementation of a vending machine utilizing EVC-Plus technology in the context of Somalia. The machine shows features such as flexibility, customizability, and accuracy. This technology possesses the capability to facilitate the sale of various items, while also offering the flexibility to adapt and cater to the unique requirements of both enterprises and individuals. The machine initiates its operation by initially receiving a command from the user. Subsequently, the automated system verifies the payment and transmits the order to a designated database. The order is stored within the database and subsequently transmitted to a Node MCU microcontroller. The Node MCU microcontroller subsequently transmits the command to the servos, which proceed to deliver the product to the user. The machine also has a controller app that allows the owner to monitor the machine's state and track its transactions. In order to optimize the functionality of this system and improve the overall usability of the solution, the following element could be taken into account for potential future integration: One potential AI technology that can be implemented is a camera system equipped with face recognition capabilities. This system would be able to classify individuals based on predetermined criteria, such as determining if a person is a potential robber or a client. Additionally, it would have the ability to detect and raise an alarm in the event of any illegal activities being conducted by those within its field of view. Implementing this measure would serve as a deterrent against instances of theft and damage.

References

[1] P. Pradeepa, T. Sudhalavanya, K. Suganthi, N. Suganthi, M. Menagadevi, Design and implementation of vending machine using Verilog HDL, Int. J. Adv. Eng. Technol. 4 (2013) 51–53.

[2] E. Mrena, V. Sibanda, S. Sibanda, K. Mpofu, Designof a control system for a vending machine, Procedia CIRP 91 (2020) 758–763. Available from: https://doi.org/10.1016/j.procir.2020.04.136.

[3] HBA SOFFAR, Automatic vending machines advantages and disadvantages. <https://www.online-sciences.com/technology/automatic-vendingmachines-advantages-and-disadvantages/>, 2016.

[4] Smith Big, Importance of vending machine. <https://myventurepad.com/importance-vending-machines/>, 2014.

[5] A. Mlama, P. Mudenda, A. Ng'ombe, L. Makashini, H. Aband, The effects of the introduction of prepayment meters on the energy usage behaviour of different housing consumer groups in Kitwe, Zambia, AIMS Energy 2 (3) (2014) 237–259.

[6] F.L. Zhu, Z. Lodhi, Q. Saleem, G. Xiong, F. Wang, Design and implementation of RFID based smart shopping booth, in: 2019 6th International Conference on Information Science and Control Engineering (ICISCE), Shanghai, China, 2019, pp. 1017–1021, Available from: https://doi.org/10.1109/ICISCE48695.2019.00205.

Index

Note: Page numbers followed by "*f,*" "*t,*" and "*b*" refer to figures, tables, and boxes, respectively.

A

Access controls, 227
Acute appendicitis (AA), 89
ADHD. *See* Attention deficit hyperactivity disorder (ADHD)
AI-powered personalized learning platforms, 80–81
Amazon, 2
ANN. *See* Artificial neural networks (ANN)
Apollo Currency Team, 5
Arrhythmias, 157, 159
Artificial bee colony (ABC) metaheuristics, 41
Artificial intelligence (AI), 2, 6–7, 13, 124, 157
  advantages and applications
    bots, 8
    breach risk, prediction of, 8
    endpoint security, 9
    identifying fresh threats, 8
  algorithms, 9
  benefits of, 8
  and blockchain applications, in energy industry
    customer engagement, 69
    energy fraud detection, 69
    energy performance improvement, using AI, 67
    energy storage, 69
    energy trading, 67, 69
    grid administration and efficiency, 68
    in grid management, 67
    grid security, 68
    increased productivity, 68
    intelligent grids, 68
    microgrids, 69
    power theft, 69
    predictive analytics, 68
    solar coin, for renewables, 67
    in solar energy, 60–67
  breach risk prediction, 7
  capacity to act, 122–123
  capacity to right, 122–123
  control effectiveness, 7
  cutting-edge AI, 16–17
  in cybersecurity, 6–7
    advantages and applications, 8–9
    benefits of, 8
    breach risk prediction, 7
    control effectiveness, 7
    incident response, 7
    threat exposure, 7
  edge AI, 15–16
  in education applications, 80–82
    interviews with, educators, 81
    materials and methods, 78–80
    past history, 78
  education evaluation methods, 171
    data analysis, 169–170
    data collection, 169
    data collection tool, 168–169
    findings, 170–171, 170*t*, 171*t*
    research model, 168
    working group, 169
  incident response, 7
  jurisdiction, 127–128
    creating law, 130–131
    realizing law, 128–130
  manager's perspective, of work life using AI, 185
    findings, 184–185
    literature survey, 182–183
    methodology, 183–184
  personality, 122
    with legal personality, 124
    without legal personality, 123–124
  persons, 122
  threat exposure, 7
  in tourism developments, 176, 179

Artificial intelligence (AI) (*Continued*)
  findings, 177–179
  in hotels, 176–177
  methodology, 177
  participant's views, 178–179, 178*t*
Artificial Intelligence Act, 115–116
Artificial neural networks (ANN), 60–67, 89
Associated autonomous vehicles, 14–15
Atherosclerosis (ATS), 89
Attention deficit hyperactivity disorder (ADHD),
       133–134
Authentication system, 3
Autoimmune diseases, 85–86

B
Back propagation neural network (BPNN),
       162–163
Beginning block, 14
BFT. *See* Byzantine fault tolerance (BFT)
Bidirectional encoder representations from
       transformers (BERT) architecture, 147–148
  dataset, 149
  method, 149–151
  performance metrics, 153*t*
  results and analysis, 152–153
  review, 148–149
Big data, 77–78
Binary or multiple-class categorizations, 40
Bitcoin, 19–20
  blockchain, 1–2
  exchanges, 3–4
  payments, 1–2
Blockchain-based innovation, 14–15
Blockchain-based mobile applications, 208–210
  identity management, 210
  performance evaluation, 209–210
Blockchain-based security mechanisms
  machine learning (ML) algorithms, 191–192
  in unmanned aerial vehicles (UAV), 189–190
    deep learning, 191
    machine learning adoption, 192
    security and privacy, 190
    security mechanisms, 188–189
    smart contracts, 191
Blockchain-based smart applications, 192

Blockchain-based supply chain management,
       210–212
  benefits, 211
Blockchains, 2–3, 19–21
  architecture, 27*f*
  and artificial intelligence (AI) applications, in
       energy industry
    customer engagement, 69
    energy fraud detection, 69
    energy performance improvement, using AI,
       67
    energy storage, 69
    energy trading, 67, 69
    grid administration and efficiency, 68
    in grid management, 67
    grid security, 68
    increased productivity, 68
    intelligent grids, 68
    microgrids, 69
    power theft, 69
    predictive analytics, 68
    solar coin, for renewables, 67
    in solar energy, 60–67
  cybersecurity applications in
    computer software, 5
    cyber-physical infrastructure
       verification, 6
    decentralizing medium storage, 5
    DNS and DDoS protection, 5
    IoT security, 5
    private message protection, 4
    unauthorized Access, prevention, 6
  decentralized system, 25
  literature review
    consensus algorithms, 59–60, 61*t*
    distributed energy resources, 59
    history, 58–59
  Solana *vs.* Ethereum network, 70–71
  technology, 1–2
  use cases
    Energy web foundation, 70
    Powerledger, 70
    Verv, 70
Block-oriented 6G, 14–15
Boosting, 92

BPNN. *See* Back propagation neural network (BPNN)
Byzantine fault tolerance (BFT), 71

C

California Consumer Privacy Act, 217
CAPTCHA technology, 9
Car area network (CAN), 6
Carpometacarpal joints, 89
CART. *See* Customer analysis and research tool (CART) algorithm
Cart algorithm, 91
CatBoost, 92
Cinema video player plugin, 138
Civil law, 130−131
Close-field communication, 18−19
Cloudbreak, 71
Cloud computing, 2, 104−105
    schedule optimization, 41−42
CMDCS2010 spam classification dataset, 39−40
CNN. *See* Convolutional neural networks (CNN)
Colitis, 85−86
Communication module, 246
Computer-assisted diagnostics, 41−42
Computer-based intelligence, 21−22
Computer-based intelligence-fueled edge figuring, 14−15
Computerized medical records, 103
Confidentiality, 104
Controller app, 283−285
Convolutional neural networks (CNN), 147
Coronary heart disease, 159
COVID-19, 41−42, 97−99, 108−110
Crohn's disease, 85
Cryptocurrency, 2
    Bitcoin, 205−206
    wallets, 208
Cryptographic hashes, 14, 19−20
Cryptographic technology, 3−4
Cryptography, 1−2, 26
Crypto wallet information, 32*f*
CSDMC2010 dataset, 48
Cumulative harms, 117−118
Current population's diversity, 45−46

Customer analysis and research tool (CART) algorithm, 94
Customer investments, 70
Custom-tailored education, 136
Cutting-edge data security technologies, 102
Cutting-edge encryption mechanisms, 3
Cutting-edge transactive applications, 59
Cyber-attacks, 219
Cybercrimes, 3, 97−99
Cyber-hygiene, 105−106
    procedures, 108
Cyber-physical medical systems, 103−104
Cyber risk, 97−101
Cybersecurity, 1−2, 97−99
    artificial intelligence technologies, 6−7
        advantages and applications, 8−9
        benefits of, 8
        breach risk prediction, 7
        control effectiveness, 7
        incident response, 7
        threat exposure, 7
    blockchain applications in
        computer software, 5
        cyber-physical infrastructure verification, 6
        decentralizing medium storage, 5
        DNS and DDoS protection, 5
        IoT security, 5
        private message protection, 4
        unauthorized Access, prevention, 6
    capability, 97−99
    susceptibility, 101
    using blockchain technologies in, 3−4
Cyberspace, 101−102
Cyber-vigilance, 107

D

Dangerous medical cyber-physical systems, 102
Data backup, 229
Data collection tool, 168−169
Data encryption, 229
Data privacy, 104
Data tampering, system, 6
DDoS. *See* Distributed denial of service (DDoS) attacks
Decarbonization, 57

Decentralization, 26
Decentralized cryptocurrency, 1–2
Decentralized marketplaces, 208
Decentralized mobile cloud computing
    architectures, 205–206
Decision trees (DT), 194–195
Deep learning, 87–88
Delegated proof-of-stake (DPoS), 61t
Denial of service, 1–2
DER, 68
DESI. *See* Digital Economy and Society Index
    (DESI)
Determination of unlawfulness, 127
Device-to-device communications, 19
Diagnostic model, 89
Digital Decade Communication, 113
Digital DNA, 113
Digital Economy and Society Index (DESI), 114
Digital health records, 103
Distributed blockchain network, 14
Distributed denial of service (DDoS) attacks,
    97–101
Distributed energy resources, 59
Distributed ledger technology (DLT), 215–216
Distributed mobile cloud computing (DMCC)
    services, 206–207
  blockchain-based supply chain management,
    210–212
  integration of, blockchain technology,
    206–207
  results, 212–213
  smart contracts, 208–210
    blockchain-based identity management, 210
    blockchain-based mobile applications,
    208–210
Distributed record technology, 13–14
DLT. *See* Distributed ledger technology (DLT)
DMCC. *See* Distributed mobile cloud computing
    (DMCC) services
DNS. *See* Domain name system (DNS)
Docked ships, 59
Domain name system (DNS), 3
DPoS. *See* Delegated proof-of-stake (DPoS)
Dubbed diversity-oriented SNS (DOSNS), 46
  method pseudocode, 47b

Duncan's test, 184
Dynamic diversity threshold, 45

E
Earthly remote mobile, 17–18
ECG. *See* Electrocardiogram (ECG)
ECR-20 protocols, 71
Edge devices, 5
Educational process, 77
Education management information systems, 201
EDuRLLC. *See* Event Portrayed uRLLC
    (EDuRLLC)
Electrical grid, 68
Electrical stimulation, 158–159
Electricity system, 59
Electrocardiogram (ECG), 157
  defined, 158–159
  detecting diseases, 159, 159f
  signal, 160–161
  technique used in, 165t
    artificial neural network (ANN), 163–164
    back propagation neural network (BPNN),
    162–163
    genetic algorithm-back propagation neutral
      network (GA-BPNN), 161–162
    heart wave, 160f
    IoT-based ECG system, 158
Electro-conduction system, 158–159
Electronic health records (EHR), 103, 255–256
  access to IoT, in local area, 262
  blockchain-based data recorder, 260–261
  findings and evaluation, 262–265
  healthcare data management systems, 258–260
  patient dealings process, 261–262
  scope, 256–258
e-Medical services, 19
Employee cybersecurity, 108
Encryption, 225
Endpoint device administration, 101
Enemy tissues, 85–86
Energy fraud detection, 69
Energy market, 59
Energy web foundation, 70
English 500 dataset, 51f, 52f
  error box plots, 52f

Estimation Arranged Correspondences (COC), 21–22
Ethereum network, 1–2, 30
European Certificate of Conformity (CE), 116
European Commission, 113
European Continental and Common Law, 130
European Digital Rights and Principles, 114
European Parliament, 114
European Union Agency for Cybersecurity, 223
European Union (EU) artificial intelligence regulation
  history, 113–115
    Digital Decade targets, 114
    multicountry projects, 114–115
    plan, 115
    2030 targets, of European Union (EU), 114
  scope
    Artificial Intelligence Act, 115–116
    current European Union (EU) legislation, 118
    harm requirement, 117–118
    innovation and implementation, 117
  risk assessment, 116–117, 117t
EVC-Plus mobile payment platform, 278
Event Portrayed uRLLC (EDuRLLC), 21–22
e-Wallet, 30
Excavators, 14
Experimental control/internal validity, 140
Extended reality (AR), 15–16

F
Facebook, 4, 88
Face2Gene, 88
Face-to-face interview technique, 168–169
False-positive estimation, 93
FBA. *See* Federated Byzantine Agreement (FBA)
Feature selection task, 41–42
Federated Byzantine Agreement (FBA), 61t
FFE. *See* Fitness function evaluations (FFE)
Fidelity, 140
Firebase real-time database, 251f
Firewalls, 229
Fitness function evaluations (FFE), 49
Flood-control mechanism, 233
Flooding, 233
Flood risk monitoring, 242

Flood warning, 233
Fraud detection, 41–42
Fuzzy logic systems, 88

G
GDPR. *See* General Data Protection Regulation (GDPR)
Gem Health Network, 257–258
General Data Protection Regulation (GDPR), 217
Genetic algorithm-back propagation neutral network (GA-BPNN), 161–162
Genetic predisposition, 85
GINI algorithm, 91
Global media communications sector, 15–16
Gmail, 2–3
Google, 2–3
Google-developed BERT architecture, 148
Google Meeting, 169
Gradient boosting machines, 92
  algorithm, 94
Grid contract management, 57–58
Gulf Stream, 71

H
Hashimoto's thyroid, 85–86
HCS. *See* Healthcare systems (HCS)
HE. *See* Homomorphic encryption (HE)
Healthcare cybersecurity, 97–101, 108–110
  cloud computing, 104–105
  current and future trends, 103
  cyber-physical medical systems, 103–104
  difficulties
    budget and requirement, 102
    dangerous medical cyber-physical systems, 102
    endpoint device administration, 101
    humans role, in cybersecurity, 101
    ineffective incident response coordination, 102
    ineffective risk assessment communication, 102
    poor business continuity strategies, 102
    security assurance for remote work, 101
    security disregard, 101–102
  health application, security of, 105

Healthcare cybersecurity (*Continued*)
  insider danger, 105–106
  malware, 105
  tools and techniques
    cryptographic systems, 106
    cyber-hygiene procedures, 108
    cyber maturity and capability, 108
    governance and risk assessment, 106–107
    instruction and simulated settings, 108
    laws and regulations, 107
    proactive cybersecurity culture, 107
Healthcare data breach, 106–107
Healthcare industry data audits, 259
Healthcare leadership, 107
Healthcare systems (HCS), 97–99
Health data, 104
Health Insurance Portability and Accountability
    Act, 257–258
High-end 5G communication networks, 17–18
HIPAA Omnibus Rules, 107
Holographic beamforming, 17–18
Homogeneous disorder, 133
Homomorphic encryption (HE), 106
Hostage credit, 61*t*
Human intelligence, 2
Human safety, 6
Human teams, 7
Hybrid machine learning method, 89
Hybrid metaheuristics
  inner functioning and complexity, of algorithm,
    46–47
  novel initialization procedure, 44–45
  population heterogeneity, preserving, 45–46
  social network search algorithm, 42–44
Hydrologic forecasting, 233
Hyperledger Fabric, 1–2

I

Identity management systems, 209
IDS. *See* Intrusion detection systems (IDS)
Image processing, 88
Immune system, 86
Improved versatile broadband (eMBB), 17–18
IMS. *See* Inertial estimation frameworks (IMS)
Industrial IoT (IIoT) network, 260–261

Industrial revolution (IR 4.0), 2, 262
Inertial estimation frameworks (IMS),
    17–18
Information security, 101
Information technologies, 99–101
InfoSec teams, 7
Innovative blockchain, 3–4
Intelligent grids, 68
Intelligently Capable eMBB Exchanges (CAeC),
    21–22
International Telecommunication Union, 223
Internet of Everything, 21–22
Internet of nanothings, 16–17
Internet of things (IoT), 2, 13, 157, 217, 234, 245,
    278
  IoT-based smart agriculture, 245
  by 6G, 18–19
Internet of things (IoT)-based river monitoring
    and alerting system
  analysis and design, 236–237
  information transmission, 237*f*
  literature review, 234–235
  mobile short message service message,
    241–242, 242*f*
  proposed system
    hardware requirements, 235
    software requirement, 235–236
  results
    daily flood figure records, 240
    daily flood record, 240
    daily flood report, 241, 242*f*
    dashboard page, 239
    flow rate assessment, 238, 239*f*
    login form, 238
  sensor for, monitoring, 237*f*
  system architecture, 237–238
  system's circuitry, 236*f*
Internet security infrastructures, 1–2
Interoperability, 101
Inter-rater agreement, 140
Intrusion, 41–42
Intrusion detection systems (IDS), 147, 229
IoT. *See* Internet of things (IoT)
IT asset inventory, 7
Item Portrayed Association, 21–22

J

Job displacement, 272
Joint localizations, 89
Judgment of fact/judgment of reality, 128
Jumper wires, 236

K

K-nearest neighbors (KNN), 90, 195
Knowledge consolidation, 2–3
Knowledge Discovery and Data Mining (KDD), 149
    Cup'99 dataset, 149, 153

L

Language learning method, 137
Learning, 135
Legal person, 122
Lengthened reality (XR), 15–16
LightGBM, 92
Likert-type research scale, 183–184
Load scheduling, 59
Lofty emission reduction, 57
Logistic function, 40
Logistic regression (LR), 39–41
    classifiers, 39–40
    LR coefficients, 48–49
    performance metrics, classification error, 50t
    results and english dataset, 50t
Low dormancy correspondences (URLLC), 17–19
Low-earth orbit satellites, 19
Low-energy bluetooth, 18–19
Low-security maturity, 97–101

M

Machine learning (ML) algorithms, 2–3, 20–21, 39, 87–88
    experimental results, 92–93
    materials and methods
        artificial neural network (ANN), 91
        Cart algorithm, 91
        CatBoost, 92
        Gaussian naive Bayes, 90
        gradient boosting machines, 92
        K-nearest neighbor (KNN), 90
        LightGBM, 92
        logistic regression, 90
        mean and standard deviation, 93t
        radial basis function, 91
        random forest, 91
        success metric criteria, 93t
        support vector classification, 91
        XGBoost, 92
Machine-to-machine communications, 19
Machine-type correspondences (mMTC), 17–18
Malware, 105
Manipulative AI systems, 117–118
Massachusetts Institute of Technology (MIT), 270–271
Massachusetts Institute of Technology Lincoln Laboratory, 149
Mathematical Laboratory (MATLAB), 163–164
MCPS. *See* Medical cyber-physical system (MCPS)
MD5, 5
Medical cyber-physical system (MCPS), 102–104
Medical data
    data and security breaches, 259
    data ownership, 260
    electronic prescription problem, 260
    handling costs, 258–259
    interoperability, 258
    obstacles, 259
    reliability of, 258
    security, 258
    storage requirements issues, 259
    technologies and protocols, 259
    trust b/w hospitals, 259–260
Medical internet of things, 103–104
Merkle tree, 19–20
Metaheuristic optimization, 41–42
Metamask transactions, 30
Microgrid control systems, 69
mmWave spectrum, 17–18
Mobile cloud computing (MCC) security, 215
    in smart cities, 218, 229
        data breaches, 215
        encryption techniques, 216
        MCC environments, 220
        monitoring and logging, 227
        privacy, 220
        results, 224–226

Mobile cloud computing (MCC) security
    (*Continued*)
    security protocols, 220, 223–224, 230
    security threats, 216
    studies, 221–223
Mobile computing, 205–206
Model accuracy, 93
Modern spam filtering systems, 39
Multicurrency, 31
Multilayer sensors, 89
Multiple machine learning algorithms, 89
Multiple sclerosis, 85
My Health Record (MHR), 97–99

N
Naive Bayes classification, 90
National eHealth Security and Access Framework
    (NESAF) v4.0, 106–107
National Health Service (NHS), 97–101
National Institute of Standards and Technology
    (NIST) Framework, 106–107, 223
Natural language processing (NLP), 147–148
Natural logarithm, 41
Natural person, 122
Network virtualization techniques, 15–16
Neural networks (NN), 194
    tuning, 41–42
NHS. *See* National Health Service (NHS)
NLP. *See* Natural language processing (NLP)
NN. *See* Neural networks (NN)
Node MCU microcontroller, 285–286
Nonlinear transform, 39
Nonprobabilistic linear classifier, 91
Normal distribution, 44–45
Novel initialization procedure, 44–45
Novel model, 46
NVivo, 79

O
OmniPHR architecture, 257–258
Online payments, 25
    goals, 25
    Metamask API, using Python, 28–30
    money transfer, 26, 28*f*
        from user to company, 28*f*, 29*b*

payment form, 31, 33*f*
Postman application, 36*f*
research and design
    architecture, 26–28
    blockchain technology and application, 26
user interface design, 30–35
Optimized hyperparameters, 151*t*
Organizational cyber-hygiene policies, 108

P
Past block hash field, 14
Payment processing, 208
Peer-to-peer (P2P), 14
    energy trading, 57–58, 72
    network of nodes, 14
Personal health records (PHR), 257–258
Phishing, 99–101
PHR. *See* Personal health records (PHR)
Plant classification, 41–42
Plant environment monitoring application, using
    IoT sensors, 248*f*
    implementation of, 247
    literature review, 246
    methodology, 246–247
    monitoring soil temperature, 252
    Nede-MCU, 246–247
    results and analysis
        login page, 249*f*
        panel data viewer, 251*f*
        plant testing, 250*f*
        splash screen, 249*f*
PoH-based data structure, 71
Population-based metaheuristics, 41–42
Population diversification, 45
Porter Stemmer, 48
Powerledger, 71
Power purchase agreement (PPA), 69
Power theft, 69
POWR. *See* Primary token powerledger (POWR)
PPA. *See* Power purchase agreement (PPA)
Primary token powerledger (POWR), 71
Proactive cybersecurity culture, 107
Profound learning, 20–21
Proof-of-activity (PoAc), 61*t*
Proof-of-authority (PoAu), 61*t*

Proof-of-burn (PoB), 61*t*
Proof-of-capacity (PoC), 61*t*
Proof-of-elapsed time (PoET), 61*t*
Proof-of-exercise (PoX), 61*t*
Proof-of-history (PoH), 60, 61*t*
Proof-of-importance (PoI), 61*t*
Proof-of-inclusion (PoI), 61*t*
Proof-of-Job, 60
Proof-of-labor, 59–60
Proof-of-ownership (PoO), 61*t*
Proof-of-property, 59–60
Proof-of-space-time, 61*t*
Proof-of-stake (PoS), 59–60, 61*t*, 189
Proof-of-work (PoW), 59–60, 61*t*
Psoriasis, 85–87, 94
    on arms, 86*f*
    over body, 87*f*
Public-key cryptography, 19–20
Python language, 90, 235–236

Q
QoS. *See* Quality of service (QoS)
QRL. *See* Quasireflection-based learning (QRL)
Qualitative research methods, 168, 177
Quality of service (QoS), 182
Quasireflection-based learning (QRL), 44–45
    QRL-based initialization mechanism
        pseudocode, 46*b*

R
Radial basis function, 91
Radiocarpal joint, 89
Radio frequency identification, 18–19
Random forest (RF) model, 91, 191
Randomized conversation topic vector, 43
Ransomware, 1–2, 99–101
Raspberry Pi 3 Model B1 microprocessor, 237
Recurrent neural network (RNN), 191
Replicators, 71
RFID technology, 278
Rheumatoid arthritis, 85
Right eye autism test, 88
rnd function, 45
RNN. *See* Recurrent neural network (RNN)
Robots, 68

Round () function, 43
Rule-based intelligent diabetes diagnosis system,
    88–89

S
Sanction imposition, 127
Scaling factor, 40–41
Scaphocapitate joint, 89
School administrators, 169
SCP. *See* Stellar consensus protocol (SCP)
Sealevel, 71
Secure super dependable low-idleness
    correspondences, 18
Security mechanisms, 188–189
Self-learning ML/DL models, 21–22
Self-learning system, 7
Seller app, 281–282
Sensor networks, 18–19
    enhancements, 41–42
Sequential decision-making processes, 182
Server-side attack, 3
Service level agreements (SLA), 208
Service monitoring, 208
Service provisioning, 208
Shock's magnitude, 42
Short message service (SMS) alarm, 234
Significant learning, 21–22
Single-point attacks, 3
Single-run analysis of variance (ANOVA) test,
    183–184
Single-run T-test, 183–184
6G biological system, 15
6G communications, 15–16
6G correspondence technology, 16–17
6G-empowered IoT (6G-IoT), 18
6G-IoT biological systems, 19
SLA. *See* Service level agreements (SLA)
Smart cities, 217, 224, 226–227, 269–270
    with artificial intelligence and blockchain,
        271–274
    history, 270–271
    result, 272–273
Smart contracts, 26
    management, 57–58
Smart medical care framework, 16–17

Smart switches, 5
Smart tourism ecosystem, 176
Social networks, 43
Social network search (SNS) algorithm, 39–40,
    42–44
Social validity, 140
SolarCoin, 67
Solenoid valve, 246–247
Somalia, 245
Spam classification
    experiments and comparative analysis
        dataset and preprocessing, 48
        experimental setup, 48–49
        simulation outcomes, 49–53
    history
        logistic regression (LR), 40–41
        metaheuristic optimization, 41–42
    hybrid metaheuristics
        inner functioning and complexity, of
            algorithm, 46–47
        novel initialization procedure, 44–45
        population heterogeneity, preserving, 45–46
        social network search algorithm, 42–44
State of the Digital Decade, 114
Statistical measurement, 183–184
Statistical package for social sciences (SPSS),
    183–184
    SPSS 19 method, 89
Stellar consensus protocol (SCP), 61t
Structured query language (SQL), 235–236
Supply chain management systems, 209
Support vector machines (SVM), 194–195
Sustainable Development Goals (SDG), 199
Sustainable educational systems
    artificial intelligence (AI), 203
        and education, 200–201
        ethical and inclusive use of, 202
        planning, 201
    policy-makers, guidelines, 202–203
SVM. See Support vector machines (SVM)
Swarm intelligence algorithms, 40

T
Tera-Hertz (THz), 13
Tesla, 71

Three-layered integrated correspondences (3D-
    InteCom), 18
Transaction tracking, 58–59
Transparency, 26
Trustworthy transactions, 1–2
Tumor identification, 41–42
Turbine, 71
Twitter, 4
Two-factor authentication, 229

U
UI payment information, 31f
Unlawfulness, allegation of, 127
Unmanned aerial vehicles (UAV), 187, 195
    machine learning (ML) algorithms, 188, 192
        benefits, in blockchain methodology,
            193–194
        blockchain-based security mechanisms,
            189–192
        challenges of, in blockchain methodology,
            194
        current state of, in blockchain methodology,
            193
        review result analysis, 194–195
        security mechanisms, 188–189
Unpredictable information correspondences
    (UCDC), 18
Untrustworthy network participants, 1–2
Untrustworthy passwords, 4
US Department of Health and Human Services,
    99–101, 108–110
US Department of Homeland Security, 3–4
US Office of Personnel Management, 97–99

V
Vending machine, 277, 285
    implementation, 285–286
        controller app, 283–285
        seller app, 281–282
    methods and materials
        requirements, 279
        system design, 279–280
    payment API, 283f
    reports, 285f
    studies, 278

Verv, 70
Virtual currency trends, 41−42
Virtual reality (VR), 135−136
   VR-based teaching material, 139
Virtual reality (VR)-based technology
   attention deficit hyperactivity disorder
         (ADHD)
      impact on students, 134
      interventions for students, 134−135
   in education, 135
   environments, for education, 135−137
   interventions, in clinic, 135
   method
      intervention procedure, 139
      limitations, 139
      materials, 138−139
      participants, 138
      validity, 140
   results, 140−142
   virtual reality-based teaching, 141*f*, 142
Voting systems, 209
VR learning environment (VRLE), 136

W
Walmart, 2
WannaCry, 107
Water distribution system, 272
Wavelet packet decomposition (WPD), 161
Web of Everything, 20−21
Whale optimization algorithm (WOA), 41
WhatsApp, 105
White sphere number (WBC), 89
Wi-Fi-enabled microcontroller, 246−247
WOA. *See* Whale optimization algorithm (WOA)
WPD. *See* Wavelet packet decomposition (WPD)

X
XGBoost, 92

Y
YF-S201 water flow meter sensor, 242

Z
Zero-day cyberattacks, 108
ZigBee, 18−19

Printed in the United States
by Baker & Taylor Publisher Services

Printed in the United States
by Baker & Taylor Publisher Services